Book 2: Financial Reporting and Analysis and Corporate Finance

SchweserNotes™ 2019

Level II CFA®

KAPLAN® SCHWESER

SCHWESERNOTES™ 2019 LEVEL II CFA® BOOK 2: FINANCIAL REPORTING AND ANALYSIS AND CORPORATE FINANCE

Published in 2018 by Kaplan, Inc.

Printed in the United States of America.

ISBN: 978-1-4754-7969-0

CONTENTS

STUDY SESSION 5—Financial Reporting and Analysis (1)

READING 14

READING 15

READING 16

STUDY SESSION 7—Corporate Finance (1)

READING 20

READING 21

READING 22

STUDY SESSION 8—Corporate Finance (2)

READING 23

READING 24

READING 25

LEARNING OUTCOME STATEMENTS (LOS)

STUDY SESSION 5

The topical coverage corresponds with the following CFA Institute assigned reading:

14. Intercorporate Investments

The candidate should be able to:

a. describe the classification, measurement, and disclosure under International Financial Reporting Standards (IFRS) for 1) investments in financial assets, 2) investments in associates, 3) joint ventures, 4) business combinations, and 5) special purpose and variable interest entities. (page 1)
b. distinguish between IFRS and US GAAP in the classification, measurement, and disclosure of investments in financial assets, investments in associates, joint ventures, business combinations, and special purpose and variable interest entities. (page 1)
c. analyze how different methods used to account for intercorporate investments affect financial statements and ratios. (page 30)

The topical coverage corresponds with the following CFA Institute assigned reading:

15. Employee Compensation: Post-Employment and Share-Based

The candidate should be able to:

a. describe the types of post-employment benefit plans and implications for financial reports. (page 37)
b. explain and calculate measures of a defined benefit pension obligation (i.e., present value of the defined benefit obligation and projected benefit obligation) and net pension liability (or asset). (page 39)
c. describe the components of a company's defined benefit pension costs. (page 43)
d. explain and calculate the effect of a defined benefit plan's assumptions on the defined benefit obligation and periodic pension cost. (page 49)
e. explain and calculate how adjusting for items of pension and other post-employment benefits that are reported in the notes to the financial statements affects financial statements and ratios. (page 53)
f. interpret pension plan note disclosures including cash flow related information. (page 54)
g. explain issues associated with accounting for share-based compensation. (page 57)
h. explain how accounting for stock grants and stock options affects financial statements, and the importance of companies' assumptions in valuing these grants and options. (page 58)

The topical coverage corresponds with the following CFA Institute assigned reading:

16. Multinational Operations

The candidate should be able to:

a distinguish among presentation (reporting) currency, functional currency, and local currency. (page 65)
b. describe foreign currency transaction exposure, including accounting for and disclosures about foreign currency transaction gains and losses. (page 66)

c. analyze how changes in exchange rates affect the translated sales of the subsidiary and parent company. (pagc 68)
d. compare the current rate method and the temporal method, evaluate how each affects the parent company's balance sheet and income statement, and determine which method is appropriate in various scenarios. (page 68)
e. calculate the translation effects and evaluate the translation of a subsidiary's balance sheet and income statement into the parent company's presentation currency. (page 77)
f. analyze how the current rate method and the temporal method affect financial statements and ratios. (page 84)
g. analyze how alternative translation methods for subsidiaries operating in hyperinflationary economies affect financial statements and ratios. (page 91)
h. describe how multinational operations affect a company's effective tax rate. (page 95)
i. explain how changes in the components of sales affect the sustainability of sales growth. (page 96)
j. analyze how currency fluctuations potentially affect financial results, given a company's countries of operation. (page 97)

The topical coverage corresponds with the following CFA Institute assigned reading:

17. Analysis of Financial Institutions

The candidate should be able to:

a. describe how financial institutions differ from other companies. (pagc 107)
b. describe key aspects of financial regulations of financial institutions. (page 108)
c. explain the CAMELS (capital adequacy, asset quality, management, earnings, liquidity, and sensitivity) approach to analyzing a bank, including key ratios and its limitations. (page 109)
d. describe other factors to consider in analyzing a bank. (page 119)
e. analyze a bank based on financial statements and other factors. (page 121)
f. describe key ratios and other factors to consider in analyzing an insurance company. (page 125)

STUDY SESSION 6

The topical coverage corresponds with the following CFA Institute assigned reading:

18. Evaluating Quality of Financial Reports

The candidate should be able to:

a. demonstrate the use of a conceptual framework for assessing the quality of a company's financial reports. (page 137)
b. explain potential problems that affect the quality of financial reports. (page 138)
c. describe how to evaluate the quality of a company's financial reports. (page 142)
d. evaluate the quality of a company's financial reports. (page 142)
e. describe the concept of sustainable (persistent) earnings. (page 145)
f. describe indicators of earnings quality. (page 145)
g. explain mean reversion in earnings and how the accruals component of earnings affects the speed of mean reversion. (page 147)
h. evaluate the earnings quality of a company. (page 147)

i. describe indicators of cash flow quality. (page 150)
j. evaluate the cash flow quality of a company. (page 151)
k. describe indicators of balance sheet quality. (page 151)
l. evaluate the balance sheet quality of a company. (page 151)
m. describe sources of information about risk. (page 153)

The topical coverage corresponds with the following CFA Institute assigned reading:

19. Integration of Financial Statement Analysis Techniques

The candidate should be able to:

a. demonstrate the use of a framework for the analysis of financial statements, given a particular problem, question, or purpose (e.g., valuing equity based on comparables, critiquing a credit rating, obtaining a comprehensive picture of financial leverage, evaluating the perspectives given in management's discussion of financial results). (page 165)
b. identify financial reporting choices and biases that affect the quality and comparability of companies' financial statements and explain how such biases may affect financial decisions. (page 167)
c. evaluate the quality of a company's financial data, and recommend appropriate adjustments to improve quality and comparability with similar companies, including adjustments for differences in accounting standards, methods, and assumptions. (page 184)
d. evaluate how a given change in accounting standards, methods, or assumptions affects financial statements and ratios. (page 186)
e. analyze and interpret how balance sheet modifications, earnings normalization, and cash flow statement related modifications affect a company's financial statements, financial ratios, and overall financial condition. (page 177)

STUDY SESSION 7

The topical coverage corresponds with the following CFA Institute assigned reading:

20. Capital Budgeting

The candidate should be able to:

a. calculate the yearly cash flows of expansion and replacement capital projects and evaluate how the choice of depreciation method affects those cash flows. (page 203)
b. explain how inflation affects capital budgeting analysis. (page 209)
c. evaluate capital projects and determine the optimal capital project in situations of 1) mutually exclusive projects with unequal lives, using either the least common multiple of lives approach or the equivalent annual annuity approach, and 2) capital rationing. (page 212)
d. explain how sensitivity analysis, scenario analysis, and Monte Carlo simulation can be used to assess the stand-alone risk of a capital project. (page 216)
e. explain and calculate the discount rate, based on market risk methods, to use in valuing a capital project. (page 219)
f. describe types of real options and evaluate a capital project using real options. (page 222)
g. describe common capital budgeting pitfalls. (page 225)

h. calculate and interpret accounting income and economic income in the context of capital budgeting. (page 226)
i. distinguish among the economic profit, residual income, and claims valuation models for capital budgeting and evaluate a capital project using each. (page 230)

The topical coverage corresponds with the following CFA Institute assigned reading:

21. Capital Structure

The candidate should be able to:

a. explain the Modigliani–Miller propositions regarding capital structure, including the effects of leverage, taxes, financial distress, agency costs, and asymmetric information on a company's cost of equity, cost of capital, and optimal capital structure. (page 246)
b. describe target capital structure and explain why a company's actual capital structure may fluctuate around its target. (page 254)
c. describe the role of debt ratings in capital structure policy. (page 254)
d. explain factors an analyst should consider in evaluating the effect of capital structure policy on valuation. (page 255)
e. describe international differences in the use of financial leverage, factors that explain these differences, and implications of these differences for investment analysis. (page 255)

The topical coverage corresponds with the following CFA Institute assigned reading:

22. Dividends and Share Repurchases: Analysis

The candidate should be able to:

a. describe the expected effect of regular cash dividends, extra dividends, liquidating dividends, stock dividends, stock splits, and reverse stock splits on shareholders' wealth and a company's financial ratios. (page 265)
b. compare theories of dividend policy and explain implications of each for share value given a description of a corporate dividend action. (page 267)
c. describe types of information (signals) that dividend initiations, increases, decreases, and omissions may convey. (page 268)
d. explain how clientele effects and agency costs may affect a company's payout policy. (page 269)
e. explain factors that affect dividend policy in practice. (page 271)
f. calculate and interpret the effective tax rate on a given currency unit of corporate earnings under double taxation, dividend imputation, and split-rate tax systems. (page 272)
g. compare stable dividend, constant dividend payout ratio, and residual dividend payout policies, and calculate the dividend under each policy. (page 276)
h. compare share repurchase methods. (page 278)
i. calculate and compare the effect of a share repurchase on earnings per share when 1) the repurchase is financed with the company's surplus cash and 2) the company uses debt to finance the repurchase. (page 279)
j. calculate the effect of a share repurchase on book value per share. (page 280)
k. explain the choice between paying cash dividends and repurchasing shares. (page 281)
l. describe broad trends in corporate payout policies. (page 284)

m. calculate and interpret dividend coverage ratios based on 1) net income and 2) free cash flow. (page 285)
n. identify characteristics of companies that may not be able to sustain their cash dividend. (page 285)

STUDY SESSION 8

The topical coverage corresponds with the following CFA Institute assigned reading:

23. Corporate Performance, Governance, and Business Ethics

The candidate should be able to:

a. compare interests of key stakeholder groups and explain the purpose of a stakeholder impact analysis. (page 297)
b. discuss problems that can arise in principal–agent relationships and mechanisms that may mitigate such problems. (page 300)
c. discuss roots of unethical behavior and how managers might ensure that ethical issues are considered in business decision making. (page 301)
d. compare the Friedman doctrine, Utilitarianism, Kantian Ethics, and Rights and Justice Theories as approaches to ethical decision making. (page 302)

The topical coverage corresponds with the following CFA Institute assigned reading:

24. Corporate Governance

The candidate should be able to:

a. describe objectives and core attributes of an effective corporate governance system and evaluate whether a company's corporate governance has those attributes. (page 310)
b. compare major business forms and describe the conflicts of interest associated with each. (page 310)
c. explain conflicts that arise in agency relationships, including manager–shareholder conflicts and director–shareholder conflicts. (page 312)
d. describe responsibilities of the board of directors and explain qualifications and core competencies that an investment analyst should look for in the board of directors. (page 313)
e. explain effective corporate governance practice as it relates to the board of directors and evaluate strengths and weaknesses of a company's corporate governance practice. (page 313)
f. describe elements of a company's statement of corporate governance policies that investment analysts should assess. (page 316)
g. describe environmental, social, and governance risk exposures. (page 317)
h. explain the valuation implications of corporate governance. (page 318)

The topical coverage corresponds with the following CFA Institute assigned reading:

25. Mergers and Acquisitions

The candidate should be able to:

a. classify merger and acquisition (M&A) activities based on forms of integration and relatedness of business activities. (page 330)
b. explain common motivations behind M&A activity. (page 331)
c. explain bootstrapping of earnings per share (EPS) and calculate a company's post-merger EPS. (page 333)
d. explain, based on industry life cycles, the relation between merger motivations and types of mergers. (page 335)

e. contrast merger transaction characteristics by form of acquisition, method of payment, and attitude of target management. (page 337)
f. distinguish among pre-offer and post-offer takeover defense mechanisms. (page 340)
g. calculate and interpret the Herfindahl–Hirschman Index and evaluate the likelihood of an antitrust challenge for a given business combination. (page 343)
h. compare the discounted cash flow, comparable company, and comparable transaction analyses for valuing a target company, including the advantages and disadvantages of each. (page 356)
i. calculate free cash flows for a target company and estimate the company's intrinsic value based on discounted cash flow analysis. (page 345)
j. estimate the value of a target company using comparable company and comparable transaction analyses. (page 350)
k. evaluate a takeover bid and calculate the estimated post-acquisition value of an acquirer and the gains accrued to the target shareholders versus the acquirer shareholders. (page 360)
l. explain how price and payment method affect the distribution of risks and benefits in M&A transactions. (page 364)
m. describe characteristics of M&A transactions that create value. (page 365)
n. distinguish among equity carve-outs, spin-offs, split-offs, and liquidation. (page 366)
o. explain common reasons for restructuring. (page 366)

The following is a review of the Financial Reporting and Analysis (1) principles designed to address the learning outcome statements set forth by CFA Institute. Cross-Reference to CFA Institute Assigned Reading #14.

READING 14

Intercorporate Investments

Study Session 5

EXAM FOCUS

There are no shortcuts here. Spend the time necessary to learn how and when to use each method of accounting for intercorporate investments because the probability of this material being tested is high. Be able to determine the effects of each method on the financial statements and ratios. Pay particular attention to the examples illustrating the difference between the equity method and the acquisition method.

MODULE 14.1: CLASSIFICATIONS

Video covering this content is available online.

CATEGORIES OF INTERCORPORATE INVESTMENTS

LOS 14.a: Describe the classification, measurement, and disclosure under International Financial Reporting Standards (IFRS) for 1) investments in financial assets, 2) investments in associates, 3) joint ventures, 4) business combinations, and 5) special purpose and variable interest entities.

LOS 14.b: Distinguish between IFRS and US GAAP in the classification, measurement, and disclosure of investments in financial assets, investments in associates, joint ventures, business combinations, and special purpose and variable interest entities.

CFA® Program Curriculum, Volume 2, page 10

Intercorporate investments in marketable securities are categorized as either (1) investments in financial assets (when the investing firm has no significant control over the operations of the investee firm), (2) investments in associates (when the investing firm has significant influence over the operations of the investee firm, but not control), or (3) business combinations (when the investing firm has control over the operations of the investee firm).

Percentage of ownership (or voting control) is typically used to determine the appropriate category for financial reporting purposes. However, the ownership percentage is only a guideline. Ultimately, the category is based on the investor's ability to influence or control the investee.

Investments in financial assets. An ownership interest of less than 20% is usually considered a passive investment. In this case, the investor cannot significantly influence or control the investee.

IFRS currently (current standards) classifies investments in financial assets as held-to-maturity, available-for-sale, or fair value through profit or loss (which includes held-for-trading and securities designated at fair value). Under U.S. GAAP, the accounting treatment for investment in financial assets is similar to current IFRS. IFRS 9 (the new standards) is applicable for annual periods beginning January 1, 2018, (early adoption is allowed). Similarly, FASB issued ASC 825 in January 2016, which is applicable for periods after December 15, 2017.

Investments in associates. An ownership interest between 20% and 50% is typically a noncontrolling investment; however, the investor can usually significantly influence the investee's business operations. Significant influence can be evidenced by the following:

- Board of directors representation.
- Involvement in policy making.
- Material intercompany transactions.
- Interchange of managerial personnel.
- Dependence on technology.

It may be possible to have significant influence with less than 20% ownership. In this case, the investment is considered an investment in associates. Conversely, without significant influence, an ownership interest between 20% and 50% is considered an investment in financial assets.

The equity method is used to account for investments in associates.

Business combinations. An ownership interest of more than 50% is usually a controlling investment. When the investor can control the investee, the acquisition method is used.

It is possible to own more than 50% of an investee and not have control. For example, control can be temporary or barriers may exist such as bankruptcy or governmental intervention. In these cases, the investment is not considered controlling.

Conversely, it is possible to control with less than a 50% ownership interest. In this case, the investment is still considered a business combination.

Joint ventures. A joint venture is an entity whereby control is shared by two or more investors. Both IFRS and U.S. GAAP require the equity method for joint ventures. In rare cases, IFRS and U.S. GAAP allow proportionate consolidation as opposed to the equity method.

Figure 14.1 summarizes the accounting treatment for investments.

Figure 14.1: Accounting for Investments

Ownership	Degree of Influence	Accounting Treatment
Less than 20% (investments in financial assets)	No significant influence	Held-to-maturity, available-for-sale, fair value through profit or loss.*
20%–50% (investment in associates)	Significant influence	Equity method
More than 50% (business combinations)	Control	Acquisition method

*Under the current standards

MODULE QUIZ 14.1

To best evaluate your performance, enter your quiz answers online.

1. Tall Company owns 30% of the common equity of Short Incorporated. Tall has been unsuccessful in its attempts to obtain representation on Short's board of directors. For financial reporting purposes, Tall's ownership interest is *most likely* considered a(n):
   A. investment in financial assets.
   B. investment in associates.
   C. business combination.

MODULE 14.2: FINANCIAL ASSETS, PART 1

Video covering this content is available online.

REPORTING OF INTERCORPORATE INVESTMENTS (PRIOR TO ISSUANCE OF IFRS 9)

Financial Assets

Investment ownership of less than 20% is usually considered passive. The acquisition of financial assets is recorded at cost (presumably the fair value at acquisition), and any dividend or interest income is recognized in the investor's income statement.

Recognizing the change in the fair value of financial assets depends on their classification as either held-to-maturity, held-for-trading, or available-for-sale. Firms can also designate financial assets and financial liabilities at fair value.

1. **Held-to-maturity.** Held-to-maturity securities are debt securities acquired with the intent and ability to be held-to-maturity. The securities cannot be sold prior to maturity except in unusual circumstances.

   Long-term held-to-maturity securities are reported on the balance sheet at amortized cost. Amortized cost is the original cost of the debt security plus any discount, or minus any premium, that has been amortized to date.

PROFESSOR'S NOTE

Amortized cost is simply thc present value of the remaining cash flows (coupon payments and face amount) discounted at the market rate of interest at issuance.

Interest income (coupon cash flow adjusted for amortization of premium or discount) is recognized in the income statement but subsequent changes in fair value are ignored.

2. **Fair value through profit or loss (held-for-trading or designated at fair value)**
   a. **Held-for-trading.** Held-for-trading securities are debt and equity securities acquired for the purposes of profiting in the near term, usually less than three months. Held-for-trading securities are reported on the balance sheet at fair value. The changes in fair value, both realized and unrealized, are recognized in the income statement along with any dividend or interest income.
   b. **Designated at fair value.** Firms can choose to report debt and equitysecurities that would otherwise be treated as held-to-maturity or available-for-sale securities at fair value. Designating financial assets and liabilities at fair value can reduce volatility and inconsistencies that result from measuring assets and liabilities using different valuation bases. Unrealized gains and losses on designated financial assets and liabilities are recognized on the income statement, similar to the treatment of held-for-trading securities.
3. **Available-for-sale**. Available-for-sale securities are debt and equity securities that are neither held-to-maturity nor held-for-trading. Like held-for-trading securities, available-for-sale securities are reported on the balance sheet at fair value. However, only the realized gains or losses, and the dividend or interest income, are recognized in the income statement. The unrealized gains and losses (net of taxes) are excluded from the income statement and are reported as a separate component of stockholders' equity (in other comprehensive income). When the securities are sold, the unrealized gains and losses are removed from other comprehensive income, as they are now realized, and recognized in the income statement.

The treatment under IFRS is similar to U.S. GAAP, except for unrealized gains or losses that result from foreign exchange movements. Foreign exchange gains and losses on available-for-sale *debt* securities are recognized in the income statement under IFRS. The entire unrealized gain or loss is recognized in equity under U.S. GAAP. For available for-sale *equity* securities, the treatment under IFRS is similar to the treatment under U.S. GAAP.

Let's look at an example of the different classifications for financial assets.

EXAMPLE: Investment in financial assets

At the beginning of the year, Midland Corporation purchased a 9% bond with a face value of $100,000 for $96,209 to yield 10%. The coupon payments are made annually at year-end. Let's suppose the fair value of the bond at the end of the year is $98,500.

Determine the impact on Midland's balance sheet and income statement if the bond investment is classified as held-to-maturity, held-for-trading (or fair value through profit or loss), and available-for-sale.

Answer:

Held-to-maturity: The balance sheet value is based on amortized cost. At year-end, Midland recognizes interest revenue of $9,621 ($96,209 beginning bond investment × 10% market rate at issuance). The interest revenue includes the coupon payment of $9,000 ($100,000 face value × 9% coupon rate) and the amortized discount of $621 ($9,621 interest revenue – $9,000 coupon payment).

At year-end, the bond is reported on the balance sheet at $96,830 ($96,209 beginning bond investment + $621 amortized discount).

Held-for-trading: The balance sheet value is based on fair value of $98,500. Interest revenue of $9,621 ($96,209 beginning bond investment × 10% yield-to-maturity at issuance) and an unrealized gain of $1,670 ($98,500 – $96,209 – $621) are recognized in the income statement.

Available-for-sale: The balance sheet value is based on fair value of $98,500. Interest revenue of $9,621 ($96,209 beginning bond investment × 10% yield-to-maturity at issuance) is recognized in the income statement. The unrealized gain of $1,670 ($98,500 – $96,209 – $621) is reported in stockholders' equity as a component of other comprehensive income.

Now let's imagine that the bonds are called on the first day of the next year for $101,000. Calculate the gain or loss recognition for each classification.

Held-to-maturity: A realized gain of $4,170 ($101,000 – $96,830 carrying value) is recognized in the income statement.

Held-for-trading: A net gain of $2,500 ($101,000 – $98,500 carrying value) is recognized in the income statement.

Available-for-sale: The unrealized gain of $1,670 is removed from equity, and a realized gain of $4,170 ($101,000 – $96,830) is recognized in the income statement.

Figure 14.2 summarizes the effects of the different classifications for financial assets on the balance sheet and income statement.

Figure 14.2: Summary of Classifications of Financial Assets

	Held-to-Maturity	Fair Value Through Profit or Loss	Available-for-Sale
Balance sheet	Amortized cost	Fair value	Fair value with unrealized G/L recognized in equity
Income statement	Interest (including amortization) Realized G/L*	Interest Dividends Realized G/L Unrealized G/L	Interest Dividends Realized G/L

* G/L = Gain and losses.

MODULE QUIZ 14.2

To best evaluate your performance, enter your quiz answers online.

Use the following information to answer Questions 1 through 5.

Kirk Company acquired shares in the equity of both Company A and Company B. We have the following information from the public market about Company A and Company B's investment value at the time of purchase and at two subsequent dates:

Security	Cost	t = 1	t = 2
A	$950	$850	$900
B	250	180	350

1. Kirk Company will report the initial value of its investment in financial assets as:
   A. $1,030.
   B. $1,200.
   C. $1,250.
2. At t = 1, Kirk will:
   A. carry the financial assets at cost.
   B. write down the financial assets to $1,030 and recognize an unrealized loss of $170.
   C. write down the financial assets to $1,030 and recognize a realized loss of $170.
3. At t = 2, Kirk will report the carrying value of its financial assets as:
   A. $1,030.
   B. $1,200.
   C. $1,250.
4. Based on the information provided, which of the following statements is *most accurate*?
   A. Classifying the shares as trading securities would result in greater reported earnings volatility for Kirk.
   B. Classifying the shares as available-for-sale securities would result in a $220 realized gain for Kirk between t = 1 and t = 2.
   C. It is optimal for Kirk to classify its shares in Company A and Company B as available-for-sale securities since it results in a net $50 gain recognized on the income statement at t = 2.
5. Suppose for this question only that Security A and Security B are both debt securities held-to-maturity and purchased initially at par. At t = 2, Kirk will report the carrying value of these securities as:
   A. $1,030.
   B. $1,200.
   C. $1,250.

MODULE 14.3: FINANCIAL ASSETS, PART 2—IMPAIRMENTS, RECLASSIFICATIONS

Video covering this content is available online.

Reclassification of Investments in Financial Assets

IFRS typically does not allow reclassification of investments into or out of the designated at fair value category. Reclassification of investments out of the held-for-trading category is severely restricted under IFRS.

Debt securities classified as available-for-sale can be reclassified as held-to-maturity if the holder intends to (and is able to) hold the debt to its maturity date. The security's balance sheet value is remeasured to reflect its fair value at the time it is reclassified. Any difference between this amount and the maturity value, and nany gain or loss that had been recorded in other comprehensive income, is amortized over the security's remaining life.

Held-to-maturity securities can be reclassified as available-for-sale if the holder no longer intends or is no longer able to hold the debt to maturity. The carrying value is remeasured to the security's fair value, with any difference recognized in other comprehensive income. Note that reclassifying a held-to-maturity security may prevent the holder from classifying other debt securities as held-to-maturity, or even require other held-to-maturity debt to be reclassified as available-for-sale.

U.S. GAAP does permit securities to be reclassified into or out of held-for-trading or designated at fair value. Unrealized gains are recognized on the income statement at the time the security is reclassified. For investments transferring out of available-for-sale category into held-for-trading category, the cumulative amount of gains and losses previously recorded under other comprehensive income is recognized in income. For a debt security transferring out of the available-for-sale category into the held-to-maturity category, the cumulative amount of gains and losses previously recorded under other comprehensive income is amortized over the remaining life of the security. For transferring investments into the available-for-sale category from the held-to-maturity category, the unrealized gain/loss is transferred to comprehensive income. Figure 14.3 summarizes the rules of reclassification.

Figure 14.3: Reclassification of Financial Assets

From	To	Unrealized Gain or Loss
Fair value through profit or loss*	Any	Income Statement (to extent not recognized)
Held-to-maturity	Fair value through profit or loss*	Income Statement
Held-to-maturity	Available-for-sale	Other comprehensive income
Available-for-sale	Held-to-maturity	Amortize out of other comprehensive income
Available-for-sale	Fair value through profit or loss*	Transfer out of other comprehensive income

*Restricted under IFRS

All transfers occur at fair value as of the transfer date.

Impairment of Financial Assets

If the value that can be recovered for a financial asset is less than its carrying value and is expected to remain so, the financial asset is impaired. IFRS and U.S. GAAP require that held-to-maturity (HTM) and available-for-sale (AFS) securities be evaluated for impairment at each reporting period. This is not necessary for held-for-trading and designated at fair value securities because declines in their values are recognized on the income statement as they occur.

U.S. GAAP

Under U.S. GAAP, a security is considered impaired if its decline in value is determined to be other than temporary. For both HTM and AFS securities, the write-down to fair value is treated as a realized loss (i.e., recognized on the income statement).

U.S. GAAP—Reversals

A subsequent reversal of impairment losses is *not* allowed.

IFRS

As under U.S. GAAP, impairments under IFRS are recognized in the income statement. Impairment of a debt or equity security is indicated if at least one loss event has occurred, and its effect on the security's future cash flows can be estimated reliably. Losses due to occurrences of future events (regardless of the probability of occurrence) are not recognized.

For debt securities, loss events can include default on payments of interest or principal, likely bankruptcy or reorganization of the issuer, concessions from the bondholders, or other indications of financial difficulty on the part of the issuer. However, a credit rating downgrade or the lack of a liquid market for the debt are not considered to be indications of impairment in the absence of other evidence.

For equities, a loss event has occurred if the fair value of the security has experienced a substantial or extended decline below its carrying value or if changes in the business environment facing the equity issuer (such as economic, legal, or technological developments) have made it unlikely that the value of the equity will recover to its initial cost.

If a held-to-maturity security has become impaired, its carrying value is decreased to the present value of its estimated future cash flows, using the same effective interest rate that was used when the security was purchased. *This may not be equal to its fair value.*

IFRS—Reversals

If the held-to-maturity security's value recovers in a later period, and its recovery can be attributed to an event (such as a credit upgrade), the impairment loss can be reversed. Impairments of available-for-sale debt securities may be reversed under the same conditions as impairments of held-to-maturity securities. Reversals of impairments are not permitted for equity securities.

Analysis of Investments in Financial Assets

When analyzing a firm with investments in financial assets, it is important to separate the firm's operating results from its investment results (e.g., interest, dividends, and gains and losses).

For comparison purposes, using market values for financial assets is generally preferred. Also, it is necessary to remove nonoperating assets when calculating the return on operating assets ratio.

Finally, the analyst must assess the effects of investment classification on reported performance. Investment results may be misleading because of inconsistent treatment of unrealized gains and losses. For example, if security prices are increasing, an investor that classifies an investment as held-for-trading will report higher earnings than if the investment is classified as available-for-sale. This is because the unrealized gains are recognized in the income statement for a held-for-trading security. The unrealized gains are reported in stockholders' equity for an available-for-sale security.

IFRS 9 New Standards for 2018

These new standards became effective for periods starting January 1, 2018.

IFRS 9 does away with the terms held-for-trading, available-for-sale, and held-to-maturity. Instead, the three classifications are **amortized cost**, **fair value through profit or loss** (FVPL), and **fair value through other comprehensive income** (FVOCI).

Amortized Cost (for Debt Securities Only)

Debt securities that meet two criteria are accounted for using the amortized cost method (which is the same as the held-to-maturity method discussed before).

Criteria for amortized cost accounting:

1. Business model test: Debt securities are being held to collect contractual cash flows.
2. Cash flow characteristic test: The contractual cash flows are either principal, or interest on principal, only.

Fair Value Through Profit or Loss (for Debt and Equity Securities)

Debt securities may be classified as fair value through profit or loss (FVPL) if held for trading, or if accounting for those securities at amortized cost results in an accounting mismatch. Equity securities that are held for trading must be classified as FVPL. Other equity securities may be classified as either fair value through profit or loss, or fair value through OCI. Once classified, the choice is irrevocable. Derivatives that are not used for hedging are always carried at FVPL. If an asset has an embedded derivative (e.g., convertible bonds), the asset as a whole is valued at FVPL.

Fair Value Through OCI (for Debt and Equity Securities)

The accounting treatment under fair value through OCI is the same as under the previously used available-for-sale classification.

Reclassification Under IFRS 9

Reclassification of equity securities under the new standards is not permitted as the initial designation (FVPL or FVOCI) is irrevocable. Reclassification of debt securities is permitted only if the business model has changed. For example, unrecognized gains/losses on debt securities carried at amortized cost and reclassified as FVPL are recognized in the income statement. Debt securities that are reclassified out of FVPL as measured at amortized cost are transferred at fair value on the transfer date, and that fair value will become the carrying amount.

Loan Impairment Under IFRS 9

A key feature of IFRS 9 was that the incurred loss model for loan impairment was replaced by the *expected credit loss model*. This requires companies to not only evaluate current and historical information about loan (including loan commitments and lease receivables) performance, but to also use forward-looking information. The new criteria results in an earlier recognition of impairment (12-month expected losses for performing loans and lifetime expected losses for nonperforming loans).

Video covering this content is available online.

MODULE 14.4: INVESTMENT IN ASSOCIATES, PART 1—EQUITY METHOD

Investments in Associates

Investment ownership of between 20% and 50% is usually considered influential. Influential investments are accounted for using the equity method. Under the equity method, the initial investment is recorded at cost and reported on the balance sheet as a noncurrent asset.

In subsequent periods, the proportionate share of the investee's earnings increases the investment account on the investor's balance sheet and is recognized in the investor's income statement. Dividends received from the investee are treated as a return of capital and thus, reduce the investment account. Unlike investments in financial assets, dividends received from the investee are not recognized in the investor's income statement.

If the investee reports a loss, the investor's proportionate share of the loss reduces the investment account and also lowers earnings in the investor's income statement. If the investee's losses reduce the investment account to zero, the investor usually discontinues use of the equity method. The equity method is resumed once the proportionate share of the investee's earnings exceed the share of losses that were not recognized during the suspension period.

Fair Value Option

U.S. GAAP allows equity method investments to be recorded at fair value. Under IFRS, the fair value option is only available to venture capital firms, mutual funds, and similar entities. The decision to use the fair value option is irrevocable and any changes in value (along with dividends) are recorded in the income statement.

EXAMPLE: Implementing the equity method

Suppose that we are given the following:

- December 31, 20X5, Company P (the investor) invests $1,000 in return for 30% of the common shares of Company S (the investee).
- During 20X6, Company S earns $400 and pays dividends of $100.
- During 20X7, Company S earns $600 and pays dividends of $150.

Calculate the effects of the investment on Company P's balance sheet, reported income, and cash flow for 20X6 and 20X7.

Answer:

Using the equity method for 20X6, Company P will:

- Recognize $120 ($400 × 30%) in the income statement from its proportionate share of the net income of Company S.
- Increase its investment account on the balance sheet by $120 to $1,120, reflecting its proportionate share of the net assets of Company S.
- Receive $30 ($100 × 30%) in cash dividends from Company S and reduce its investment in Company S by that amount to reflect the decline in the net assets of Company S due to the dividend payment.

At the end of 20X6, the carrying value of Company S on Company P's balance sheet will be $1,090 ($1,000 original investment + $120 proportionate share of Company S net income – $30 dividend received).

For 20X7, Company P will recognize income of $180 ($600 × 30%) and increase the investment account by $180. Also, Company P will receive dividends of $45 ($150 × 30%) and lower the investment account by $45. Hence, at the end of 20X7, the carrying value of Company S on Company P's balance sheet will be $1,225 ($1,090 beginning balance + $180 proportionate share of Company S net income – $45 dividend received).

Excess of Purchase Price Over Book Value Acquired

Rarely does the price paid for an investment equal the proportionate book value of the investee's net assets, since the book value of many assets and liabilities is based on historical cost.

At the acquisition date, the excess of the purchase price over the proportionate share of the investee's book value is allocated to the investee's identifiable assets and liabilities based on their fair values. Any remainder is considered goodwill.

In subsequent periods, the investor recognizes expense based on the excess amounts assigned to the investee's assets and liabilities. The expense is recognized consistent with the investee's recognition of expense. For example, the investor might recognize additional depreciation expense as a result of the fair value allocation of the purchase price to the investee's fixed assets.

It is important to note that the purchase price allocation to the investee's assets and liabilities is included in the investor's balance sheet, not the investee's. In addition, the additional expense that results from the assigned amounts is not recognized in the investee's income statement. Under the equity method of accounting, the investor must adjust its balance sheet investment account and the proportionate share of the income reported from the investee for this additional expense.

PROFESSOR'S NOTE

Under the equity method, the investor does not actually report the separate assets and liabilities of the investee. Rather, the investor reports the investment in one line on its balance sheet. This one-line investment account includes the proportionate share of the investee's net assets at fair value and the goodwill.

EXAMPLE: Allocation of purchase price over book value acquired

At the beginning of the year, Red Company purchased 30% of Blue Company for $80,000. On the acquisition date, the book value of Blue's identifiable net assets was $200,000. Also, the fair value and book value of Blue's assets and liabilities were the same except for Blue's equipment, which had a book value of $25,000 and a fair value of $75,000 on the acquisition date. Blue's equipment is depreciated over ten years using the straight-line method. At the end of the year, Blue reported net income of $100,000 and paid dividends of $60,000.

Part A: Calculate the goodwill created as a result of the purchase.

Part B: Calculate Red's income at the end of the year from its investment in Blue.

Part C: Calculate the investment in Blue that appears on Red's year-end balance sheet.

Answer:

Part A

The excess of purchase price over the proportionate share of Blue's book value is allocated to the equipment. The remainder is goodwill.

Purchase price:	$80,000	
Less: Pro-rata book value of net assets:	60,000	($200,000 book value × 30%)
Excess of purchase price:	$20,000	
Less: Excess allocated to equipment:	15,000	[($75,000 FV – $25,000 BV) × 30%]
Goodwill:	$5,000	

Part B

Red recognizes its proportionate share of Blue's net income for the year. Also, Red must recognize the additional depreciation expense that resulted from the purchase price allocation.

Red's proportionate share of Blue's net income:	$30,000 ($100,000 NI × 30%)
Less: Additional depreciation from excess of purchase price allocated to Blue's equipment:	1,500 ($15,000 excess / 10 years)
Equity income:	$28,500

Part C

The beginning balance of Red's investment account is increased by the equity income from Blue and is decreased by the dividends received from Blue.

Investment balance at beginning of year:	$80,000 (Purchase price)
Equity income:	28,500 (From Part B)
Less: Dividends:	18,000 ($60,000 × 30%)
Investment balance at end of year:	$90,500

PROFESSOR'S NOTE

An alternative method of calculating the year-end investment is as follows:

% acquired × (book value of net assets at beginning of year + net income – dividends) + unamortized excess purchase price
= [0.3 × (200,000 + 100,000 – 60,000)] + (20,000 – 1,500) = $90,500

MODULE QUIZ 14.3, 14.4

To best evaluate your performance, enter your quiz answers online.

1. If a company uses the equity method to account for an investment in another company:
   A. income is combined to the extent of ownership.
   B. all income of the affiliate is included except intercompany transfers.
   C. earnings of the affiliate are included but reduced by any dividends paid to the company.

Use the following information to answer Questions 2 through 4.

Suppose Company P acquired 40% of the shares of Company A for $1.5 million on January 1, 2016. During the year, Company A earned $500,000 and paid dividends of $125,000.

2. At the end of 2016, Company P reported investment in Company A as:
   A. $1.5 million.
   B. $1.65 million.
   C. $1.7 million.
3. For 2016, Company P reported investment income of:
   A. $50,000.
   B. $150,000.
   C. $200,000.
4. For 2016, Company P received cash flow from the investee of:
   A. $50,000.
   B. $150,000.
   C. $200,000.

Video covering this content is available online.

MODULE 14.5: INVESTMENT IN ASSOCIATES, PART 2

Impairments of Investments in Associates

Equity method investments must be tested for impairment. Under U.S. GAAP, if the fair value of the investment falls below the carrying value (investment account on the balance sheet) and the decline is considered other-than-temporary, the investment is written-down to fair value and a loss is recognized on the income statement. Under IFRS, impairment needs to be evidenced by one or more loss events. Under both IFRS and U.S. GAAP, if there is a recovery in value in the future, the asset cannot be written-up.

Transactions With the Investee

So far, our discussion has ignored transactions between the investor and investee. Because of its ownership interest, the investor may be able to influence transactions with the investee. Thus, profit from these transactions must be deferred until the profit is confirmed through use or sale to a third party.

Transactions can be described as upstream (investee to the investor) or downstream (investor to the investee). In an upstream sale, the investee has recognized all of the profit in its income statement. However, for profit that is unconfirmed (goods have not been used or sold by the investor), the investor must eliminate its proportionate share of the profit from the equity income of the investee.

For example, suppose that Investor owns 30% of Investee. During the year, Investee sold goods to Investor and recognized $15,000 of profit from the sale. At year-end, half of the goods purchased from Investee remained in Investor's inventory.

All of the profit is included in Investee's net income. Investor must reduce its equity income of Investee by Investor's proportionate share of the unconfirmed profit. Since half of the goods remain, half of the profit is unconfirmed. Thus, Investor must reduce its equity income by $2,250 [($15,000 total profit × 50% unconfirmed) × 30% ownership interest]. Once the inventory is sold by Investor, $2,250 of equity income will be recognized.

In a downstream sale, the investor has recognized all of the profit in its income statement. Like the upstream sale, the investor must eliminate the proportionate share of the profit that is unconfirmed.

For example, imagine again that Investor owns 30% of Investee. During the year, Investor sold $40,000 of goods to Investee for $50,000. Investee sold 90% of the goods by year-end.

In this case, Investor's profit is $10,000 ($50,000 sales – $40,000 COGS). Investee has sold 90% of the goods; thus, 10% of the profit remains in Investee's inventory. Investor must reduce its equity income by the *proportionate share* of the unconfirmed profit: $10,000 profit × 10% unconfirmed amount × 30% ownership interest = $300. Once Investee sells the remaining inventory, Investor can recognize $300 of profit.

Analytical Issues for Investments in Associates

When an investee is profitable, and its dividend payout ratio is less than 100%, the equity method usually results in higher earnings as compared to the accounting methods used for minority passive investments. Thus, the analyst should consider if the equity method is appropriate for the investor. For example, an investor could use the equity method in order to report the proportionate share of the investee's earnings, when it cannot actually influence the investee.

Also, the investee's individual assets and liabilities are not reported on the investor's balance sheet. The investor simply reports its proportionate share of the investee's equity in one line on the balance sheet. By ignoring the investee's debt, leverage is lower. In addition, the margin ratios are higher since the investee's revenues are ignored.

Finally, the proportionate share of the investee's earnings is recognized in the investor's income statement, but the earnings may not be available to the investor in the form of cash flow (dividends). That is, the investee's earnings may be permanently reinvested.

Under the *acquisition method*, all of the assets, liabilities, revenues, and expenses of the subsidiary are combined with the parent. Intercompany transactions are excluded.

In the case where the parent owns less than 100% of the subsidiary, it is necessary to create a noncontrolling (minority) interest account for the proportionate share of the subsidiary's net assets that are not owned by the parent.

MODULE 14.6: BUSINESS COMBINATIONS: BALANCE SHEET

Video covering this content is available online.

Business Combinations

Under IFRS, business combinations are not differentiated based on the structure of the surviving entity. Under U.S. GAAP, business combinations are categorized as:

- **Merger.** The acquiring firm absorbs all the assets and liabilities of the acquired firm, which ceases to exist. The acquiring firm is the surviving entity.
- **Acquisition.** Both entities continue to exist in a parent-subsidiary relationship. Recall that when less than 100% of the subsidiary is owned by the parent, the parent prepares consolidated financial statements but reports the unowned (minority or noncontrolling) interest on its financial statements.
- **Consolidation.** A new entity is formed that absorbs both of the combining companies.

Historically, two accounting methods have been used for business combinations: (1) the purchase method and (2) the pooling-of-interests method. However, the pooling method has been eliminated from U.S. GAAP and IFRS. Now, the **acquisition method** (which replaces the purchase method) is required.

The **pooling-of-interests method**, also known as **uniting-of-interests method** under IFRS, combined the ownership interests of the two firms and viewed the participants as equals—neither firm acquired the other. The assets and liabilities of the two firms were simply combined. Key attributes of the pooling method include the following:

- The two firms are combined using historical book values.
- Operating results for prior periods are restated as though the two firms were always combined.
- Ownership interests continue, and former accounting bases are maintained.

Note that fair values played no role in accounting for a business combination using the pooling method—the actual price paid was suppressed from the balance sheet and income statement. Analysts should be aware that transactions reported under the pooling (uniting-of-interests) method prior to 2001 (2004) may still be reported under that method.

Let's look at an example of the acquisition method.

Suppose that on January 1, 2010, Company P acquires 80% of the common stock of Company S by paying $8,000 *in cash* to the shareholders of Company S. The preacquisition balance sheets of Company P and Company S are shown in Figure 14.4.

Figure 14.4: Preacquisition Balance Sheets

Preacquisition Balance Sheets **January 1, 2010**	**Company P**	**Company S**
Current assets	$48,000	$16,000
Other assets	32,000	8,000
Total	$80,000	$24,000
Current liabilities	$40,000	$14,000
Common stock	28,000	6,000
Retained earnings	12,000	4,000
Total	$80,000	$24,000

Under the equity method of accounting, Company P will report its 80% interest in Company S in a one-line investment account on the balance sheet.

In an acquisition, the assets and liabilities of Company P and Company S are combined, and the stockholders' equity of Company S is ignored. It is also necessary to create a minority interest account for the portion of Company S's equity that is not owned by Company P. Figure 14.5 compares the acquisition method and the equity method on Company P's post-acquisition balance sheet.

Figure 14.5: Balance Sheet Comparison of the Acquisition and Equity Methods

Company P Post-Acquisition Balance Sheet January 1, 2010	Acquisition Method	Equity Method
Current assets	$56,000	$40,000
Investment in S		8,000
Other assets	40,000	32,000
Total	$96,000	$80,000
Current liabilities	$54,000	$40,000
Minority interest	2,000	
Common stock	28,000	28,000
Retained earnings	12,000	12,000
Total	$96,000	$80,000

Post-acquisition, Company P's current assets are lower by the $8,000 cash used to acquire 80% of Company S. Under the acquisition method, the current assets are $56,000 ($48,000 P current assets + $16,000 S current assets – $8,000 cash). With the equity method, current assets are $40,000 ($48,000 P current assets – $8,000 cash).

PROFESSOR'S NOTE

Where does the $8,000 go? It goes to the departing shareholders from whom the shares were purchased.

When using the acquisition method, Company P reports 100% of Company S's assets and liabilities even though Company P only owns 80%. The remaining 20% of Company S is owned by minority investors and the difference is accounted for using a noncontrolling (minority) interest account. The minority interest is created by multiplying the subsidiary's equity by the percentage of the subsidiary not owned by the parent. In our example, the minority interest is $2,000 ($10,000 S equity × 20%). Noncontrolling interest is reported in stockholders' equity.

MODULE QUIZ 14.5, 14.6

To best evaluate your performance, enter your quiz answers online.

Use the following information to answer Questions 1 though 3.

Suppose Company P acquires 80% of the common stock of Company S on December 31, 2016, by paying $120,000 cash to the shareholders of Company S. The two firms' pre-acquisition balance sheets as of December 31, 2016, and pre-acquisition pro forma income statements for the year ending December 31, 2017, follow:

Pre-Acquisition Balance Sheets December 31, 2016	**Company P**	**Company S**
Current assets	$720,000	$240,000
Other assets	480,000	120,000
Total assets	$1,200,000	$360,000
Current liabilities	$600,000	$210,000
Common stock	420,000	90,000
Retained earnings	180,000	60,000
Total liabilities & equity	$1,200,000	$360,000

Unconsolidated Income Statements December 31, 2017	**Company P**	**Company S**
Revenue	$900,000	$300,000
Expenses	600,000	240,000
Net income	$300,000	$60,000
Dividends		$15,000

1. Immediately after the acquisition, Company P will report total assets of:
   A. $1,080,000.
   B. $1,440,000.
   C. $1,560,000.
2. For the year ended December 31, 2017, Company P's pro forma consolidated net income is:
   A. $300,000.
   B. $348,000.
   C. $360,000.
3. On its December 31, 2017, pro forma consolidated balance sheet, Company P should report a minority ownership interest of:
   A. $0.
   B. $39,000.
   C. $42,000.

MODULE 14.7: BUSINESS COMBINATIONS: INCOME STATEMENT

Video covering this content is available online.

Now let's look at the income statements. Figure 14.6 contains the separate income statements of Company P and Company S for the year ended December 31, 2010.

Figure 14.6: Company P and S Income Statements

Income Statements Year ended December 31, 2010	Company P	Company S
Revenue	$60,000	$20,000
Expenses	40,000	16,000
Net income	$20,000	$4,000

Under the equity method, Company P will report its 80% share of Company S's net income in a one-line account in the income statement. Under the acquisition method, the revenue and expenses of Company P and Company S are combined. It is also necessary to create a minority interest in the income statement for the portion of Company S's net income that is not owned by Company P.

Figure 14.7 compares the income statement effects of the acquisition method and equity method.

Figure 14.7: Income Statement Comparison of Acquisition and Equity Methods

Company P Income Statement Year ended December 31, 2010	Acquisition Method	Equity Method
Revenue	$80,000	$60,000
Expenses	56,000	40,000
Operating income	$24,000	$20,000
Equity in income of S		3,200
Minority interest	(800)	
Net income	$23,200	$23,200

Similar to the consolidated balance sheet, Company P reports 100% of Company S's revenues and expenses even though Company P only owns 80%. Thus, a minority interest is created by multiplying the subsidiary's net income by the percentage of the subsidiary not owned. In our example, the minority interest is $800 ($4,000 S net income × 20%). The minority interest is subtracted in arriving at consolidated net income.

Notice the acquisition method results in higher revenues and expenses, as compared to the equity method, but net income is the same.

PROFESSOR'S NOTE

This example assumed that the parent company acquired its interest in the subsidiary by paying the proportionate share of the subsidiary's book value. If the parent pays more than its proportionate share of book value, the excess is allocated to tangible and intangible assets. The minority interest computation in the example also would be different. This will be covered later in this topic review.

MODULE QUIZ 14.7

To best evaluate your performance, enter your quiz answers online.

Use the following information to answer Questions 1 and 2.

Company M acquired 20% of Company N for $6 million on January 1, 2017. Company N's debt and equity securities are publicly traded on an organized exchange. Company N reported the following for the year ended 2017:

Year	Net Income (Loss)	Dividends
2017	($450,000)	$600,000

1. If Company M can significantly influence Company N, what is the balance sheet carrying value of Company M's investment at the end of 2017?
   A. $5,790,000.
   B. $5,970,000.
   C. $6,000,000.
2. If Company M can significantly influence Company N, what amount of income should Company M recognize from its investment for the year ended 2017?
   A. ($90,000).
   B. ($210,000).
   C. $30,000.
3. Selected operating results for Lowdown, Inc., in 2016 and 2017 are shown in the following table:

Lowdown, Inc.	2016	2017
Sales and operating revenues	$1,000	$1,140
Investment income	$45	$160
Total revenues	1,045	1,300
Operating costs	500	640
Pre-tax operating income	545	660

Martha Patterson, an analyst with Cauldron Associates, has been assigned the task of separating Lowdown's operating and investment results. She intends to do this by removing the effects of the returns on Lowdown's marketable securities portfolio and forecasting operating income for 2018. Patterson assumes that growth trend in operating income from 2016 to 2017 will continue in 2018.

The appropriate forecast of Lowdown's operating income in 2018 based on Patterson's analysis is *closest* to:
   A. $500.
   B. $650.
   C. $700.

MODULE 14.8: BUSINESS COMBINATIONS: GOODWILL

Video covering this content is available online.

Under the acquisition method, the purchase price is allocated to the *identifiable* assets and liabilities of the acquired firm on the basis of fair value. Any remainder is reported on the balance sheet as goodwill. Goodwill is said to be an *unidentifiable* asset that cannot be separated from the business.

Under U.S. GAAP, goodwill is the amount by which the fair value of the subsidiary is greater than the fair value of the acquired company's identifiable net assets (*full goodwill*). Under IFRS, goodwill is the excess of the purchase price over the fair value of the acquiring company's proportion of the acquired company's identifiable net assets (*partial goodwill*). However, IFRS permits the use of the full goodwill approach also.

Full goodwill (required under U.S. GAAP; allowed under IFRS):

> full goodwill = (fair value of equity of whole subsidiary) – (fair value of net identifiable assets of the subsidiary)

Partial goodwill (only allowed under IFRS):

> partial goodwill = purchase price – (% owned × FV of net identifiable assets of the subsidiary)

or

> partial goodwill = % owned × full goodwill

Let's look at an example of calculating acquisition goodwill.

EXAMPLE: Goodwill

Wood Corporation paid $600 million for all of the outstanding stock of Pine Corporation. At the acquisition date, Pine reported the condensed balance sheet below:

Pine Corporation Condensed Balance Sheet

	Book Value (in millions)
Current assets	$80
Plant and equipment, net	760
Goodwill	30
Liabilities	400
Stockholders' equity	470

The fair value of the plant and equipment was $120 million more than its recorded book value. The fair values of all other identifiable assets and liabilities were equal to their recorded book values. Calculate the amount of goodwill Wood should report in its consolidated balance sheet.

Answer:

(in millions)

Purchase price		$600
Current assets	$80	
Plant and equipment, net	880	
Liabilities	(400)	
Less: Fair value of net assets		560
Acquisition goodwill		$40

Goodwill is equal to the excess of purchase price over the fair value of identifiable assets and liabilities acquired. The plant and equipment was *written-up* by $120 million to reflect fair value. The goodwill reported on Pine's balance sheet is an unidentifiable asset and is thus ignored in the calculation of Wood's goodwill.

EXAMPLE: Full goodwill vs. partial goodwill

Continuing the previous example, suppose that Wood paid $450 million for 75% of the stock of Pine. Calculate the amount of goodwill Wood should report using the full goodwill method and the partial goodwill method.

Answer:

Full goodwill method:

Wood's balance sheet goodwill is the excess of the fair value of the subsidiary ($450 million / 0.75 = $600 million) over the fair value of identifiable net assets acquired, just as in the previous example. Acquisition goodwill = $40 million.

Partial goodwill method:

Wood's balance sheet goodwill is the excess of the acquisition price over Wood's proportionate share of the fair value of Pine's identifiable net assets:

Purchase price		$450 million
Less: 75% of fair value of net assets	0.75 × $560 =	$420 million
Acquisition goodwill		$30 million

Goodwill is lower using the partial goodwill method. How is this reflected on the liabilities-and-equity side of the balance sheet?

The value of *noncontrolling interest* also depends on which method is used. If the full goodwill method is used, noncontrolling interest is based on the acquired company's fair value. If the partial goodwill method is used, noncontrolling interest is based on the fair value of the acquired company's identifiable net assets.

In the previous example, noncontrolling interest using the full goodwill method is 25% of Wood's fair value of $600 million, or $150 million. Using the partial goodwill method, noncontrolling interest is 25% of the fair value of Pine's identifiable net assets, or $140 million. The difference of $10 million balances the $10 million difference in goodwill.

The full goodwill method results in higher total assets and higher total equity than the partial goodwill method. Thus, return on assets and return on equity will be lower if the full goodwill method is used.

Goodwill is not amortized. Instead, it is tested for impairment at least annually. Impairment occurs when the carrying value exceeds the fair value. However, measuring the fair value of goodwill is complicated by the fact that goodwill cannot be separated from the business. Because of its inseparability, goodwill is valued at the reporting unit level.

Under IFRS, testing for impairment involves a single step approach. If the carrying amount of the cash generating unit (where the goodwill is assigned) exceeds the recoverable amount, an impairment loss is recognized.

Under U.S. GAAP, goodwill impairment potentially involves two steps. In the first step, if the carrying value of the reporting unit (including the goodwill) exceeds the fair value of the reporting unit, an impairment exists.

Once it is determined the goodwill is impaired, the loss is measured as the difference between the carrying value of the goodwill and the *implied* fair value of the goodwill. The impairment loss is recognized in the income statement as a part of continuing operations.

PROFESSOR'S NOTE

Notice that the impairment test for goodwill is based on the decline in value of the reporting unit, while the loss is based on the decline in value of the goodwill.

The *implied* fair value of the goodwill is calculated in the same manner as goodwill at the acquisition date. That is, the fair value of the reporting unit is allocated to the identifiable assets and liabilities as if they were acquired on the impairment measurement date. Any excess is considered the *implied* fair value of the goodwill.

Let's look at an example.

EXAMPLE: Impaired goodwill

Last year, Parent Company acquired Sub Company for $1,000,000. On the date of acquisition, the fair value of Sub's net assets was $800,000. Thus, Parent reported acquisition goodwill of $200,000 ($1,000,000 purchase price – $800,000 fair value of Sub's net assets).

At the end of this year, the fair value of Sub is $950,000, and the fair value of Sub's net assets is $775,000. Assuming the carrying value of Sub is $980,000, determine if an impairment exists and calculate the loss (if applicable) under U.S. GAAP and under IFRS.

Answer:

U.S. GAAP (two-step approach):

1. Since the carrying value of Sub exceeds the fair value of Sub ($980,000 carrying value > $950,000 fair value), an impairment exists.
2. In order to measure the impairment loss, the implied goodwill must be compared to the carrying value of the goodwill. At the impairment

measurement date, the implied value of the goodwill is $175,000 ($950,000 fair value of Sub – $775,000 fair value of Sub's net assets). Since the carrying value of the goodwill exceeds the implied value of the goodwill, an impairment loss of $25,000 is recognized ($200,000 goodwill carrying value – $175,000 implied goodwill) thereby reducing goodwill to $175,000.

IFRS (one-step approach):

Goodwill impairment and loss under IFRS is 980,000 (carrying value) – 950,000 (fair value) = $30,000.

Bargain Purchase

In rare cases, acquisition purchase price is less than the fair value of net assets acquired. Both IFRS and U.S. GAAP require that the difference between fair value of net assets and purchase price be recognized as a gain in the income statement.

MODULE QUIZ 14.8

To best evaluate your performance, enter your quiz answers online.

1. According to U.S. GAAP, goodwill is considered impaired if the:
   A. implied goodwill at the measurement date exceeds the carrying value of goodwill.
   B. carrying value of the reporting unit is greater than fair value of the reporting unit.
   C. goodwill can be separated from the business and valued separately.
2. Adam Corporation acquired Hardy Corporation recently using the acquisition method. Adam is preparing to report its year-end results to include Hardy according to IFRS. Which of the following statements regarding goodwill is *most accurate*?
   A. Adam would amortize its goodwill over no more than 20 years.
   B. Adam would test its goodwill annually to ensure the carrying value is not greater than the recoverable amount.
   C. Adam would test its goodwill annually to ensure the fair value is not greater than the carrying value.

MODULE 14.9: JOINT VENTURES

Video covering this content is available online.

Joint Ventures

Recall that a joint venture is an entity in which control is shared by two or more investors. Joint ventures are created in various legal, operating, and accounting forms and are often used to invest in foreign markets, special projects, or risky ventures. Both U.S. GAAP and IFRS require the equity method of accounting for joint ventures.

In rare circumstances, the proportionate consolidation method may be allowed under U.S. GAAP and IFRS. Proportionate consolidation is similar to a business acquisition, except the investor (venturer) only reports the proportionate share of the assets, liabilities, revenues, and expenses of the joint venture. Since only the proportionate share is reported, no minority owners' interest is necessary.

Let's return to our earlier acquisition example. Recall that Company P acquired 80% of Company S on January 1, 2010, for $8,000 cash. Figure 14.8 compares the proportionate consolidation method and the equity method on the post-acquisition balance sheet of Company P.

Figure 14.8: Balance Sheet Comparison of Proportionate Consolidation and Equity Methods

Company P Post-Acquisition Balance Sheet January 1, 2010	Proportionate Consolidation Method	Equity Method
Current assets	$52,800	$40,000
Investment in S		8,000
Other assets	38,400	32,000
Total	$91,200	$80,000
Current liabilities	$51,200	$40,000
Common stock	28,000	28,000
Retained earnings	12,000	12,000
Total	$91,200	$80,000

Under proportionate consolidation, Company P's current assets are $52,800 [$48,000 P current assets – $8,000 cash paid + ($16,000 S current assets × 80%)].

With proportionate consolidation, Company P reports its 80% share of each of Company S's assets and liabilities. No minority ownership interest is necessary. Just like a regular consolidation, Company S's equity is ignored.

Notice that proportionate consolidation results in higher assets and liabilities, compared to the equity method, but stockholders' equity (or net assets) is the same.

Figure 14.9: Income Statement Comparison of Proportionate Consolidation and Equity Methods

Company P Income Statement Year ended December 31, 2010	Proportionate Consolidation Method	Equity Method
Revenue	$76,000	$60,000
Expenses	52,800	40,000
Operating income	$23,200	$20,000
Equity in income of S	______	3,200
Net income	$23,200	$23,200

With proportionate consolidation, Company P reports its 80% share of Company S's revenues and expenses. Once again, no minority ownership interest is necessary.

Notice that proportionate consolidation results in higher revenues and expenses compared to the equity method, but net income is the same.

MODULE QUIZ 14.9

To best evaluate your performance, enter your quiz answers online.

Use the following information to answer Questions 1 through 3.

Company C owns a 50% interest in a joint venture, JVC, and accounts for it using the equity method. JVC's assets and liabilities have a book value equal to their fair value. They have each reported the following 2017 financial results.

Balance Sheets	Company C	JVC
Cash	$1,550	$300
Accounts receivable	3,500	700
Inventory	3,000	800
Fixed assets	5,000	2,600
Investment in JVC	400	
Total assets	**$13,450**	**$4,400**
Accounts payable	$3,500	$1,200
Long-term debt	4,000	2,400
Equity	5,950	800
Total liabilities and equity	**$13,450**	**$4,400**

Income Statements	Company C	JVC
Revenues	$17,430	$2,800
Equity in JVC earnings	100	
Cost of goods sold	7,000	2,000
Other expenses	9,600	600
Net income	**$930**	**$200**

1. Assuming consolidation using the acquisition method, Company C's stockholders' equity at the end of 2017 is *closest* to:
   A. $5,950.
   B. $6,350.
   C. $6,750.
2. Assuming consolidation using the acquisition method, Company C's total assets at the end of 2017 is *closest* to:
   A. $15,250.
   B. $15,650.
   C. $17,450.
3. Assuming proportionate consolidation, Company C's cost of goods sold and net income for the year ended 2017 are *closest* to:

	Cost of goods sold	Net income
A.	$8,000	$930
B.	$9,000	$1,030
C.	$8,000	$830

4. According to U.S. GAAP, which of the following statements about the method used to account for a joint venture whereby each party owns 50% is *most accurate*?
   A. The investor can choose between the acquisition method and the equity method.
   B. The equity method is required.
   C. The acquisition method is required.

MODULE 14.10: SPECIAL PURPOSE ENTITIES

Video covering this content is available online.

Special Purpose and Variable Interest Entities

A special purpose entity (SPE) is a legal structure created to isolate certain assets and liabilities of the sponsor. An SPE can take the form of a corporation, partnership, joint venture, or trust. The typical motivation is to reduce risk and thereby lower the cost of financing. SPEs are often structured such that the sponsor company has control over the SPE's finances or operating activities while third parties have controlling interest in the SPE's equity.

In the past, SPEs were often maintained off-balance-sheet, thereby enhancing the sponsor's financial statements and ratios.

The FASB uses the term variable interest entity (VIE) to describe a special purpose entity that meets certain conditions. According to FASB ASC Topic 810, *Consolidation*, a VIE is an entity that has one or both of the following characteristics:

1. At-risk equity that is insufficient to finance the entity's activities without additional financial support.
2. Equity investors that lack any one of the following:
   - Decision making rights.
   - The obligation to absorb expected losses.
   - The right to receive expected residual returns.

If an SPE is considered a VIE, it must be consolidated by the primary beneficiary. The primary beneficiary is the entity that absorbs the majority of the risks or receives the majority of the rewards.

PROFESSOR'S NOTE

In a VIE, the capital source labeled as stockholders' equity is not truly equity, as the amount is insufficient to have the risk/return characteristics of equity. Generally, in these companies, "variable interest" refers to a stake in the company (or guarantees given) by the primary beneficiary. This stake has the same economic characteristics as "normal" equity.

The IASB continues to use the term special purpose entity. According to IFRS 10, *Consolidated Financial Statements,* the sponsoring entity must consolidate if it controls the SPE.

EXAMPLE: Special purpose entity

Company P, a textile manufacturer, wants to borrow $100 million. It has two options:

Option A: Borrow $100 million from Bank B.

Option B: Sell $100 million worth of accounts receivable to Company S, an SPE created for this purpose. The SPE will fund the purchase by borrowing the money from Bank B.

Company P's balance sheet before the borrowing is provided below:

Assets	$ millions	Liabilities and Equity	$ millions
Cash	$50	Current liabilities	$500
Accounts receivable	$200	Debt	$1,200
Fixed assets	$2,000	Equity	$550
Total assets	$2,250	Total	$2,250

Prepare company P's balance sheet under both options assuming that the SPE in option B meets the requirements for consolidation.

Answer:

Option A: Company P's cash and debt will both increase by the new borrowing of $100 million.

Company P's balance sheet after the borrowing:

Assets	$ millions	Liabilities and Equity	$ millions
Cash	$150	Current liabilities	$500
Accounts receivable	$200	Debt	$1,300
Fixed assets	$2,000	Equity	$550
Total	$2,350	Total	$2,350

Option B: Company P's (nonconsolidated) balance sheet will reflect a reduction in accounts receivable of $100 million and an increase in cash by the same amount.

Company P's balance sheet after the sale of accounts receivable to the SPE:

Assets	$ millions	Liabilities and Equity	$ millions
Cash	$150	Current liabilities	$500
Accounts receivable	$100	Debt	$1,200
Fixed assets	$2,000	Equity	$550
Total	$2,250	Total	$2,250

SPE's balance sheet after purchase of accounts receivable and bank loan:

Assets	$ millions	Liabilities and Equity	$ millions
Accounts receivable	$100	Debt	$100
Total	$100	Total	$100

After consolidation, the SPE's debt gets included with company P's debt, and accounts receivable for company P increase by the same amount.

Company P's balance sheet after consolidation:

Assets	$ millions	Liabilities and Equity	$ millions
Cash	$150	Current liabilities	$500
Accounts receivable	$200	Debt	$1,300
Fixed assets	$2,000	Equity	$550
Total	$2,350	Total	$2,350

The balance sheet of company P under either option is the same. Company P cannot hide the borrowing "off the books."

OTHER ISSUES IN BUSINESS COMBINATIONS THAT WEAKEN COMPARABILITY

Contingent Assets and Liabilities

Under IFRS, only contingent liabilities whose fair value can be measured reliably are recognized at the time of acquisition. (Contingent *assets* are never recognized.) In subsequent periods, contingent liabilities are measured at the higher of the value initially recognized, or the best estimate of the amount needed to settle the liabilities.

U.S. GAAP divides contingent assets and liabilities into contractual and noncontractual. Contractual contingent assets and liabilities are recorded at their fair values on the acquisition date. Noncontractual contingent assets are also recorded if, "more likely than not" they meet the definition of an asset or liability. Subsequently, measurement of contingent liabilities is similar under IFRS, while contingent assets are recognized at the *lower* of the initial value and the best estimate of the future settlement amount.

Contingent Consideration

If the terms of the acquisition involve a contingent consideration (e.g., a specific extra amount is payable to the former shareholders of the subsidiary if certain earnings or revenue targets are met), such consideration is recognized at fair value under both IFRS and U.S. GAAP as an asset, liability, or equity. Subsequent changes in value are recognized in the income statement, unless the value was originally classified in equity (any changes then settle within equity and not via the income statement).

In-Process R&D

In-process R&D is capitalized as an intangible asset and included as an asset under both U.S. GAAP and IFRS. In-process R&D is subsequently amortized (if successful) or impaired (if unsuccessful).

Restructuring Costs

Restructuring costs are expensed when incurred—and not capitalized as part of the acquisition cost—under both IFRS and U.S. GAAP.

LOS 14.c: Analyze how different methods used to account for intercorporate investments affect financial statements and ratios.

CFA® Program Curriculum, Volume 2, page 34

The effects of the choice of accounting methods on reported financial results have been covered earlier in this topic review, so we won't repeat the discussion here. Instead, we'll compare the effects of the equity method, the proportionate consolidation method, and the acquisition method.

There are four important effects on the balance sheet and income statement items that result from the choice of accounting method (in most situations):

1. All three methods report the same net income.
2. Equity method and proportionate consolidation report the same equity. Acquisition method equity will be higher by the amount of minority interest.
3. Assets and liabilities are highest under the acquisition method and lowest under the equity method; proportionate consolidation is in-between.
4. Revenues and expenses are highest under the acquisition method and lowest under the equity method; proportionate consolidation is in-between.

Figure 14.10: Reported Financial Results from Different Accounting Methods

	Equity Method	Proportionate Consolidation	Acquisition Method
Net profit margin	Higher—sales are lower and net income is the same	In-between	Lower
ROE	Higher—equity is lower and net income is the same	Same as equity method	Lower
ROA	Higher—net income is the same and assets are lower	In-between	Lower

MODULE QUIZ 14.10

To best evaluate your performance, enter your quiz answers online.

1. A company accounts for its investment in a subsidiary using the equity method. The reported net profit margin is 14%. An analyst adjusts the financials and determines that the company's own net profit margin is 8% while the subsidiary's profit margin is 10%. The net profit margin based on consolidation would *most likely* be:
   A. less than 8%.
   B. more than 14%.
   C. between 8% and 14%.

KEY CONCEPTS

LOS 14.a

Accounting for investments:

Ownership	Degree of Influence	Accounting Treatment
Less than 20% (investments in financial assets)	No significant influence	Held-to-maturity, fair value through profit or loss, available-for-sale
20%–50% (investments in associates)	Significant influence	Equity method
More than 50% (business combinations)	Control	Acquisition method

Investments in financial assets: Dividends and interest income are recognized in the investor's income statement. Held-to-maturity securities are reported on the balance sheet at amortized cost. Subsequent changes in fair value are ignored. Fair value through profit or loss securities are reported at fair value, and the unrealized gains and losses are recognized in the income statement. Available-for-sale securities are also reported at fair value, but the unrealized gains and losses are reported in stockholders' equity.

Investments in associates/joint ventures: With the equity method, the proportionate share of the investee's earnings increase the investor's investment account on the balance sheet and are recognized in the investor's income statement. Dividends received reduce the investment account. Dividends received are not recognized in the investor's income statement under the equity method. In rare cases, proportionate consolidation may be allowed. Proportionate consolidation is similar to a business combination, except the investor only includes the proportionate share of the assets, liabilities, revenues, and expenses of the joint venture. No minority owners' interest is required.

Business combinations: In an acquisition, all of the assets, liabilities, revenues, and expenses of the subsidiary are combined with the parent. Intercompany transactions are excluded. When the parent owns less than 100% of the subsidiary, it is necessary to create a noncontrolling interest account for the proportionate share of the subsidiary's net assets and net income that is not owned by the parent.

Under IFRS, the sponsor of a special purpose entity (SPE) must consolidate the SPE if their economic relationship indicates that the sponsor controls the SPE. U.S. GAAP requires that a variable interest entity (VIE) must be consolidated by its primary beneficiary.

LOS 14.b

Differences between IFRS and U.S. GAAP treatment of intercorporate investments include:

- Unrealized foreign exchange gains and losses on available-for-sale securities are recognized on the income statement under IFRS and as other comprehensive income under U.S. GAAP.
- IFRS permits either the partial goodwill or full goodwill method to value goodwill and noncontrolling interest in business combinations. U.S. GAAP requires the full goodwill method.

LOS 14.c

The effects of the equity method versus the acquisition method:

- Both report the same net income.
- Acquisition method equity will be higher by the amount of minority interest.
- Assets and liabilities are higher under the acquisition method.
- Sales are higher under the acquisition method.

ANSWER KEY FOR MODULE QUIZZES

Module Quiz 14.1

1. **A** Usually an ownership interest between 20% and 50% would indicate the ability to significantly influence. However, in this case, Tall is unable to influence Short as evidenced by its failure to obtain board representation; thus, Tall's ownership interest should be considered an investment in financial assets. (LOS 14.a)

Module Quiz 14.2

1. **B** Initially, the carrying value of all security investments is cost.

   initial cost = $950 + 250 = $1,200 (LOS 14.a)

2. **B** Both available-for-sale and fair value through profit or loss securities are carried at market value on the balance sheet. Also, both classifications call for recognition of unrealized losses and gains. Market value at t = 1 is $850 + $180 = $1,030. Unrealized loss is ($850 – $950) + ($180 – $250) = –$170. Note that the recognition differs. With available-for-sale securities, the recognition is only on the balance sheet. With fair value through profit or loss securities, the recognition impacts the income statement. (LOS 14.a)

3. **C** The increase in value requires that investment securities be written up to $900 + $350 = $1,250. Because these are equity securities, the held-to-maturity classification is not available. (LOS 14.a)

4. **A** Classifying the shares as trading requires both realized and unrealized gains and losses to be recognized on the income statement. As a result, this would have the effect of greater reported earnings volatility. There is actually a $220 *unrealized* gain between t = 1 and t = 2; the gain is unrealized because the shares were not actually sold. The net gain of $50 between the acquisition date and t = 2 is unrealized; therefore, by classifying as available-for-sale, the gain is not recognized on the income statement (it goes directly to equity). Classification as either trading or available-for-sale securities results in the same fair market value of $1,250 reported on the balance sheet at t = 2. (LOS 14.a)

5. **B** Debt securities held-to-maturity are securities that a company has the positive intent and ability to hold to maturity. They are carried at amortized cost ($1,200), and no unrealized or realized gains or losses are recognized until disposition. Because these securities were purchased at par, there is no amortization of premium/discount. (LOS 14.a)

Module Quiz 14.3, 14.4

1. **A** With the equity method, the proportional share of the affiliate's income (% ownership × affiliate earnings) is reported on the investor's income statement. (Module 14.4, LOS 14.a)

2. **B** $1,500,000 + 0.4($500,000 – $125,000) = $1,650,000. (Module 14.4, LOS 14.a)

3. **C** $500,000 × 0.4 = $200,000; dividends are not included in income under the equity method. (Module 14.4, LOS 14.a)

4. **A** $125,000 × 0.4 = $50,000; the dividend is cash flow = $50,000. (Module 14.4, LOS 14.a)

Module Quiz 14.5, 14.6

1. **B** Total assets = $1,200,000 + $360,000 – $120,000 = $1,440,000. (Module 14.6, LOS 14.a)

2. **B** Minority interest income = $60,000(0.2) = $12,000.

   Consolidated net income (after minority interest income is subtracted) = $300,000 + $60,000 – $12,000 = $348,000. (Module 14.5, LOS 14.a)

3. **B** The beginning balance of the minority interest is $30,000 ($150,000 S equity × 20%). The minority interest is increased by the minority share of Company S's income of $12,000 ($60,000 × 20%) and is decreased by the minority share of the dividends paid by Company S of $3,000 ($15,000 × 20%). Thus, the ending balance is $39,000 ($30,000 + $12,000 – $3,000). Note that the value of goodwill at the time of acquisition is zero; hence, there is no need to specify whether full or partial goodwill accounting is used. (Module 14.5, LOS 14.a)

Module Quiz 14.7

1. **A** $6,000,000 + 0.2(–$450,000) – 0.2($600,000) = $5,790,000. (Module 14.6, LOS 14.a)

2. **A** 0.2(–$450,000) = –$90,000. (Module 14.7, LOS 14.a)

3. **A** After removing the investment gains in 2016 and 2017, operating income is $500 each year. Based on a growth trend of 0%, the appropriate operating income forecast for 2018 is also $500.

	2016	2017
Sales and operating revenues	$1,000	$1,140
Operating costs	500	640
Adjusted operating income	500	500

(Module 14.7, LOS 14.a)

Module Quiz 14.8

1. **B** In testing goodwill for impairment, the carrying value of the reporting unit (including goodwill) is compared to the fair value of the reporting unit. Once an impairment has been detected, the loss is equal to the difference in the book value of the goodwill and the implied value of the goodwill. (LOS 14.a)

2. **B** Adam is required to perform an annual impairment test. The carrying value cannot exceed the fair value; if it does, then an impairment has taken place and the goodwill must be written down. (LOS 14.a)

Module Quiz 14.9

1. **B** Company C would include minority interest (50% of $800) along with its own equity of $5,950 in the consolidated financial statements. (Module 14.6, LOS 14.a)

2. **C** Company C would include all the assets of JVC and remove its equity investment in the consolidated balance sheet. $13,450 – $400 + $4,400 = $17,450. (Module 14.7, LOS 14.a)

3. **A** COGS = $7,000 Company C + 50% of $2,000 JVC = $8,000.

   Net income of $930 is not affected by proportionate consolidation. (Module 14.9, LOS 14.a)

4. **B** Under U.S. GAAP (and IFRS), equity method is required to be used to account for joint ventures. Only in rare cases is proportionate consolidation allowed. (Module 14.9, LOS 14.b)

Module Quiz 14.10

1. **C** The equity method typically yields a higher measure of net profit margin. Consolidation is most likely to result in a net profit margin somewhere between the profit margins of the two entities. (LOS 14.c)

The following is a review of the Financial Reporting and Analysis (1) principles designed to address the learning outcome statements set forth by CFA Institute. Cross-Reference to CFA Institute Assigned Reading #15.

READING 15 Employee Compensation: Post-Employment and Share-Based

Study Session 5

EXAM FOCUS

This is a complicated topic, but don't be intimidated. Accounting for pension plans may be complex, but the economic reasoning is not too difficult to grasp. Despite convergence between U.S. GAAP and IFRS, significant differences remain, particularly with respect to recognition of periodic pension cost in income statement versus in OCI. You should be able to explain how reported results are affected by management's assumptions. You should also be able to adjust the reported financial results for economic reality by calculating total periodic pension cost. Share-based compensation is also introduced. Compensation expense is based on fair value on the grant date, and it is often necessary to use an option pricing model to estimate fair value. Make sure you understand the effects of changing the model inputs on fair value.

MODULE 15.1: TYPES OF PLANS

Video covering this content is available online.

LOS 15.a: Describe the types of post-employment benefit plans and implications for financial reports.

CFA® Program Curriculum, Volume 2, page 77

A pension is a form of deferred compensation earned over time through employee service. The most common pension arrangements are defined-contribution plans and defined benefit plans.

A **defined contribution plan** is a retirement plan whereby the firm contributes a certain sum each period to the employee's retirement account. The firm's contribution can be based on any number of factors including years of service, the employee's age, compensation, profitability, or even a percentage of the employee's contribution. In any event, the firm makes no promise to the employee regarding the future value of the plan assets. The investment decisions are left to the employee, who assumes all of the investment risk.

The financial reporting requirements for defined-contribution plans are straightforward. Pension expense is simply equal to the employer's contribution. There is no future obligation to report on the balance sheet. The remainder of this topic review will focus on accounting for a defined-benefit plan.

In a **defined-benefit plan**, the firm promises to make periodic payments to the employee after retirement. The benefit is usually based on the employee's years of service and the employee's compensation at, or near, retirement. For example, an employee might earn a retirement benefit of 2% of her final salary for each year of service. Consequently, an employee with 20 years of service and a final salary of $100,000 would receive $40,000 ($100,000 final salary × 2% × 20 years of service) each year upon retirement until death.

Since the employee's future benefit is defined, the employer assumes the investment risk.

Financial reporting for a defined-benefit plan is much more complicated than for a defined-contribution plan because the employer must estimate the value of the future obligation to its employees. This involves forecasting a number of variables such as future compensation levels, employee turnover, retirement age, mortality rates, and an appropriate discount rate.

A company that offers defined pension benefits typically funds the plan by contributing assets to a separate legal entity, usually a trust. The plan assets are managed to generate the income and principal growth necessary to pay the pension benefits as they come due.

The difference in the benefit obligation and the plan assets is referred to as the **funded status of the plan**. If the plan assets exceed the pension obligation, the plan is said to be "overfunded." Conversely, if the pension obligation exceeds the plan assets, the plan is "underfunded."

Other post-employment benefits, primarily health care benefits for retired employees, are similar to a defined-benefit pension plan: the future benefit is defined today but is based on a number of unknown variables. For example, in a post-employment health care plan, the employer must forecast health care costs that are expected once the employee retires.

Funding is an area where other post-employment benefit plans differ from defined-benefit pension plans. Pension plans are typically funded at some level, while other post-employment benefit plans are usually unfunded. In the case of an unfunded plan, the employer recognizes expense in the income statement as the benefits are earned; however, the employer's cash flow is not affected until the benefits are actually paid to the employee.

MODULE QUIZ 15.1

To best evaluate your performance, enter your quiz answers online.

1. Which of the following statements about retirement plans is *most accurate*?
   A. Total periodic pension cost is equal to the change in PBO minus the firm's contributions.
   B. In a defined-contribution plan, periodic pension cost is calculated as the difference in the contribution amount and the actual return on plan assets.
   C. In a defined-benefit plan, the employer assumes the majority of the investment risk.

MODULE 15.2: DEFINED BENEFIT PLANS—BALANCE SHEET

Video covering this content is available online.

LOS 15.b: Explain and calculate measures of a defined benefit pension obligation (i.e., present value of the defined benefit obligation and projected benefit obligation) and net pension liability (or asset).

CFA® Program Curriculum, Volume 2, page 79

The **projected benefit obligation** (PBO) [known as **present value of defined benefit obligation (PVDBO)** under IFRS] is the actuarial present value (at an assumed discount rate) of all future pension benefits earned to date, *based on expected future salary increases*. It measures the value of the obligation, assuming the firm is a going concern and that the employees will continue to work for the firm until they retire.

From one period to the next, the benefit obligation changes as a result of current service cost, interest cost, past (prior) service cost, changes in actuarial assumptions, and benefits paid to employees.

Current service cost is the present value of benefits earned by the employees during the current period. Service cost includes an estimate of compensation growth (future salary increases) if the pension benefits are based on future compensation. In rare cases, the pension plan may have a provision for employees to share in the service cost. Current service cost in that case would only represent the employer's share of the cost. Employee contributions would be added to both beginning PBO and beginning plan assets in PBO and FV plan asset reconciliation respectively.

Interest cost is the increase in the obligation due to the passage of time. Benefit obligations are discounted obligations; thus, interest accrues on the obligation each period. Interest cost is equal to the pension obligation at the beginning of the period multiplied by the discount rate.

Past (prior) service costs are retroactive benefits awarded to employees when a plan is initiated or amended. Under IFRS, past service costs are expensed immediately. Under U.S. GAAP, past service costs are amortized over the average service life of employees.

Changes in actuarial assumptions are the gains and losses that result from changes in variables such as mortality, employee turnover, retirement age, and the discount rate. An actuarial gain will decrease the benefit obligation and an actuarial loss will increase the obligation.

Benefits paid reduce the PBO.

Consider the following example of calculating the PBO.

EXAMPLE: Calculating PBO

John McElwain was hired on January 1, 2016, as the only employee of Transfer Trucking, Inc., and is eligible to participate in the company's defined-benefit pension plan. Under the plan, he is promised an annual payment of 2% of his final annual salary for each year of service. The pension benefit will be paid at the end of each year, beginning one year after retirement. McElwain's starting annual salary is $50,000.

In order to calculate the PBO at the end of the first year, we will assume the following:

- The **discount rate** is 8%.
- McElwain's salary will increase by 4% per year (this is called the **rate of compensation growth**).
- McElwain will work for 25 years.
- McElwain will live for 15 years after retirement and receive 15 annual pension benefit payments.

Answer:

Based on a starting salary of $50,000 in 2016 and 4% annual pay increases over 24 years, McElwain's salary at retirement will be $50,000 \times (1 + 0.04)^{24} =$ $128,165.21. (If McElwain works for 25 years, he will receive 24 pay increases.)

If McElwain is expected to earn $128,165.21 in his last year of employment (2040), he will be entitled to an annual end-of-year pension payment equal to 2% of his final salary for each year of service. Thus, at the end of one year of service, McElwain's benefit is $2,563.30 per year from retirement until death ($128,165.21 × 2% × 1 year). Assuming he lives 15 years past retirement, the present value of the payments on the retirement date (2040) is $21,940.55 (PV of 15 year annuity of $2,563.30 at PMT = –2,563.30; N = 15; I/Y = 8; FV = 0; CPT PV → 21,940.55). At the end of his first year of employment (2016), the present value of the annuity that begins in 24 years is $3,460.01 ($21,940.55 discounted at 8% for 24 years).

Therefore, the PBO at the end of 2016 (McElwain's first year of employment) is $3,460.01. A table outlining these cash flows follows.

Calculation of the PBO at the End of 2016

Year	Years of Service	Projected Salary	Years in Retirement	Benefit Payment (end of year)	Present Value (end of year)
2016	1	$50,000.00			PBO = $3,460.01
2017	2	$52,000.00			
2018	3	$54,080.00			
2038	23	$118,495.94			
2039	24	$123,235.78			
2040	25	$128,165.21			$21,940.55
2041			1	$2,563.30	
2042			2	$2,563.30	
2043			3	$2,563.30	
2054			14	$2,563.30	
2055			15	$2,563.30	

After two years of employment, McElwain's benefit is $5,126.61 ($128,165.21 × 2% × 2 years). The present value of the payments on the retirement date (2040) is $43,881.09 (PV of 15 year annuity of $5,126.61 at 8%). At the end of his second year of employment (2017), the present value of the annuity that begins in 23 years is $7,473.62 ($43,881.09 discounted at 8% for 23 years).

Therefore, the PBO at the end of 2017 (McElwain's second year of employment) is $7,473.62. A table outlining these cash flows follows.

Calculation of the PBO at the End of 2017

Year	Years of Service	Projected Salary	Years in Retirement	Benefit Payment (end of year)	Present Value (end of year)
2016	1	$50,000.00			
2017	2	$52,000.00			PBO = $7,473.62
2018	3	$54,080.00			
2038	23	$118,495.94			
2039	24	$123,235.78			
2040	25	$128,165.21			$43,881.09
2041			1	$5,126.61	
2042			2	$5,126.61	
2043			3	$5,126.61	
2054			14	$5,126.61	
2055			15	$5,126.61	

During 2017, the PBO increased $4,013.61. The increase is a result of current service cost and interest cost as follows:

	2016 PBO	$3,460.01	
+	Current service cost	3,736.81	(PV of 15 payments of $2,563.30 beginning in 23 years)
+	Interest cost	276.80	($3,460.01 × 8%)
	2017 PBO	$7,473.62	

The current service cost is the present value of the benefits earned during 2017 and the interest cost is the increase in the PBO due to the passage of time.

Balance Sheet Effects

Figure 15.1: Funded Status of a Pension Plan

Plan Assets
Fair value at the beginning of the year
(+) Contributions
(+) Actual return
(–) Benefits paid
= Fair value at the end of the year

PBO
PBO at the beginning of the year
(+) Service cost
(+) Interest cost
(+) Past service cost (plan amendments during the year)
(+/–) Actuarial losses/gains during the year
(–) Benefits paid
= PBO at the end of the year

Difference is funded status of the plan:
Plan assets > PBO → Overfunded plan
Plan assets < PBO → Underfunded plan

The funded status reflects the economic standing of a pension plan:

funded status = fair value of plan assets – PBO

The balance sheet presentation under both U.S. GAAP and IFRS is as follows:

balance sheet asset (liability) = funded status

If the funded status is negative, it is reported as a liability. If the funded status is positive, it is reported as an asset *subject to a ceiling of present value of future economic benefits (such as future refunds or reduced contributions).*

PROFESSOR'S NOTE

An overfunded pension plan would lead to either lower future contributions (i.e., savings in contributions for employers) or future withdrawals (refunds). Both IFRS and U.S. GAAP limit the asset recognition to the present value of such refunds or reduced contributions.

MODULE QUIZ 15.2

To best evaluate your performance, enter your quiz answers online.

1. Which of the following components of the projected benefit obligation is *most likely* to increase every year as a direct result of the employee working another year for the company?
   A. Current service cost.
   B. Interest cost.
   C. Benefits paid.

MODULE 15.3: DEFINED BENEFIT PLANS, PART 1—PERIODIC COST

Video covering this content is available online.

LOS 15.c: Describe the components of a company's defined benefit pension costs.

CFA® Program Curriculum, Volume 2, page 82

The periodic pension cost (i.e., total periodic pension cost or net periodic pension cost) for a period is the employer's contributions adjusted for changes in funded status. In other words, the expense to the company is either paid (via contributions) or deferred (via a worsening of the plan's funded status).

total periodic pension cost (TPPC)
= employer contributions – (ending funded status – beginning funded status)

Alternatively,

total periodic pension cost = current service cost + interest cost – actual return on plan assets +/– actuarial losses/gains due to changes in assumptions affecting PBO + prior service cost

PROFESSOR'S NOTE

The main difference between U.S. GAAP and IFRS is the allocation of total periodic pension cost between the income statement (i.e., reported pension expense) and OCI. Hence under both GAAP and IFRS, total periodic pension cost = periodic pension cost in P&L + periodic pension cost in OCI.

Let's look at the components of periodic pension cost reported in P&L (or income statement). We have already discussed current service cost and interest cost, but it will help to review them again.

Periodic Pension Cost Reported in P&L

Current service cost. As previously discussed, current service cost is the present value of benefits earned by the employees during the current period. Current service cost is the increase in the PBO that is the result of the employees working one more period. Current service cost is immediately recognized in the income statement.

Interest cost. Interest cost is the increase in the PBO due to the passage of time. It is calculated by multiplying the PBO at the beginning of the period by the discount rate. Interest cost is immediately recognized as a component of pension expense.

Under IFRS, net interest expense/income is defined as the discount rate multiplied by the beginning funded status (i.e., interest cost is offset against expected plan return). If the plan is reporting a liability (i.e., an underfunded plan), an expense is reported. Conversely, if the plan reports an asset, interest income is reported.

Expected return on plan assets. The employer contributes assets to a separate entity (trust) to be used to satisfy the pension obligation in the future. The return on the plan assets has no effect on the PBO. However, the expected return on the assets is a component of reported pension expense. Expected return (instead of actual return) on plan assets is used for the computation of reported pension expense. The difference in the expected return and the actual return is combined with other items related to changes in actuarial assumptions into the "actuarial gains and losses" account. *Under IFRS, the expected rate of return on plan assets is implicitly assumed to be the same as the discount rate used for computation of PBO and a net interest expense/income is reported as discussed above.*

PROFESSOR'S NOTE

While TPPC uses *actual* return on plan assets as an offset to pension cost, periodic pension cost reported in the income statement uses *expected* return on plan assets. The difference between actual and expected return results in deferred gains (when actual return > expected return) or losses (when actual return < expected return) as discussed next.

Actuarial gains and losses. Earlier, we defined actuarial gains/losses as changes in PBO due to changes in actuarial assumptions. However, there are two components within actuarial gains and losses. The first component is the gain (loss) due to decrease (increase) in PBO occurring on account of changes in actuarial assumptions; the second component is the difference between actual and expected return on plan assets.

Actuarial gains and losses are recognized in *other comprehensive income* (OCI). Under IFRS, actuarial gains and losses are not amortized. Under U.S. GAAP, actuarial gains and losses are amortized using the corridor approach.

Corridor Approach (U.S. GAAP only)

For any period, once the beginning balance of actuarial gains and losses exceed 10% of the greater of the beginning PBO or plan assets, amortization is required. This arbitrary 10% "corridor" represents a materiality threshold whereby gains and losses should offset over time. The excess amount over the "corridor" is amortized as a component of periodic pension cost in P&L over the remaining service life of the employees. The amortization of an actuarial gain reduces periodic pension cost in P&L and the amortization of an actuarial loss increases periodic pension cost in P&L. Companies can choose to amortize actuarial gains and losses more quickly than implied by the corridor method. However, the application has to be consistent for gains as well as losses and over time.

Past (prior) service costs. When a firm adopts or amends its pension plan, the PBO is immediately increased. Under U.S. GAAP, instead of expensing the cost immediately, it is reported as a part of other comprehensive income and amortized over the remaining service life of the affected employees.

Under IFRS, the past service costs are recognized in periodic pension cost in P&L immediately (i.e., they are expensed immediately and not amortized).

Under U.S. GAAP, the amortization of actuarial gains and losses and the amortization of past service costs reduces the volatility of periodic pension cost in P&L. Thus, the amortization process results in periodic pension cost in P&L that is "smoothed." Under IFRS, there is no amortization. Actuarial gains and losses are not subject to the corridor method and hence never transferred out of OCI into income statement.

In summary, total periodic pension cost for a period is the employer's contributions adjusted for changes in funded status. U.S. GAAP and IFRS differ in recognizing this expense between income statement and OCI as summarized in Figure 15.2.

Figure 15.2: Difference Between Recognition of Components of Pension Costs Under U.S. GAAP and IFRS

Component	U.S. GAAP	IFRS
Current service cost	Income statement	Income statement
Past service cost	OCI, amortized over service life	Income statement
Interest cost	Income statement	Income statement
Expected return	Income statement	Income statement*
Actuarial gains/losses	Amortized portion in income statement. Unamortized in OCI.	All in OCI—not amortized (called 'Remeasurements')

*Under IFRS, the expected rate of return on plan assets equals the discount rate and net interest expense/income is reported.

MODULE QUIZ 15.3

To best evaluate your performance, enter your quiz answers online.

1. Company Z has a defined-benefit plan. The projected benefit obligation is $60 million, and prior service cost is $10 million. The fair value of the plan's assets is $40 million. Under U.S. GAAP, what amount should Company Z report on its balance sheet as a result of the pension plan?
   A. $10 million liability.
   B. $10 million asset.
   C. $20 million liability.

2. Jacklyn King has been asked to do some accounting for Alexeeff Corp.'s pension plan. Alexeeff reports under U.S. GAAP. At the beginning of the period, the PBO was $12 million, and the fair market value of plan assets totaled $8 million. The discount rate is 9%, expected return on plan assets is $0.96 million, and the anticipated compensation growth rate is 4%. At the end of the period, it was determined that the actual return on assets was 14%, plan assets equaled $9 million, and the service cost for the year was $0.9 million. Ignore amortization of unrecognized prior service costs and actuarial gains and losses. Periodic pension cost reported in the income statement for the year is *closest* to:
   A. $0.72 million.
   B. $0.86 million.
   C. $1.02 million.

Video covering this content is available online.

MODULE 15.4: DEFINED BENEFIT PLANS, PART 2—PERIODIC COST EXAMPLE

EXAMPLE: Periodic pension cost

The following information is provided about the defined benefit pension plan of Zenith Industries for the fiscal year ending 20X5:

Employer contributions	€ 1,200
Current service costs	€ 1,850
Past service costs	€ 120
Beginning of year benefit obligation	€ 38,750
End of year benefit obligation	€ 43,619
Increase in benefit obligation due to changes in actuarial assumption	€ 628
Beginning of year plan assets	€ 28,322
End of year plan assets	€ 30,682
Actual return on plan assets	€ 1,795
Benefits paid	€ 635
Unamortized actuarial losses (U.S. GAAP only)	€ 3,150
Expected rate of return on plan assets	6%
Discount rate used in estimating benefit obligation	7.5%

Calculate:

1. Beginning and ending funded status.
2. Total periodic pension cost.
3. Periodic pension cost reported in P&L under U.S. GAAP (ignore amortization of past service cost).
4. Periodic pension cost in reported in P&L under IFRS.
5. Periodic pension cost reported in OCI under U.S. GAAP.
6. Periodic pension cost reported in OCI under IFRS.

Answer:

While not necessary for answering any of the questions, reconciliation of beginning PBO to ending PBO and beginning plan assets to ending plan assets would be informative.

PBO

Beginning of year benefit obligation	€ 38,750
(+) Current service costs	€ 1,850
(+) Interest cost [beg. PBO × 7.5%]	€ 2,906
(+) Past service costs	€ 120
(+) Actuarial loss/(gain)	€ 628
(–) Benefits paid	€ 635
(=) End of year benefit obligation	€ 43,619

Plan Assets

Beginning of year plan assets	€ 28,322
(+) Employer contributions	€ 1,200
(+) Actual return	€ 1,795
(–) Benefits paid	€ 635
(=) End of year plan assets	€ 30,682

1. Beginning funded status = beginning plan assets – beginning PBO

   = 28,322 – 38,750 = –€10,428

   Ending funded status = ending plan assets – ending PBO

   = 30,682 – 43,619 = –€12,937

2. Total periodic pension cost = employer contribution – change in funded status

   = 1,200 – [–12,937 – (–10,428)] = €3,709

   Alternatively,

   total periodic pension cost = current service cost + interest cost + past service cost + actuarial losses – actual return

   = 1,850 + 2,906 + 120 + 628 – 1,795 = €3,709

3. Periodic pension cost in P&L (U.S. GAAP):

   a. Corridor approach:
      Since beginning PBO > beginning plan assets, we take 10% of beginning PBO: €3,875.

      Since unamortized actuarial losses do not exceed 10% of beginning PBO, no amortization is necessary.

b. Periodic pension cost in P&L:

Current service costs	€1,850
(+) Interest cost	€2,906
(–) Expected return on plan assets[1]	€1,699
(=) Pension expense reported in P&L	€3,057

[1]Expected return = expected rate of return × beginning plan assests

= 6% × €28,322 = €1,699

4. Periodic pension cost in P&L (IFRS):

Current service costs	€1,850
(+) Past service cost (total)	€120
(+) Net interest cost[2]	€782
(=) Pension expense reported in P&L	€2,752

[2] Net interest cost = discount rate × beginning funded status

= 7.5% × €10,428 = €782

5. Periodic pension cost in OCI = total periodic pension cost – periodic pension cost in P&L

   Periodic pension cost in OCI (U.S. GAAP) = €3,709 – €3,057 = €652

6. Periodic pension cost in OCI (IFRS) = €3,709 – €2,752 = €957

Presentation

The presentation of pension expense differs between IFRS and U.S. GAAP. Under U.S. GAAP, all components of periodic pension cost that are reported in the income statement are aggregated and presented as a single line item. Under IFRS, components *may* be presented separately. Both U.S. GAAP and IFRS require disclosure of total periodic pension cost in the notes to financial statements.

Capitalizing Pension Costs

Pension costs included in the cost of production of goods (e.g., labor costs included in the value of work-in-process or finished goods) may be capitalized as part of valuation of ending inventory. When this inventory is eventually sold, such costs are expensed as a component of cost of goods sold.

PROFESSOR'S NOTE

One key to understanding this reading is to avoid confusing these two measures: 1) periodic pension cost in the income statement (i.e., reported pension expense) and 2) TPPC.

Reported pension expense:

- is what we report in the income statement.
- uses EXPECTED return on plan assets.
- is computed differently depending on whether we're using IFRS or US GAAP.

Total periodic pension cost (TPPC):

- is the true (i.e., economic) cost of the pension plan.
- does not change depending on the accounting system chosen.
- uses ACTUAL return on plan assets.

MODULE QUIZ 15.4

To best evaluate your performance, enter your quiz answers online.

1. The net amount of the cost components of Heritage Bakery's pension plan for 2016 was \$38 million. Cost components include current service cost and interest cost. The fair market value of plan assets on January 1, 2016, was \$159 million. The projected benefit obligation (PBO) on January 1, 2016, was \$193 million, and the PBO on December 31, 2016, was \$220 million. There are no effects of foreign currency exchange rate changes, business combinations, divestitures, curtailments, settlements, special terminations, or contributions by the employer or plan participants. Actual return on assets in 2016 was \$32 million. The expected return on plan assets for 2016 was 10%. The fair value of plan assets on December 31, 2016, is *closest* to:
   A. \$148 million.
   B. \$164 million.
   C. \$180 million.

MODULE 15.5: PLAN ASSUMPTIONS

Video covering this content is available online.

LOS 15.d: Explain and calculate the effect of a defined benefit plan's assumptions on the defined benefit obligation and periodic pension cost.

CFA® Program Curriculum, Volume 2, page 85

The firm discloses three assumptions used in its pension calculations: the discount rate, the rate of compensation growth, and the expected return on plan assets.

The **discount rate** is the interest rate used to compute the present value of the benefit obligation and the current service cost component of periodic pension cost. The discount rate is not the risk-free rate. Rather, it is based on interest rates of high quality fixed income investments with a maturity profile similar to the future obligation. The discount rate assumption affects the PBO as well as periodic pension cost.

The **rate of compensation growth** is the average annual rate by which employee compensation is expected to increase over time. The rate of compensation growth affects both the PBO and periodic pension cost.

The **expected return on plan assets** is the assumed long-term rate of return on the plan's investments. Recall that the expected return reduces periodic pension cost in P&L and the differences between the expected return and actual return are deferred. Also, recall that expected return is assumed only under U.S. GAAP. Under IFRS, it is always equal to the discount rate.

Firms can improve reported results by *increasing* the discount rate, *reducing* the compensation growth rate, or (under U.S. GAAP) *increasing* the expected return on plan assets.

Increasing the discount rate will:

- Reduce present values; hence, PBO is lower. A lower PBO improves the funded status of the plan.
- Usually results in lower total periodic pension cost because of lower current service cost. Recall that current service cost is a present value calculation; thus, an increase in the discount rate reduces the present value of a future sum.
- Usually reduce interest cost (beginning PBO × the discount rate) unless the plan is mature. Note that beginning PBO is reduced when the discount rate increases. For a nonmature plan this decrease more than offsets the impact of the increased rate at which we compute the interest cost.

Decreasing the compensation growth rate will:

- Reduce future benefit payments; hence, PBO is lower. A lower PBO improves the funded status of the plan.
- Reduce current service cost and lower interest cost; thus, total periodic pension cost will decrease.

Increasing the expected return on plan assets (under U.S. GAAP) will:

- Reduce periodic pension cost reported in P&L (but will leave the total periodic pension cost unchanged).
- Not affect the benefit obligation or the funded status of the plan.

Figure 15.3 summarizes the effects of changes in these assumptions on the PBO.

Figure 15.3: Effect of Changing Pension Assumptions on Balance Sheet Liability and Periodic Pension Cost

Effect on...	Increase Discount Rate	Decrease Rate of Compensation Growth	Increase Expected Rate of Return
Balance sheet liability	Decrease	Decrease	No effect
Total periodic pension cost	Decrease*	Decrease	No effect
Periodic pension cost in P&L	Decrease*	Decrease	Decrease**

*For mature plans, a higher discount rate might increase interest costs. In rare cases, interest cost will increase by enough to offset the decrease in the current service cost, and periodic pension cost will increase.

**Under U.S. GAAP only. Not applicable under IFRS.

The assumptions are similar for other post-employment benefits except the compensation growth rate is replaced by a health care inflation rate. Generally, the presumption is the inflation rate will taper off and eventually become constant. This constant rate is known as the **ultimate health care trend rate**.

All else equal, firms can reduce the post-employment benefit obligation and periodic expense by decreasing the near term health care inflation rate, by decreasing the ultimate health care trend rate, or by reducing the time needed to reach the ultimate health care trend rate.

Analysts must compare the pension and other post-employment benefit assumptions over time and across firms to assess the quality of earnings. Earnings quality deals with the conservatism of management's financial reporting assumptions.

In addition, analysts should consider whether the assumptions are internally consistent. For example, the discount rate and compensation growth rate should reflect a consistent view of inflation. Under U.S. GAAP, the assumed expected rate of return should be consistent with plan's asset allocation. If the assumptions are inconsistent, the firm may be manipulating the financial statements by using aggressive assumptions.

MODULE QUIZ 15.5

To best evaluate your performance, enter your quiz answers online.

1. Which of the following statements *best* describes the impact of an increase in the discount rate on PBO and periodic pension cost reported in P&L of a defined-benefit retirement plan covering a relatively young workforce?
   A. Decrease the PBO and increase periodic pension cost reported in P&L.
   B. Decrease the PBO and decrease periodic pension cost reported in P&L.
   C. Increase the PBO and decrease periodic pension cost reported in P&L.

2. Under U.S. GAAP, all else equal, which of the following statements *best* describes the impact of an increase in the expected return on plan assets?
   A. Increase in plan assets and decrease in periodic pension cost reported in P&L.
   B. Decrease in PBO and increase in service cost.
   C. Increase in net income.

Use the following information to answer Questions 3 and 4.

You have just been hired as the controller at Vincent, Inc. Vincent has a defined-benefit retirement plan for its employees. The firm has a relatively young workforce with a low percentage of retirees. Your first task is to analyze the effects of changing assumptions on different variables used to calculate certain pension amounts.

3. Which of the following *best* describes the impact of an increase in the compensation growth rate?
   A. Retained earnings are lower.
   B. PBO is lower.
   C. The plan assets are higher.
4. All else equal, a decrease in the discount rate will *most likely* have what impact on the funded status?
   A. Increase.
   B. Decrease.
   C. No effect.
5. SCP Incorporated disclosed the following information related to its defined-benefit pension plan:

	2016	**2015**	**2014**
Discount rate	4.4%	4.3%	4.1%
Expected return on assets	5.2%	4.9%	4.9%
Expected salary growth rate	3.1%	3.1%	3.1%
Actual inflation rate	2.3%	2.5%	2.6%
Allocation of plan assets:			
Debt investments	40.0%	30.0%	30.0%
Equity investments	60.0%	70.0%	70.0%

   SCP's pension assumptions are internally consistent with regard to:
   A. inflation expectations but not asset returns.
   B. asset returns but not inflation expectations.
   C. neither asset returns nor inflation expectations.

MODULE 15.6: ANALYST ADJUSTMENTS

Video covering this content is available online.

LOS 15.e: Explain and calculate how adjusting for items of pension and other post-employment benefits that are reported in the notes to the financial statements affects financial statements and ratios.

CFA® Program Curriculum, Volume 2, page 92

Comparative financial analysis using published financial statements can be difficult when there are differences between firms' accounting treatments for pensions. Analysts may need to make several adjustments for analytical purposes:

1. **Gross vs. net pension assets/liabilities:**

   There are two reasons for netting pension assets and liabilities:

   - The employer largely controls the plan assets and the obligation and, therefore, bears the risks and potential rewards.
   - The company's decisions regarding funding and accounting for the pension plan are more likely to be affected by the net pension obligation, not the gross amounts, because the plan assets can only be used for paying pension benefits to its employees.

   This unique netting procedure affects certain ratios because the firm's total assets and total liabilities are both less than if the firm reported the gross amounts. For example, return on assets (ROA) would likely be lower if the gross amounts were reported on the balance sheet (higher denominator). In addition, leverage ratios would likely be higher with the gross amounts.

2. **Differences in assumptions used:**

   For example, an analyst is comparing two companies in the same industry. Both companies offer a defined benefit plan but assume different discount rates. The company assuming a higher discount rate would be underestimating its pension liabilities (i.e., PBO) and underestimating periodic pension cost in P&L (and hence reporting higher net income).

3. **Differences between IFRS and U.S. GAAP in recognizing total periodic pension cost (in income statement vs. OCI):**

   As mentioned previously, some components of total periodic pension cost may be treated differently depending on the accounting standards being followed. For comparison purposes, an analyst may need to make adjustments to ensure uniform treatment of components. Alternatively, the analyst could simply use comprehensive income (i.e., net income plus OCI) as the metric for comparison.

4. **Differences due to classification in the income statement:**

   Classification of the components of periodic pension cost in P&L as operating/nonoperating differs under U.S. GAAP versus IFRS. Under U.S. GAAP, the entire periodic pension cost in P&L (including interest) is shown as an operating expense. Under IFRS, the components of periodic pension cost can be included in various line items. Analysts can adjust GAAP-reported income by adding back the periodic pension cost in P&L and subtracting only service cost in determining operating income. Interest cost should be added to the firm's interest expense, and the actual return on plan assets should be added to nonoperating income. Note that this adjustment excludes (ignores) any amortizations.

EXAMPLE: Reclassifying periodic pension cost for analytical purposes

Use the following information to reclassify the components of periodic pension cost between operating and nonoperating items:

Partial Income Statement	
Operating profit	$145,000
Interest expense	(12,000)
Other income	2,000
Income before tax	$135,000
Other Data	
Current service cost	$7,000
Interest cost	5,000
Expected return on assets	8,000
Actual return on assets	9,500

Answer:

Periodic pension cost (in P&L) of $4,000 ($7,000 current service cost + $5,000 interest cost – $8,000 expected return on assets) is added back to operating profit. Then, service cost of $7,000 is subtracted from operating profit, interest cost of $5,000 is added to interest expense, and the actual return on assets of $9,500 is added to other income. Following is the adjusted partial income statement:

Partial Income Statement	**Reported**	**Adjustments**	**Adjusted**
Operating profit	$145,000	+ 4,000 – 7,000	$142,000
Interest expense	(12,000)	– 5,000	(17,000)
Other income	2,000	+ 9,500	11,500
Income before tax	$135,000		$136,500

LOS 15.f: Interpret pension plan note disclosures including cash flow related information.

CFA® Program Curriculum, Volume 2, page 101

If the firm's contributions exceed its total periodic pension cost, the difference can be viewed as a reduction in the overall pension obligation, similar to an excess principal payment on a loan. Conversely, if the total periodic pension cost exceeds the contributions, the difference can be viewed as a source of borrowing.

If the difference between cash flow and total periodic pension cost is material, the analyst should consider reclassifying the difference from operating activities to financing activities in the cash flow statement.

EXAMPLE: Adjusting cash flow

Bhaskar Thakur is analyzing the financial statements of Box Car (BC) Inc., a manufacturer of equipment for the railroad industry. Thakur notices that BC has a defined benefit pension plan in place. He finds out that the company made a €340 million contribution to the plan during the year. He collects the following additional information about the company:

Funded status (beginning of the year)	€2,530
Funded status (end of the year)	€2,180

BC reported a net income during the year of €812 million. Cash flow from operating activities and financing activities were reported as €948 million and €112 million respectively. BC's tax rate was 40% during the year.

Compute:

1. The total periodic pension cost during the year.
2. Cash flow from operating and financing activities after making appropriate adjustments.

Answer:

1. Total periodic pension cost

   = contributions – [ending funded status – beginning funded status]

   = 340 – (2,180 – 2,530) = 340 – (–350) = €690 million

2. BC's contributions were €350 million less than the total periodic pension cost.

   after tax shortfall = 350(1 – 0.4) = €210 million

   adjusted cash flow from operating activities = 948 – 210 = €738 million

   adjusted cash flow from financing activities = 112 + 210 = €322 million

PROFESSOR'S NOTE

You might be asking yourself why we adjust over- or under- contributions for tax. The coverage here is (mostly) based on the U.S. tax code, where companies can deduct only actual cash contributions made to their pension plan.

MODULE QUIZ 15.6

To best evaluate your performance, enter your quiz answers online.

Use the following information to answer Questions 1 through 6.

Tanner, Inc., is a large chain of tanning salons in the United States. Tanner prepares financial statements under U.S. GAAP. The financial statements of Tanner, Inc., for the year ended December 31, 20X9, include the following (in $ millions):

PBO at January 1, 20X9	$435
Current service cost	63
Interest cost	29
Benefits paid	– 44
PBO at December 31, 20X9	$483
Fair value of plan assets at January 1, 20X9	$522
Actual return on plan assets	77
Employer contributions	48
Benefits paid	– 4
Fair value of plan assets at December 31, 20X9	$603
Average remaining years of service for employees	10
Expected return on plan assets: 12 months ended 12/31/X9	$32

1. Assuming there were no deferred or unamortized amounts as of January 1, 20X9, Tanner's periodic pension cost reported in P&L (in millions) for the year ended December 31, 20X9, is *closest* to:
   A. $15.
   B. $60.
   C. $92.
2. The funded status of the Tanner pension plan (in millions) as of December 31, 20X9, is *closest* to:
   A. underfunded by $212.
   B. underfunded by $120.
   C. overfunded by $120.
3. Tanner's total periodic pension cost (in millions) for the year ended 20X9 is *closest* to:
   A. $0.
   B. $15.
   C. $41.
4. For analytical purposes, what adjustment to the cash flow statement would *best* reflect the substance of Tanner's pension contributions?
   A. Increase operating cash flow and decrease financing cash flow.
   B. Decrease operating cash flow and increase financing cash flow.
   C. No adjustment is necessary for analytical purposes.

5. Suppose Tanner changes its assumption related to mortality rates of its employees, which results in an increase in the projected benefit obligation (PBO). The increase in the PBO is *most likely* to be reported as:
   A. an increase in prior service cost.
   B. an actuarial loss.
   C. an actuarial gain.
6. For this question only, suppose that Tanner reported under IFRS. The *most likely* impact of an increase in the discount rate for the year ending December 31, 20X9, would be:
   A. a decrease in the reported balance sheet asset.
   B. an increase in the net interest expense.
   C. an increase in the net interest income.
7. Hiten Reshmiya is analyzing the financial statements of Tarun Textiles. He collects the following information for the year ending December 31, 201X:

Item	**Rs. Millions**
PBO at the beginning of the year	1,822
PBO at the end of the year	1,915
Fair value of plan assets at the beginning of the year	2,015
Fair value of plan assets at the end of the year	2,232
Contributions made during the year	321
Cash flow from operating activities	469
Cash flow from financing activities	113
Tax rate	30%

   Tarun's adjusted cash flow from operating activities is *closest* to:
   A. Rs. 556 million.
   B. Rs. 506 million.
   C. Rs. 593 million

MODULE 15.7: SHARE-BASED COMPENSATION

Video covering this content is available online.

LOS 15.g: Explain issues associated with accounting for share-based compensation.

CFA® Program Curriculum, Volume 2, page 102

Share-based compensation plans can take several forms, including stock options and outright share grants. They have the advantages of serving to motivate and retain employees as well as being a way to reward employees with no additional outlay of cash.

Recording cash compensation expense is straightforward; it is recorded as the compensation is earned. Stock options and share grants raise several issues. If the shares are not publicly traded, an estimate of value must be used for stock grants. Unless the market price of the options is available, the value of stock options must be estimated using an options valuation model.

Shares or options may be granted with contingencies. In these cases, the estimated expense may be spread over a period of time. For example, if shares are granted, but cannot be sold for a period of time, the compensation expense recorded is spread over the period of time from the grant date until the date on which they can be sold by the employee. The overall principle here is that the compensation expense should be spread over the period for which they reward the employee, referred to as the service period.

LOS 15.h: Explain how accounting for stock grants and stock options affects financial statements, and the importance of companies' assumptions in valuing these grants and options.

CFA® Program Curriculum, Volume 2, page 105

Accounting for share-based compensation is similar under IFRS and U.S. GAAP.

Stock Options

Compensation expense is based on the fair value of the options on the grant date based on the number of options that are expected to vest. The vesting date is the first date the employee can actually exercise the options. The compensation expense is allocated in the income statement over the service period, which is the time between the grant date and the vesting date. Recognition of compensation expense will decrease net income and retained earnings; however, paid-in capital is increased by an identical amount. This results in no change to total equity.

Determining Fair Value

The fair value of the option is based on the observable market price of a similar option if one is available. Absent a market-based instrument, the firm can use an option-pricing model such as Black-Scholes or the binomial model. There is no preference of a specific model in either IFRS or U.S. GAAP.

PROFESSOR'S NOTE

Since market options differ from the custom terms of employee options, a comparable market option is not usually available. See the section on derivatives for a complete discussion of option-pricing models.

Option-pricing models typically incorporate the following six inputs:

1. Exercise price.
2. Stock price at the grant date.
3. Expected term.
4. Expected volatility.
5. Expected dividends.
6. Risk-free rate.

Many of the inputs require subjective estimates that can significantly affect the fair value of the option and, ultimately, compensation expense. For example, lower volatility, a shorter term or a lower risk-free rate, will typically decrease the estimated fair value of the options, decreasing compensation expense. A higher expected dividend yield will also decrease the estimated fair value and compensation expense.

Stock grants. Compensation expense for stock granted to an employee is based on the fair value of the stock on the grant date. The compensation expense is allocated over the employee's service period.

A stock grant can involve an outright transfer of stock without conditions, restricted stock, and performance stock. With restricted stock, the transferred stock cannot be sold by the employee until vesting has occurred. Performance stock is contingent on meeting performance goals, such as accounting earnings or other financial reporting metrics like return on assets or return on equity. Unfortunately, tying performance to accounting earnings and other metrics may result in manipulation of the accounting metric used.

Stock appreciation rights. The difference between a stock appreciation right and an option is the form of payment. A stock appreciation award gives the employee the right to receive compensation based on the increase in the price of the firm's stock over a predetermined amount. With stock appreciation rights, employees have limited downside risk and unlimited upside potential, thereby limiting the risk aversion problem discussed earlier. Also, since no shares are actually issued, there is no dilution to existing shareholders. A disadvantage of stock appreciation rights is that they require current period cash outlay.

Phantom stock. Phantom stock is similar to stock appreciation rights except the payoff is based on the performance of hypothetical stock instead of the firm's actual shares. Phantom stock can be used in privately held firms and firms with highly illiquid stock.

MODULE QUIZ 15.7

To best evaluate your performance, enter your quiz answers online.

1. Which of the following are necessary inputs in order to compute share-based compensation expense using an option pricing model?
   A. The exercise price and the stock price one year after the grant date.
   B. The expected dividend yield and the firm's cost of capital.
   C. The expected term of the option and the expected volatility of the stock price.
2. Which of the following statements about share-based compensation is *most accurate*?
   A. Compensation expense is only recognized if an employee stock option has intrinsic value on the grant date.
   B. In a restricted stock plan, the employer recognizes compensation expense when the employee sells the stock.
   C. The compensation expense for employee stock options is allocated over the employee's service period.

KEY CONCEPTS

LOS 15.a

In a defined-contribution plan, the firm contributes a certain amount each period to the employee's retirement account. The firm makes no promise regarding the future value of the plan assets; thus, the employee assumes all of the investment risk. Accounting is straight-forward; pension expense is equal to the firm's contribution.

In a defined-benefit plan, the firm promises to make periodic payments to the employee after retirement. The benefit is usually based on the employee's years of service and the employee's salary at, or near, retirement. Since the employee's future benefit is defined, the employer assumes the investment risk. Accounting is complicated because many assumptions are involved.

LOS 15.b

The projected benefit obligation (PBO) is the actuarial present value of future pension benefits earned to date, based on expected future salary increases.

balance sheet asset (liability) = fair value of plan assets – PBO

LOS 15.c

Components of periodic pension cost reported in P&L:

- Current service cost—the present value of benefits earned by the employees during the current period. Expensed in income statement.
- Interest cost—the increase in the PBO due to the passage of time. Expensed in income statement.
- Expected return on plan assets—offsets reported pension cost. Under U.S. GAAP, the expected rate of return is assumed. Under IFRS, the expected rate of return is the same as the discount rate.
- Amortization of actuarial gains and losses—under U.S. GAAP only, the losses (or gains) during the year due to changes in actuarial assumptions and due to differences between expected and actual return are recognized in OCI and amortized using the corridor method. Under IFRS, the actuarial gains and losses during the year are recognized in OCI and are not amortized.
- Amortization of past service cost—under U.S. GAAP only, an increase in PBO resulting from plan amendments granting a retroactive increase in benefits is amortized. Under IFRS, past service costs are immediately expensed in the income statement.

Total periodic pension cost includes costs reflected in the income statement (discussed above) as well as in OCI.

total periodic pension cost = contributions – change in funded status

or

total periodic pension cost = current service cost + interest cost – actual return on plan assets +/– actuarial losses/gains due to changes in assumptions affecting PBO + prior service cost

LOS 15.d

Firms can improve reported results by increasing the discount rate, lowering the compensation growth rate, or, in the case of U.S. GAAP, increasing the expected return on plan assets.

LOS 15.e

Comparative financial analysis using published financial statements is complicated by differences in accounting treatment for pensions:

- Gross vs. net pension assets/liabilities.
- Differences in assumptions used.
- Differences between IFRS and U.S. GAAP in recognizing periodic pension cost in the income statement.
- Differences due to classification in the income statement.

LOS 15.f

If the firm's contributions exceed the total periodic pension cost, the difference can be viewed as a reduction in the overall pension obligation, similar to an excess principal payment on a loan. Conversely, if the total periodic pension cost exceeds the firm's contributions, the difference can be viewed as a source of borrowing.

If the differences in cash flow and total periodic pension cost are material, the analyst should consider reclassifying the difference from operating activities to financing activities in the cash flow statement.

LOS 15.g

Share-based compensation raises issues about the valuation of the specific compensation as well as about the period in which, or periods over which, the compensation expense should be recorded.

LOS 15.h

Share-based compensation expense is based on the fair value of the option or stock at the grant date. To determine fair value, it is often necessary to use imperfect pricing models.

Many of the option pricing model inputs require subjective estimates that can significantly affect the fair value of the option and, ultimately, compensation expense. For example, lower volatility, a shorter term or a lower risk-free rate, will usually decrease the estimated fair value and compensation expense. A higher expected dividend yield will also decrease the estimated fair value and compensation expense.

ANSWER KEY FOR MODULE QUIZZES

Module Quiz 15.1

1. **C** In a defined-benefit pension plan, the employer assumes the investment risk. Total periodic pension cost is calculated as a firm's contributions minus the change in funded status. In a defined-contribution plan, pension expense is equal to the employer's contribution to the plan. (LOS 15.a)

Module Quiz 15.2

1. **A** The current service cost is the present value of new benefits earned by the employee working another year. Current service cost increases the PBO. Note that the interest cost increases every year regardless of whether the employee works another year or not. (LOS 15.b)

Module Quiz 15.3

1. **C** The funded status equals plan assets minus PBO. This plan is underfunded by $20 million ($40 million plan assets – $60 million PBO), which is reported as a liability on the balance sheet. Prior service cost is already included in the PBO (remember, PBO represents present value of all pension payments, whether reported in the income statement or not). (LOS 15.c)

2. **C** periodic pension cost in P&L = current service cost + interest cost – expected return on assets

   current service cost = $0.90 million (given)

   interest cost = PBO at the beginning of the period × discount rate
   = $12 million × 0.09
   = $1.08 million

   expected return on plan assets = $0.96 million (given)

   periodic pension cost in P&L = $0.90 million + $1.08 million – $0.96 million = $1.02 million

   (LOS 15.c)

Module Quiz 15.4

1. **C** The first step is to solve for benefits paid. The beginning PBO balance plus the cost components minus benefits paid is equal to the ending PBO balance: $193 + $38 – benefits paid = $220 million, which implies benefits paid are equal to $11 million. The question specifies that there are no contributions during the year. The ending fair value of plan assets is equal to beginning value plus actual return on assets less benefits paid: $159 + $32 – $11 = $180 million. (LOS 15.c)

Module Quiz 15.5

1. **B** The use of a higher discount rate will result in lower present values and, hence, lower current service cost. Lower service cost will result in a lower PBO and lower periodic pension cost in P&L. (LOS 15.d)

2. **C** The expected return on assets does not affect the calculation of the PBO. Periodic pension cost reported in P&L is decreased by the expected return on assets. If the expected return assumption is increased, then periodic pension cost in P&L decreases. Lower reported pension expense will result in higher net income. (LOS 15.d)

3. **A** A higher compensation growth rate will increase periodic pension cost reported in P&L (as well as the total periodic pension cost) and, thus, lower net income. Lower net income results in lower retained earnings. A higher compensation growth rate will increase the PBO. The compensation growth rate does not affect the plan assets. (LOS 15.d)

4. **B** A decrease in the discount rate will increase the PBO. A higher PBO lowers the funded status (plan assets – PBO). (LOS 15.d)

5. **C** Neither inflation expectations nor asset returns are internally consistent. The discount rate is increasing, but the inflation rate is decreasing. There is usually a direct relationship between the discount rate and the inflation rate. In 2016, the expected rate of return increased; however, SPC decreased its allocation to equity investments. Normally, reducing exposure to equity investments in favor of debt investments will decrease returns. (LOS 15.d)

Module Quiz 15.6

1. **B** Where there are no amortizations, the periodic pension cost reported in P&L is equal to service cost + interest cost – the expected return on assets ($63 + $29 – $32 = $60). (Module 15.3, LOS 15.c)

2. **C** A plan is overfunded when the fair value of plan assets exceeds the PBO. The Tanner plan is $120 overfunded ($603 – $483). (Module 15.2, LOS 15.b)

3. **B** Total periodic pension cost = current service cost + interest cost – *actual* investment return ($63 + $29 – $77 = $15). No figures for actuarial losses and prior service costs were given, so we assume they are zero. (Module 15.2, LOS 15.c)

4. **A** Tanner's contributions of $48 exceeded the total periodic pension cost of $15. Thus, the difference of $33 should be treated similar to an excess principal payment on a loan. Principal payments are reported as financing activities in the cash flow statement. The adjustment calls for increasing operating cash flow and decreasing financing cash flow. (Module 15.6, LOS 15.f)

5. **B** An actuarial loss resulting from changes in actuarial assumptions (such as mortality rates) leads to an increase in the PBO. Prior service cost increases the PBO as a result of amendments to the pension plan. (Module 15.2, LOS 15.b)

6. **C** Beginning of the year funded status = 522 – 435 = 87 (overfunded). Tanner would have reported an asset of $87 million. An increase in discount rate would lower the PBO but would not affect fair value of plan assets—increasing the funded status of the plan (higher reported asset).

   Under IFRS, Tanner would report a net interest income of the discount rate multiplied by the asset value. If Tanner had reported a liability, it would have reported a net interest expense. An increase in discount rate when a pension asset is reported results in an increase in net interest income (because the asset is multiplied by a higher rate). (Module 15.3, LOS 15.c)

7. **A**

   total periodic pension cost = contributions – change in funded status
   = 321 – [(2,232 – 1,915) – (2,015 – 1,822)]
   = 197 million

   after-tax excess contribution = (1 – 0.3) × (321 – 197) = 86.8 million

   adjusted cash flow from operating activities = 469 + 86.8 = 555.8 million (Module 15.6, LOS 15.f)

Module Quiz 15.7

1. **C** The stock price after the grant date and the firm's required cost of capital are not inputs to option pricing models. (LOS 15.h)

2. **C** For share-based compensation, expense is recognized based on the fair value of the compensation as of the grant date and allocated over the employee's service period. No expense is recognized when the option is exercised or the stock is sold. (LOS 15.h)

The following is a review of the Financial Reporting and Analysis (1) principles designed to address the learning outcome statements set forth by CFA Institute. Cross-Reference to CFA Institute Assigned Reading #16.

READING 16 Multinational Operations

Study Session 5

EXAM FOCUS

This topic review covers a detailed discussion of accounting for foreign subsidiaries and operations of multinational firms. The main issue is how to convert the results of a foreign subsidiary into the parent's consolidated financial statements. You have several significant tasks to master. First, you need to become familiar with the terminology of translation. Second, you need to be able to distinguish between and implement the two methods of accounting for foreign operations (i.e., remeasurement via the temporal method or translation via the current rate method). Third, you need to be able to analyze the impact of these two methods on reported earnings, cash flows, and financial ratios for both the subsidiary and the parent. This reading is important and challenging. Begin by concentrating on the examples of each method and then move on to the analysis section.

MODULE 16.1: TRANSACTION EXPOSURE

Video covering this content is available online.

LOS 16.a: Distinguish among presentation (reporting) currency, functional currency, and local currency.

CFA® Program Curriculum, Volume 2, page 131

Foreign currency can affect a multinational firm's financial statements in two ways: (1) the multinational firm may engage in business transactions that are denominated in a foreign currency, and (2) the multinational firm may invest in subsidiaries that maintain their books and records in a foreign currency. In both cases, special accounting treatment is required.

Before we move on, we need to define the different currencies that are involved in multinational accounting.

- The **local currency** is the currency of the country being referred to.
- The **functional currency**, determined by management, is the currency of the primary economic environment in which the entity operates. It is usually the currency in which the entity generates and expends cash. The functional currency can be the local currency or some other currency.
- The **presentation (reporting) currency** is the currency in which the parent company prepares its financial statements.

LOS 16.b: Describe foreign currency transaction exposure, including accounting for and disclosures about foreign currency transaction gains and losses.

CFA® Program Curriculum, Volume 2, page 132

Foreign currency denominated transactions, including sales, are measured in the presentation (reporting) currency at the spot rate on the transaction date. Foreign currency risk arises when the transaction date and the payment date differ.

For example, let's consider a U.S. firm that sells goods to a company located in Italy for €10,000 when the spot exchange rate is $1.60 per euro. Payment is due in 30 days. When payment is actually received, the euro has depreciated to $1.50.

On the transaction date, the U.S. firm recognizes a sale, and an account receivable, in the amount of $16,000 (€10,000 × $1.60). On the payment date, the U.S. firm receives €10,000 and immediately converts the euros to $15,000 (€10,000 × $1.50). As a result of the depreciating euro, the U.S. firm recognizes a $1,000 loss in the income statement [€10,000 × ($1.50 – $1.60)]. If the euro had appreciated to $1.70, the U.S. firm would have recognized a $1,000 gain [€10,000 × ($1.70 – $1.60)]. Note that the Italian firm recognized no gain or loss since the purchase and settlement transactions were both denominated in euros.

If the balance sheet date occurs before the transaction is settled, gains and losses on foreign currency transactions are recognized. Accordingly, the balance sheet amounts are adjusted based on the exchange rate on the balance sheet date, and an unrealized gain or loss is recognized in the income statement. Once the transaction is settled, additional gain or loss is recognized if the exchange rate changes after the balance sheet date.

Returning to our earlier example, let's assume the sale occurred on December 15 of last year when the euro exchange rate was $1.60. At the end of the year, the euro depreciated to $1.56. The transaction was settled on January 15 when the euro exchange rate was $1.50.

At the end of the year, the U.S. firm will reduce its account receivable by $400 and recognize a $400 loss [€10,000 × ($1.56 – $1.60)] in the December income statement. When the receivable is collected, the U.S. firm receives €10,000 and immediately converts the euros to $15,000 (€10,000 × $1.50). As a result, a loss of $600 [€10,000 × ($1.50 – $1.56)] is recognized in the January income statement.

If the U.S. firm purchases goods (denominated in euros) from the Italian firm with payment due in 30 days, the same concepts are applied except that the U.S. firm would recognize a gain on the payment date. In this case, the U.S. firm has an account payable denominated in euros. If the euro depreciates relative to the dollar, the U.S. firm recognizes a gain in the income statement because it will take less U.S. dollars to buy the necessary euros to settle the transaction.

Analyst Issues

While transaction gains and losses are recognized in the income statement, the accounting standards do not provide any guidance to include them within operating or non-operating income. IFRS requires disclosure of the "amount of exchange rate differences recognized in profit or loss" while U.S. GAAP requires disclosure of "the aggregate transaction gain or loss included in determining net income for the period." However, neither standard requires disclosure of where such gains/losses would be recorded. Obviously, the comparability of operating margins between entities would be diminished if the compared entities used different methods.

MODULE QUIZ 16.1

To best evaluate your performance, enter your quiz answers online.

1. On December 15, 2015, a U.S. firm with a fiscal year end of December 31, 2015, sold merchandise to a Mexican firm. Payment (in pesos) was due in 30 days but was actually received on January 20, 2016. Using the following exchange rates, what is the effect on the U.S. firm's income statement when payment is received?

	MXN/USD
December 15, 2015	10.0
December 31, 2015	12.0
January 15, 2016	12.5
January 20, 2016	11.5

A. Gain.
B. Loss.
C. No effect.

Video covering this content is available online.

MODULE 16.2: TRANSLATION

LOS 16.c: Analyze how changes in exchange rates affect the translated sales of the subsidiary and parent company.

LOS 16.d: Compare the current rate method and the temporal method, evaluate how each affects the parent company's balance sheet and income statement, and determine which method is appropriate in various scenarios.

CFA® Program Curriculum, Volume 2, page 144 and 148

There are two methods used to remeasure or translate the financial statements of a foreign subsidiary to the parent's presentation (reporting) currency.

- **Remeasurement** involves converting the local currency into functional currency using the temporal method.
- **Translation** involves converting the functional currency into the parent's presentation (reporting) currency using the current rate method. The current rate method is also known as the all-current method.

PROFESSOR'S NOTE

The term "translation" is used in two different ways in this topic review. First, translation refers to a specific method of converting account and transaction balances to another currency. Second, translation is used to describe (without identifying a specific methodology) the general process of converting account and transaction balances from one currency to another. Thus, both the remeasurement methodology and the translation methodology result in "translation," or the conversion of account and transaction balances to another currency. The ensuing discussion should make this distinction clear.

The translation method, current rate or temporal, is determined by the functional currency relative to the parent's presentation currency. Since the functional currency is chosen by management, it may not be completely objective.

According to the IASB, management should consider the following factors in deciding on the functional currency:

- The currency that influences sales prices for goods and services.
- Currency of the country whose competitive forces and regulations mainly determine the sale price of goods and services.
- The currency that influences labor, material, and other costs.
- The currency from which funds are generated.
- The currency in which receipts from operating activities are usually retained.

The FASB provides similar guidance.

Generally, we can use the following to determine the appropriate translation method:

- If the functional currency and the parent's presentation currency differ, the *current rate method* is used to translate the foreign currency financial statements.

Translation usually involves self-contained, independent subsidiaries whose operating, investing, and financing activities are decentralized from the parent. See Column 1 of Figure 16.1.

- If the functional currency is the same as the parent's presentation currency, the *temporal method* is used to remeasure the foreign currency financial statements. Remeasurement usually occurs when a subsidiary is *well integrated* with the parent (i.e., the parent makes the operating, investing, and financing decisions). See Column 2 of Figure 16.1.
- In the case where the local currency, the functional currency, and the presentation currency all differ, both the temporal method and the current rate method are used. For example, consider a U.S. firm that owns a German subsidiary whose functional currency is the Swiss franc. In this case, the temporal method is used to remeasure from the local currency (euros) into the functional currency (Swiss francs). Then, the current rate method is used to translate from the functional currency (Swiss francs) to the presentation currency (U.S. dollar). See Column 3 of Figure 16.1.
- If a subsidiary is operating in a hyperinflationary environment, the functional currency is considered to be the parent's presentation currency, and the temporal method is used under U.S. GAAP. Under IFRS, the subsidiary's financial statements are restated for inflation and then translated using the current exchange rate. Hyperinflation will be discussed in more detail later in this topic review.

Figure 16.1 illustrates the three ways the local currency may be remeasured and/or translated into the presentation currency of the parent. Note that the choice of the functional currency determines the method used for conversion.

Figure 16.1: Three Methods for Remeasurement/Translation of Local Currencies

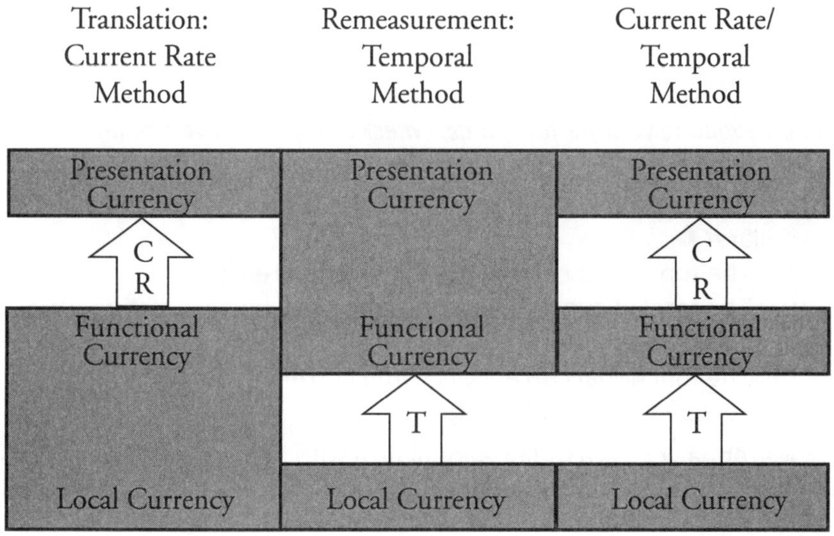

Let's look at an example.

EXAMPLE: Determining the appropriate translation method (1)

A U.S. multinational firm has a Japanese subsidiary. The subsidiary's functional currency is the Japanese yen (¥). The subsidiary's books and records are maintained in yen. The parent's presentation currency is the U.S. dollar. Determine which foreign currency translation method is appropriate.

Answer:

Since the functional currency and the parent's presentation currency differ, the current rate method is used to translate the subsidiary's financial statements from yen to U.S. dollars.

EXAMPLE: Determining the appropriate translation method (2)

Now imagine the Japanese subsidiary's functional currency is the U.S. dollar. Determine which foreign currency translation method is appropriate.

Answer:

Since the functional currency and the parent's presentation currency are the same, the temporal method is used to remeasure the subsidiary's financial statements from yen to U.S. dollars.

Before discussing the specific procedures used in applying the current rate and the temporal methods, we need to define a few exchange rates.

- The **current rate** is the exchange rate on the balance sheet date.
- The **average rate** is the average exchange rate over the reporting period.
- The **historical rate** is the actual rate that was in effect when the original transaction occurred. For example, if a firm bought machinery on January 2, 2016, the historical rate for that transaction at every balance sheet date in the future would be the exchange rate on January 2, 2016.

MODULE QUIZ 16.2

To best evaluate your performance, enter your quiz answers online.

1. Which of the following is *least likely* a condition that requires the use of the temporal method for a U.S. parent that reports results in U.S. dollars?
   A. The functional currency is the local currency.
   B. The foreign subsidiary is operating in a highly inflationary economy.
   C. The functional currency is some currency other than the local currency or the U.S. dollar.
2. Mazeppa, Inc., is a multinational firm with its home office located in Toronto, Canada. Its main foreign subsidiary is located in Paris, but the primary economic environment in which the foreign subsidiary generates and expends cash is in the United States (New York). The:
   A. local currency is the U.S. dollar.
   B. functional currency is the euro.
   C. presentation (reporting) currency is the Canadian dollar.

3. How many of the following situations *might* result in a translation gain?
   - Total assets exceed total liabilities when the foreign currency is depreciating using the current rate method.
   - Monetary liabilities exceed monetary assets when the foreign currency is appreciating using the temporal method.
   - Monetary assets exceed monetary liabilities when the foreign currency is depreciating using the temporal method.
   - Total assets equal total liabilities when the foreign currency is appreciating using the current rate method.

   A. None.
   B. One.
   C. Two.

Use the following information to answer Questions 4 and 5.

Gila Sailing and Fishing, Inc. (Gila), is a subsidiary of Sea of Cortez Unlimited Boating Adventures, Inc. (Cortez), a multinational organization headquartered in Tempe, Arizona. Gila is located in the Sonora Valley and sells fishing trips off the coast of the Sea of Cortez. Cortez accounts for Gila using the temporal method. Gila's current balance sheet (denominated in pesos) is as follows:

Cash	1,000,000
Accounts receivable	11,000,000
Fixed assets	43,000,000
Total assets	55,000,000
Accounts payable	9,000,000
Deferred revenue	2,000,000*
Long-term debt	8,000,000
Equity	36,000,000
Total liabilities and equity	55,000,000

* Note: Deferred revenue relates to a wealthy customer who paid for several trips in advance but has been unable to find enough spare time to come back to Sonora.

4. Nonmonetary assets less nonmonetary liabilities are:
   A. 5,000,000.
   B. 41,000,000.
   C. 43,000,000.

5. Cortez is concerned about depreciation of the peso and would like to change Gila's capital structure. This would be *best* accomplished by:
   A. borrowing pesos and reducing equity.
   B. using cash to reduce accounts payable.
   C. selling receivables and using the proceeds to pay down long-term debt.

Video covering this content is available online.

MODULE 16.3: TEMPORAL METHOD

Applying the Temporal Method

The temporal method is applied using the following procedures:

- Monetary assets and liabilities are remeasured using the current exchange rate. Monetary assets and liabilities are fixed in the amount of currency to be received or paid and include: cash, receivables, payables, and short-term and long-term debt.
- All other assets and liabilities are considered nonmonetary and are remeasured at the historical (actual) rate. The most common nonmonetary assets include inventory, fixed assets, and intangible assets. An example of a nonmonetary liability is unearned (deferred) revenue.

PROFESSOR'S NOTE

There is one exception. Nonmonetary assets and liabilities measured on the balance sheet at "fair value" (e.g., inventory carried at market value) are remeasured at the current exchange rate, not the historical rate.

- Just like the current rate method, common stock and dividends paid are remeasured at the historical (actual) rate.
- Expenses related to nonmonetary assets such as COGS, depreciation expense, and amortization expense are remeasured based on the historical rates prevailing at the time of purchase.
- Revenues and all other expenses are translated at the average rate.
- Remeasurement gain or loss is recognized in the income statement. This results in more volatile net income as compared to the current rate method whereby the translation gain or loss is reported in shareholders' equity.

Inventory and COGS Under the Temporal Method

Remember, the historical rate is the actual rate in effect when the original transaction occurred. Thus, there can be numerous historical rates to keep track of as a firm purchases nonmonetary assets (e.g., inventory, fixed assets, and intangibles) over time. Inventory can be particularly complicated since the firm's cost flow assumption (i.e., FIFO, LIFO, or average cost) must also be considered.

Recall that ending inventory under FIFO consists of the costs from the most recently purchased goods. Thus, FIFO ending inventory is remeasured based on more recent exchange rates. On the other hand, FIFO COGS consists of costs that are older; thus, the exchange rates used to remeasure COGS are older.

Under LIFO, ending inventory consists of older costs; thus, the inventory is remeasured at older exchange rates. LIFO COGS, however, consists of costs from the most recently purchased goods; thus, COGS is remeasured based on more recent exchange rates.

Not surprisingly, under the weighted-average method, ending inventory and COGS are remeasured at the weighted-average exchange rate for the period.

MODULE 16.4: CURRENT RATE METHOD

Video covering this content is available online.

Applying the Current Rate Method

The current rate method is applied using the following procedures:

- All income statement accounts are translated at the average rate.
- All balance sheet accounts are translated at the current rate *except for common stock*, which is translated at the historical (actual) rate that applied when the stock was issued.
- Dividends are translated at the rate that applied when they were declared.
- Translation gain or loss is reported in shareholders' equity as a part of the cumulative translation adjustment (CTA).

Figure 16.2 summarizes the impact of changing exchange rates on the parent's exposure.

Figure 16.2: Impact of Changing Exchange Rates on Exposure

	Local Currency	
Exposure	**Appreciating**	**Depreciating**
Current rate method:		
Net assets	Gain	Loss
Net liabilities	Loss	Gain
Temporal method:		
Net monetary assets	Gain	Loss
Net monetary liabilities	Loss	Gain

Calculating the Translation/Remeasurement Gain or Loss

Recall that under the current rate method, the translation gain or loss is reported in shareholders' equity as a part of the CTA. The CTA is simply a "plug" figure that forces the basic accounting equation (A = L + E) to balance.

Let's try an example.

EXAMPLE: Calculating the ending balance of the CTA under the current rate method

Given the following balance sheet data, calculate the ending balance of the CTA.

Assets	$1,000
Liabilities	600
Common stock	150
Beginning retained earnings	175
Current period net income	50
Dividends paid	25

Answer:

First, we need to calculate the ending balance of retained earnings. Given the beginning balance of retained earnings, the current period net income, and the dividends paid, we can calculate the ending balance of retained earnings as $200($175 beginning retained earnings + $50 net income – $25 dividends paid). Now, we can force the accounting equation to balance with a CTA of $50 ($1,000 assets – $600 liabilities – $150 common stock – $200 ending retained earnings).

It is important to understand that the CTA is an accumulated balance of all of the translation gains and losses at a point in time. In order to compute the translation gain or loss for a specific period, we need the *change* in the CTA for the period. Returning to our example, if the beginning balance of the CTA was $20 and the ending balance (plug) was $50, the translation gain for the period was $30.

Under the temporal method, no CTA is reported in shareholders' equity. Instead, the remeasurement gain or loss is recognized in the income statement. The remeasurement gain or loss is also a plug figure and is simply the difference in the earnings before the gain or loss and the earnings after the gain or loss.

Let's summarize what we have learned about the temporal and current rate methods.

PROFESSOR'S NOTE

Figure 16.3 is a must-know for the exam. Memorize it!

Figure 16.3: Summary of Temporal Method and Current Rate Method

	Temporal Method	Current Rate Method
Monetary assets and liabilities	Current rate	Current rate
Nonmonetary assets and liabilities	Historical rates	Current rate
Common stock	Historical rates	Historical rates
Equity (taken as a whole)	Mixed*	Current rate**
Revenues and SG&A	Average rate	Average rate
Cost of goods sold	Historical rates	Average rate
Depreciation and amortization	Historical rates	Average rate
Net income	Mixed rate*	Average rate
Exposure	Net monetary assets	Net assets
Exchange rate gain or loss	Income statement	Equity

* Net income is remeasured at a "mixed rate" (i.e., a mix of the average rate and the historical rate) under the temporal method because (1) the FX gain or loss is shown in the income statement, and (2) revenues and SG&A are remeasured at the average rate while COGS, depreciation, and amortization are remeasured at the historical rate. Equity is "mixed" because the change in retained earnings (which includes net income) is mixed.

** Under the current rate method, total assets and liabilities are translated at the current rate. The total equity (equity taken as a whole) would then have to be translated at the current rate for the balance sheet to balance.

Exposure to Changing Exchange Rates

Before calculating the gain or loss that results from changing exchange rates, it is necessary to understand the parent's *exposure* under the two methods. Under the current rate method, exposure is defined as the net asset position of the subsidiary. A firm has a net asset position when its assets exceed its liabilities. Recall that under the current rate method, all of the assets and liabilities are translated at the current rate. Thus, it is the net assets, that is, the subsidiary's equity, that are exposed to changing exchange rates. So, if the subsidiary has a net asset exposure and the local currency is appreciating, a gain is recognized. Conversely, a net asset exposure in a depreciating environment will result in a loss.

PROFESSOR'S NOTE

Although it is possible for a firm to have a net liability position under the current rate method, it is unusual. Most firms can't survive very long when their liabilities exceed their assets.

Recall that under the temporal method, the nonmonetary assets and liabilities are remeasured at historical rates. Thus, only the monetary assets and liabilities are exposed to changing exchange rates. Therefore, under the temporal method, exposure is defined as the subsidiary's net monetary asset or net monetary liability position. A firm has net monetary assets if its monetary assets exceed its monetary liabilities. If the monetary liabilities exceed the monetary assets, the firm has a net monetary liability exposure.

Since very few assets are considered to be monetary (mainly cash and receivables), most firms have net monetary liability exposures. If the parent has a net monetary liability exposure when the foreign currency is appreciating, the result is a loss. Conversely, a net monetary liability exposure coupled with a depreciating currency will result in a gain.

Under the temporal method, firms can eliminate their exposure to changing exchange rates by balancing monetary assets and monetary liabilities. When balanced, no gain or loss is recognized. For example, imagine that a U.S. multinational firm has a net monetary liability exposure of €1 million. In this case, a loss will occur if the euro appreciates relative to the dollar. To eliminate the exposure, the firm could sell euro denominated nonmonetary assets, such as fixed assets or inventory, and use the proceeds to reduce the monetary liabilities.

Eliminating exposure under the current rate method is more difficult because it is necessary to balance total assets and total liabilities. Balancing assets and liabilities would eliminate shareholders' equity.

PROFESSOR'S NOTE

There are other ways of eliminating exposure using various hedging techniques. However, the specifics of hedging are beyond the scope of this topic review.

MODULE QUIZ 16.3, 16.4

To best evaluate your performance, enter your quiz answers online.

1. Which of the following statements is *most accurate* regarding foreign currency translation? Under the:
   A. temporal method, the monetary asset accounts of a foreign subsidiary are translated using the current rate.
   B. temporal method, the nonmonetary asset accounts of a foreign subsidiary are translated using the current rate.
   C. current rate method, all balance sheet accounts of a foreign subsidiary are translated using the average rate.
2. Which of the following statements about the temporal method and the current rate method is *least accurate*?
   A. Net income is generally more volatile under the temporal method than under the current rate method.
   B. Subsidiaries that operate in highly inflationary environments will generally use the temporal method under U.S. GAAP.
   C. Subsidiaries whose operations are well integrated with the parent will generally use the current rate method.
3. If a foreign subsidiary's functional currency and the parent's reporting currency are the same, the parent's exposure to changing exchange rates is based on:
   A. total assets minus total liabilities.
   B. monetary assets minus monetary liabilities.
   C. nonmonetary assets minus nonmonetary liabilities.
4. XYZ Company is a U.S. subsidiary that operates in the United Kingdom where the functional currency is the British pound (£). XYZ's income statement shows £400 of net income and a £100 dividend that was paid on October 31 when the exchange rate was $1.60 per £. The current exchange rate is $1.70 per £, and the average rate is $1.55 per £. The change in retained earnings for the period in U.S. dollars is *closest* to:
   A. $460.
   B. $465.
   C. $480.
5. A foreign subsidiary is operating in a country where the local currency is depreciating relative to the parent's presentation currency. Assuming the subsidiary is a FIFO firm, which accounting method will result in the highest gross profit margin reported in the parent's consolidated income statement?
   A. Current rate method.
   B. Temporal method.
   C. The current rate method and the temporal method will result in the same COGS.

MODULE 16.5: EXAMPLE

Video covering this content is available online.

Study Session 5

LOS 16.e: Calculate the translation effects and evaluate the translation of a subsidiary's balance sheet and income statement into the parent company's presentation currency.

CFA® Program Curriculum, Volume 2, page 157

Let's look at extended examples of both translation methods.

CURRENT RATE METHOD

EXAMPLE: The current rate method

FlexCo International is a U.S. company with a subsidiary, Vibrant, Inc., located in the country of Martonia. Vibrant was acquired by FlexCo on 12/31/2014. FlexCo reports its financial results in U.S. dollars. The currency of Martonia is the loca (LC). Vibrant's financial statements for 2015 are shown in the following two figures.

Vibrant December 31, 2014 and 2015 Balance Sheet

	2014	2015
Cash	LC100	LC100
Accounts receivable	500	650
Inventory	1,000	1,200
Current assets	LC1,600	LC1,950
Fixed assets	800	1,600
Accumulated depreciation	(100)	(700)
Net fixed assets	LC700	LC900
Total assets	LC2,300	LC2,850
Accounts payable	400	500
Current debt	100	200
Long-term debt	1,300	950
Total liabilities	LC1,800	LC1,650
Common stock	400	400
Retained earnings*	100	800
Total equity	LC500	LC1,200
Total liabilities and equity	LC2,300	LC2,850

* Retained earnings on December 31, 2014, were $50.

Vibrant 2015 Income Statement

	2015
Revenue	LC5,000
Cost of goods sold	(3,300)
Gross margin	1,700
Other expenses	(400)
Depreciation expense	(600)
Net income	LC700

The following exchange rates between the U.S. dollar and the loca were observed:

- December 31, 2014: \$0.50 = LC1.00.
- December 31, 2015: \$0.4545 = LC1.00.
- Average for 2015: \$0.4762 = LC1.00.
- Historical rate for equity: \$0.50 = LC1.00.
- Historical rate for PP&E and depreciation: \$0.4881 = LC1.00.
- Historical rate for beginning and ending inventory \$0.52/LC and \$0.456/LC respectively.
- Purchases were made evenly throughout the year.

The majority of Vibrant's operational, financial, and investment decisions are made locally in Martonia, although Vibrant does rely on FlexCo for information technology expertise.

Use the appropriate method to translate Vibrant's 2015 balance sheet and income statement into U.S. dollars.

Answer:

Vibrant is relatively self-contained, which likely means the loca is the functional currency. Since the functional currency ≠ the parent's presentation currency, the current rate method is used to translate Vibrant's financial statements from the functional currency to the parent's presentation currency. The current rate method uses the current rate for all balance sheet accounts (except common stock, which is translated at the historical rate) and the average rate for all income statement accounts. The translation gain or loss is included in the CTA, which is reported in the equity section of the balance sheet as a part of other comprehensive income.

Vibrant's translated 2015 income statement is shown in the following table. Notice that we translate the income statement first with the current rate method to derive net income, which we then use to calculate retained earnings on the balance sheet.

Vibrant's 2015 Translated Income Statement Under the Current Rate Method

	2015 (LC)	Rate	2015 ($)
Revenue	LC5,000	$0.4762	$2,381.0
Cost of goods sold	(3,300)	$0.4762	(1,571.5)
Gross margin	1,700		809.5
Other expenses	(400)	$0.4762	(190.5)
Depreciation expense	(600)	$0.4762	(285.7)
Net income	LC700		$333.3

Vibrant's 2015 translated balance sheet is shown in the next table.

Vibrant 2015 Translated Balance Sheet Under the Current Rate Method

	2015 (LC)	Rate	2015 ($)
Cash	LC100	$0.4545	$45.5
Accounts receivable	650	$0.4545	295.4
Inventory	1,200	$0.4545	545.4
Current assets	LC1,950		$886.3
Fixed assets	1,600	$0.4545	727.2
Accumulated depreciation	(700)	$0.4545	(318.2)
Net fixed assets	LC900		$409.0
Total assets	LC2,850		$1,295.3
Accounts payable	500	$0.4545	227.2
Current debt	200	$0.4545	90.9
Long-term debt	950	$0.4545	431.8
Total liabilities	LC1,650		$749.9
Common stock	400	$0.50	200.0
Retained earnings	800	(a)	383.3
Cumulative translation adjustment	—	(b)	(37.9)
Total equity	LC1,200		$545.4
Total liabilities and shareholders' equity	LC2,850		$1,295.3

(a) Beginning (2015) retained earnings were $50, so ending (2015) retained earnings are $50 + $333.3 = $383.3.

(b) The CTA is a plug figure that makes the accounting equation balance: $1,295.3 assets – $749.9 liabilities – $200.0 common stock – $383.3 retained earnings = –$37.9.

Notice the change in the CTA from 2014 to 2015 is equal to –$37.9 (–$37.9 ending CTA – $0 beginning CTA). Because Vibrant was acquired at the end of 2014, the CTA was zero on that date. Thus, the depreciating loca resulted in translation loss of $37.9 for the year ended 2015. The translation loss occurred because Vibrant had a net asset exposure (assets > liabilities) and the loca depreciated relative to the dollar.

TEMPORAL METHOD

Now let's apply the temporal method to Vibrant.

EXAMPLE: The temporal method

Suppose instead that the majority of Vibrant's operational, financial, and investment decisions are made by the parent company, FlexCo. In this case, Vibrant's functional currency and FlexCo's presentation currency are likely the same; thus, the temporal method is used to remeasure the loca to the dollar. All other information is the same.

Use the appropriate method to translate Vibrant's 2015 balance sheet and income statement into U.S. dollars.

Under the temporal method, we'll start with the balance sheet.

Vibrant 2015 Remeasured Balance Sheet Under the Temporal Method

	2015 (LC)	Rate	2015 ($)
Cash	LC100	$0.4545	$45.5
Accounts receivable	650	$0.4545	295.4
Inventory	1,200	$0.4560	547.2
Current assets	LC1,950		888.1
Fixed assets	1,600	$0.4881	781.0
Accumulated depreciation	(700)	$0.4881	(341.7)
Net fixed assets	LC900		$439.3
Total assets	LC2,850		$1,327.4
Accounts payable	500	$0.4545	227.3
Current debt	200	$0.4545	90.9
Long-term debt	950	$0.4545	431.8
Total liabilities	LC1,650		$750.0
Common stock	400	$0.50	200.0
Retained earnings	800	(a)	377.4
Total equity	LC1,200		577.4
Total liabilities and shareholders' equity	LC2,850		$1,327.4

(a) Retained earnings is a plug figure that makes the accounting equation balance:

$1,327.4 assets – $750.0 liabilities – $200.0 common stock = $377.4 retained earnings.

Vibrant's remeasured income statement using the temporal method is shown in the following table. Remember the remeasurement gain or loss appears in the income statement under the temporal method.

Vibrant's 2015 Remeasured Income Statement Under the Temporal Method

	2015 (LC)	Rate	2015 ($)
Revenue	LC5,000	$0.4762	$2,381.0
Cost of goods sold	(3,300)	(c)	(1,639.5)
Gross margin	1,700		741.5
Other expenses	(400)	$0.4762	(190.5)
Depreciation expense	(600)	$0.4881	(292.9)
Income before remeasurement gain	700		258.1
Remeasurement gain	—	(b)	69.3
Net income	LC700	(a)	$327.4

(a) Net income is derived from the beginning and ending balances of retained earnings and dividends paid: ($50.0 beginning balance + net income – $0 dividends paid = $377.4 ending balance). Solving for net income, we get $327.4.

(b) The remeasurement gain is a plug that is equal to the difference in net income and income before remeasurement gain: $327.4 – $258.1 = $69.3.

(c) LC purchases = LC COGS + LC ending inventory – LC beginning inventory

LC purchases = 3,300 + 1,200 – 1,000 = LC 3,500

$ COGS = $ beginning inventory + $ purchases – $ ending inventory = (1,000 × 0.52) + (3,500 × 0.4762) – (1,200 × 0.456) = $1,639.5

The remeasurement gain occurred because Vibrant had a net monetary liability exposure (monetary liabilities > monetary assets), and the loca depreciated relative to the dollar.

Why Do the Two Methods Report Significantly Different Results?

You should immediately notice that the two different methods report very different results, particularly related to the size and sign of the translation gain/loss, net income, and total assets. These comparisons are shown in Figure 16.4.

Figure 16.4: Vibrant Example: Current Rate vs. Temporal Method

	Current Rate	Temporal
Income before translation gain/loss	$333.3	$258.1
Translation gain/loss	–$37.9	$69.3
	(on the balance sheet)	(on the income statement)
Net income	$333.3	$327.4
Total assets	$1,295.3	$1,327.4

We can make the following observations.

Income before translation gain/loss is different between the two methods. This is because COGS and depreciation are translated/remeasured at different rates under the two methods. Under the current rate method, COGS and depreciation expense are translated at the average rate thereby reflecting the depreciating local currency. Under the temporal method, COGS and depreciation expense are remeasured at historical (actual) rates, and thus, do not reflect the depreciating local currency.

The translation gain/loss is different between the two methods; it's not even the same sign. The current rate method results in a translation loss, while the temporal method results in a translation gain. This is NOT an unusual occurrence. Under the current rate method, Vibrant's net assets (assets > liabilities) are exposed to the depreciating local currency. Holding net assets in a depreciating environment results in a loss. Under the temporal method, Vibrant's net monetary liabilities (monetary liabilities > monetary assets) are exposed. Holding net monetary liabilities in a depreciating environment results in a gain.

Net income is different between the two methods. This is because of the different exchange rates used to translate/remeasure COGS and depreciation expense as previously discussed. In addition, the gain/loss recognized under the two methods are reported in different financial statements. Under the current rate method, the translation loss is reported in shareholders' equity as a part of the CTA. Under the temporal method, the remeasurement gain is reported in the income statement. Reporting the gain or loss in the income statement results in more volatile net income.

Total assets are different between the two methods because inventory and net fixed assets are different. Inventory and fixed assets are translated at the current rate under the current rate method thereby reflecting the depreciating local currency. Under the temporal method, the historical rate is used, thus, inventory and fixed assets do not reflect the depreciating local currency.

Comparing Subsidiary Results to Translated Results Under the Current Rate Method

A side-by-side comparison of Vibrant's 2015 balance sheet and income statement before and after translation is presented in Figure 16.5.

Figure 16.5: Vibrant LC and Translated Balance Sheet and Income Statement

	2015 (LC)	2015 ($) Current Rate Method
Cash	LC100	$45.5
Accounts receivable	650	295.4
Inventory	1,200	545.4
Current assets	LC1,950	$886.3
Fixed assets	1,600	727.2
Accumulated depreciation	(700)	(318.2)
Net fixed assets	LC900	$409.0
Total assets	LC2,850	$1,295.3
Accounts payable	500	227.2
Current debt	200	90.9
Long-term debt	950	431.8
Total liabilities	LC1,650	$749.9
Common stock	400	200.0
Retained earnings	800	383.3
Cumulative translation adjustment	—	(37.9)
Total equity	LC1,200	$545.4
Total liabilities and shareholders' equity	LC2,850	$1,295.3
Revenue	LC5,000	$2,381.0
Cost of goods sold	(3,300)	(1,571.5)
Gross margin	1,700	809.5
Other expenses	(400)	(190.5)
Depreciation expense	(600)	(285.7)
Net income	LC700	$333.3

MODULE 16.6: RATIOS

Video covering this content is available online.

LOS 16.f: Analyze how the current rate method and the temporal method affect financial statements and ratios.

CFA® Program Curriculum, Volume 2, page 167

Pure Balance Sheet and Pure Income Statement Ratios

Pure income statement and pure balance sheet ratios are *unaffected* by the application of the current rate method. In other words, the local currency trends and relationships are "preserved." What we mean by "pure" is that all of the components of the ratio are from the balance sheet, or all of the components are from the income statement.

For example, the current ratio (current assets / current liabilities) is a pure balance sheet ratio because both the numerator and denominator are from the balance sheet and are translated at the current rate. If you multiply both numerator and denominator by the same exchange rate, the rate cancels, and you're left with the same ratio.

All profit margin measures are pure income statement ratios because both the numerator (gross profit, operating profit, or net profit) and the denominator (revenue) are from the income statement and are translated at the average rate.

Selected pure balance sheet and pure income statement ratios from the Vibrant example are presented in Figure 16.6. Notice the current rate method preserves the original LC ratio in each case.

Figure 16.6: Vibrant Pure Balance Sheet and Pure Income Statement Ratios

Ratio	2015 (LC)	2015 ($) Current Rate Method
	Pure Balance Sheet Ratios	
Current ratio	2.79	2.79
Quick ratio	1.07	1.07
LTD-to-total capital	0.44	0.44
	Pure Income Statement Ratios	
Gross profit margin	34.0%	34.0%
Net profit margin	14.0%	14.0%

PROFESSOR'S NOTE

Interest coverage (EBIT / interest expense) is another example of a pure income statement ratio.

Mixed Balance Sheet/Income Statement Ratios

A **mixed ratio** combines inputs from both the income statement and balance sheet. The current rate method results in small changes in mixed ratios because the numerator and the denominator are almost always translated at different exchange rates. The change will likely be small and the direction will depend on the relationship between the exchange rate used to translate the denominator and the exchange rate used to translate the numerator.

Our analysis of mixed ratios isn't as clear-cut as the analysis of pure ratios, but we can make one definitive statement: *mixed ratios calculated from financial statements translated using the current rate method will be different than the same ratio calculated from the local currency statements before translation*. However, we can't make any definitive statements about whether specific ratios will be larger or smaller after translation unless we make the assumption that all mixed ratios are calculated using end-of-period balance sheet figures. The analysis that follows does not necessarily apply for mixed ratios calculated using beginning or average balance sheet figures.

This is a very important point so we'll repeat it again: the conclusions drawn in the following section assume we're using end-of-period balance sheet figures.

Selected mixed balance sheet and income statement ratios from the Vibrant example are presented in Figure 16.7. Recall that during 2015, the loca depreciated relative to the parent's presentation currency, the U.S. dollar.

Figure 16.7: Vibrant Mixed Balance Sheet/Income Statement Ratios (Depreciating LC)

Ratio*	2015 (LC)	2015 ($) Current Rate Method
Return on assets	24.6%	25.7%
Return on equity	58.3%	61.1%
Total asset turnover	1.75	1.84
Inventory turnover	2.75	2.88
Accounts receivable turnover	7.69	8.06

*Ratios are calculated using end-of-period balance sheet numbers.

Notice that in each case the translated ratio is larger than the original ratio. This will always be the case when the foreign currency is depreciating because the average rate (which is used in the numerator of the ratio) is greater than the ending rate (which is used in the denominator of the ratio). When the foreign currency is appreciating, each of these ratios will decrease.

PROFESSOR'S NOTE

In the Level II curriculum, we don't run across many mixed ratios with a balance sheet item in the numerator and an income statement item in the denominator. However, one example is the receivables collection period. Just remember that if accounts receivable turnover increases, receivables collection period will decrease. The same is true for the inventory processing period.

On the exam, remember these key points regarding the original versus the translated financial statements and ratios:

- Pure balance sheet and pure income statement ratios will be the same.
- If the foreign currency is depreciating, translated mixed ratios (with an income statement item in the numerator and an end-of-period balance sheet item in the denominator) will be larger than the original ratio.
- If the foreign currency is appreciating, translated mixed ratios (with an income statement item in the numerator and an end-of-period balance sheet item in the denominator) will be smaller than the original ratio.

Comparing Results Using the Temporal Method and Current Rate Method

Now, let's compare the results of the temporal method and current rate method as they relate to Vibrant's 2015 balance sheet and income statement.

Figure 16.8: Comparison of Vibrant's Balance Sheet and Income Statement Using the Temporal Method and the Current Rate Method

	2015 ($) Temporal Method	2015 ($) Current Rate Method
Cash	$45.5	$45.5
Accounts receivable	295.4	295.4
Inventory	547.2	545.4
Current assets	$881.1	$886.3
Fixed assets	781.0	727.2
Accumulated depreciation	(341.7)	(318.2)
Net fixed assets	439.3	409.0
Total assets	$1,327.4	$1,295.3
Accounts payable	227.3	227.2
Current debt	90.9	90.9
Long-term debt	431.8	431.8
Total liabilities	$750.0	$749.9
Common stock	200.0	200.0
Retained earnings	377.4	383.3
Cumulative translation adjustment	—	(37.9)
Total equity	577.4	$545.4
Total liabilities and shareholders' equity	$1,327.4	$1,295.3
Revenue	$2,381.0	$2,381.0
Cost of goods sold	(1,639.5)	(1,571.5)
Gross margin	741.5	809.5
Other expenses	(190.5)	(190.5)
Depreciation expense	(292.9)	(285.7)
Income before remeasurement gain	258.1	333.3
Remeasurement gain	69.3	—
Net income	$327.4	$333.3

Please note that this analysis assumes **end-of-period balance sheet figures**.

Analyzing the effect on the financial ratios of the choice of accounting method is a little more difficult in this case, but the basic procedure is as follows:

- Determine whether the foreign currency is appreciating or depreciating.

- Determine which rate (historical rate, average rate, or current rate) is used to convert the numerator under both methods. Determine whether the numerator of the ratio will be the same, larger, or smaller under the temporal method versus the current rate method.
- Determine which rate (historical rate, average rate, or current rate) is used to convert the denominator under both methods. Determine whether the denominator of the ratio will be the same, larger, or smaller under the temporal method versus the current rate method.
- Determine whether the ratio will increase, decrease, or stay the same based on the direction of change in the numerator and the denominator.

For example, let's analyze the fixed asset turnover ratio, which is equal to revenue divided by fixed assets. Assume the foreign currency is depreciating.

- The numerator (revenue) is converted at the same rate (the average rate) under both methods.
- The denominator (fixed assets) is converted at the historical rate under the temporal method and the current rate under the current rate method. If the foreign currency is depreciating, the historical rate will be higher than the current rate, which means fixed assets will be higher under the temporal method.
- Since fixed assets are higher, turnover will be lower under the temporal method (higher denominator).

MODULE QUIZ 16.5, 16.6

To best evaluate your performance, enter your quiz answers online.

1. Which of the following ratios may be larger in the presentation currency versus the local currency when translated under the current rate method?
   A. Current ratio.
   B. Return on assets.
   C. Net profit margin.

Use the following information to answer Questions 2 through 5.

This information is a continuation of the FlexCo/Vibrant example from the topic review. Suppose it is now the end of 2016 and Vibrant reports the operating results shown in the following table.

Vibrant December 31, 2015 and 2016 Balance Sheet

	2015	2016
Cash	LC100	LC150
Accounts receivable	650	800
Inventory	1,200	1,400
Current assets	LC1,950	LC2,350
Fixed assets	1,600	2,500
Accumulated depreciation	(700)	(1,500)
Net fixed assets	LC900	LC1,000
Total assets	LC2,850	LC3,350
Accounts payable	500	500
Current debt	200	100
Long-term debt	950	1,150
Total liabilities	LC1,650	LC1,750
Common stock	400	400
Retained earnings*	800	1,200
Total equity	LC1,200	LC1,600
Total liabilities and equity	LC2,850	LC3,350

*At the beginning of 2016, retained earnings were $383.3.

Vibrant 2016 Income Statement

	2016
Revenue	LC5,500
Cost of goods sold	(3,800)
Gross margin	1,700
Other expenses	(500)
Depreciation expense	(800)
Net income	LC400

The following exchange rates between the U.S. dollar and the loca were observed:

- December 31, 2015: USD/LC 0.4545.
- December 31, 2016: USD/LC 0.4000.
- Average for 2016: USD/LC 0.4292.
- Historical rate for fixed assets, inventory, and equity: USD/LC 0.5000.

The CTA at the end of 2015 was equal to –$37.9 under the current rate method.

2. Assume for this question only that Vibrant operates relatively independently from FlexCo. For 2016, FlexCo *most likely* will report a cumulative translation loss on the consolidated:
   A. income statement of $77.1 related to Vibrant.
   B. balance sheet of $77.1 related to Vibrant.
   C. balance sheet of $115.0 related to Vibrant.

3. The gross profit margin ratio and the return on ending assets ratio from Vibrant's 2016 U.S. dollar financial statements translated using the current rate method are *closest* to:

	Gross profit margin	Return on assets
A.	22.7%	14.2%
B.	30.9%	12.8%
C.	33.6%	11.9%

4. The gross profit margin ratio from Vibrant's 2016 U.S. dollar financial statements remeasured using the temporal method is:
   A. lower.
   B. the same.
   C. higher.

5. As compared to the current rate method, which of the following *best* describes the impact of the temporal method on accounts receivable turnover from Vibrant's 2016 U.S. dollar financial statements?
   A. Higher.
   B. Lower.
   C. The same.

6. Bob Haskell, CFA, is analyzing the financial statements of a U.S.-based company called Seriev Motor. Seriev has a foreign subsidiary located in Japan. Seriev translates the subsidiary results using the current rate method. Haskell determines that the following four ratios will remain the same after translation from yen into U.S. dollars:
   - Gross profit margin.
   - Interest coverage (EBIT/interest expense).
   - Return on assets.
   - Quick ratio.

   The dollar has depreciated against the yen during the most recent year. Haskell is correct in his analysis of:
   A. all four ratios.
   B. three of the four ratios.
   C. two of the four ratios.

MODULE 16.7: HYPERINFLATION

Video covering this content is available online.

LOS 16.g: Analyze how alternative translation methods for subsidiaries operating in hyperinflationary economies affect financial statements and ratios.

CFA® Program Curriculum, Volume 2, page 154

In a hyperinflationary environment, the local currency will rapidly depreciate relative to the parent's presentation currency because of a deterioration of purchasing power. In this case, using the current rate to translate all of the balance sheet accounts will result in much lower assets and liabilities after translation. Using the lower values, the subsidiary seems to disappear in the parent's consolidated financial statements.

In reality, the real value of the nonmonetary assets and liabilities is typically not affected by hyperinflation because the local currency-denominated values increase to offset the impact of inflation (e.g., real estate values rise with inflation). Unfortunately, adjusting the nonmonetary asset and liabilities for inflation is not allowed under U.S. GAAP; although, adjusting for inflation is permitted under IFRS. As a result, IFRS and U.S. GAAP differ significantly when dealing with a subsidiary operating in a hyperinflationary environment.

According to the FASB, a hyperinflationary environment is one where cumulative inflation exceeds 100% over a 3-year period. Assuming compounding, an annual inflation rate of more than 26% over three years will result in cumulative inflation over 100% ($1.26^3 - 1$ is approximately equal to 100%). When hyperinflation is present, the functional currency is considered to be the parent's presentation currency; thus, the temporal method is used to remeasure the financial statements.

The IASB does not specifically define hyperinflation; however, cumulative inflation of over 100% in a 3-year period is one indication that hyperinflation exists.

Unlike U.S. GAAP, the temporal method is not used in a hyperinflationary environment under IFRS. Instead, the foreign currency financial statements are restated for inflation and then translated using the current exchange rate. Restating for inflation involves the following procedures:

- Nonmonetary assets and nonmonetary liabilities are restated for inflation using a price index. Since most nonmonetary items are reported at historical cost, simply multiply the original cost by the change in the price index for the period between the acquisition date and the balance sheet date.
- It is not necessary to restate monetary assets and monetary liabilities.
- The components of shareholders' equity (other than retained earnings) are restated by applying the change in the price index from the beginning of the period or the date of contribution if later.
- Retained earnings is the plug figure that balances the balance sheet.
- In the statement of retained earnings, net income is the plug figure.

- The income statement items are restated by multiplying by the change in the price index from the date the transactions occur.
- The net purchasing power gain or loss is recognized in the income statement based on the net monetary asset or liability exposure. Holding monetary assets during inflation results in a purchasing power loss. Conversely, holding monetary liabilities during inflation results in a purchasing power gain. This figure forces the net income to be same as the net income figure that was the plug figure in the statement of retained earnings.

Let's look at an example.

EXAMPLE: Adjusting financial statements for inflation

Imagine that a foreign subsidiary was created on December 31, 2014. The LC is the currency of the country where the foreign subsidiary is located. The subsidiary's balance sheets for 2014 and 2015, and income statement for the year-ended 2015, are shown below:

(in LCs)	2014	2015
Cash	5,000	8,000
Supplies	25,000	25,000
Total assets	30,000	33,000
Accounts payable	20,000	20,000
Common stock	10,000	10,000
Retained earnings	0	3,000
Liabilities and equity	30,000	33,000
Revenue		15,000
Expenses		(12,000)
Net income		3,000

Also, use the following price indices:

December 31, 2014	100
December 31, 2015	150
Average for 2015	125

Prepare an inflation adjusted balance sheet and income statement for 2015.

Answer:

(in LCs)	2015	Adjustment Factor	Inflation Adjusted
Cash	8,000		8,000
Supplies	25,000	150 / 100	37,500
Total assets	33,000		45,500
Accounts payable	20,000		20,000
Common stock	10,000	150 / 100	15,000
Retained earnings	3,000		10,500
Liabilities and equity	33,000		45,500
Revenue	15,000	150 / 125	18,000
Expenses	(12,000)	150 / 125	(14,400)
Net purchasing power gain			6,900
Net income	3,000		10,500

The nonmonetary assets (supplies) and the common stock are inflation adjusted based on the change in the beginning and ending price index because the amounts were outstanding for the entire year. Thc rcvcnues and expenses occurred throughout the year and are inflation adjusted using the change in the average and ending price index. Notice the monetary assets (cash) and monetary liabilities (accounts payable) are not inflation adjusted. Instead, the purchasing power gains and losses are calculated.

In this example, 2015 was the first year—hence, there were no beginning retained earnings. Therefore, the plug figure of LC10,500 has to be net income minus dividends for the current year. Given that dividends = 0, net income has to be LC10,500. But it is not; hence, again, a plug figure (this time, in income statement) is needed to make sure that net income is equal to LC10,500. This plug (in income statement) is the net purchasing power gain or loss. Here, the gain is LC6,900.

Alternatively, inflation results in a purchasing power loss of LC2,500 on the beginning cash balance [–LC5,000 × (150 – 100) / 100] and a loss of LC600 on the increase in cash [–LC3,000 × (150 – 125) / 125]. Additionally, inflation results in a purchasing power gain of LC10,000 on the accounts payable [LC20,000 × (150 – 100) / 100]. Thus, adjusting for inflation will result in a net purchasing power gain of LC6,900 (–LC2,500 loss on beginning cash – LC600 loss on increase in cash + LC10,000 gain on accounts payable).

Notice the similarities of adjusting the financial statements for inflation and remeasuring the financial statements using the temporal method.

- Under the temporal method, the monetary assets and liabilities are exposed to changing exchange rates. Similarly, it is the monetary assets and liabilities that are exposed to the risk of inflation.

- Purchasing power gains and losses are analogous to exchange rate gains and losses when the foreign currency is depreciating. For example, if a subsidiary has net monetary liability exposure in a depreciating environment, a gain is recognized under the temporal method. Likewise, a purchasing power gain is recognized when a net monetary liability exposure is adjusted for the effects of inflation.
- The gain or loss from remeasurement is recognized in the income statement as is the net purchasing power gain or loss that results from inflation.

Under IFRS, once the subsidiary's financial statements are adjusted for inflation, the restated financial statements are translated into the parent's reporting currency using the current exchange rate.

Analyzing Foreign Currency Disclosure

Up to this point, we have examined a multinational parent with only one subsidiary. This made the analysis easier (although it sure doesn't seem that way) because we were able to link the effect of the choice of translation method to the consolidated financial statements for the specific subsidiary.

However, in practice, multinational firms may have many foreign subsidiaries, which means that the CTA on the balance sheet, the remeasurement gain or loss in the income statement, and the parent company's ratios include the effects of all of the subsidiaries. Unfortunately, disclosure requirements are limited, so it is difficult for the analyst to get information about the firm's currencies and the specific exposure to the currencies. In some cases, it is even difficult to determine what accounting method (temporal or current rate) the firm uses for its various foreign operations.

What little information that is available is found in the financial statement footnotes and the management discussion and analysis section of the annual report.

As previously discussed, management judgment is involved in deciding on the functional currency of a foreign subsidiary. Firms operating in the same industry may use different methods for translation purposes thereby making comparisons more difficult. One solution involves adding the change in the CTA to the firm's net income. Recall the change in the CTA is equal to the translation gain or loss for the period. By bringing the translation gain or loss into the income statement, comparisons with a temporal method firm are improved. The solution does not totally resolve the problem but it is a good start.

The same solution can be applied to all non-owner changes in shareholders' equity. For example, adding the unrealized gains and losses from available-for-sale securities to net income would allow an analyst to compare the company to a firm that owns held-for-trading securities.

Including the gains and losses (that are reported in shareholders' equity) in net income is known as *clean-surplus accounting* in the analytical community. The term *dirty-surplus* is used to describe gains and losses that are reported in shareholders' equity.

MODULE QUIZ 16.7

To best evaluate your performance, enter your quiz answers online.

1. Barkley Corporation, a wholly-owned subsidiary of a U.S. firm, is located in a country that is experiencing hyperinflation. Barkley's functional currency and the parent's presentation currency differ. What exchange rate should be used to convert Barkley's intangible assets into U.S. dollars according to U.S. GAAP?
   A. Historical rate.
   B. Current rate.
   C. Prime rate.
2. Tiny Company, a subsidiary of Large Corporation, operates in a country that is experiencing hyperinflation. Assuming Large follows IFRS, which of the following exposures will result in a net purchasing power gain?
   A. Nonmonetary assets and current liabilities.
   B. Monetary liabilities.
   C. Nonmonetary assets and nonmonetary liabilities.

MODULE 16.8: TAX, SALES GROWTH, FINANCIAL RESULTS

Video covering this content is available online.

LOS 16.h: Describe how multinational operations affect a company's effective tax rate.

CFA® Program Curriculum, Volume 2, page 183

Tax Implications of Multinational Operations

Multinational corporations are subject to multiple tax jurisdictions with differing laws and tax rates. In the United States, for example, the tax code allows a credit for foreign taxes paid by U.S. companies, effectively taxing the company at the U.S. tax rate.

Effective tax rate is the tax expense in the income statement divided by pretax profit. **Statutory tax rate** is provided by the tax code of the home country. Accounting standards require companies to provide a reconciliation between the effective tax rate and the statutory tax rate. This reconciliation disclosure can be used by the analyst to project future tax expense.

Changes in effective tax rate on account of foreign operations can be due to:

- Changes in the mix of profits from different countries (with varying tax rates).
- Changes in the tax rates.

EXAMPLE: Analysis of reconciliation of effective tax rate

The reconciliation between the statutory tax rate and effective tax rate for two companies (Amco and Bianco) for the year 2017 is provided.

Item	Amco	Bianco
Statutory tax rate	25.0%	30.0%
Effect of disallowed expenses	3.0%	1.0%
Effect of exempt income	(2.0%)	(0.5%)
Effect of taxes in foreign jurisdictions	3.4%	(1.2%)
Effect of recognition of prior losses	(0.8%)	(3.0%)
Effective tax rate	28.6%	26.3%

1. Which company benefited from the lowering of tax expense on account of its foreign operations?
2. If the mix of foreign operations for both companies is expected to increase over time, which company is most likely to report lower effective tax rate in the future? Assume that the statutory tax rates do not change.

Answer:

1. The effect of foreign operations resulted in an increase in effective tax rate for Amco by 3.4% and a decrease for Bianco by 1.2%. Hence, Bianco benefited from its foreign operations in reducing its effective tax rate and tax expense.
2. If the mix of foreign operations increases, assuming no change to the tax rate, Bianco would see its effective tax rate decrease further and Amco would see its effective tax rate increase.

LOS 16.i: Explain how changes in the components of sales affect the sustainability of sales growth.

CFA® Program Curriculum, Volume 2, page 186

Financial statements for multinational companies report sales denominated in the reporting currency even though the actual sales may have occurred in many different currencies. Changes in currency values affect the value of translated sales. Sales growth owing to an increase in volumes or prices is considered more sustainable than sales growth due to appreciation of the foreign currencies in which sales were made.

Organic growth in sales is defined as growth in sales excluding the effects of acquisitions/divestitures and currency effects. Companies often report foreign currency effects on sales in the MD&A section of their annual reports. This information can be used by analysts to improve the accuracy of their forecasts of future sales.

EXAMPLE: Analysis of sales components

BCN, Inc., an American multinational, reported the following in its MD&A for the year 2017:

Region	% Change in Sales	Impact of Currency	% Change in Sales Excluding Currency Effect
North America ex-U.S.	3%	–2%	5%
Asia (incl. Japan)	2%	0%	2%
Europe	2%	3%	–1%

Comment on the growth rates observed in different markets for BCN.

Answer:

BCN experienced highest growth in North America ex-U.S. Excluding the loss in translation (due to depreciation of the foreign currency in which sales are denominated) for North America ex-U.S., the revenue growth would have been 5% due to an increase in volumes and/or price.

In Europe, the revenue growth is 2%, but that was due to appreciation of the currencies in which sales occurred. Excluding the currency effect, sales were down in Europe by 1%.

In Asia, the revenue growth of 2% is solely due to price/volume changes.

LOS 16.j: Analyze how currency fluctuations potentially affect financial results, given a company's countries of operation.

CFA® Program Curriculum, Volume 2, page 189

Major Sources of Foreign Exchange Risk

Foreign exchange risks reflect the effect of changes in currency values on the assets and liabilities of a business as well as on future sales. We discussed transaction and translation exposure earlier in this topic review and the impact of each on reported profits.

Disclosures as part of MD&A may include the impact of currency value changes on profits. Such disclosures help an analyst estimate the potential impact of currency value changes on a company's earnings going forward. If such information is not provided, analysts can conduct their own sensitivity analysis to further improve their forecasts and understand risks faced by the company. Analysts also should inquire about any hedging tools employed by the company to manage its currency exposures.

EXAMPLE: Walmart's foreign exchange risk management practice

An excerpt from Walmart's 2015 Annual Report:

> We are exposed to fluctuations in foreign currency exchange rates as a result of our net investments and operations in countries other than the U.S. For fiscal 2015, movements in currency exchange rates and the related impact on the translation of the balance sheets of the Company's subsidiaries in Canada, the United Kingdom, Japan, Mexico, and Chile were the primary cause of the $3.6 billion net loss in the currency translation and other category of accumulated other comprehensive income (loss). We hedge a portion of our foreign currency risk by entering into currency swaps and designating certain foreign-currency-denominated long-term debt as net investment hedges.
>
> We hold currency swaps to hedge the currency exchange component of our net investments and also to hedge the currency exchange rate fluctuation exposure associated with the forecasted payments of principal and interest of non-U.S.-denominated debt. The aggregate fair value of these swaps was in a liability position of $110 million at January 31, 2015, and in an asset position of $550 million at January 31, 2014. The change in the fair value of these swaps was due to fluctuations in currency exchange rates, primarily the strengthening of the U.S. dollar relative to other currencies in the latter half of fiscal 2015. A hypothetical 10% increase or decrease in the currency exchange rates underlying these swaps from the market rate at January 31, 2015, would have resulted in a loss or gain in the value of the swaps of $435 million. A hypothetical 10% change in interest rates underlying these swaps from the market rates in effect at January 31, 2015, would have resulted in a loss or gain in value of the swaps of $20 million.

MODULE QUIZ 16.8

To best evaluate your performance, enter your quiz answers online.

1. Suparna, Inc., is a U.S.-based multinational engineering company specializing in advanced water management solutions. Outside the United States, Suparna has extensive operations in Asia-Pacific, Europe, and Latin America.

   The following information is collected from the MD&A section of Suparna's annual report for 2015:

   Reconciliation of the Statutory Tax Rate

Item	Suparna
Statutory tax rate	35.0%
Effect of disallowed provisions	2.0%
Effect of taxes in foreign jurisdictions	(1.9%)
Other	0.3%
Effective tax rate	35.4%

   Due to its foreign operations, Suparna's effective tax rate was *most likely*:

   A. higher than the prior year's effective tax rate.
   B. lower than its statutory tax rate.
   C. higher than the statutory tax rate.

Answer Questions 2 and 3 based on the following information.

IBM's 2012 annual report includes the following excerpts:

> *Foreign currency fluctuations often drive operational responses that mitigate the simple mechanical translation of earnings. During periods of sustained movements in currency, the marketplace and competition adjust to the changing rates. For example, when pricing offerings in the marketplace, the company may use some of the advantage from a weakening U.S. dollar to improve its position competitively, and price more aggressively to win the business, essentially passing on a portion of the currency advantage to its customers. Competition will frequently take the same action. Consequently, the company believes that some of the currency based changes in cost impact the prices charged to clients. The company also maintains currency hedging programs for cash management purposes which mitigate, but do not eliminate, the volatility of currency impacts on the company's financial results. The company translates revenue, cost and expense in its non-U.S. operations at current exchange rates in the reported period.*
>
> *References to "adjusted for currency" or "constant currency" reflect adjustments based upon a simple constant currency mathematical translation of local currency results using the comparable prior period's currency conversion rate. However, this constant currency methodology that the company utilizes to disclose this information does not incorporate any operational actions that management may take in reaction to fluctuating currency rates. Based on the currency rate movements in 2012, total revenue decreased 2.3 percent as reported and was flat at constant currency versus 2011. On a pre-tax income basis, these translation impacts offset by the net impact of hedging activities resulted in a theoretical maximum (assuming no pricing or sourcing actions) decrease of approximately $100 million in 2012. The same mathematical exercise resulted in an increase of approximately $600 million in 2011. The company views these amounts as a theoretical maximum impact to its as-reported financial results. Considering the operational responses mentioned above, movements of exchange rates, and the nature and timing of hedging instruments, it is difficult to predict future currency impacts on any particular period, but the company believes it could be substantially less than the theoretical maximum given the competitive pressure in the marketplace.*

2. IBM's 2012 revenue growth excluding the impact of currency rate movements was *most likely*:
   A. higher than as reported in the financial statements.
   B. lower than as reported in the financial statements.
   C. the same as reported in the financial statements.

3. The *most likely* impact of currency fluctuations on IBM's 2011 pre-tax earnings net of hedging activities is that pre-tax earnings were:
   A. lower by $600 million.
   B. lower by $100 million.
   C. higher by $600 million.

KEY CONCEPTS

LOS 16.a

The local currency is the currency of the country to which it refers.

The functional currency, determined by management, is the currency of the primary economic environment in which the entity operates. The functional currency is usually the currency in which the entity generates and expends cash. It can be the local currency or some other currency.

The presentation (reporting) currency is the currency in which the entity prepares its financial statements.

LOS 16.b

Foreign currency denominated transactions, including sales, are measured in the presentation (reporting) currency at the spot rate on the transaction date. If the exchange rate changes, gain or loss is recognized on the settlement date. If the balance sheet date occurs before the transaction is settled, the gain or loss is based on the exchange rate on the balance sheet date. Once the transaction is settled, additional gain or loss is recognized if the exchange rate changes after the balance sheet date.

The standards do not provide guidance as to where such gains/losses are recognized and, hence, reduce comparability of financial statements.

LOS 16.c

Revenues are translated at average exchange rate under both the temporal method and under the current rate method.

LOS 16.d

If the functional currency and the parent's presentation currency differ, the current rate method is used to translate the subsidiary's financial statements. This usually occurs when the subsidiary is relatively independent of the parent. Under the current rate method, all assets and liabilities are translated at the current rate; common stock and dividends paid at the historic rate; and revenues and expenses at the average rate. Translation gains and losses are reported in equity in the CTA account. The CTA is a plug figure that makes the accounting equation balance.

If the functional currency is the same as the parent's presentation currency, the temporal method is used to remeasure the subsidiary's financial statements. This usually occurs when the subsidiary is well integrated with the parent. Under the temporal method:

- Monetary assets and liabilities are remeasured at the current rate.
- Nonmonetary assets and liabilities are remeasured at the historical rate.
- Common stock and dividends paid are remeasured at the historical rate.
- COGS, depreciation, and amortization expense are remeasured at the historical rate.

- All other revenues and expenses are remeasured at the average rate.
- Remeasurement gains and losses are reported in the income statement.

LOS 16.e

Under the current rate method, exposure is defined as the net asset position (assets – liabilities) of the subsidiary. Under the temporal method, exposure is defined as the net monetary asset or net monetary liability position of the subsidiary. When assets are exposed to a depreciating foreign currency, a loss results. When liabilities are exposed to a depreciating foreign currency, a gain results.

The local currency trends and relationships of pure balance sheet and income statement ratios are preserved under the current rate method. When compared to the local currency mixed ratios will differ after translation.

LOS 16.f

In comparing the ratio effects of the temporal method and current rate method, it is necessary to:

- Determine whether the local currency is appreciating or depreciating.
- Determine which rate (historical rate, average rate, or current rate) is used to convert the numerator under both methods and analyze the effects on the ratio.
- Determine which rate (historical rate, average rate, or current rate) is used to convert the denominator under both methods and analyze the effects on the ratio.
- Determine whether the ratio will increase, decrease, or stay the same based on the direction of change in the numerator and the denominator.

LOS 16.g

A hyperinflationary environment is one where cumulative inflation exceeds 100% over a 3-year period (more than 26% annual inflation). Under U.S. GAAP, the temporal method is required when the subsidiary is operating in a hyperinflationary environment. Under IFRS, the foreign currency financial statements are first restated for inflation and then translated using the current rate method. Restating for inflation results in recognition of the net purchasing power gain or loss which is based on the net monetary asset or liability of the subsidiary.

LOS 16.h

Earnings of multinational companies are subject to multiple tax jurisdictions; hence, the statutory tax rate often differs from the effective tax rate. Expected changes in the mix of profits from different countries can be used by the analyst to forecast future tax expenses for the company.

LOS 16.i

Revenues of multinational companies may be denominated in different currencies but are translated into the reporting currency for the purpose of preparing financial statements. Revenue growth can occur due to price or volume changes and due to changes in exchange rates. Analysts separate the two because the growth in revenues due to changes in price or volume is considered more sustainable.

LOS 16.j

Foreign exchange risks include the impact of changes in currency values on assets and liabilities of a business, as well as on future sales. Disclosures may enable an analyst to evaluate the impact of changes in currency values on a company's business.

ANSWER KEY FOR MODULE QUIZZES

Module Quiz 16.1

1. **A** This is an indirect quotation from the perspective of the U.S. firm. Since the peso depreciated from the sale date to the end of 2015, a loss is recognized in 2015. However, the peso appreciated from the end of 2015 to the payment date on January 20, 2016. Thus, a gain is recognized in 2016. (LOS 16.b)

Module Quiz 16.2

1. **A** If the functional currency is the local currency, then the functional currency and the parent's presentation currency are different. In this case, the current rate method is used. (LOS 16.a)

2. **C** As a multinational firm, the location of Mazeppa's head office would most likely determine the currency to be used to prepare its final, consolidated financial statements. Since Mazeppa's is located in Canada, the presentation currency is likely the Canadian dollar. Based on the facts, the local currency is the euro and the functional currency is the U.S. dollar. (LOS 16.a)

3. **A** None of the situations will result in a gain. When total assets equal total liabilities, net assets are zero; thus, no gain or loss is recognized as a result of changing exchange rates. The other situations would result in a translation loss. (LOS 16.c)

4. **B** Fixed assets are the only nonmonetary assets. Deferred revenue is the only nonmonetary liability. Equity is not relevant to this question. (LOS 16.c)

5. **A** Reducing equity and increasing peso liabilities would be most effective in reducing currency risk to the parent. The other options leave the net exposure unchanged, since there is a one-for-one reduction in both monetary assets and monetary liabilities. (LOS 16.c)

Module Quiz 16.3, 16.4

1. **A** Monetary asset accounts of a foreign subsidiary are translated using the current rate under the temporal method. (Module 16.3, LOS 16.d)

2. **C** Subsidiaries whose operations are well integrated with the parent will generally use the parent's currency as the functional currency. Remeasurement from the local currency to the functional currency is done with the temporal method. (Module 16.3, LOS 16.a)

3. **B** If the functional currency is the same as the parent's presentation currency, the temporal method is used. Under the temporal method, the subsidiary's net monetary asset or net monetary liability position is exposed to changing exchange rates. (Module 16.3, LOS 16.e)

4. **A** Since the functional currency (£) differs from the parent's presentation currency ($), the current rate method is used. Under the current rate method, net income is translated at the average rate. Dividends are translated at the historical rate on the date the dividends were paid.

   ($1.55/£ × £400) – ($1.60/£ × £100) = $460

   (Module 16.4, LOS 16.c)

5. **A** The current rate method will result in higher gross profit in a depreciating environment. Under the temporal method, the subsidiary's COGS will be remeasured at the historical rate. This means that COGS will be relatively less affected by the depreciating currency. Sales, however, will be affected by the depreciating currency. Thus, gross profit margin will be lower. Under the current rate method, both sales and COGS will be affected by the depreciating currency. (Module 16.4, LOS 16.d)

Module Quiz 16.5, 16.6

1. **B** All pure income statement and balance sheet ratios are unaffected by the application of the current rate method. What we mean by "pure" is that the components of the ratio all come from the balance sheet, or the components of the ratio all come from the income statement. Return on assets is a "mixed ratio" because assets come from the balance sheet and are translated at the current rate and net income is translated at the average rate. Unless the exchange rate doesn't change during the year, the two inputs will be translated at different rates, and the local currency value of the ratio will change when translated into the reporting currency. The other ratios will *always* be the same using the current rate method. (Module 16.6, LOS 16.f)

2. **C** If Vibrant operates independently from FlexCo, the functional currency is the loca and the current rate method applies.

   The first step is to compute the ending balance of retained earnings of $555 [$383.3 beginning retained earnings + (LC400 net income × $0.4292)].

   Next, translate assets, liabilities, and common stock. Assets are $1,340 (LC3350 × 0.4), liabilities are $700 (LC1,750 × 0.4), and common stock is $200 (LC400 × 0.5).

   Finally, make the accounting equation balance with the CTA of –$115 ($1,340 assets – $700 liabilities – $200 common stock – $555 ending retained earnings). (Module 16.2, LOS 16.c)

3. **B** It might look like you have to construct the translated financial statements to answer this question, but you actually don't have to if you remember the relationships between the original subsidiary ratios measured in the local currency and the translated ratios measured in U.S. dollars.

Pure income statement ratios like gross profit margin will be the same. The gross profit margin measured in the local currency is LC1,700 gross profit / LC5,500 revenue = 30.9%; the gross margin measured in U.S. dollars must also be 30.9%.

Mixed ratios like ROA will be different. In this case, since the local currency is depreciating, the translated ROA will be greater than the original ROA. This occurs because net income (in the numerator) is translated at the higher average rate, and ending total assets (in the denominator) will be translated at the lower current rate. ROA measured in the local currency is LC400 net income / LC3,350 ending total assets = 11.9%. The ROA measured in U.S. dollars must be greater than 11.9%, which means 12.8% is the only possible answer.

If you did go through the process of calculating the translated ratios, you should have arrived at these numbers:

$$\text{translated gross margin} = \frac{1,700 \times 0.4292}{5,500 \times 0.4292} = \frac{\$729.60}{2,360.60} = 30.9\%$$

$$\text{translated ROA} = \frac{400 \times 0.4292}{3,350 \times 0.40} = \frac{\$171.70}{\$1,340} = 12.8\%$$

(Module 16.6, LOS 16.f)

4. **A** The local currency is depreciating, so the gross profit margin remeasured in U.S. dollars using the temporal method will be lower than the gross profit margin translated into U.S. dollars using the current rate method. This is because COGS will be measured at the higher historical rate under the temporal method and at the lower average rate under the current rate method. With temporal method COGS greater than current rate COGS, temporal method gross margin will be less than current rate method gross margin. Current rate gross margin is the same as in the original currency (from the previous problem), which means the only possible answer is "lower." (Module 16.6, LOS 16.f)

5. **C** Accounts receivable turnover will be the same under both methods. The numerator (sales) is converted at the average rate under both methods. The denominator (accounts receivable) is converted at the current rate under both methods. (Module 16.6, LOS 16.f)

6. **B** Gross profit margin and interest coverage are pure income statement ratios that will not change. The quick ratio is a pure balance sheet ratio that will not change. Return on assets is a mixed ratio (income statement item in the numerator and balance sheet item in the denominator), so it will change as long as the average and current exchange rates are different. Given that the dollar is depreciating against the yen, the current and average rates are likely to be different.

   Therefore, Haskell is correct in his analysis of three of the four ratios: gross profit margin, interest coverage, and the quick ratio. (Module 16.6, LOS 16.f)

Module Quiz 16.7

1. **A** In an inflationary environment, the temporal method is required under U.S. GAAP, even if the functional currency and the parent's presentation currency differ. Under the temporal method, inventory, fixed assets, and intangible assets are remeasured at the historical rate; that is, the actual rate when the assets were purchased. (LOS 16.g)

2. **B** Nonmonetary items are not exposed to purchasing power gains or losses during inflation. Monetary assets will result in purchasing power losses, and monetary liabilities will result in purchasing power gains. (LOS 16.g)

Module Quiz 16.8

1. **B** Suparna's effective tax rate was lowered by 1.9% due to the effect of taxes in foreign jurisdictions. (LOS 16.h)

2. **A** Per the annual report, total revenue decreased 2.3% as reported and was flat at constant currency versus 2011. Hence, the constant currency growth rate was higher than the reported growth rate. (LOS 16.i)

3. **C** Pre-tax earnings offset by the net impact of hedging activities decreased approximately $100 million in 2012 and increased by approximately $600 million due to currency translation effects. (LOS 16.j)

The following is a review of the Financial Reporting and Analysis (1) principles designed to address the learning outcome statements set forth by CFA Institute. Cross-Reference to CFA Institute Assigned Reading #17.

READING 17 Analysis of Financial Institutions

Study Session 5

EXAM FOCUS

This topic review covers financial analysis techniques that are specific to banks and insurance companies. Know the CAMELS framework of analysis for a bank (this is the main focus of the topic review). Also know and be able to interpret the key ratios in analyzing both P&C and L&H insurance companies.

MODULE 17.1: FINANCIAL INSTITUTIONS

Video covering this content is available online.

LOS 17.a: Describe how financial institutions differ from other companies.

CFA® Program Curriculum, Volume 2, page 213

Financial institutions provide a broad range of products and services, including serving as an intermediary between providers and users of capital, asset and risk management, and transaction executions.

Financial institutions differ from other companies as follows:

1. Systemic importance. Financial institutions are necessary for the smooth functioning and overall health of the economy. As an intermediary between providers and users of capital, there are often inter-linkages between financial institutions. These inter-dependencies introduce a system-wide risk of failure when one of the member institutions fails—*the contagion effect.* As a deposit-taking institution, banks are especially prone to the risk of a bank run. To avoid financial contagion, bank deposits are often insured up to a certain limit by the government.

2. Regulated. Given the significance of financial institutions, they are often highly regulated. Regulations include minimum capital requirements, minimum liquidity requirements, and limits on risk-taking.
3. Assets. The assets of financial institutions tend to be financial assets such as loans and securities that are usually reported at fair value. This contrasts with other companies that primarily own tangible assets reported at depreciated historic cost.

LOS 17.b: Describe key aspects of financial regulations of financial institutions.

CFA® Program Curriculum, Volume 2, page 219

Due to global inter-linkages between financial institutions, financial contagion may spread beyond a single economy. To manage this global systemic risk, global and regional regulatory bodies coordinate rules and oversight. Uniformity in standards also seeks to prevent regulatory arbitrage.

One of the most important global organizations is the Basel Committee on Banking Supervision, a standing committee of the Bank of International Settlements. The Basel committee develops the regulatory framework for banks (currently **Basel III**) with the objective of increasing the banking sector's ability to absorb economic and financial shocks.

The three pillars of the Basel III framework are the maintenance of minimum levels of capital, liquidity, and stable funding.

- Minimum required capital for a bank is based on the risk of the bank's assets. The riskier a bank's assets are, the higher its required capital.
- Basel III specifies that a bank should hold enough liquid assets to meet demands under a 30-day liquidity stress scenario.
- The Basel III framework requires stable funding relative to a bank's liquidity needs over a one-year time horizon. Stability in funding is proportional to the tenor of the bank's deposits; longer-term deposits are more stable than shorter-term deposits. Stability also depends on the type of deposit (e.g., consumer deposits are more stable than interbank market funds).

Other global organizations that coordinate regulations include the:

1. Financial Stability Board, which seeks to coordinate actions of participating jurisdictions in identifying and managing systemic risks.
2. International Association of Deposit Insurers, which seeks to improve the effectiveness of deposit insurance systems.
3. International Organization of Securities Commissions (IOSCO), which seeks to promote fair and efficient security markets.
4. International Association of Insurance Supervisors (IAIS), which seeks to improve supervision of the insurance industry.

MODULE QUIZ 17.1

To best evaluate your performance, enter your quiz answers online.

1. Which of the following is *least likely* to be recommended by the Basel III framework?
   A. Minimum percentage of risk-weighted assets that needs to be held as capital.
   B. Rate spread earned on assets over the deposit crediting rate should be positive.
   C. The minimum required stable funding level to cover one-year time-horizon liquidity needs.
2. Which international organization strives to maintain fair and efficient security markets?
   A. IOSCO.
   B. Basel III Committee.
   C. IAIS.

MODULE 17.2: CAPITAL ADEQUACY AND ASSET QUALITY

Video covering this content is available online.

LOS 17.c: Explain the CAMELS (capital adequacy, asset quality, management, earnings, liquidity, and sensitivity) approach to analyzing a bank, including key ratios and its limitations.

CFA® Program Curriculum, Volume 2, page 221

The CAMELS approach is a six-factor analysis of a bank, including capital adequacy, asset quality, management, earnings, liquidity, and sensitivity.

Capital Adequacy

To prevent financial insolvency, a bank must maintain adequate capital to sustain business losses. Capital adequacy is based on risk-weighted assets (RWA); more risky assets require a higher level of capital. Risk-weighting is specified by individual regulators.

EXAMPLE: Risk-weighted assets

Mega Bank is regulated by the Central Bank of Zima. Per the central bank rules, the following risk weightings are applied to the bank's assets.

Asset Type	Risk Weight
Cash and Central Bank deposits	0%
Corporate loans—performing	100%
Corporate loans—nonperforming	200%
Consumer real estate loans	90%

An Analysis of Mega Bank's balance sheet for 20X8 reveals the following.

Asset Type	Amount ('000)
Cash and Central Bank deposits	$120
Corporate loans—performing	$1,130
Corporate loans—nonperforming	$920
Consumer real estate loans	$2,450
Total assets	$4,620

Calculate Mega Bank's RWA.

Answer:

Asset Type	Risk Weight	Amount ('000)	RWA ('000)
Cash and Central Bank deposits	0%	$120	$0
Corporate loans—performing	100%	$1,130	$1,130
Corporate loans—nonperforming	200%	$920	$1,840
Consumer real estate loans	90%	$2,450	$2,205
Total risk-weighted assets			$5,175

Basel III defines a bank's capital in a tiered, hierarchical approach:

1. Tier 1 capital:
   a. **Common Equity Tier 1 capital** (the most important component): Common stock, additional paid-in capital, retained earnings, and OCI less intangibles and deferred tax assets.
   b. **Other Tier 1 capital**: subordinated instruments with no specified maturity and no contractual dividends (e.g., preferred stock with discretionary dividends).
2. Tier 2 capital: Subordinated instruments with *original* (i.e., when issued) maturity of more than five years.

Tier 1 capital plus Tier 2 capital makes up the total capital of a bank.

Again, individual jurisdictions specify the minimum capital requirements. Basel III guidelines specify a minimum Common Equity Tier 1 capital of 4.5% of RWA, minimum total Tier 1 capital of 6% of RWA, and minimum total capital of 8% of RWA.

EXAMPLE: Capital position

Mega Bank's RWA for 20X7 and 20X8 were $4,700,000 and $5,175,000, respectively. An analysis of bank's capital for the two years reveals the following information.

Capital Type	Amount ('000)	
	20X7	20X8
Common Equity Tier 1	$200	$190
Subordinated debt, no maturity, no dividends/interest	$85	$95
Subordinated debt, maturity 5+ years	$110	$120

1. Determine the Common Equity Tier 1 capital ratio, Tier 1 capital ratio and total capital ratio for both years.
2. Comment on capital adequacy for Mega Bank.

Answer:

1. Mega Bank's capital ratios as a percentage of its RWA for the two years are shown in the following table.

Capital Type	% of RWA	
	20X7	20X8
Common Equity Tier 1	4.26%	3.67%
Subordinated debt, no maturity, no dividends/interest	1.81%	1.84%
Subordinated debt, maturity 5+ years	2.34%	2.32%
Total capital	8.40%	7.83%

total Tier 1 ratio for 20X7 = 4.26% + 1.81% = 6.07%

total Tier 1 ratio for 20X8 = 3.67% + 1.84% = 5.51%

2. Mega Bank's Common Equity Tier 1 ratio is less than Basel III guideline of 4.5%. Furthermore, it has worsened from 20X7 to 20X8. Given that this is the most important component of capital, it should be a cause for concern for the bank's regulators. The bank's total Tier 1 ratio was above the Basel III guideline of 6% in 20X7, but it has fallen below the guideline for 20X8. The total capital ratio is above the Basel III guideline of 8% for 20X7 but again has fallen short in 20X8.

Asset Quality

In a broad context, asset quality derives from the processes of generating assets, managing them, and controlling overall risk. Evaluation of asset quality includes analysis of current and potential credit risk associated with the bank's assets.

Bank assets include loans (the largest component) and investments in securities. While loans are generally carried on the balance sheet at amortized cost (net of allowances), the accounting treatment for investments in securities differs between U.S. GAAP and IFRS. Under IFRS 9, depending on the business model, debt securities may be carried at amortized cost, fair value through OCI, or fair value through profit or loss. Equity securities are always carried at fair value (either through OCI or through profit or loss). Under U.S. GAAP, equity investments are carried at fair value through profit or loss, while debt securities can be carried at amortized cost (held-to-maturity classification), fair value through OCI (available for sale classification) or fair value through profit or loss (trading classification).

PROFESSOR'S NOTE:

The curriculum covers the latest U.S. GAAP standards (applicable for periods starting December 15, 2017) for this topic review.

It helps to be familiar with a couple of terms used in bank balance sheets (even though terms used can vary quite a bit among banks):

1. *Reverse repurchase agreements* are bank loans advanced under a repurchase agreement (i.e., against a high-quality collateral).
2. *Assets held for sale* pertain to discontinued operations whose value in the balance sheet assumes disposition (as opposed to long-term holding).

Credit Risk Analysis

The nature of a bank's busincss cntails a large exposure to credit risk. Credit risk is present in debt securities that the bank invests in, loans the bank makes, as well as in the bank's off-balance-sheet liabilities (e.g., unused lines of credit, or letters of credit). Analyzing the credit quality of a bank's assets can provide an analyst key insights into the bank's solvency and future profitability.

EXAMPLE: Credit analysis

The following table provides information for loans held by Small Bank at the end of 20X8 and 20X7.

Loans	20X8	20X7
Very strong credit quality	661	596
Strong credit quality	882	894
Good credit quality	1,488	1,292
Satisfactory credit quality	606	696
Sub-standard credit quality	992	894
Past due but not yet impaired	276	199
Impaired	441	298
Seriously impaired	165	99
Total	5,511	4,968

1. It appears that from 20X7 to 20X8, the credit quality of Small Bank's loan assets has *most likely*:

   A. worsened.

   B. improved.

   C. remained essentially the same.

2. The proportion of loans at the end of 20X8 that are either past due or impaired is *closest* to:

   A. 12%.

   B. 16%.

   C. 19%.

Answers:

The following table summarizes the percentage of loans in each category for both years.

Loans	20X8	20X7	20X8	20X7
Very strong credit quality	661	596	12%	12%
Strong credit quality	882	894	16%	18%
Good credit quality	1,488	1,292	27%	26%
Satisfactory credit quality	606	696	11%	14%
Sub-standard credit quality	992	894	18%	18%
Past due but not yet impaired	276	199	5%	4%
Impaired	441	298	8%	6%
Seriously impaired	165	99	3%	2%
Total	5,511	4,968	100%	100%

1. **A** It appears that proportion of better quality loans (at least satisfactory credit quality) has declined while that of poor credit quality (past due, impaired and seriously impaired) has increased.

2. **B** The total of loans that were either past due or impaired (including seriously impaired) at the end of 20X8 = 5% + 8% + 3% = 16%. Though not asked for in this question, the total for 20X7 was 4% + 6% + 2% = 12%.

Loan Loss Provisions

For a bank, loans represent a large portion of its total assets. Accordingly, the credit quality of loans and loss provisions are critical in evaluating the bank's financial position and performance. **Allowance for loan losses** is a contra asset account to loans and is the result of **provision for loan losses,** an expense subject to management discretion. Analysts need to evaluate the bank's policy of setting aside adequate provisions relative to actual loan performance. Actual losses (net of recoveries) are then written off against these provisions.

Several ratios are useful in this evaluation:

1. Ratio of allowance for loan losses to nonperforming loans.
2. Ratio of allowance for loan losses to net loan charge-offs.
3. Ratio of provision for loan losses to net loan charge-offs.

Each ratio compares a discretionary metric (i.e., allowance or provision) to a more objective measure.

EXAMPLE: Loan loss provisions

The following information is collected for Mega Bank.

Loans	20X8	20X7
Total loans	5,511	4,968
Nonperforming loans	606	397
Provisions for loan losses	122	108
Allowance for loan losses	338	404
Write-offs	202	178
Recoveries	(14)	(19)
Net write-offs	188	159

Calculate the appropriate ratios to evaluate the adequacy of loan loss reserves as well as provisions for loan losses for Mega Bank.

Answer:

Ratios		
Allowance for loan losses to nonperforming loans	0.56	1.02
Allowance for loan losses to net loan charge-offs	1.80	2.54
Provision for loan losses to net loan charge-offs	0.65	0.68

The allowance for loan losses to nonperforming loans ratio has declined from 1.02 to 0.56, indicating that the bank has not made sufficient provisions for loan losses (i.e., possible aggressive accounting).

This aggressive accounting is also evidenced by the provision for loan losses to net loan charge-offs ratio, which is also declining from 0.68 to 0.65. In other words, for 20X8, the expense recorded for loan losses was only 65% of actual losses during that year. The allowance for loan losses to net loan charge-offs ratio has decreased for 20X8, indicating that the rate of increase in allowance for loan losses is significantly below the growth rate of actual write-offs.

MODULE QUIZ 17.2

To best evaluate your performance, enter your quiz answers online.

1. The most important source of capital for a bank is:
   A. Tier 1 capital.
   B. Common Equity Tier 1 capital.
   C. Total capital.
2. According to Basel III guidelines, total Tier 1 capital must be at *least*:
   A. 4.5% of risk-weighted assets.
   B. 6% of risk-weighted assets.
   C. 8% of risk-weighted assets.
3. Securities issued by a bank that are subordinate to deposits and other debt obligations and without specified maturity or contractual payments are *most likely* part of:
   A. Tier 1 capital.
   B. Common Equity Tier 1 capital.
   C. Tier 2 capital.

4. Under current accounting standards, equity securities in a bank's portfolio are *most likely* shown on the balance sheet at:
   A. Fair value.
   B. Fair value under US GAAP and fair value or amortized cost under IFRS.
   C. Fair value under IFRS and fair value or amortized cost under US GAAP.

MODULE 17.3: MANAGEMENT CAPABILITIES AND EARNINGS QUALITY

Video covering this content is available online.

Management Capabilities

The quality of a bank's management influences the success with which the bank is able to exploit profitable opportunities while also controlling the level of risks taken. Risk management and control is critical for banks. This includes identification and control of different types of risk (e.g., credit, market, operating, legal, and other). A bank's internal control and governance systems (including an independent board) ensure that managers do not take undue risks or engage in self-serving behavior. The board also sets appropriate levels of maximum allowable risk for the managers. Internal control systems should continuously measure and monitor the myriad risks that the bank may be exposed to.

Earnings

Earnings are considered high quality if they are adequate (providing a rate of return above the cost of capital) as well as sustainable. Ideally, the trend in earnings should be positive and the underlying accounting estimates (used to arrive at reported earnings) should be unbiased. Finally, earnings should ideally be derived from recurring sources.

A major source of earnings of a bank is from investment in securities. Estimates used in the valuation of these securities may lead to biased earnings. Both IFRS and U.S. GAAP use the concept of a *fair value hierarchy* based on types of inputs used in determining the fair value of financial assets.

Level 1 inputs are quoted market prices of identical assets. Level 2 inputs are observable but not quoted prices of identical assets. Examples of Level 2 inputs include quoted prices of similar assets, quoted prices of identical assets in non-active markets, observable interest rates, spreads, and implied volatility. Level 3 inputs are non-observable and hence subjective. For example, fair value may be derived from models or based on estimated future cash flows discounted at an estimated discount rate.

In practice, banks often use the fair value hierarchy to label their assets (e.g., Level 2 securities are those whose value was determined using Level 2 inputs) or to label their valuation methodology (e.g., Level 2 methodology is defined as one that uses Level 2 inputs).

Similar to other companies, other subjective estimates (e.g., goodwill impairment, recognition of deferred tax assets, and recognition of contingent liabilities) affects the quality of a bank's earnings.

For a typical bank, major sources of earnings are (1) net interest income, (2) service income, and (3) trading income. Of these, trading income is the most volatile year-to-year, and, hence, on a relative basis, banks with proportionally higher net interest income and service income would have more sustainable earnings.

MODULE QUIZ 17.3

To best evaluate your performance, enter your quiz answers online.

1. Regarding inputs into valuation of securities, Level 1 inputs are *most accurately* described as:
   A. quoted market prices of identical securities.
   B. quoted market prices of similar securities.
   C. inputs derived from market prices.
2. Which of the following sources of earnings for a bank is *most* volatile?
   A. Service income.
   B. Net interest income.
   C. Trading income.

Video covering this content is available online.

MODULE 17.4: LIQUIDITY POSITION AND SENSITIVITY TO MARKET RISK

Liquidity Position

Having adequate liquidity is critical for a bank. The Basel III framework introduced two minimum liquidity standards:

1. **Liquidity coverage ratio (LCR)** is calculated as the value of a bank's highly liquid assets divided by its expected cash outflows.

   $$\text{LCR} = \frac{\text{highly liquid assets}}{\text{expected cash outflows}}$$

   Highly liquid assets are those that are easily convertible into cash, while expected cash flows are the estimated one-month liquidity needs *in a stress scenario*. The standards recommend a minimum LCR of 100%.

2. **Net stable funding ratio (NSFR)** is the percentage of required stable funding that is sourced from *available* stable funding.

   $$\text{NSFR} = \frac{\text{available stable funding}}{\text{required stable funding}}$$

   Available stable funding is a function of the composition and maturity distribution of a bank's funding sources (i.e., capital, deposits, and other liabilities). Required stable funding is a function of the composition and maturity distribution of the bank's asset base.

   Available stable funding (ASF) is determined based on an ASF factor that is assigned to each funding source, as shown in Figure 17.1.

Figure 17.1: Available Stable Funding Components

Funding Component	ASF Factor
Regulatory capital minus Tier 2 instruments maturing in a year	100%
Other capital instruments and liabilities with maturity > 1 year	
Stable demand deposits and term deposits (maturity < 1 year) from retail and small business customers	95%
Less-stable demand deposits and term deposits (maturity < 1 year) from retail and small business customers	90%
Funding from nonfinancial corporates (maturity < 1 year), operational deposits, funding from sovereigns, public sector (maturity < 1 year), multilateral and national development banks	50%
All other liabilities	0%

NSFR relates the liquidity needs of a bank's assets to the liquidity provided by the bank's liabilities (i.e., funding sources). Longer-dated liabilities are considered more stable and hence would be suitable to fund assets with longer maturities (e.g., long-term loans). Deposits from retail and small business clients are considered more stable than deposits from corporate clients. The standards recommend a minimum NSFR of 100%.

Other liquidity monitoring metrics recommended by Basel III include *concentration of funding* and *maturity mismatch*. Relatively concentrated funding indicates a bank's reliance on relatively few funding sources. This lack of diversification may pose a problem when the sources withdraw funding, resulting in heightened liquidity risk for the bank. Maturity mismatch occurs when the asset maturities differ meaningfully from maturity of the liabilities (funding sources). The higher the mismatch, the higher the liquidity risk for the bank. For example, sometimes banks try to maximize the spread between lending and borrowing rates by borrowing at low, short-term rates and lending at higher, longer-term rates. This mismatch in assets and liabilities may expose the bank to a liquidity crunch if it is unable to roll over its borrowings at reasonable rates.

EXAMPLE: Liquidity analysis

The following information is collected for Mega Bank.

Description	20X9	20X8
Highly liquid assets	1,250	1,100
Average monthly withdrawals	900	750
Expected monthly outflows in a stress scenario	1,300	1,050

Describe the liquidity risk faced by Mega Bank.

Answer:

LCR for 20X8 = (1,100/1,050) = 104.76%

LCR for 20X9 = (1,250/1,300) = 96.15%

For 20X9, the bank's LCR has dropped from prior year, dropping even below the minimum requirement of 100%, indicating higher liquidity risk.

Sensitivity to Market Risk

Bank earnings are affected by various market risks (e.g., volatility of security prices, currency values, interest rates). The most critical of these is interest rate risk. A bank's interest rate risk is the result of differences in maturity, rates, and repricing frequency between the bank's assets and its liabilities. For example, in a rising interest rate scenario, if the assets are repriced more frequently than liabilities, the bank's net interest income would increase.

Banks respond to opportunities presented in the market and alter their balance sheets. For example, following the financial crisis of 2008, central banks around the world reduced short-term interest rates, allowing banks to borrow at lower rates. To benefit from this interest rate scenario, many banks increased their duration risk (i.e., borrowed more short-term funds while lending long term).

Similarly, the impact of a change in the shape of the yield curve differs among banks, based on differences in the composition of their assets and liabilities. In the MD&A section of their annual reports, banks often disclose exposure to a wide variety of market and nonmarket risks. For example, a bank may disclose the impact of a change in yield on its earnings.

The impact of market risk can be captured by value at risk (VaR). We will discuss this important risk metric in the portfolio management topic area of the curriculum.

MODULE QUIZ 17.4

To best evaluate your performance, enter your quiz answers online.

1. For a bank, a maturity mismatch between assets and liabilities is *most likely* to contribute to the bank's:
   A. earnings quality risk.
   B. liquidity risk.
   C. capital adequacy risk.
2. What does NSFR measure?
   A. Liquidity of a bank's funding sources relative to the liquidity needs of its assets.
   B. Stability of a bank's funding sources relative to its assets.
   C. A bank's capital relative to its stable funding sources.
3. What is the *minimum* NSFR recommended by the Basel III standards?
   A. 10%.
   B. 50%.
   C. 100%.

4. Based on the information below, which bank has the *highest* liquidity risk in a stress scenario?

Bank	LCR	NSFR
Alpha	125%	121%
Beta	141%	118%
Charlie	108%	132%
Delta	111%	89%

A. Beta.
B. Delta.
C. Charlie.

5. Based on the information below, which bank has the *highest* liquidity risk measured by funding stability?

Bank	LCR	NSFR
Alpha	125%	121%
Beta	141%	118%
Charlie	108%	132%
Delta	111%	89%

A. Charlie.
B. Beta.
C. Delta.

MODULE 17.5: OTHER FACTORS

Video covering this content is available online.

LOS 17.d: Describe other factors to consider in analyzing a bank.

CFA® Program Curriculum, Volume 2, page 238

Apart from the CAMELS approach to analyzing bank, other factors that analysts should consider include the following.

Government Support

Apart from providing deposit insurance, governments often serve as a backstop against bank failure. This is usually due to the systemic importance of the banking sector. During the financial crisis of 2008, the U.S. government created the Troubled Asset Relief Program (TARP) to prop up numerous banks that had taken on more risk than their capital could handle. The expected level of government support is related to the inter-linkages in the banking sector. Usually, the larger the bank and more inter-linked it is, the more likely that its failure will have a contagion effect. Therefore, larger banks enjoy a higher probability of implicit government support. Further, the current status of the banking sector in the country should be considered. A healthy overall sector may be able absorb the failure of an isolated bank. Hence, the implicit support level is inversely related to the overall health of the banking sector; during good times, support levels are low.

Government Ownership

Public ownership of banks may be due to the strategic importance of banks in promoting economic development. In some countries, absent government ownership, depositors may not have faith in the banking sector, a critical element for a bank's existence. Public ownership increases faith (of implicit government backing) in a bank. Shrinking public ownership and divestment would conversely reduce this security blanket.

During the financial crisis of 2008, some governments became reluctant owners of struggling banks. When the governments eventually exited their ownership stakes, it was perceived as a sign of confidence in the bank's balance sheet.

Bank Mission

Apart from profit-making, banks may also pursue other objectives. For example, community banks may be guided by community development in their lending decisions. If the community is dependent on a primary industry (e.g., banks in Houston, TX, had their fortunes tied to the oil industry in the 1980s), it may lead to concentration of risk in a community bank's asset portfolio. Global banks, on the other hand, have well-diversified asset bases, reducing their overall risk.

Culture

A bank's culture influences its propensity to seek risky investments. A relatively conservative culture may result in calculated risk-taking, while a risk-seeking culture may lead to an overly aggressive risk stance. There is a need for balance, because if the culture is too risk-averse, it may fail to provide an adequate return on investment.

Culture evaluation can be conducted by a review of:

- Diversity of a bank's assets. Banks that have generated losses due to an investment strategy with a narrow focus may be too aggressive.
- Accounting restatements due to failures of internal controls pertaining to financial reporting. Restatements may indicate an unethical culture.
- Management compensation. Excessive compensation that is too closely tied to the performance of the bank's stock may lead to a culture of excessive risk-taking.
- Speed with which a bank adjusts its loan loss provisions relative to actual loss behavior. A slower response rate generally indicates aggressive accounting practices and a risk-taking culture.

Apart from these factors, there are general factors that are relevant to analysis of any company (not just banks). These include:

- *A competitive environment* affects a bank's culture and risk-taking behavior. For example, a regional bank may be satisfied with its current market position and may not be tempted to take excessive risk. Global banks may end up taking excessive risk as their management seeks to outdo their large rivals.

- *Off-balance-sheet assets and/or liabilities* may seriously affect an entity if the underlying risks turn out to be larger than the available resources. Often, key information about a bank's off-balance-sheet exposures may be opaque or not readily available to analysts, making it very difficult to examine. However, all off-balance-sheet items are not equally nefarious. Operating leases, for example, are a lot less risky compared to selling protection in a CDS. Bank analysts should look out for variable interest (or special purpose) entities, which are usually required to be consolidated. In some instances, if an SPE is not deemed to be a VIE and therefore does not get consolidated, there may be a significant off-balance-sheet risk not reflected in the financial statements.
  - *Segment information* may provide insights into different lines of business or different geographical markets that the bank operates in. Each segment may be exposed to different levels or types of risk, such as sensitivity to markets, geo-political risks, or cyclicality.
  - *Currency exposure* is significant for large, global banks trading in currencies or holding significant assets or liabilities in different currencies whose values fluctuate. Volatility in currency values can have a significant impact on a bank's earnings.

LOS 17.e: Analyze a bank based on financial statements and other factors.

CFA® Program Curriculum, Volume 2, page 242

We have already described the CAMELS framework that should be used to analyze a bank. Due to the limitation of time allocated to each question on the exam, focus on different types of analysis (e.g., of capital adequacy, asset quality, liquidity risk, etc.) rather than a comprehensive analysis.

EXAMPLE: Asset quality

The following excerpts are from the annual report of JP Morgan Chase & Co. (Source: JP Morgan Chase & Co. 2017 Annual Report).

Excerpt 1: Asset Composition

Assets	2017	2016
Cash and due from banks	$ 25,827	$ 23,873
Deposits with banks	$ 404,294	$ 365,762
Federal funds sold and securities purchased under resale agreements	$ 198,422	$ 229,967
Securities borrowed	$ 105,112	$ 96,409
Trading assets	$ 381,844	$ 372,130
Securities	$ 249,958	$ 289,059
Loans	$ 930,697	$ 894,765
Allowance for loan losses	$ (13,604)	$ (13,776)
Loans, net of allowance for loan losses	$ 917,093	$ 880,989
Accrued interest and accounts receivable	$ 67,729	$ 52,330
Premises and equipment	$ 14,159	$ 14,131
Goodwill, MSRs, and other intangible assets	$ 54,392	$ 54,246
Other assets	$ 114,770	$ 112,076
Total assets	$ 2,533,600	$ 2,490,972

Notes: Cash and due from banks and deposits with banks are the bank's most liquid assets. Fed funds sold and securities purchased under repurchase agreements, and securities borrowed are loans made against high-quality collateral.

Excerpt 2: Capital Ratios

Ratio	2017	2016	2015	2014	2013
Common Equity Tier 1 ("CET1") capital ratio	12.20%	12.30%	11.80%	10.20%	10.70%
Tier 1 capital ratio	13.9	14.0	13.5	11.6	11.9
Total capital ratio	15.9	15.5	15.1	13.1	14.3

Excerpt 3: Fair Value Assets

December 31, 2017 (in billions, except ratio data)	Total assets at fair value	Total Level 3 assets
Trading debt and equity instruments	$325.3	$5.4
Derivative receivables	56.5	6.0
Trading assets	381.8	11.4
AFS securities	202.2	0.3
Loans	2.5	0.3
MSRs	6.0	6.0
Other	33.2	1.2
Total assets measured at fair value on a recurring basis	625.7	19.2
Total assets measured at fair value on a nonrecurring basis	1.3	0.8
Total assets measured at fair value	$627.0	$20.0
Total Firm assets	$2,533.6	
Level 3 assets as a percentage of total Firm assets		0.8%
Level 3 assets as a percentage of total Firm assets at fair value		3.2%

Using information in Excerpt 1:

1. What portion of bank assets is held in most liquid assets? What was the change from 2016 to 2017?
2. On a relative basis, what is the change in loans (including reverse repurchase agreements) from 2016 to 2017?
3. On a relative basis, what is the change in the bank's exposure to investments from 2016 to 2017?

Using information in Excerpt 2:

4. Comment on the bank's capital adequacy.

Using information in Excerpt 3:

5. What portion of bank's fair value assets are Level 1 and Level 2 assets?
6. What portion of bank's total assets are assets measured at fair value?
7. What portion of bank's total assets are Level 3 assets?

Answers:

For answers 1 to 3, calculation of each asset as a percentage of total assets is shown as follows.

Assets	2017	2016	2017	2016
Cash and due from banks	$25,827	$23,873	1.02%	0.96%
Deposits with banks	$404,294	$365,762	15.96%	14.68%
Federal funds sold and securities purchased under resale agreements	$198,422	$229,967	7.83%	9.23%
Securities borrowed	105,112	$96,409	4.15%	3.87%
Trading assets	$381,844	$372,130	15.07%	14.94%
Securities	$249,958	$289,059	9.87%	11.60%
Loans	$930,697	$894,765	36.73%	35.92%
Allowance for loan losses	$(13,604)	$(13,776)	–0.54%	–0.55%
Loans, net of allowance for loan losses	$ 917,093	$880,989	36.20%	35.37%
Accrued interest and accounts receivable	$ 67,729	$52,330	2.67%	2.10%
Premises and equipment	$ 14,159	$14,131	0.56%	0.57%
Goodwill, MSRs, and other intangible assets	$ 54,392	$54,246	2.15%	2.18%
Other assets	$114,770	$112,076	4.53%	4.50%
Total assets	$2,533,600	$2,490,972	100.00%	100.00%

1. liquid assets for 2017 = 1.02% + 15.96% = 16.98%

   liquid assets for 2016 = 0.96% + 14.68% = 15.64%

   Bank's liquidity position improved from 2016 to 2017.
2. Loans (net of allowances) and including repurchase agreement loans and securities borrowed are:

   2017: 7.83% + 4.15% + 36.20% = 48.18%

   2016: 9.23% + 3.87% + 35.37% = 48.47%

   On a relative basis, the bank's lending activities have not changed significantly from 2016 to 2017.
3. investments for 2016 = 14.94% + 11.60% = 26.54%

   Investments seem to have declined slightly on a relative basis from 2016 to 2017.
4. J.P. Morgan's capital levels have generally been increasing over time indicating a strengthening of capital position. Additionally, Common Equity Tier 1 ratio of 1 12.20% for 2017 exceeds the minimum level of 4.5% specified by the Basel III framework. Total Tier 1 capital ratio of 13.90% exceeds the minimum recommended level of 6%, and the total capital of ratio of 15.90% exceeds the minimum recommended level of 8%.

5. Level 3 assets represent 3.2% of total fair value assets. Hence, Level 1 and 2 assets must be 96.8% (100 – 3.2) of total fair value assets.
6. fair value assets as a proportion of total assets = 627 / 2,533.6 = 24.75%
7. Level 3 assets are given to be 0.8% of the bank's total assets.

MODULE QUIZ 17.5

To best evaluate your performance, enter your quiz answers online.

1. While analyzing a bank, elements of culture evaluation are *least likely* to include:
   A. the speed with which the bank adjusts its loss provisions.
   B. any prior restatements of financial statements.
   C. the tenure of the current management team.
2. Government ownership of a significant stake in a bank is *most likely* to indicate that:
   A. there is a high likelihood of government support in the event of failure.
   B. required liquidity ratios are lower than for privately owned banks.
   C. the ratio of Common Equity Tier 1 to risk-weighted assets is high.
3. Implicit government backing of the banking sector is *most likely* to be:
   A. positively related to the health of the banking sector.
   B. positively related to the size of the bank.
   C. negatively related to the degree of inter-linkages in the banking sector.
4. Community banks are *least likely* to have:
   A. a well-diversified asset base.
   B. a community lending focus.
   C. mission statements that promote community development.

MODULE 17.6: INSURANCE COMPANIES

Video covering this content is available online.

LOS 17.f: Describe key ratios and other factors to consider in analyzing an insurance company.

CFA® Program Curriculum, Volume 2, page 264

Insurance company revenues include premium income and income on **float** (i.e., income earned on premiums between their collection and the payment of claims). Property and casualty (P&C) insurers differ from life and health (L&H) insurers in terms of variability of claims and contract duration. Claims for P&C insurers tend to be lumpier as compared to relatively stable and predictable claims for L&H insurers. Contract duration (i.e., policy period) is much higher for L&H insurers relative to that of P&C insurers. Regulatory requirements that focus on solvency of insurance companies often result in different reporting standards compared to IFRS or U.S. GAAP.

P&C Insurance Companies

Premium income is usually the highest source of income for a P&C insurer. Keys to the profitability of an insurer are prudence in underwriting, pricing of adequate premiums for bearing risk, and diversification of risk. To diversify their risks, insurers often *reinsure* some risks. The policy period is often very short, with premiums received at the beginning of the period and invested during the float period. Claim events (e.g., fire, accident, etc.) are clearly defined but may take a long time to emerge.

Property insurance covers specific assets against loss due to insured events. Casualty insurance (also called liability insurance) protects against a legal liability (often to a third party) due to the occurrence of a covered event. Sometimes a policy, known as *multiple peril policy*, may cover both property and casualty losses occurring during a covered event.

P&C Profitability

P&C margins are cyclical. During periods of heightened competition, price cutting to obtain new business leads to slim or negative margins (*soft pricing* period). This soft pricing period leads to losses and a shrinking capital base for many insurers, who either leave the industry or stop underwriting new policies. The resulting reduction in competition leads to a healthier pricing environment (*hard pricing* period), which in turn results in fatter margins. Higher margins during the hard pricing period attract new competition, perpetuating the cycle.

Major expenses for P&C insurers include claims expense and the expense of obtaining new policy business. The cost of writing new policies depends on whether the insurer uses a direct-to-customer model (in which case it would bear the fixed cost of staffing) or the agency model (in which case it would pay variable commissions). Soft or hard pricing is driven by the industry's combined ratio (total insurance expenses divided by net premiums earned). When the ratio is low (high), it is a hard (soft) market.

For a single insurer, a combined ratio in excess of 100% indicates an underwriting loss.

The combined ratio, per Statutory Accounting Practices, is the sum of the **underwriting loss ratio** and the **expense ratio**.

$$\text{underwriting loss ratio} = \frac{\text{claims paid} + \Delta\text{ loss reserves}}{\text{net premium earned}}$$

$$\text{expense ratio} = \frac{\text{underwriting expenses including commissions}}{\text{net premium written}}$$

The underwriting loss ratio measures the relative efficiency of the company's underwriting standards (whether the policies are priced appropriately relative to risks borne), while the expense ratio measures the efficiency of the company's operations. The underwriting loss ratio is also called the loss and loss adjustment expense (discussed later). The expense ratio is also called the *underwriting expense ratio*.

Notice that the denominator in the two ratios is different. For reporting purposes, sometimes insurers use U.S. GAAP, which calls for net premium earned as the denominator for both ratios.

The **loss reserve** is an estimated value of unpaid claims (based on estimated losses incurred during the reporting period). Subject to management discretion in measurement, the loss reserve is a highly material amount. Insurers revise their estimate of the loss reserve as more information becomes available. Downward revisions indicate that the company was conservative in estimating their losses in the first place. Upward revisions indicate aggressive profit booking, a warning sign for analysts.

Other Profitability Ratios

Loss and loss adjustment expense ratio measures the relative success in estimation of risks insured (lower is more successful).

$$\text{loss and loss adjustment expense ratio} = \frac{\text{loss expense + loss adjustment expense}}{\text{net premiums earned}}$$

Dividends to policyholders (shareholders) ratio is a liquidity measure measuring cash outflow on account of dividends relative to premium income.

$$\text{dividends to policyholders} = \frac{\text{dividends to policy holders (shareholders)}}{\text{net premiums earned}}$$

Combined ratio after dividends (CRAD) measures total efficiency and is more comprehensive than the combined ratio.

$$\text{CRAD} = \text{combined ratio} - \text{dividends to policyholders ratio}$$

EXAMPLE: P&C profitability ratios

Andy Miranda is evaluating three P&C insurers and has collected selected information for the latest fiscal year.

Description ($ millions)	ABC, Inc.	PDQ, Inc.	XYZ, Inc.
Loss and loss adjustment expense	5,400	3,212	2,467
Underwriting expense	2,111	1,860	1,387
Dividends to policyholders (shareholders)	412	232	148
Net premiums earned	8,114	5,445	4,087
Net premiums written	8,217	5,348	4,299

1. Calculate the loss and loss adjustment expense ratio, underwriting expense ratio, combined ratio, and CRAD to policyholders.
2. Which insurer is *most profitable* on a combined ratio basis?
3. Which insurer has the *most efficient* operations?
4. Which insurer is *most profitable* overall?

Answers:

1. The computation of ratios is shown below.

Ratio	ABC, Inc.	PDQ, Inc.	XYZ, Inc.
Loss and loss adjustment expense ratio	66.55%	58.99%	60.36%
Underwriting expense ratio	25.69%	34.78%	32.26%
Combined ratio	92.24%	93.77%	92.63%
Dividends to policyholders ratio	5.08%	4.26%	3.62%
Combined ratio after dividends	87.16%	89.51%	89.00%

2. On a combined ratio basis, ABC, Inc., has the lowest combined ratio and is most profitable.
3. ABC, Inc., has the most efficient operations as evidenced by its lowest underwriting expense ratio.
4. ABC, Inc., is the most profitable as evidenced by the lowest CRAD to policyholders (shareholders).

Investment Returns

After premium income, investment return is an important source of P&C insurers' profitability. Due to the inherent risk of the insurance business, insurers tend to invest premiums conservatively. An evaluation of a P&C insurer's investment portfolio should look for diversification by asset class and concentration by type, maturity, industry classification, and geographic location. The total investment return ratio is used to evaluate the performance of an insurer's investment operations.

$$\text{total investment return ratio} = \text{total investment income} \div \text{invested assets}$$

Instead of total investment income, computing the ratio after excluding unrealized capital gains from income provides information about the importance of unrealized gains and losses to the insurer's total income.

Liquidity

Liquidity is an important consideration for P&C insurers as they stand ready to meet their claim obligations. One way to gauge the liquidity of the investment portfolio is to look at their fair value hierarchy reporting. As stated earlier for banks, Level 1 assets are based on readily available prices for traded securities and therefore tend to be most liquid. Level 2 assets tend to have lower liquidity, and Level 3 assets are generally the least liquid.

Capitalization

There are no global risk-based capital requirement standards for insurers. Regionally, the E.U. has adopted the Solvency II standards, while NAIC in the United States has specified minimum capital levels based on size and risk (including asset, credit, liquidity, underwriting, and other relevant risks).

L&H Insurance Companies

Similar to P&C insurers, L&H insurers derive their revenue primarily from premiums, while investment income is the secondary source. Life insurance policies can be basic term-life, whereby the insurer makes payment if death occurs during the policy period. Other types of policies may include other investment products attached to pure life policies. Health insurance policies vary globally by the type of coverage provided.

Primary considerations in analysis of L&H insurers include:

1. Revenue diversification. The proportion of income generated from premiums, investments, and fees can vary over time and among insurers. While diversification is a desirable attribute, premium income tends to be more stable over time relative to other sources.
2. Earnings characteristics. An L&H insurer's profitability reflects a number of accounting items that require judgment and estimates. Actuarial assumptions affect the value of the future liabilities due to policyholders. Current period claim expense includes not only actual claim payments, but also interest on the estimated liability to policyholders. L&H insurers also capitalize the cost of acquiring new and renewal policies and amortize it based on actual and estimated future profits from that business. Therefore, estimates influence the amount that is amortized in any given period. Estimates also affect the value of securities and, hence, investment returns (discussed in the next section). Finally, mismatches between the valuation approaches for assets and liabilities can distort values when the interest rate environment changes.

   Apart from standard ratios such as ROA, ROE, and EBIT margins, industry-specific cost ratios include:

   a. total benefits paid ÷ net premiums written and deposits.

   b. commissions and expenses ÷ net premiums written and deposits.
3. Investment returns. L&H insurers have a longer float period than P&C insurers, so investment returns are a key component of the insurer's profitability. A large portion of the investment portfolio is often long-term debt. Duration mismatch between the insurer's assets and liabilities is an area of concern. Similar to P&C insurers, the total investment income ratio (investment income divided by amount of invested assets) is often used to evaluate an L&H insurer's investment portfolio performance. Analysts often recalculate this ratio after removing unrealized gains and losses from investment income to remove the impact of estimated fair values for some of the investment assets.
4. Liquidity. While policy surrenders can be unpredictable, the liquidity needs of L&H insurers are generally fairly predictable. Hence, keeping excess liquidity is not as much of a concern for L&H insurers compared to P&C insurers. Analysis of liquidity for an insurer includes analyzing the insurer's investment portfolio. Non-investment grade bonds and equity real estate are typically relatively illiquid as compared to investment grade debt.

   A liquidity measure used by Standard and Poor's, for example, takes a ratio of adjusted investment assets to adjusted obligations. Assets are adjusted based on their ready convertibility into cash, while obligations are adjusted based on assumptions about withdrawals. This ratio is estimated both under normal market conditions and under stress scenarios to assess the liquidity risk for the insurer.

5. Capitalization. Similar to P&C insurers, there are no global minimum capitalization standards. Domestic regulators often do specify risk-adjusted minimum capital requirements. Due to duration mismatches between assets and liabilities for L&H insurers, risk-adjusted capital requirements usually incorporate interest rate risk.

MODULE QUIZ 17.6

To best evaluate your performance, enter your quiz answers online.

1. Relative to P&C insurers, L&H insurers are *most likely* to have:
   A. a longer contract period.
   B. lumpier claims.
   C. a higher liquidity risk.
2. Relative to P&C insurers, L&H insurers are *most likely* to have:
   A. a higher float.
   B. a shorter contract period.
   C. a lower interest rate risk.
3. Relative to P&C insurers, L&H insurers are *most likely* to have:
   A. higher interest rate risk.
   B. longer soft pricing period.
   C. lumpier claims.
4. A soft pricing period is *most accurately* characterized by a period in which the combined ratio is:
   A. higher for P&C insurers.
   B. higher for L&H insurers.
   C. lower for P&C insurers.
5. For a single insurer, a combined ratio of greater than 100% would *most accurately* indicate:
   A. an underwriting loss.
   B. an underwriting profit.
   C. high liquidity.

Use the following information to answer Questions 6 through 10.

Jia Li, CFA, is reviewing the relative performance of three P&C insurers. Li has collected the following information for the year 20X9.

Description ($ millions)	IPCO	SYMCO	DELPHI
Loss and loss adjustment expense	4,512	2,278	3,265
Underwriting expense	1,322	1,799	1,867
Dividends to policyholders (shareholders)	122	198	148
Net premiums earned	7,598	4,978	5,994
Net premiums written	7,682	5,222	6,322

6. Which insurer has the *highest* loss and loss adjustment expense ratio?
   A. IPCO.
   B. SYMCO.
   C. DELPHI.
7. Which insurer with the *lowest* underwriting expense ratio?
   A. IPCO.
   B. SYMCO.
   C. DELPHI.
8. Which insurer with the *highest* combined ratio?
   A. IPCO.
   B. SYMCO.
   C. DELPHI.
9. Which insurer with the *lowest* dividend to policyholders (shareholders) ratio?
   A. IPCO.
   B. SYMCO.
   C. DELPHI.
10. Which insurer with the *highest* combined ratio after dividends?
    A. IPCO.
    B. SYMCO.
    C. DELPHI.

KEY CONCEPTS

LOS 17.a

Financial institutions differ from other companies due to their systemic importance and regulated status. The assets of financial institutions tend to be primarily financial assets as opposed to tangible assets for other companies.

LOS 17.b

The Basel Committee on Banking Supervision provides the framework (currently Basel III) that specifies minimum levels of capital and liquidity as well as stability of funding.

Other global institutions include the Financial Stability Board, International Association of Deposit Insurers, International Organization of Securities Commissions (IOSCO), and International Association of Insurance Supervisors (IAIS).

LOS 17.c

CAMELS approach:

- Capital adequacy: based on risk-weighted assets (RWA); more risky assets require a higher level of capital. Total capital is composed of Tier 1 capital (which includes Common Equity Tier 1 and other Tier 1 capital) and Tier 2 capital. Basel III specifies minimums for Common Equity Tier 1 capital of 4.5% of RWA, total Tier 1 capital of 6% of RWA, and total capital of 9% of RWA.
- Assets: include loans and investments. Loans are evaluated on their credit quality. Valuation and accounting treatment of investment securities differs between standards (IFRS vs. U.S. GAAP).
- Management quality: influences how prudent management is at seeking and managing risks that the bank takes. Internal control systems should continuously measure and monitor different risks that the bank is exposed to.
- Earnings quality: influenced by numerous estimates (loss provisions, valuation of securities, goodwill impairment, etc.). In the fair value hierarchy for valuation of financial assets, Level 1 inputs are quoted market prices of identical assets; Level 2 inputs are observable but not quoted prices of identical assets; and Level 3 inputs are non-observable.
- Liquidity: critical for a bank. Ratios to evaluate liquidity risk include the following:

$$\text{liquidity coverage ratio} = \frac{\text{highly liquid assets}}{\text{expected cash outflows}}$$

$$\text{net stable funding ratio} = \frac{\text{available stable funding}}{\text{required stable funding}}$$

Liquidity coverage ratio (LCR) measures the availability of liquid funds (in highly liquid assets) relative to expected one-month liquidity needs in a stress scenario. Net stable funding ratio (NSFR) is the ratio of required stable funding that is sourced from available stable funding. Basel III standards recommend minimum 100% for both ratios.

- Sensitivity to market risk: banks are exposed to a variety of market risks including market risk of their investment portfolio, currency risk, credit risk, and interest rate risk. Interest rate risk is key for a bank due to mismatches between assets and liabilities with respect to maturity and repricing frequency.

LOS 17.d

Other than the CAMELS framework, analysts may also consider any government support for the banking sector, government ownership of a bank, and a bank's mission and culture. Additional factors (not unique to the banking sector) include the competitive environment, off-balance-sheet obligations, segment information, and currency exposure.

LOS 17.e

A comprehensive analysis of a bank involves using the CAMELS framework as well as evaluation of other factors that affect the bank's liquidity position, its ability to withstand shocks, and its profitability.

LOS 17.f

P&C insurers have cyclical soft and hard pricing markets, driven by the industry's combined ratio (total insurance expenses divided by net premiums earned). When the ratio is low (high), it is a hard (soft) market.

Ratios include:

$$\text{underwriting loss ratio} = \frac{\text{claims paid} + \Delta\ \text{loss reserves}}{\text{net premium earned}}$$

$$\text{expense ratio} = \frac{\text{underwriting expenses including commissions}}{\text{net premium written}}$$

$$\text{loss and loss adjustment expense ratio} = \frac{\text{loss expense} + \text{loss adjustment expense}}{\text{net premiums earned}}$$

$$\text{dividends to policyholders} = \frac{\text{dividends to policy holders (shareholders)}}{\text{net premiums earned}}$$

combined ratio after dividends = combined ratio – dividends to policyholders

total investment return ratio = total investment income ÷ invested assets

L&H Insurers have a longer contract period, higher float, and higher interest rate risk than P&C insurers. Ratios include:

total benefits paid / net premiums written and deposits

commissions and expenses / net premiums written and deposits

ANSWER KEY FOR MODULE QUIZZES

Module Quiz 17.1

1. **B** The three pillars of Basel III framework are minimum capital requirements (as a proportion of risk-weighted assets), minimum liquidity, and stable funding. While a positive spread on deposit is always needed for a bank to be profitable, it is not a recommendation of the Basel III framework. (LOS 17.b)

2. **A** The International Organization of Securities Commissions (IOSCO) seeks to promote fair and efficient securities markets. The Basel III Committee provides a framework for analyzing and regulating banks. The International Association of Insurance Supervisors (IAIS) seeks to promote effective supervision of insurance sector. (LOS 17.b)

Module Quiz 17.2

1. **B** The most important tier of capital is the Common Equity Tier 1 capital, which includes common stock, additional paid-in capital, retained earnings, other comprehensive income and adjustments pertaining to deductions for intangible assets, and deferred tax assets. (LOS 17.c)

2. **B** Under Basel III guidelines, total Tier 1 capital must be at least 6% of risk-weighted assets. (LOS 17.c)

3. **A** Subordinated instruments without specified maturity or dividend/interest are considered part of Tier 1 capital. Together with Common Equity Tier 1 capital, it forms total Tier 1 capital. (LOS 17.c)

4. **A** Equity securities are carried on the balance sheet at fair value (and unrealized gains are shown in the income statement) under current U.S. GAAP standards. Under IFRS, equity is also carried at fair value on the balance sheet, but unrealized gains can be in OCI (fair value through OCI classification) or in the income statement (fair value through profit or loss classification). (LOS 17.c)

Module Quiz 17.3

1. **A** Level 1 inputs are quoted prices of identical assets. (LOS 17.c)

2. **C** Out of service income, net interest income, and trading income, trading income is most volatile. (LOS 17.c)

Module Quiz 17.4

1. **B** Maturity mismatch is a liquidity risk metric and measures the mismatch in maturity of a bank's assets and liabilities. (LOS 17.c)

2. **A** NSFR is the ratio of available stable funding sources to the required stable funding and measures liquidity of funding sources relative to liquidity needs of the assets. (LOS 17.c)

3. **C** Basel III standards recommend a minimum NSFR of 100%. (LOS 17.c)

4. **C** Liquidity risk in a stress scenario is measured by LCR. Charlie has the lowest LCR and hence the highest liquidity risk. (LOS 17.c)

5. **C** Funding stability is captured by NSFR. Delta has the lowest NSFR (below the recommended 100%), indicating the highest liquidity risk. (LOS 17.c)

Module Quiz 17.5

1. **C** While slower speed of adjustments of loss provisions and restatements of financial statements are used as an indicator of aggressive, risk-seeking culture, the tenure of the bank's management team is typically not included in an evaluation of the bank's culture. (LOS 17.d)

2. **A** Government ownership of part or all of a bank is an indication of implied government backing of the bank should the bank's capital prove inadequate to absorb losses. (LOS 17.d)

3. **B** Due to the significance of the banking sector to the overall economy, and to minimize the contagion effect of banking failures, governments often bail out troubled banks. This implicit government backing increases during times of economic stress (i.e., negatively related to the health of the banking sector) and is more likely for larger banks with a higher likelihood of causing contagion. Higher inter-linkages in the banking sector lead to a higher risk of bank failure–induced contagion and a higher probability of government backing. (LOS 17.d)

4. **A** Mission statements of many community banks include promoting community development and, hence, lead to community-focused lending. Often, this leads to a larger concentration of loan assets tied to the fortunes of a single industry. (LOS 17.d)

Module Quiz 17.6

1. **A** The contract period (the time between receipt of premium and payment of claim) is typically much longer for L&H insurers than for P&C insurers. (LOS 17.f)

2. **A** Due to their longer contract period, float for L&H insurers is typically higher than for P&C insurers. (LOS 17.f)

3. **A** Due to duration mismatches between assets and liabilities of L&H insurers, interest rate risk is more of concern for L&H insurers compared to P&C insurers. (LOS 17.f)

4. **A** During a soft pricing period, price competition among P&C insurers leads to high combined ratios. (LOS 17.f)

5. **A** For a single insurer, a combined ratio in excess of 100% indicates a loss. (LOS 17.f)

Use the following information for answers to Questions 6 through 10.

Ratio	IPCO	SYMCO	DELPHI
Loss and loss adjustment expense ratio	59.38%	45.76%	54.47%
Underwriting expense ratio	17.21%	34.45%	29.53%
Combined ratio	76.59%	80.21%	84.00%
Dividends to policyholders ratio	1.61%	3.98%	2.47%
Combined ratio after dividends	74.99%	76.23%	81.53%

6. **A** IPCO with a loss and loss adjustment expense ratio of 59.38% has the highest ratio. (LOS 17.f)

7. **A** IPCO has the lowest underwriting expense ratio of 17.21%. (LOS 17.f)

8. **C** DELPHI has the highest combined ratio of 84%. (LOS 17.f)

9. **A** IPCO's dividend to policyholders ratio is lowest at 1.61%. (LOS 17.f)

10. **C** DELPHI has the highest combined ratio after dividends of 81.53%. (LOS 17.f)

The following is a review of the Financial Reporting and Analysis (2) principles designed to address the learning outcome statements set forth by CFA Institute. Cross-Reference to CFA Institute Assigned Reading #18.

READING 18 Evaluating Quality of Financial Reports

Study Session 6

EXAM FOCUS

It is important for an analyst to evaluate the quality of a company's financial reports before relying on the reports for information to make investment decisions. Financial reports can be low-quality due to non-compliance with accounting standards, fraud, bias, and other factors.

MODULE 18.1: QUALITY OF FINANCIAL REPORTS

Video covering this content is available online.

LOS 18.a: Demonstrate the use of a conceptual framework for assessing the quality of a company's financial reports.

CFA® Program Curriculum, Volume 2, page 291

FINANCIAL REPORT QUALITY

The quality of financial reports can be viewed along two highly related dimensions: **earnings quality** and **reporting quality**. Reporting quality is an assessment of the information disclosed in the financial reports. High-quality reporting provides *decision-useful information*; information that is accurate as well as relevant. Low-quality reporting impedes assessment while high-quality reporting enables it.

The term *high-quality earnings* refers to a high level of earnings (i.e., meets the required return on investment) as well as sustainability of earnings. Good economic performance and sustainable earnings are considered higher quality. Conversely, low-quality earnings arise either due to genuinely bad performance or due to misrepresentation of economic performance. Earnings quality is also referred to as **results quality**. High-quality earnings increase the value of a company more than low-quality earnings.

One cannot have both low-quality reporting and high-quality earnings; high-quality earnings assume high-quality reporting. However, one could have a situation in which the company has high quality reporting but low-quality earnings. For example, a strike during the reporting period may have resulted in LIFO liquidation and, hence, given a one-off boost (i.e., earnings have low persistence) to reported earnings. However, the underlying reporting was accurate and decision-useful.

The conceptual framework for assessing the quality of a company's reports entails answering two questions:

1. Are the underlying financial reports GAAP compliant *and* decision-useful?
2. Are the earnings of high quality?

For this discussion, GAAP is used in a generic sense and refers to either U.S. GAAP or IFRS.

Based on the answer to the previous two questions, the overall quality of financial reports can be classified along a continuum of high to low quality as shown in Figure 18.1.

Figure 18.1: Financial Reports Quality (High to Low)

1. GAAP compliant and decision-useful, high-quality earnings.
2. GAAP compliant and decision-useful, low-quality earnings.
3. GAAP compliant but not decision-useful (biased choices).
4. Non-compliant accounting.
5. Fraudulent accounting.

Biased accounting provides information that hinders an analyst's ability to generate accurate forecasts of the future performance of the company. Biased accounting can be aggressive (recognizing future revenues/earnings in the current period) or conservative (postponing current earnings to the future). A related bias is 'earnings management' (e.g., earnings smoothing).

LOS 18.b: Explain potential problems that affect the quality of financial reports.

CFA® Program Curriculum, Volume 2, page 293

Potential problems that affect the quality of financial reports may arise from:

- Measurement and timing issues and/or
- Classification issues.

Measurement and Timing Issues

Errors in measurement and/or timing typically affect multiple financial statement elements. For example, aggressive revenue recognition practices increase reported revenues, profits, equity, and assets. Similarly, conservative revenue recognition practices reduce reported revenues, profits, equity, and assets. Similarly, omission or postponement of expense recognition would increase profits, equity, and assets.

Classification Issues

Classification issues refer to how an individual financial statement element is categorized within a particular financial statement (e.g., classification of expenses as operating vs. non-operating in the income statement). While timing/measurement issues affect multiple financial statement elements, classification issues typically affect one element. Figure 18.2 provides some examples of classification issues and the effects of misclassification.

Figure 18.2: Examples of Misclassification

Misclassification	Effect
Removing accounts receivable by selling or transferring receivables to a related entity or by treating them as long-term receivables.	Reduces days' sales outstanding and enhances the receivables turnover ratio. May be done to mask aggressive revenue recognition practices.
Reclassifying inventory as other (long-term) assets.	Increases inventory turnover ratio. Current ratio will decrease.
Reclassifying non-core revenues as revenues from core continuing operations.	Misleads analysts about the sustainability of future revenues.
Reclassifying expenses as non-operating.	Causes analysts to treat recurring expenses as one-time costs.
Treating investing cash flows (e.g., sale of long-term assets) as operating cash flows.	Operating cash flow is considered to be recurring and increasing it may lead to higher equity valuation.

BIASED ACCOUNTING

Biased accounting choices seek to further a specific agenda—to sell a story. Some examples of biased accounting choices and their related warning signs are shown next.

Mechanisms to misstate profitability:

- Aggressive revenue recognition, including channel stuffing (aggressively selling products to distributors on generous terms such as lax return policies), bill and hold sales (where economic title to goods may not truly pass to customers), and outright fake sales.
- Lessor use of finance lease classification.
- Classifying non-operating revenue/income as operating, and operating expenses as non-operating.
- Channeling gains through net income and losses through OCI.

Warnings signs of misstated profitability:

- Revenue growth higher than peers'.
- Receivables growth higher than revenue growth.
- High rate of customer returns.
- High proportion of revenue is received in final quarter.

- Unexplained boost to operating margin.
- Operating cash flow lower than operating income.
- Inconsistency in operating versus non-operating classification over time.
- Aggressive accounting assumptions (e.g., high estimated useful lives).
- Executive compensation largely tied to financial results.

Mechanisms to misstate assets/liabilities:

- Choosing inappropriate models and/or model inputs and thus affecting estimated values of financial statement elements (e.g., estimated useful lives for long-lived assets).
- Reclassification from current to non-current.
- Over- or understating allowances and reserves.
- Understating identifiable assets (and overstating goodwill) in acquisition method accounting for business combinations.

Warnings signs of misstated assets/liabilities:

- Inconsistency in model inputs for valuation of assets versus valuation of liabilities.
- Typical current assets (e.g., inventory, receivables) being classified as non-current.
- Allowances and reserves differ from those of peers and fluctuate over time.
- High goodwill relative to total assets.
- Use of special purpose entities.
- Large fluctuations in deferred tax assets/liabilities.
- Large off-balance-sheet liabilities.

Mechanisms to overstate operating cash flows:

- Managing activities to affect cash flow from operations (e.g., stretching payables).
- Misclassifying investing cash flow as cash flow from operations.

Warnings signs of overstated operating cash flows:

- Increase in payables combined with decreases in inventory and receivables.
- Capitalized expenditures (which flow through investing activities).
- Increases in bank overdraft.

BUSINESS COMBINATIONS—ACQUISITION METHOD ACCOUNTING

Mergers and acquisitions often provide opportunities and motivations to manage financial results. For example, companies with declining operating cash flow may be motivated to acquire other cash-generating entities to increase cash flow from operations. Cash acquisitions are reflected in cash flow from investing activities. If acquisitions are paid for using stock, such a payment would bypass the cash flow statement altogether.

Stock acquisitions provide an incentive for the acquiring company management to pursue aggressive accounting so as to inflate their stock price prior to acquisition. Similarly, target company managers may also be motivated to inflate their firm's stock price to fetch an attractive price at acquisition.

In some cases, misreporting is actually the impetus for acquisitions: acquiring company managers may pursue acquisitions to hide pre-acquisition accounting irregularities. Such companies may acquire targets with dissimilar operations or with less publicly available information to reduce the comparability and consistency of their own financial statements.

At the time of acquisition, acquiring company must allocate the purchase price to fair value of identifiable net assets of the subsidiary and the balance to goodwill. Acquiring companies often underestimate the value of identifiable net assets—thereby overestimating goodwill on acquisition. Fair value adjustments for identifiable assets typically result in excess depreciation which reduces profits for future reporting periods. Since goodwill is not amortized, the effect of overestimating goodwill (and underestimating the value of identifiable assets) is to increase future reported profits. Such inflated goodwill will eventually have to be written down as part of impairment testing but such losses can be timed. In addition, impairment losses can be downplayed as a one-off, non-recurring event.

GAAP ACCOUNTING BUT NOT ECONOMIC REALITY

Sometimes, an accounting treatment may conform to reporting standards but, nonetheless, result in financial reporting that does not faithfully represent economic reality. For example, prior to mandatory consolidation requirements for variable interest entities under U.S. GAAP, Enron was able to avoid consolidation of various special purpose entities on technical grounds—thereby keeping large losses and liabilities off-balance-sheet.

Restructuring provisions and impairment losses provide opportunities to time the recognition of losses (i.e., earnings management). Typically, recognition of impairment or restructuring losses in a period reflects overstatement of income in prior periods. Conversely, impairment or restructuring provisions may be strategically timed to shift future expenses into the current period. For example, impairment losses on long-lived assets recognized in the current period will reduce future depreciation expense. Similarly, restructuring provisions allow managers to effectively set aside profits in the current period to be used in the future. Provisions are non-cash expenses charged in the current period; future expenses from such provisions bypass the income statement. In such cases, losses recognized in the current period will boost income in the future when reversed.

Video covering this content is available online.

MODULE 18.2: EVALUATING EARNINGS QUALITY, PART 1

LOS 18.c: Describe how to evaluate the quality of a company's financial reports.

LOS 18.d: Evaluate the quality of a company's financial reports.

CFA® Program Curriculum, Volume 2, page 305 and 306

Steps in evaluating the quality of financial reports:

Step 1: Understand the company, its industry, and the accounting principles it uses and why such principles are appropriate.

Step 2: Understand management including the terms of their compensation. Also evaluate any insider trades and related party transactions.

Step 3: Identify material areas of accounting that are vulnerable to subjectivity.

Step 4: Make cross-sectional and time series comparisons of financial statements and important ratios.

Step 5: Check for warning signs as discussed previously.

Step 6: For firms in multiple lines of business or for multinational firms, check for shifting of profits or revenues to a specific part of the business that the firm wants to highlight. This is particularly a concern when a specific segment shows dramatic improvement while the consolidated financials show negative or zero growth.

Step 7: Use quantitative tools to evaluate the likelihood of misreporting.

QUANTITATIVE TOOLS

The Beneish Model

The Beneish model is a probit regression model that estimates the probability of earnings manipulation using eight dependent variables. The M-score determines the probability of earnings manipulation – higher values indicate higher probabilities.

$$\text{M-score} = -4.84 + 0.920\ (\text{DSRI}) + 0.528\ (\text{GMI}) + 0.404\ (\text{AQI}) + 0.892\ (\text{SGI}) + 0.115\ (\text{DEPI}) - 0.172\ (\text{SGAI}) + 4.679\ (\text{Accruals}) - 0.327\ (\text{LEVI})$$

where:

M-score > –1.78 (i.e., less negative) indicates a higher-than-acceptable probability of earnings manipulation.

- Days sales receivable index (DSRI): Ratio of days' sales receivables in year t relative to year $t - 1$. A large increase in DSRI could be indicative of revenue inflation.

- Gross margin index (GMI): Ratio of gross margin in year $t - 1$ to that in year t. When this ratio is greater than 1, the gross margin has deteriorated. A firm with declining margins is more likely to manipulate earnings.
- Asset quality index (AQI): Ratio of non-current assets other than plant, property, and equipment to total assets in year t relative to year $t - 1$. Increases in AQI could indicate excessive capitalization of expenses.
- Sales growth index (SGI): Ratio of sales in year t relative to year $t - 1$. While not a measure of manipulation by itself, growth companies tend to find themselves under pressure to manipulate earnings to meet ongoing expectations.
- Depreciation index (DEPI): Ratio of depreciation rate in year $t - 1$ to the corresponding rate in year t. The depreciation rate is depreciation expense divided by depreciation plus PPE. A DEPI greater than 1 suggests that assets are being depreciated at a slower rate in order to manipulate earnings.
- Sales, general and administrative expenses index (SGAI): Ratio of SGA expenses (as a % of sales) in year t relative to year $t - 1$. Increases in SGA expenses might predispose companies to manipulate.
- Accruals = (income before extraordinary items – cash flow from operations) / total assets.
- Leverage index (LEVI): Ratio of total debt to total assets in year t relative to year $t - 1$.

PROFESSOR'S NOTE

Don't memorize the model or coefficients—instead be able to interpret the model as illustrated in the following example.

PROFESSOR'S NOTE

You might wonder why, given the variables' descriptions, the coefficients on SGAI and LEVI are negative rather than positive. Beneish expected positive coefficient on these variables, but actual regression results produced negative values.

This is likely why Beneish created an alternate model (not included in the curriculum) that excludes SGAI and LEVI.

EXAMPLE: Beneish model interpretation

Beneish's M-score analysis for Pattern Processors Inc., (PPI) is shown below:

Variable	Value
DSRI	1.19
GMI	0.88
AQI	0.90
SGI	1.12
DEPI	1.19
SGAI	0.78
Accruals	0.12
LEVI	0.55
M-score	–1.53
Probability	9.58%

1. Using a cutoff value of –1.78 for the M-score, what would you conclude about the probability of earnings manipulation for PPI?
2. What are the implications of the DSRI and DEPI variables for PPI?

Answer:

1. The M-score for PPI is given as –1.53 which is higher than –1.78, indicating a higher-than-acceptable probability of earnings manipulation. The estimated probability of earnings manipulation is 9.58%.
2. Both DSRI and DEPI (as well as SGI) have a value greater than 1. A DSRI value greater than 1 may indicate that the firm is accelerating revenue recognition. A DEPI value greater than 1 indicates that the depreciation rate was lower than in the previous year. PPI may have used aggressive estimates for estimated useful lives or estimated salvage values or may be adopting more income friendly methods of depreciation.

Limitations of the Beneish Model

The Beneish model relies on accounting data, which may not reflect economic reality. Deeper analysis of underlying relationships may be warranted to get a clearer picture. Additionally, as managers become aware of the use of specific quantitative tools, they may begin to game the measures used. This concern is supported by evidence indicating that the predictive power of the Beneish model is decreasing over time.

Altman Model

While not directly related to earnings quality, Altman's Z-score model was developed to assess the probability that a firm will file for bankruptcy.

Altman's model relies on discriminant analysis to generate a Z-score using five variables. The variables used include net working capital as a proportion of total assets, retained earnings as a proportion of total assets, operating profit as a proportion of total assets, market value of equity relative to book value of liabilities, and sales relative to total assets. Each variable is positively related to the Z-score, and a higher Z-score is better (less likelihood of bankruptcy). Hence, higher values of any of the five variables reduce the probability of bankruptcy under Altman's model.

One limitation of the Altman model is that it is a single-period static model and, hence, does not capture the change in key variables over time. Additionally, similar to the Beneish model, Altman's model mostly uses accounting data. Other market based data sources may provide more meaningful information for evaluation of default risk.

PROFESSOR'S NOTE

We present the next LOS out of order for ease of exposition.

LOS 18.f: Describe indicators of earnings quality.

CFA® Program Curriculum, Volume 2, page 310

High-quality earnings are characterized by two elements:

1. Sustainable: high-quality earnings tend to persist in the future.
2. Adequate: high-quality earnings cover the company's cost of capital.

As stated previously, high-quality earnings assume high-quality reporting. In other words, low-quality earnings come about due to (a) earnings that are below the firm's cost of capital and/or (b) earnings that are not sustainable and/or (c) poor reporting quality (i.e., the reported information does not provide a useful indication of a firm's performance).

LOS 18.e: Describe the concept of sustainable (persistent) earnings.

CFA® Program Curriculum, Volume 2, page 310

Sustainable or **persistent** earnings are earnings that are expected to recur in the future. Earnings comprised of a high proportion of non-recurring items are considered to be non-sustainable (and hence low-quality).

Classification of items as non-recurring is highly subjective and, hence, is open for gaming. Classification shifting does not affect the total net income but rather is an attempt to mislead the user of the financial statements into believing that the "core" or "recurring" portion of earnings is higher than it actually is. One way to overstate persistent earnings is to mis-classify normal operating expenses as expenses from discontinued operations. Analysts should be wary of large special items or when the company is reporting unusually large operating income for a period. Companies may include non-GAAP metrics such as pro forma income which excludes non-recurring elements. Analysts should review the disclosures reconciling pro forma income to reported income to evaluate whether the items that are labeled as non-recurring are truly non-recurring.

One way to gauge earnings persistence is to use a regression model such as:

$$\text{earnings}_{(t+1)} = \alpha + \beta_1 \text{ earnings}_{(t)} + \varepsilon$$

In this model, a higher value of β_1 indicates higher persistence of earnings.

Accruals

Under the accrual basis of accounting, revenues are recognized when earned and expenses are recognized when incurred, regardless of the timing of cash flow. Unfortunately, accrual accounting requires considerable subjectivity because of the many estimates and judgments involved with assigning revenues and expenses to appropriate periods. Due to this subjectivity in revenue and expense recognition, disaggregating income into its two major components, cash and accruals, further enhances its quality as an input for forecasting future earnings. The accrual component of income is less persistent than the cash component. In the following regression model, $\beta_1 > \beta_2$:

$$\text{earnings}_{(t+1)} = \alpha + \beta_1 \text{ cash flow}_{(t)} + \beta_2 \text{ ccuruals}_{(t)} + \varepsilon$$

It is important to recognize that some accruals occur as part of normal business. Such accruals are called as *non-discretionary accruals*. Discretionary accruals result from non-normal transactions or non-normal accounting choices, and are sometimes used to manipulate earnings. One mechanism to separate discretionary and non-discretionary accruals is to model (using regression) total accruals as a function of a set of factors that typically give rise to normal accruals (e.g., growth of credit sales, amount of depreciable assets). The residuals from such a model would be an indicator of discretionary accruals.

Finally, a major red flag about earnings quality is raised when a company reports positive net income while reporting negative operating cash flow.

Other Indicators

One metric used to identify potentially low-quality earnings is to look for those companies that repeatedly meet or barely beat consensus estimates. While this is not a foolproof metric, analysts should be wary of a company that narrowly beats its benchmarks consistently.

External indicators of low-quality earnings include enforcement actions by regulatory authorities (e.g., SEC) and restatements. External indicators are not very useful as they cannot be used to forecast deficiencies before such deficiencies are publicly known.

MODULE 18.3: EVALUATING EARNINGS QUALITY, PART 2

Video covering this content is available online.

LOS 18.g: Explain mean reversion in earnings and how the accruals component of earnings affects the speed of mean reversion.

CFA® Program Curriculum, Volume 2, page 318

When examining net income, analysts should be aware that earnings at extreme levels tend to revert back to normal levels over time. This phenomenon is known as mean reversion. (Mean reversion can be explained with basic principles of economics: the competitive marketplace corrects poor performance; thus, losses are eliminated as firms abandon negative value projects. Conversely, capital is attracted to successful projects thereby increasing competition and lowering returns.)

Because of mean reversion, analysts should not expect extreme earnings (high or low) to continue indefinitely. When earnings are largely comprised of accruals, mean reversion will occur faster—and even more so when the accruals are largely discretionary.

LOS 18.h: Evaluate the earnings quality of a company.

CFA® Program Curriculum, Volume 2, page 319

Accounting systems require many estimates and rely on many subjective choices. These estimates and choices can be misused by managers to present misleading performance.

Two major contributors to earnings manipulation are:

1. Revenue recognition issues, and
2. Expense recognition issues (capitalization).

Revenue Recognition Issues

Revenue is the largest and most important element in the income statement. Subjectivity in revenue recognition practices makes revenue highly vulnerable to manipulation and therefore should be scrutinized by analysts. Analysts should not only concern themselves with quantity of revenue, but also with the quality of revenues (i.e., how those revenues were generated). Revenues generated via deliberate channel-stuffing or as a result of bill-and-hold arrangements should be considered spurious and inferior. Even (relatively) genuine revenues, when secured via the use of heavy discounting practices, come at the expense of deteriorating margins. A higher growth rate of receivables relative to the growth rate of revenues is a red flag. Similarly, an increasing days' sales outstanding (DSO) over time is an indication of poor revenue quality.

EXAMPLE: Evaluating earnings quality

Daniel Springs Inc., (DSI) produces heavy-duty automotive components. Financial results for DSI, as well as industry comparables, are shown below:

DSI selected financial data ($ 000s):

	20X1	20X2	20X3
Sales	$12,117	$13,112	$14,766
Accounts receivable	$1,272	$1,573	$2,363

Industry average:

	20X1	20X2	20X3
DSO	22.6	22.8	22.4
Receivables turnover	16.2	16.0	16.3

1. Compute DSI's increase in revenue and receivables from 20x1 to 20x2 and from 20x2 to 20x3. Compare the change in revenues to the change in receivables.
2. Using end-of-year accounts receivables, comment on the trend in days' sales outstanding (DSO) and receivables turnover for DSI and compare it to the industry average.
3. Comment on possible revenue recognition issues at DSI.

Answers:

1. DSI's revenues increased at a slower rate compared to the growth rate in receivables indicating potential problems with collections and low quality of receivables.

	20X1	20X2	20X3
Change in sales	-	8.2%	12.6%
Change in receivables	-	23.7%	50.2%

2. DSI's days' sales outstanding is increasing over time and is significantly higher than the industry average. The receivables turnover ratio for DSI is declining over time and is lower than industry average. Finally, the change in receivables as a proportion of revenues is positive and is increasing over time.

	20X1	20X2	20X3
Receivables/revenue	10.5%	12.0%	16.0%
Change in rec/rev	-	14.3%	33.3%
DSO	38.3	43.8	58.4
Receivables turnover	9.5	8.3	6.3

3. Based on all indicators, it appears that revenues at DSI are potentially of inferior quality. Analysts should be extremely skeptical about earnings quality of DSI.

Steps in the analysis of revenue recognition practices:

Step 1: **Understand the basics.** From the information disclosed, understand the revenue recognition practices followed by the company including relevant shipping terms, return policies, rebates, and the existence of multiple deliverables.

Step 2: **Evaluate and question ageing receivables.** Compare receivables metrics with those from the past and with the industry median.

Step 3: **Cash versus accruals.** Evaluate the proportion of earnings that are cash-based versus accruals-based.

Step 4: **Compare financials with physical data provided by the company.** For example, correlate sales with capacity utilization data.

Step 5: **Evaluate revenue trends and compare with peers.** Narrow down such analysis by segments.

Step 6: **Check for related party transactions.** For example, a company might artificially boost fourth-quarter revenues by recognizing a large sale to an affiliated entity.

Expense Capitalization

One way to boost reported performance is to under-report an operating expense by capitalizing it. Capitalizing an expense does however show up on the balance sheet as an asset and an analyst should be wary of unsupported changes in major asset categories. When the proportion of PP&E increases over time in common size balance sheets, analysts should question whether there is a systematic capitalization of expenses underway.

Steps in the analysis of expense recognition practices:

Step 1: **Understand the basics.** Understand the company's cost capitalization policies based on information disclosed in the annual report. Also gather information about depreciation policies and how they compare with those of the company's peers.

Step 2: **Trend and comparative (peer) analysis.** Evaluate changes in non-current assets over time to see if there are any anomalies which could be explained by cost capitalization. Stable or improving profit margins coupled with a buildup of non-current assets would be a warning sign. Steady or rising revenue coupled with declining asset turnover ratios is another warning sign of cost capitalization.

Compare depreciation expense as a proportion of asset size over time and with peers. Finally compare capital expenditures to gross PP&E over time and with peers. Rising capital expenditures as a percentage of PP&E is another warning sign of cost capitalization.

Step 3: **Check for related party transactions.** An example of a problematic transaction would be if the company is shifting resources to a privately held company that is owned by senior managers. On the other hand, analysts should also watch for propping practices whereby profits from related entities temporarily prop up an ailing public company. (Managers might prop up a public company to preserve the option of misappropriating funds in the future.)

MODULE 18.4: EVALUATING CASH FLOW QUALITY

Video covering this content is available online.

LOS 18.i: Describe indicators of cash flow quality.

CFA® Program Curriculum, Volume 2, page 333

High-quality cash flow means the reported cash flow was high (i.e., good economic performance) and the underlying reporting quality was also high. Because operating cash flow (OCF) has the most direct impact on the valuation of a company, we will focus on OCF while evaluating cash flows.

A cash flow statement should be evaluated in the context of the corporate life cycle as well as industry norms. It would be quite normal for early-stage startups to have negative operating and investing cash flows, financed by cash flow from financing activities (e.g., equity issuance). For a mature firm, negative operating cash flow coupled with positive financing cash flow is usually problematic.

High-quality cash flow is characterized by positive OCF that is derived from sustainable sources and is adequate to cover capital expenditures, dividends, and debt repayments. Furthermore, high-quality OCF is characterized by lower volatility than that of the firm's peers. Significant differences between OCF and earnings, or differences that widen over time, can be an indicator of earnings manipulation.

While cash flows are less amenable to manipulation, management can affect cash flows via strategic decisions (timing issues). For example, OCF can be increased by slowing payments to suppliers (increasing accounts payables) or by selling receivables. Analysts can identify such practices by reviewing activity ratios (receivables and payables turnover ratios).

Management may also try to shift positive cash flows from investing or financing activities into operating activities to boost OCF (classification issues).

PROFESSOR'S NOTE:

Operating cash flow (OCF) and cash flow from operating activities (CFO) refer to the same thing: the money a company brings in from regular, ongoing business activities.

LOS 18.j: Evaluate the cash flow quality of a company.

CFA® Program Curriculum, Volume 2, page 334

Evaluation of the statement of cash flows (and more importantly cash flow from operating activities) entails:

1. **Checking for any unusual items or items that have not shown up in prior years.**
2. **Checking revenue quality.** Aggressive revenue recognition practices typically result in an increase in receivables—which reduces operating cash flow. Another common indicator of aggressive revenue recognition is an increase in inventories (and hence a cash outflow) when sham sales are reversed (i.e., treated as returns from customers).
3. **Checking for strategic provisioning.** Provisions for restructuring charges show up as an inflow (i.e., a non-cash expense) in the year of the provision and then as an outflow when ordinary operating expenses are channeled through such reserves.

Analysts should be aware that accounting standards afford some flexibility in the treatment of certain items in the statement of cash flows. For example, while interest paid, interest received, and dividends received have to be treated as operating cash flows under U.S. GAAP, interest paid can be classified as either operating or financing cash flow under IFRS. Also, interest/dividend received can be classified as either operating or investing cash flow under IFRS. A company reporting under IFRS and accounting for interest paid as an operating cash flow could instead report it as a financing cash flow, giving the appearance of an increase in operating cash flows in a year-over-year comparison. Also, cash flows from sale of available-for-sale securities are treated as investing cash flows, while cash flows from sale of trading securities are treated as operating cash flows. Remember that companies have significant flexibility in designating investments as trading or available for sale. Hence, managers can shift cash flows from one classification to another. Such variation in the classification of cash flow items reduces comparability across companies.

MODULE 18.5: EVALUATING BALANCE SHEET QUALITY

Video covering this content is available online.

LOS 18.k: Describe indicators of balance sheet quality.

LOS18.l: Evaluate the balance sheet quality of a company.

CFA® Program Curriculum, Volume 2, page 342 and 344

High-quality financial balance sheet reporting is evidenced by completeness, unbiased measurement, and clarity of presentation.

Completeness

Completeness of a balance sheet is compromised by the existence of off-balance-sheet liabilities such as incorrect use of the operating lease classification, or purchase agreements structured as take-or-pay contracts. Analysts should restate the reported balance sheet by capitalizing operating leases and recording purchase contract obligations, if significant.

PROFESSOR'S NOTE

"Take-or-pay" contractual provisions obligate a party to either take delivery of goods or pay a specified amount (i.e., a penalty).

In the case of intercorporate investments, the equity method of accounting allows one-line consolidation for investments in associates. The equity method of accounting would result in certain profitability ratios (e.g., net profit margin, return on assets) being higher than under the acquisition method. Firms consolidating several subsidiaries with close to a 50% ownership stake by using the equity method would be a cause for concern.

Unbiased Measurement

The balance sheet reflects subjectivity in the measurement of several assets and liabilities:

- Value of the pension liability (based on several actuarial assumptions).
- Value of investment in debt or equity of other companies for which a market value is not readily available.
- Goodwill value (subjectivity in impairment testing).
- Inventory valuation (subjectivity in testing for impairment).
- Impairment of PP&E and other assets.

Overstatement of asset values (i.e., not recognizing adequate impairment losses) overstates profitability and equity.

Clear Presentation

While accounting standards specify which items should be included in the balance sheet, they do not typically specify how such items must be presented. Companies have discretion regarding which items they present as a single-line item versus those that are grouped together. Clarity of presentation allows an analyst to gather relevant information as well as to make comparisons across companies. Clarity should be evaluated in conjunction with information found in the notes to financial statements and supplementary disclosures.

LOS 18.m: Describe sources of information about risk.

CFA® Program Curriculum, Volume 2, page 346

Evaluating the financial, operating, and other risks that a business is exposed to is an important part of analyst's job. There are several sources of information about such risks:

- **Financial statements.** Financial statements contain information regarding the leverage used by the company and the variability of cash flows and earnings over time. Quantitative models (e.g., Altman's Z-score) often rely on this accounting information.
- **Auditor's report.** Because an audit report provides only historical information, such a report's usefulness as an information source is limited. However, involuntary changes in auditors, a small-sized audit firm relative to the size of the company being audited, and a lack of auditor independence are red flags that an analyst should pay special attention to.
- **Notes to financial statements.** Companies are required to make certain risk related disclosures in the notes to financial statements. Both GAAP and IFRS require companies to disclose risks related to pension benefits, contingent obligations and financial instruments.

  Disclosures about contingent liabilities include a description of the liability, as well as estimated amounts and timing of the payments. Disclosures about pension benefits include information about actuarial assumptions. Disclosures about financial instruments include information about credit risk, liquidity risk and market risk.
- **Management Discussion and Analysis (MD&A).** Ideally, companies should include principal risks that are unique to the business (as opposed to risks faced by most businesses) in their MD&A. However, discussion of generic risks and "boiler plate" language often makes this information of low utility.
- **SEC Form 'NT'.** In the United States, SEC form 'NT' is filed when a firm is unable to file required reports in a timely manner. Because such an occurrence is usually due to a breakdown in accounting systems or internal controls, or the discovery of misrepresentation that needs to be investigated, such filings typically signal problems in reporting quality.
- **Financial press.** Often the initial information about accounting irregularities at a company is obtained from the financial press. Analysts should do their own due diligence to ensure that the information revealed has merit and to ascertain the magnitude of the irregularity and its impact on valuation.

MODULE QUIZ 18.1, 18.2, 18.3, 18.4, 18.5

To best evaluate your performance, enter your quiz answers online.

Use the following information to answer Questions 1 through 6.

Rana Midha, CFA, works as a freelance equity analyst in the United States. Midha's main area of expertise is in the analysis of financial statements, and he is currently reviewing the latest annual reports issued by five large companies in the retail sector.

Midha's approach to analyzing the results is to focus first on the quality of the financial reporting. To do this, he uses a conceptual framework that addresses the quality of earnings and whether the information is decision-useful. Midha then orders the companies on a quality spectrum.

Extracts from Midha's notes on three of the companies under analysis are shown in Exhibit 1.

Exhibit 1: Financial Reporting Quality

GGFT, Inc.

- Information provided adheres to GAAP without deviations.
- Disclosures provide a high level of relevant information.
- Accounting choices show a very aggressive bias.
- Earnings provide an adequate rate of return on capital.

FSKA, Inc.

- Information provided adheres to GAAP without deviations.
- Disclosures provide a high level of relevant information.
- Accounting choices show no appreciable bias.
- Earnings last year provided an adequate rate of return on capital.
- Earnings do not appear to be sustainable.

SDTT, Inc.

- Information provided adheres to GAAP without deviations.
- Disclosures provide a high level of relevant information.
- Accounting choices show no appreciable bias.
- Earnings last year provided an adequate rate of return on capital.
- Earnings appear to be sustainable.

In modeling the sustainability of earnings, Midha regresses earnings in the current period against those in the previous period using the following AR(1) model:

$$\text{earnings}_{t+1} = \alpha + \beta_1 \text{earnings}_t + \varepsilon$$

Another company that Midha is reviewing, PSAA, Inc., has released its annual report 14 days later than usual due to a disagreement with its auditors. New auditors were appointed two weeks after the financial year end. The details were widely reported in the press and an extract from an accounting journal is shown in Exhibit 2.

Exhibit 2: Accounting and Compliance Monthly (extract)

"... The disagreement stemmed from the proposed treatment of an entity set up by PSAA during the accounting year. CRAFT USA (CRAFT) was formed to develop a new range of low alcohol craft beers for the U.S. market. The entity immediately recruited a team of two head brewers from a local brewery which had gained national praise for their low-alcohol beverages. CRAFT's equity was owned entirely by the two head brewers who each had a 50% share and contributed $200,000 of share capital. In addition, PSAA provided $2,500,000 by way of convertible debt, exercisable at the end of each of the next 10 years.

PSAA's provisional accounts recognized the interest income from the convertible debt but not the operating losses CRAFT incurred during the year. PSAA's CEO commented that 'the entire share capital and, hence, voting rights reside entirely with the head brewing team ..."

Midha also likes to analyze the probability of earnings manipulation using Messod D. Beneish and colleagues' M-score. Exhibit 3 shows the model as Midha uses it and the M-scores for two companies, BDNF, Inc. and QKLK, Inc.

Exhibit 3: M-Score

M-score = –4.84 + 0.920 (DSRI) + 0.528 (GMI) + 0.404 (AQI) + 0.892 (SGI) + 0.115 (DEPI) – 0.172 (SGAI) + 4.670 (Accruals) – 0.327 (LEVI)

M-score = score indicating probability of earnings manipulation

DSRI (days sales receivable index) = $(\text{receivables}_t / \text{sales}_t) / (\text{receivables}_{t-1} / \text{sales}_{t-1})$

GMI (gross margin index) = $\text{gross margin}_{t-1} / \text{gross margin}_t$

AQI (asset quality index) = $[1 - (PPE_t + CA_t) / TA_t] / [1 - (PPE_{t-1} + CA_{t-1}) / TA_{t-1}]$, where PPE is property, plant, and equipment; CA is current assets; and TA is total assets.

SGI (sales growth index) = $\text{sales}_t / \text{sales}_{t-1}$

DEPI (depreciation index) = $\text{depreciation rate}_{t-1} / \text{depreciation rate}_t$, where depreciation rate = depreciation / (depreciation + PPE).

SGAI (sales, general, and administrative expenses index) = $(SGA_t / \text{sales}_t) / (SGA_{t-1} / \text{sales}_{t-1})$

accruals = (income before extraordinary items – cash from operations) / total assets

LEVI (leverage index) = $\text{leverage}_t / \text{leverage}_{t-1}$, where leverage is calculated as the ratio of debt to assets.

Company	M-Score
BDNF	–1.62
QKLK	–1.10

Study Session 6

1. Which of the following conclusions is Midha *most likely* to draw from the extracts shown in Exhibit 1?
   A. GGFT displays zero financial reporting quality.
   B. GGFT will be lower on the quality spectrum than FSKA.
   C. Midha will classify FSKA as having high quality earnings.
2. For this question, the companies referenced are described in Exhibit 1. If Midha runs the simple AR(1) model on earnings as described, which of the following statements is *least accurate*?
   A. FSKA will have a lower β_1 than SDTT.
   B. Higher proportions of cash-based earnings as opposed to accruals-based earnings lead to lower β_1 coefficients.
   C. A higher β_1 coefficient is consistent with higher quality earnings.
3. Which of the following statements regarding CRAFT, as detailed in Exhibit 2, is *most accurate*?
   A. CRAFT should be consolidated as a variable interest entity even if the convertible debt has no voting rights.
   B. CRAFT should be consolidated as a variable interest entity and, hence, the interest income and operating losses should be recognized separately in PSAA's consolidated income statement.
   C. CRAFT should not be consolidated as a variable interest entity if the coupon rate on the convertible debt is fixed.
4. Which of the following statements regarding the M-score model in Exhibit 3 is *most accurate*?
   A. Midha's notes incorrectly calculate the DSRI coefficient as he has not correctly calculated the days of sales receivable ratios.
   B. A company with a DEPI variable of less than one may be manipulating earnings by increasing the useful economic lives of assets.
   C. An AQI variable of greater than one may indicate excessive expenditure capitalization.
5. Which of the following statements about the M-scores Madhi calculated in Exhibit 3 is *most accurate*?
   A. BDNF's M-score indicates a larger probability of earnings manipulation than QKLK's M-score.
   B. QKLK's M-score indicates a probability of earnings manipulation of 1.10%.
   C. Using a cut off M-score of -1.78, both firms would be classified as potential manipulator companies.
6. Which of the following statements regarding sources of information about risk is *least accurate*?
   A. Frequent changes of auditor are an indication of potential risk.
   B. A clean audit report is a key piece of information regarding potential risk.
   C. An audit firm which has inadequate resources for the complexity of a company audit is a warning sign regarding potential risk.

Use the following information to answer Questions 7 through 13.

Hannah Jones, CFA, is currently reviewing the financial statements of three pharmaceutical companies she covers in her role as an equity analyst. Her primary aim is to establish the growth in operating earnings over the last year for each company. Exhibit 1 shows operating earnings for each company in 2013 and 2014.

Exhibit 1: Operating Earnings ($ Millions)

Company	2013 Operating Earnings	2014 Operating Earnings
ZZYP	142.5	140.3
AART	209.8	195.4
XXPG	220.9	233.2

While performing her review, Jones makes adjustments to the earnings figures to arrive at her "core earnings growth" figure. The adjustments she intends to make are listed below:

- ZZYP has sold two of its patents in the last two years. Both sales were forced by government anti-trust actions. Jones wants to remove the impact of these non-recurring items from operating earnings. The sale boosted operating profit by $8.2 million in 2013 and $1.9 million in 2014.
- AART uses IFRS and in 2013 capitalized development costs totaling $20.1 million. No similar costs were capitalized in 2014 but the development project was finished during the year and depreciation of $5.0 million on the previously capitalized costs was charged. Jones believes the costs should be expensed as incurred.

A colleague, Jim Hartford, recently reviewed similar calculations that Jones had performed on a group of retail companies. He was impressed with the detail, but made the following two constructive comments:

Comment 1: Break earnings down into its cash-based, discretionary accruals-based, and non-discretionary accruals-based elements. Companies with large accruals-based elements, particularly non-discretionary accruals-based elements, are more likely to be engaged in aggressive profit recognition practices.

Comment 2: Use the analysis of cash-based and accruals-based earnings to assess the likelihood of earnings reverting to the mean. Companies with large accruals-based earnings historically have seen earnings trend away from the mean for longer periods than those that have largely cash-based earnings.

Study Session 6

Jones is also aware that operating earnings do not always translate into operating cash flows. As a result, she always takes a detailed look at the reconciliation of operating profit to operating cash flows for each company analyzed. The reconciliation for ZZYP is shown in Exhibit 2.

Exhibit 2: ZZYP Operating Cash Flow Reconciliation 2013

	$ Millions
Net income	**98.5**
Depreciation, amortization and impairment	137.4
(Increase)/decrease in trade and other receivables	(11.5)
Decrease/(increase) in inventories	(4.1)
Increase/(decrease) in trade and other payables and provisions	12.4
Decrease/(increase) in short term investments	15.2
Non-cash and other movements	7.7
Interest paid	(14.2)
Tax paid	(25.1)
Net cash flow from operating activities	**216.3**

Jones is concerned with two things in the reconciliation and intends to make the following adjustments before doing any detailed analysis:

Adjustment 1: Changes in short-term investments should be classified as investing activities.

Adjustment 2: For comparative analysis, interest paid should be classified as a financing cash flow.

Jones always considers operating cash flows that are negative and those that are trending below net earnings as warnings signs of low quality cash flow. She will never advise clients to invest in a company with negative operating cash flows unless they are what she classifies as an "ESS" company, meaning an early stage start-up company that the market believes has potential. She believes that such companies differ from well-established companies because they may have negative operating and investing cash flows funded by a positive cash flow from financing.

The final part of Jones' analysis is to look at the company balance sheet. When doing so, she focuses on whether a company has any significant sources of off balance sheet financing. The most common adjustment she makes is to capitalize any operating leases a company is committed to.

An example of a typical required adjustment is shown in Exhibit 3.

Exhibit 3: Leasing Adjustment

Total equity ($ millions)	120.2
Total liabilities ($ millions)	182.1
Debt-to-equity ratio	1.5× (pre adjustment)
Interest rate applicable	7.75%

Commitment and Contingencies Footnote (extract)

The company leases asset and equipment under non-cancellable operating leases which expire in 2019. Scheduled payments are as follows ($ millions):

2015	9.9
2016	9.9
2017	9.9
2018	9.9
2019	8.0
Thereafter	-

7. Using the information in Exhibit 1 and Jones' proposed adjustments, the company with the highest "core earnings growth" from 2013 to 2014 was *most likely*:
   A. ZZYP.
   B. AART.
   C. XXPG.
8. Hartford's Comment 1 is *most likely*:
   A. correct.
   B. incorrect because non-discretionary accruals do not impact earnings.
   C. incorrect because discretionary accruals are more likely to indicate manipulation than non-discretionary.
9. Hartford's Comment 2 is *most likely*:
   A. correct.
   B. incorrect because companies with large proportions of accruals-based earnings historically have experienced more rapid reversions to the mean.
   C. incorrect because the speed at which earnings revert to the mean is not affected by the proportions of cash-based and accruals-based earnings.
10. If Jones makes the two adjustments to the operating cash flow reconciliation shown in Exhibit 2, the adjusted cash flow from operations would be *closest* to:
    A. $230.5.
    B. $215.3.
    C. $200.8.

11. Jones' statement regarding companies that she classifies as "ESS" is *most likely*:
    A. correct.
    B. incorrect because start-up companies typically have positive cash from investing due to a build-up of cash generating assets.
    C. incorrect because start-up companies cannot typically raise large amounts of debt and, hence, usually will not have positive cash flows from financing.
12. The presence of significant off-balance sheet financing *most likely* indicates:
    A. a lack of completeness, which reduces financial reporting quality.
    B. an decrease in leverage, which reduces financial results quality.
    C. a lack of clear presentation, which reduces financial reporting quality.
13. Using the information in Exhibit 3, after capitalizing the operating lease, the debt to equity ratio would be *closest* to:
    A. 1.8×.
    B. 1.5×.
    C. 1.4×.

KEY CONCEPTS

LOS 18.a

High-quality reporting provides decision-useful information; information that is accurate as well as relevant. High-quality earnings are sustainable and meet the required return on investment. High-quality earnings assume high-quality reporting.

The conceptual framework for assessing the quality of a company's reports entails answering two questions:

1. Are the underlying financial reports GAAP compliant and decision-useful?
2. Are the earnings of high quality?

LOS 18.b

Potential problems that affect the quality of financial reports can result from:

1. Measurement and timing issues and/or
2. Classification issues.

Additionally, biased accounting and accounting for business combinations can compromise the quality of financial reports. GAAP compliance is a necessary but not sufficient condition for high-quality financial reporting.

LOS 18.c

Evaluation of the quality of financial reports involves understanding the company, its management, and identifying material areas of accounting that are exposed to subjectivity. It also requires cross-sectional (with peers) and time-series (versus the past) comparison of key financial metrics, checking for any warning signs of poor quality reporting, and the use of quantitative tools.

LOS 18.d

The Beneish model is used to estimate the probability of earnings manipulation and is based on eight variables. However, as managers become aware of the use of such models, they are likely to game the model's inputs. This concern is supported by an observed decline in the predictive power of the Beneish model over time.

LOS 18.e

Sustainable or persistent earnings are those that are expected to recur in the future. Earnings with a high proportion of non-recurring items are considered to be non-sustainable (and hence low-quality).

LOS 18.f

High-quality earnings are characterized by two elements:

1. Sustainable: high-quality earnings are expected to recur in future periods.
2. Adequate: high-quality earnings cover the company's cost of capital.

LOS 18.g

Mean reversion in earnings, or the tendency of earnings at extreme levels to revert back to normal levels over time, implies that earnings at very high levels are not sustainable. Mean reversion is quicker for accruals-based earnings and faster still if such accruals are discretionary.

LOS 18.h

Two major contributors to earnings manipulation are:

1. Revenue recognition issues; and
2. Expense recognition issues (capitalization).

Bill-and-hold sales or channel stuffing are examples of aggressive revenue recognition practices. Analysis of DSO and receivables turnover (over time and compared to peers) is used to reveal red flags. Cost capitalization will result in an excessive asset base which can be spotted by evaluation of the trend and comparative analysis of common-size balance sheets.

LOS 18.i

High-quality cash flow means that the reported cash flow was high (i.e., good economic performance) and the underlying reporting quality was also high.

LOS 18.j

Elements to check for in the statement of cash flows:

- Unusual items or items that have not shown up in prior years.
- Excessive outflows for receivables and inventory due to aggressive revenue recognition.
- Provisions for, and reversals of, restructuring charges.

LOS 18.k

High financial reporting quality for a balance sheet is evidenced by completeness, unbiased measurement, and clarity of presentation.

LOS 18.l

Completeness of a balance sheet can be compromised by the existence of off-balance sheet liabilities. Also, biased measurement may be present in the measurement of pension obligations, goodwill, investments, inventory, and other assets.

LOS 18.m

Sources of information about the risk of a business include financial statements, auditor's reports, notes to financial statements, MD&A, and the financial press.

ANSWER KEY FOR MODULE QUIZ

Module Quiz 18.1, 18.2, 18.3, 18.4, 18.5

1. **B** The bias in accounting choices means GGFT is lower on the spectrum than FSKA. FSKA appears to have high-quality financial reporting, but earnings are of low quality due to the lack of sustainability.
(Module 18.1, LOS 18.a)

2. **B** Cash-based earnings are more persistent than accruals-based earnings. Hence, companies with a higher proportion of cash-based earnings will have a higher persistence of earnings and, hence, a higher beta coefficient in the AR(1) model. (Module 18.2, LOS 18.e)

3. **A** PSAA may still have to consolidate CRAFT as a VIE despite the voting rights residing with the equity holders. PSAA is exposed to a variable interest due to gains and losses on the conversion option on the convertible debt. If CRAFT is classified as a VIE, the interest income will not be recognized in the consolidated income statement. (Module 18.2, LOS 18.c)

4. **C** The AQI variable measures the change in proportion of assets other than PPE and current assets over time. A value greater than 1 for AQI indicates an increase in proportion of assets other than PPE and CA (from last period) and may indicate excessive expenditure capitalization. A DEPI variable of less than 1 results from a higher depreciation rate for the current year compared to the prior year and would not occur if the company was extending useful lives. (Module 18.2, LOS 18.d)

5. **C** The M-score is a standard normal variable. The larger (less negative) the M-score, the higher the probability of earnings manipulation. Using a cut off of –1.78, both companies would be considered to be likely manipulators of earnings. (Module 18.2, LOS 18.d)

6. **B** A clean audit report is unlikely to provide timely information about potential risks. Due to its focus on historical information, it is also unlikely to be useful to the analyst. (Module 18.5, LOS 18.m)

7. **B**

ZZYP	**2013**	**2014**	**Growth**
Op earnings	142.5	140.3	
Non recurring	(8.2)	(1.9)	
Core earnings	**134.3**	**138.4**	**3.05%**

AART	**2013**	**2014**	**Growth**
Op earnings	209.8	195.4	
Dev costs	(20.1)	5.0	
Core earnings	**189.7**	**200.4**	**5.64%**

XXPG	2013	2014	Growth
Op/core earnings	**220.9**	**233.2**	**5.57%**

(Module 18.5, LOS 18.l)

8. **C** Hartford's comment is incorrect. Discretionary accruals, and to a lesser extent non-discretionary accruals-based earnings, are more likely to be indications of manipulation than cash-based earnings. (Module 18.2, LOS 18.e)

9. **B** Studies have shown the accruals-based earnings are less sustainable than cash-based earnings and, hence, revert to the mean more quickly. (Module 18.2, LOS 18.e)

10. **B**

	$ Millions
Net income	**98.5**
Depreciation, amortization and impairment	137.4
(Increase)/decrease in trade and other receivables	(11.5)
Decrease/(increase) in inventories	(4.1)
Increase/(decrease) in trade and other payables and provisions	12.4
Decrease/(increase) in short term investments (CFI)	-
Non-cash and other movements	7.7
Interest paid (CFI)	-
Tax paid	(25.1)
Net cash flow from operating activities	**215.3**

(Module 18.4, LOS 18.j)

11. **A** Start-ups typically take time to start showing positive operating cash flows. In the early years CFI is negative because the company is spending cash to buy assets and CFF is positive due to capital raised via debt or equity. (Module 18.4, LOS 18.j)

12. **A** Off-balance sheet financing indicates a lack of completeness. Completness, along with unbiased reporting and clear presentation, is required for high quality financial reporting. (Module 18.5, LOS 18.k)

13. **A**

Year	Lease Payment
2015	9.9
2016	9.9
2017	9.9
2018	9.9
2019	8.0
PV at 7.75%	**38.48**

revised debt-to-equity = (182.1 + 38.5) / 120.2 = 1.84x

(Module 18.5, LOS 18.l)

The following is a review of the Financial Reporting and Analysis (2) principles designed to address the learning outcome statements set forth by CFA Institute. Cross-Reference to CFA Institute Assigned Reading #19.

READING 19

Integration of Financial Statement Analysis Techniques

Study Session 6

EXAM FOCUS

This is a key topic review in Financial Reporting and Analysis, and perhaps as important as any of the financial statement analysis material. Here, you are required to use material presented earlier to make appropriate adjustments to the balance sheet and income statement using a common framework. Make sure you can determine and interpret the effects of management's choice of accounting methods and assumptions on the reported financial results and ratios.

MODULE 19.1: FRAMEWORK FOR ANALYSIS

Video covering this content is available online.

LOS 19.a: Demonstrate the use of a framework for the analysis of financial statements, given a particular problem, question, or purpose (e.g., valuing equity based on comparables, critiquing a credit rating, obtaining a comprehensive picture of financial leverage, evaluating the perspectives given in management's discussion of financial results).

CFA® Program Curriculum, Volume 2, page 372

The primary purpose of financial statement analysis is to identify potential outcomes, good or bad, that could affect an investment decision.

A basic framework, presented in Figure 19.1, has been developed to assist the user based on the objectives of the analysis. The framework can be used in making decisions about an equity ownership interest in a firm, a lending decision, evaluating a credit rating, or anticipating the impact on a firm of a change in accounting standards.

Figure 19.1: Framework for Analysis

Step	Input	Output
1. Establish the objectives	■ Perspective of the analyst (e.g., evaluating a debt/equity investment or issuing a credit rating) ■ Needs or concerns communicated by the client or supervisor ■ Institutional guidelines	■ Purpose statement ■ Specific questions to be answered ■ Nature and content of the final report ■ Timetable and resource budget
2. Collect data	■ Financial statements ■ Communication with management, suppliers, customers, and competitors	■ Organized financial information
3. Process data	■ Data from Step 2	■ Adjusted financial statements ■ Common-size statements ■ Ratios ■ Forecasts
4. Analyze data	■ Data from Steps 2 and 3	■ Results
5. Develop and communicate conclusions	■ Results from analysis ■ Published report guidelines	■ Report answering questions posed in Step 1 ■ Recommendations
6. Follow up	■ Periodically updated information	■ Updated analysis and recommendations

Of course, which data are processed and analyzed will depend on the specific objectives of the analysis. In the example we present here, the objective is an analysis of a purchase decision for a long-term equity investment. The analysis focuses on the following:

- Sources of earnings and return on equity.
- Asset base.
- Capital structure.
- Capital allocation decisions.
- Earnings quality and cash flow analysis.
- Market value decomposition.
- Off-balance-sheet financing.
- Anticipating changes in accounting standards.

PROFESSOR'S NOTE

A detailed example of financial statement adjustments and analysis is the best way to address the LOS in this topic review. To make the example easier to follow, we provide the financial statement data necessary to conduct our analysis as needed, rather than all at once.

MODULE QUIZ 19.1

To best evaluate your performance, enter your quiz answers online.

1. When applying the financial analysis framework, which of the following is the *best* example of output from processing data?
   A. A written list of questions to be answered by management.
   B. Audited financial statements.
   C. Common-size financial statements.
2. When applying the financial analysis framework to the valuation of an equity security, communicating with company suppliers, customers, and competitors is an input that occurs while:
   A. establishing the objective of the analysis.
   B. processing data.
   C. collecting data.

MODULE 19.2: EARNINGS SOURCES AND PERFORMANCE

Video covering this content is available online.

LOS 19.b: Identify financial reporting choices and biases that affect the quality and comparability of companies' financial statements and explain how such biases may affect financial decisions.

CFA® Program Curriculum, Volume 2, page 386

We consider the acquisition of a minority equity interest in Thunderbird Corporation, a publicly held firm located in the United States. Thunderbird is a leading producer of electronic components used in automotive, aircraft, and marine applications.

Sources of Earnings and Return on Equity

We begin our analysis by identifying the sources of Thunderbird's earnings and determining whether these sources are sustainable over time.

Return on equity (ROE) can be decomposed using the extended DuPont equation, as follows:

	Tax Burden		Interest Burden		EBIT Margin		Total Asset Turnover		Financial Leverage
ROE =	$\frac{\text{NI}}{\text{EBT}}$	×	$\frac{\text{EBT}}{\text{EBIT}}$	×	$\frac{\text{EBIT}}{\text{revenue}}$	×	$\frac{\text{revenue}}{\text{average assets}}$	×	$\frac{\text{average assets}}{\text{average equity}}$

The DuPont decomposition allows us to identify the firm's performancedrivers, allowing us to expose effects of weaker areas of business that are being masked by the effects of other, stronger areas. For example, a firm could offset a declining EBIT margin by increasing asset turnover or increasing leverage.

We must also consider the firm's sources of income and whether the income is generated internally from operations or externally. For example, the firm has less control over income that is generated by an ownership interest in an associate than over income generated internally. If equity income from associates or joint ventures is a significant source of earnings, we should isolate these effects by removing the equity income from our DuPont analysis to eliminate any bias.

As mentioned before, the equity method is used to account for influential investments (generally an ownership interest of 20% to 50%). Under the equity method, the investor recognizes its pro-rata share of the investee's earnings on the income statement. Eliminating the equity income from the investor's earnings permits analysis of the investor's performance resulting exclusively from its own asset base. Assuming the investee is profitable, this adjustment will decrease both the investor firm's earnings and net profit margin.

Since, under the equity method, the firm's investment is reported as a balance sheet asset, total assets should be reduced by the carrying value of investment. This will increase total asset turnover (smaller denominator). We can use the extended Dupont equation to determine the overall effect on ROE.

PROFESSOR'S NOTE

In order to make the accounting equation balance, you might be tempted to adjust equity downward for the elimination of the investment asset. However, without information about how the investment is financed (e.g., debt, stock, cash, or a combination), it would be arbitrary to adjust assets and equity for purposes of calculating financial leverage. Unless the question specifically provides this information, don't adjust the leverage (you are implicitly assuming that the investment was financed using the same leverage as the rest of the company).

We begin our extended example using the selected financial data for Thunderbird presented in Figure 19.2. Thunderbird owns a 30% equity interest in one of its suppliers, Eagle Corporation.

Figure 19.2: Selected Financial Data—Thunderbird Corporation

$ in millions	2016	2015	2014	2013
Income statement				
Revenue	$75,286	$68,921	$63,781	•
EBIT	10,517	9,311	8,313	•
EBT	9,463	8,474	7,258	•
Income from associates and joint ventures[1]	896	674	627	•
Net income	7,967	6,894	6,023	•
Balance sheet				
Total assets	$80,261	$71,264	$71,903	$61,731
Equity method investment	6,255	5,901	4,951	3,638
Stockholders' equity	37,964	36,994	34,348	27,382

[1] Not included in EBIT and EBT

Using these data, we can decompose Thunderbird's ROE using the extended DuPont equation.

Figure 19.3: Extended DuPont Analysis (as reported)

	Tax Burden	×	Interest Burden	×	EBIT Margin	×	Total Asset Turnover	×	Financial Leverage	=	ROE
2014	82.98%		87.31%		13.03%		0.955		2.165		19.51%
2015	81.35%		91.01%		13.51%		0.963		2.007		19.33%
2016	84.19%		89.98%		13.97%		0.994		2.021		21.26%

Note the slight improvement in ROE over the period, from 19.51% to 21.26%. The decomposition reveals that this is the result of an increasing EBIT margin and decreased effects of taxes and interest, which is offset to some degree by a reduction in financial leverage. Note that an increase in the interest and tax burden ratios indicates that the effective tax rate and impact of interest charges on operating earnings have *decreased*.

By removing the equity income of Eagle from earnings and the equity investment from total assets, we can examine Thunderbird's performance on a standalone basis. Another common adjustment made by analysts is to remove the effects of any unusual items (e.g., provisions for restructuring and litigation, goodwill impairment, etc.) from reported operating earnings (EBIT) before computing the EBIT margin and the tax burden ratios.

Figure 19.4: Extended DuPont Analysis (excluding equity income and investment asset)

	Tax Burden[1]	×	Interest Burden	×	EBIT Margin	×	Total Asset Turnover[2]	×	Financial Leverage	=	ROE
2014	74.35%		87.31%		13.03%		1.020		2.165		18.68%
2015	73.40%		91.01%		13.51%		1.042		2.007		18.87%
2016	74.72%		89.98%		13.97%		1.080		2.021		20.51%

[1] (net income – equity income) / EBT

[2] revenue / [(beginning total assets – beginning equity investment + ending total assets – ending equity investment) / 2]

As compared to the reported ROE (Figure 19.3), adjusted ROE (Figure 19.4) has been decreased by eliminating equity income and the investment asset. Note that EBIT margin did not change because Thunderbird did not include equity income from Eagle as a part of EBIT.

PROFESSOR'S NOTE

We did not adjust the financial leverage because (in the absence of any specific information) we assume that the investment in associate used the same capital structure (i.e., mix of debt and equity) as the parent company.

MODULE QUIZ 19.2

To best evaluate your performance, enter your quiz answers online.

1. Lorenzo Company recently reported EBIT margin of 11%, total asset turnover of 1.2, a financial leverage ratio of 1.5, and interest burden of 70%. Assuming an income tax rate of 35%, Lorenzo's return on equity is *closest* to:
   A. 9%.
   B. 10%.
   C. 11%.
2. McAdoo Corporation recently reported the following:

Earnings before interest and taxes	$246,500
Interest expense	(10,000)
Earnings before taxes	$236,500
Income taxes	(94,600)
Income from associates	16,750
Net income	$158,650

   Tax burden, without the regard to the investments in associates, is *closest* to:
   A. 57.6%.
   B. 60.0%.
   C. 67.1%.

3. Selected financial information from Westcreek Corporation follows:

	2016	2015
Revenue	$848,000	$732,800
Fixed assets	$146,800	$114,400
Investment in Creston Corp.	$56,400	$42,100
Total assets	$468,000	$363,600

At the end of 2016, Westcreek's total asset turnover, without regard to the investment in Creston, is *closest* to:
A. 2.0.
B. 2.3.
C. 2.5.

4. Rainbow Corporation recently reported the following financial information for its two separate divisions:

Division	EBIT Margin	Total Assets %	Total CapEx %
Green	9.5%	60%	30%
Red	3.2%	40%	70%

Rainbow is *most likely* overallocating resources to:
A. Red only.
B. Green only.
C. Red and Green.

MODULE 19.3: ASSET BASE AND CAPITAL STRUCTURE

Video covering this content is available online.

Asset Base

Analysis of the asset base requires an examination of changes in the composition of balance sheet assets over time. Presenting balance sheet items in a common-size format (i.e., as a proportion of total assets) is a useful starting point.

We begin by examining a common-size presentation of Thunderbird's assets in Figure 19.5.

Figure 19.5: Total Assets

$ in millions	2016		2015		2014	
Current assets	$25,039	31.2%	$24,714	34.7%	$29,236	40.7%
PP&E	15,445	19.2%	14,161	19.9%	13,293	18.5%
Identifiable intangibles	5,052	6.3%	2,641	3.7%	1,996	2.8%
Goodwill	23,396	29.1%	19,959	28.0%	18,893	26.3%
Other noncurrent assets	11,329	14.1%	9,789	13.7%	8,485	11.8%
Total assets	$80,261		$71,264		$71,903	

A manufacturing firm, such as Thunderbird, is expected to have considerable investments in both current assets (primarily receivables and inventory) and fixed assets (primarily plant, property, and equipment). However, note the significance of goodwill, which is 29.1% of total assets at the end of 2016. Goodwill is an unidentifiable intangible asset representing the difference between the purchase price and market value of identifiable assets with finite lives in a business acquisition reported under the purchase method.

According to Figure 19.5, goodwill has increased since 2014, indicating Thunderbird has completed a number of business acquisitions.

The increases in Thunderbird's EBIT margin and ROE (Figure 19.3) may be partially due to successful acquisitions. However, since goodwill is no longer amortized through the income statement, we must consider the possibility of losses in the future if goodwill is determined to have been impaired.

Capital Structure

A firm's capital structure must be able to support management's strategic objectives as well as to allow the firm to honor its future obligations.

Referring to Figure 19.3, Thunderbird's financial leverage ratio has decreased over the last three years from 2.2 in 2014 to 2.0 in 2016. Unfortunately, the ratio does not reveal the true nature of the leverage, as some liabilitics are more burdensome than others. Financial liabilities and bond liabilities, for example, can be placed in default if not paid on time, or in the event of noncompliance with the lending covenants (i.e., technical default). On the other hand, liabilities such as employee benefit obligations, deferred taxes, and restructuring provisions are less burdensome and may or may not require a cash outflow in the future.

Next, we will examine the components of Thunderbird's long-term capital.

Figure 19.6: Long-Term Capital

$ in millions	2016		2015		2014	
Long-term debt	$4,290	8.6%	$4,866	10.0%	$5,794	12.4%
Other long-term liabilities	7,679	15.4%	6,669	13.7%	6,663	14.2%
Stockholders' equity	37,964	76.0%	36,994	76.2%	34,348	73.4%
Total long-term capital	$49,933		$48,529		$46,805	

Thunderbird's long-term debt has decreased from 12.4% of long-term capital in 2014 to 8.6% in 2016, a significant decrease in financial leverage.

Given that Thunderbird's long-term debt has decreased, we consider the possibility of an offsetting change in the firm's working capital. Various working capital ratios are presented in Figure 19.7.

Figure 19.7: Selected Working Capital Data and Ratios

$ in millions	2016	2015	2014	2013
Balance sheet				
Cash and equivalents	$4,616	$3,695	$3,261	$3,431
Marketable securities	2,031	4,338	8,915	7,266
Accounts receivable	10,795	10,204	10,004	8,266
Inventories	6,490	5,620	5,713	4,918
Other current assets	1,107	857	1,343	818
Current assets	$25,039	$24,714	$29,236	$24,699
Accounts payable	$9,925	$8,800	$7,782	$6,352
Notes payable	17,179	10,846	13,189	10,305
Other current liabilities	3,224	3,089	4,127	3,732
Current liabilities	$30,328	$22,735	$25,098	$20,389
Other data				
Revenue	$75,286	$68,921	$63,781	•
Cost of goods sold	31,526	28,499	26,542	•
Purchases*	32,396	28,406	27,337	•
Average daily expenditures	173.3	159.5	148.4	•
Working capital ratios				
Current ratio	0.83	1.09	1.16	•
Quick ratio	0.58	0.80	0.88	•
Defensive interval ratio	100.6	114.3	149.4	•
Days' sales outstanding (DSO)	50.9	53.5	52.3	•
Days' inventory on hand (DOH)	70.1	72.6	73.1	•
Days' payables	(105.5)	(106.5)	(94.4)	•
Cash conversion cycle	15.5	19.6	31.0	•

* Purchases = COGS + ending inventory – beginning inventory

Both the current ratio and quick ratio have declined as a result of both the increase in notes payable and the decrease in marketable securities. The defensive interval ratio has been declining due to both an increase in daily expenditures and a decrease in marketable securities.

On the other hand, the firm appears to be better managing its receivables, inventory, and payables, as shown by a decrease in the cash conversion cycle from 31.0 days to 15.5 days. Receivables are being collected sooner (declining DSO), inventory turnover has increased (declining DOH), and the firm is paying suppliers more slowly (increasing days' payables).

Video covering this content is available online.

MODULE 19.4: CAPITAL ALLOCATION

Capital Allocation Decisions

Consolidated financial statements can hide the individual characteristics of dissimilar subsidiaries. As a result, firms are required to disaggregate financial information by segments to assist users.

Recall that a business segment is a portion of a larger company that accounts for more than 10% of the company's revenues or assets, and is distinguishable from the company's other line(s) of business in terms of risk and return characteristics. Geographic segments are also identified based on the same criteria.

Although required disclosure under U.S. GAAP and IFRS is limited, the disclosures are valuable in identifying each segment's contribution to revenue and profit, the relationship between capital expenditures and rates of return, and which segments should be de-emphasized or eliminated.

Continuing our example, Thunderbird operates four different divisions: aircraft, automotive, marine, and specialty products. Figure 19.8 presents Thunderbird's revenue and EBIT by segment.

Figure 19.8: Revenue and EBIT by Segment

$ in millions	2016		2015		2014	
Revenue						
Aircraft	$11,027	14.6%	$8,856	12.8%	$7,863	12.3%
Automotive	34,631	46.0%	32,754	47.5%	30,276	47.5%
Marine	22,345	29.7%	20,566	29.8%	19,491	30.6%
Specialty	7,283	9.7%	6,745	9.8%	6,151	9.6%
	$75,286		$68,921		$63,781	
EBIT						
Aircraft	$2,440	23.2%	$1,955	21.0%	$1,696	20.4%
Automotive	5,059	48.1%	4,674	50.2%	4,115	49.5%
Marine	2,482	23.6%	2,160	23.2%	2,020	24.3%
Specialty	536	5.1%	522	5.6%	482	5.8%
	$10,517		$9,311		$8,313	

Figure 19.8 reveals that in terms of contributing revenue and EBIT, the automotive division is the largest segment while the specialty products division is the smallest. Also, the percentage contribution to EBIT by the specialty products division declined from 5.8% in 2014 to 5.1% in 2016.

Thunderbird's assets and capital expenditures by segment are presented in Figure 19.9.

Figure 19.9: Assets and Capital Expenditures by Segment

$ in millions	2016		2015		2014	
Assets*						
Aircraft	$14,777	27.5%	$6,861	15.4%	$5,288	12.8%
Automotive	20,059	37.4%	19,553	43.9%	19,166	46.6%
Marine	12,310	22.9%	11,927	26.8%	10,779	26.2%
Specialty	6,509	12.1%	6,219	14.0%	5,928	14.4%
	$53,655		$44,560		$41,161	
Capital expenditures						
Aircraft	$383	11.3%	$336	11.8%	$240	10.4%
Automotive	1,432	42.3%	1,199	42.1%	1,018	44.3%
Marine	841	24.8%	667	23.4%	618	26.9%
Specialty	730	21.6%	646	22.7%	421	18.3%
	$3,386		$2,848		$2,297	

* Not equal to total assets due to unallocated and non-segment assets.

Not surprisingly, Figure 19.9 reveals that the automotive division requires the greatest proportion of assets and capital expenditures. Note that the specialty products division has the least assets of all four divisions and that the aircraft division has required the least capital expenditures. Also note that the capital expenditures of the specialty products division have increased over the period.

Using the percentages from Figure 19.9, we can calculate the ratio of proportional capital expenditures to proportional assets for each segment. A ratio greater than one indicates the firm is growing the segment by allocating a greater percentage of its capital expenditures to a segment than that segment's proportion of total assets. Conversely, a ratio of less than one indicates the firm is allocating a smaller percentage of its capital expenditures to a segment than its proportion of total assets. If these trends continue, the segments will represent a more or less significant proportion of the firm over time.

By comparing the EBIT margin contributed by each segment to its ratio of capital expenditure proportion to asset proportion, we can determine if the firm is investing its capital in its most profitable segments.

Figure 19.10: EBIT Margin and CapEx % to Assets % by Segment

	EBIT Margin			CapEx % / Assets %		
	2016	2015	2014	2016	2015	2014
Aircraft	22.1%	22.1%	21.6%	0.41	0.77	0.81
Automotive	14.6%	14.3%	13.6%	1.13	0.96	0.95
Marine	11.1%	10.5%	10.4%	1.08	0.87	1.03
Specialty	7.4%	7.7%	7.8%	1.79	1.62	1.27

From Figure 19.10, we note that while the specialty products division has, by far, the lowest EBIT margin, it has the highest capital expenditures proportion to assets proportion ratio. Additionally, the specialty products division's EBIT margin is declining. If Thunderbird continues to overallocate capital resources to the specialty products division, the firm's company-wide returns may suffer.

Accrual-based measures such as EBIT may not be a good indicator of an entity's ability to generate cash flow. We would rather evaluate segmental capital allocation decisions based on cash flows generated by each segment. However, segmental cash flow data is generally not reported. We can, however, approximate cash flow as EBIT plus depreciation and amortization. Figure 19.11 provides depreciation and amortization expense by segment. Figure 19.12 shows the cash flow estimates using segmental EBIT from Figure 19.8 and segmental depreciation and amortization information from Figure 19.11.

Figure 19.11: Depreciation and Amortization Expense by Segment

$ in millions	2016	2015	2014
Aircraft	$172	$165	$142
Automotive	$644	$590	$603
Marine	$377	$328	$366
Specialty	$329	$318	$251
Total	$1,522	$1,401	$1,362

Figure 19.12: Estimated Cash Flow = EBIT + Depreciation/Amortization

$ in millions	2016	2015	2014
Aircraft	$2,612	$2,120	$1,838
Automotive	$5,703	$5,264	$4,718
Marine	$2,859	$2,488	$2,386
Specialty	$865	$840	$733
Total	$12,039	$10,712	$9,675

We then compute cash operating return on average total assets using information from Figure 19.12 and computing average total assets for 2015 and 2016 from information in Figure 19.9. Figure 19.13 shows the relevant information including EBIT margins from Figure 19.10.

Figure 19.13: Segmental Cash Generation and EBIT Margins

	Cash Flow/Average Assets		EBIT Margin	
	2016	2015	2016	2015
Aircraft	24.1%	34.9%	22.1%	22.1%
Automotive	28.8%	27.2%	14.6%	14.3%
Marine	23.6%	21.9%	11.1%	10.5%
Specialty	13.6%	13.8%	7.4%	7.7%

Average assets are calculated as beginning assets + ending assets divided by 2. Using data from Figure 19.9, the 2016 average assets for the aircraft division is ($14,777 + $6,861)/2 or $10,819. Hence, for 2016, the cash flow to average assets for the aircraft division is $2,612 / $10,819 = 24.1%. Figure 19.13 confirms poor capital allocation decision to the specialty products division. In addition, we can see that the aircraft division—while continuing to produce superior operating margins—has fallen behind in cash generation in the latest year.

MODULE 19.5: EARNINGS QUALITY AND CASH FLOW ANALYSIS

Video covering this content is available online.

LOS 19.e: Analyze and interpret how balance sheet modifications, earnings normalization, and cash flow statement related modifications affect a company's financial statements, financial ratios, and overall financial condition.

CFA® Program Curriculum, Volume 2, page 403

PROFESSOR'S NOTE

For continuity of our extended example, we present this LOS out of order.

Earnings Quality and Cash Flow Analysis

Earnings quality refers to the persistence and sustainability of a firm's earnings. Earnings that are closer to operating cash flow are considered higher quality. Of course, earnings are subject to accrual accounting events that require numerous judgments and estimates. As a result, earnings are more easily manipulated than cash flow.

We can disaggregate earnings into their cash flow and accruals components using either a balance sheet approach or a cash flow statement approach. With either approach, the ratio of accruals to average net operating assets can be used to measure earnings quality. The interpretation of both ratios is the same: the lower the ratio, the higher the earnings quality.

Accruals Ratio

Balance sheet approach. Using the balance sheet, we can measure accruals as the change in net operating assets over a period. Net operating assets (NOA) is the difference between operating assets and operating liabilities. Operating assets are equal to total assets minus cash, equivalents to cash, and marketable securities. Operating liabilities are equal to total liabilities minus total debt (both short term and long term). In summary, the formula for balance sheet based aggregate accruals is:

$$\text{accruals}^{BS} = NOA_{END} - NOA_{BEG}$$

In order to make comparisons, it is necessary to scale the accrual measure for differences in size. Just like ROA and ROE, the measure can be distorted if a firm is growing or contracting quickly. Scaling the measure also allows for comparisons with other firms. Scaling is done by dividing the accrual measure by the average NOA for the period. The result is known as the accruals ratio:

$$\text{accruals ratio}^{BS} = \frac{(NOA_{END} - NOA_{BEG})}{(NOA_{END} + NOA_{BEG})/2}$$

Cash flow statement approach. We can also derive the aggregate accruals by subtracting cash flow from operating activities (CFO) and cash flow from investing activities (CFI) from reported earnings as follows:

$$\text{accruals}^{CF} = NI - CFO - CFI$$

Recall that IFRS allows some flexibility in the classifications of certain cash flows, primarily interest and dividends paid. Thus, for firms following U.S. GAAP, it may be necessary to reclassify these cash flows from operating activities to financing activities for comparison purposes.

Like the balance sheet accrual measure, the cash flow measure must be scaled for comparison purposes. Thus, the accruals ratio based on the cash flow statement is:

$$\text{accruals ratio}^{CF} = \frac{(NI - CFO - CFI)}{(NOA_{END} + NOA_{BEG})/2}$$

Figure 19.14 contains the necessary data to calculate the accruals ratio using both approaches.

Figure 19.14: Selected Balance Sheet and Cash Flow Data

$ in Millions	2016	2015	2014
Balance sheet			
Total assets	$80,261	$71,264	$71,903
Cash and marketable securities	(6,647)	(8,033)	(12,176)
Operating assets	$73,614	$63,231	$59,727
Total liabilities	$42,297	$34,270	$37,555
Long-term debt	(4,290)	(4,866)	(5,794)
Short-term debt	(17,179)	(10,846)	(13,189)
Operating liabilities	$20,828	$18,558	$18,572
Net operating assets (NOA)[1]	$52,786	$44,673	$41,155
Balance sheet accruals[2]	$8,113	$3,518	$6,541
Cash flow statement			
Net income	$7,967	$6,894	$6,023
(–) Operating cash flow	9,407	8,173	7,144
(–) Investing cash flow	(11,027)	(7,364)	(3,261)
Cash flow accruals[3]	$9,587	$6,085	$2,140

[1] NOA totaled $34,614 at the end of 2013

[2] Year-to-year change in NOA

[3] 9,587 = (+7,967) – (+9,407) – (–11,027)

Using the data contained in Figure 19.14, we can calculate the balance sheet and cash flow statement accruals ratios in Figure 19.15.

Figure 19.15: Balance Sheet and Cash Flow Accruals Ratios

$ in millions	2016	2015	2014
Balance sheet approach			
$\frac{\text{BS accruals}}{\text{average NOA}}$	$\frac{\$8,113}{\$48,730} = 16.6\%$	$\frac{\$3,518}{\$42,914} = 8.2\%$	$\frac{\$6,541}{\$37,885} = 17.3\%$
Cash flow statement approach			
$\frac{\text{CF accruals}}{\text{average NOA}}$	$\frac{\$9,587}{\$48,730} = 19.7\%$	$\frac{\$6,085}{\$42,914} = 14.2\%$	$\frac{\$2,140}{\$37,885} = 5.6\%$

Under the balance sheet approach, the accruals ratio has fluctuated widely over the period, from 17.3%, down to 8.2% in 2015, and back up to 16.6%. Wide fluctuations like these may be an indication of earnings manipulation.

Equally disturbing, the accruals ratio calculated using the cash flow approach has steadily increased over the last three years from 5.6% in 2014 to 19.7% in 2016.

PROFESSOR'S NOTE

Although both accruals ratios are conceptually equivalent (both measure the degree of accruals present in a firm's earnings), their results can differ because of acquisitions and divestitures, exchange rate gains and losses, and inconsistent treatment of specific items on the balance sheet and on the cash flow statement. As noted earlier, Thunderbird has been involved in a number of acquisitions over the 3-year period.

Because of the potential for earnings manipulation by increasing accruals, we decide to compare Thunderbird's cash flow to its operating income. Our interest is in determining whether operating income is confirmed by cash flow. However, we cannot directly use the cash flow from operating activities as a proxy for cash flow for this purpose.

In order to compare the two measures, it is necessary to eliminate cash paid for interest and taxes from operating cash flow by adding them back. (Interest and taxes are deducted for operating cash flow but not for operating income.) This adjusted figure is the **cash generated from operations (CGO)**. CGO can also be calculated as:

CGO = EBIT + non-cash charges – increase in working capital

PROFESSOR'S NOTE

Be careful when making the cash interest and tax adjustment to operating cash flow. Firms that follow IFRS have the choice of reporting cash paid for interest as an operating cash flow or as a financing cash flow. If a firm reports the interest as a financing cash flow, no interest adjustment is necessary.

As shown in Figure 19.16, we can calculate the ratio of cash generated from operations to operating income.

Figure 19.16: Cash Flow to Operating Income

$ in Millions	2016	2015	2014
Operating cash flow (OCF)*	$9,407	$8,173	$7,144
(+) Cash interest paid	552	419	306
(+) Cash taxes paid	2,150	1,968	1,778
Cash generated from operations (CGO)	$12,109	$10,560	$9,228
Operating income	$10,517	$9,311	$8,313
Cash generated from operations / operating income	1.15	1.13	1.11

* After deducting cash paid for interest and taxes

The ratio of CGO to operating income confirms that cash generated from operations has exceeded operating income over the past three years. The results of this analysis reduce our earlier concerns of potential earnings manipulation from our accruals analysis.

In order to evaluate Thunderbird's recent acquisitions, we examine the cash return on total assets.

Figure 19.17: Cash Return on Total Assets

$ in Millions	2016	2015	2014
Cash generated from operations	$12,109	$10,560	$9,228
Average total assets	$75,763	$71,584	$66,817
CGO / average total assets	16.0%	14.8%	13.8%

The cash return on total assets has increased over the period, which seems to justify the recent acquisitions. However, since the results of the accruals ratios, calculated in Figure 19.15, gave us cause for concern, we need to calculate cash flow to reinvestment, cash flow to total debt, and cash flow interest coverage ratios.

Figure 19.18: Selected Cash Flow Ratios

$ in Millions	2016	2015	2014
Cash flow to reinvestment			
Cash generated from operations (CGO)	$12,109	$10,560	$9,228
Capital expenditures	$3,386	$2,848	$2,297
CGO / capital expenditures	3.6	3.7	4.0
Cash flow to total debt			
Cash generated from operations (CGO)	$12,109	$10,560	$9,228
Total debt	$21,469	$15,712	$18,983
CGO / total debt	56.4%	67.2%	48.6%
Cash flow interest coverage			
Cash generated from operations (CGO)	$12,109	$10,560	$9,228
Cash interest paid	$552	$419	$306
CGO / cash interest	21.9	25.2	30.2

All three cash flow measures presented in Figure 19.18 are reassuring. Although cash flow to reinvestment declined slightly over the period, cash flow still covered capital expenditures by 3.6 times in 2016. This indicates there are sufficient resources to fund Thunderbird's ongoing capital expenditures.

Cash flow to total debt of 56.4% in 2016 confirms Thunderbird's relatively low leverage. Cash flow interest coverage (the interest coverage ratio calculated on a cash-flow basis) has been declining over the past three years but, for 2016, cash flow still covered interest paid 21.9 times, which is excellent. With low leverage and high interest coverage, Thunderbird has the flexibility to increase its debt if the need arises.

MODULE QUIZ 19.3, 19.4, 19.5

To best evaluate your performance, enter your quiz answers online.

1. Suppose that we are provided the following financial data for MegaCo Industries:

Operating income	20,000
Net income	12,000
Cash from operations	33,000
Cash from investing	(30,000)
Cash from financing	(10,000)
Average total assets	90,000
Average net operating assets	180,000

MegaCo's cash flow accruals ratio is *closest* to:
A. 5.0%.
B. 7.5%.
C. 10.0%.

MODULE 19.6: MARKET VALUE DECOMPOSITION

Video covering this content is available online.

Market Value Decomposition

When a parent company has an ownership interest in an associate (subsidiary or affiliate), it may be beneficial to determine the *standalone* value of the parent; that is, the implied value of the parent without regard to the value of the associate. The implied value is equal to the parent's market value less the parent's pro-rata share of the associate's market value. If the associate's stock is traded on a foreign stock exchange, it may be necessary to convert the market value of the associate to the parent's reporting currency.

As noted earlier, Thunderbird owns a 30% equity interest in Eagle Corporation, a publicly traded firm located in Europe. Let's suppose that the market capitalization of Thunderbird is $137 billion. Also, let's imagine that the market capitalization of Eagle is €60 billion and, at year-end, the $/€ exchange rate is $1.40.

In this case, Thunderbird's pro-rata share of Eagle's market value is $25.2 billion (€60 billion × 30% × $1.40). Therefore, the implied value of Thunderbird, excluding Eagle, is $111.8 billion ($137 billion – $25.2 billion) or 81.6% of Thunderbird's market capitalization ($111.8 billion / $137 billion).

Next, let's compute Thunderbird's P/E multiple without Eagle. Let's suppose Thunderbird's P/E multiple is 17.1 ($137 billion market capitalization / $8 billion net income). Assuming the S&P 500 multiple is 20.1, Thunderbird's P/E is a 15% discount to the P/E of the S&P index.

The implied P/E multiple of Thunderbird without Eagle is 15.7 [$111.8 billion implied value / ($8 billion Thunderbird net income – $896 million equity income from Eagle)]. Thus, Thunderbird's implied P/E multiple is an even greater 22% discount to the S&P multiple.

PROFESSOR'S NOTE

Had Eagle's earnings been stated in euros, it would have been necessary to convert the earnings into dollars at the average exchange rate for the period. The average rate is used since it is assumed the earnings occurred evenly throughout the year.

The discount to the S&P multiple seems excessive given Thunderbird's low leverage and strong cash flow position. Thus, Thunderbird's stock may be undervalued relative to the market.

Thunderbird's implied P/E multiple is a crude measure because of the potential differences in accounting methods used by the two firms—Thunderbird reports under U.S. GAAP while Eagle reports under IFRS.

We can summarize our findings as follows:

Support for investment in Thunderbird

- Thunderbird's earnings growth has been generated internally from operations, through acquisitions, and by investment income from Eagle.
- Thunderbird's ROE is positive and trending upward. Investment income from Eagle has improved Thunderbird's ROE.
- Earnings quality appears to be good as operating earnings are confirmed by cash flow.
- Cash flow is sufficient to support capital expenditures and an increase in debt if necessary.
- Thunderbird is growing through acquisitions and its cash return on assets continues to increase.
- After eliminating Thunderbird's pro-rata share of Eagle's market value and equity income, Thunderbird appears to be undervalued based on its implied P/E multiple relative to that of the S&P index.

Concerns

- Potential earnings manipulation as evidenced by increasing accrual ratios. However, this concern is reduced due to Thunderbird's strong cash flow.
- Thunderbird may be overallocating capital resources to the lowest margin segment (specialty products). Future monitoring will be required.
- Recent acquisitions may result in losses from goodwill impairment in the future.

MODULE QUIZ 19.6

To best evaluate your performance, enter your quiz answers online.

Use the following information to answer Questions 1 and 2.

Big Company owns 25% of Small Company. Selected recent financial data for both firms follows:

	Big	Small
Net income	£16,000	€6,000
Market capitalization	£275,000	€150,000
Current exchange rate (£/€)	0.85	
Average exchange rate (£/€)	0.80	

1. The percentage of Big's value explained by its ownership of Small is *closest* to:
   A. 10.9%.
   B. 11.6%.
   C. 13.6%.
2. The implied P/E multiple of Big, without regard to Small, is *closest* to:
   A. 16.1.
   B. 16.4.
   C. 17.2.

Video covering this content is available online.

MODULE 19.7: OFF-BALANCE-SHEET FINANCING AND CHANGING ACCOUNTING STANDARDS

LOS 19.c: Evaluate the quality of a company's financial data, and recommend appropriate adjustments to improve quality and comparability with similar companies, including adjustments for differences in accounting standards, methods, and assumptions.

CFA® Program Curriculum, Volume 2, page 395

Off-Balance-Sheet Financing

There are a number of financing arrangements that are not reported on the balance sheet. One of the most common forms of off-balance-sheet financing is operating leases.

Recall that an operating lease is simply a rental arrangement; that is, the lessee reports neither an asset nor a liability related to the lease on its balance sheet, even though the lessee may have a contractual obligation under the lease agreement. The lessee only reports rental expense, equal to the periodic lease payment, on the income statement.

Alternatively, a finance lease (also called a "capital" lease) is, in substance, treated as a purchase of an asset financed with debt. Thus, the lessee reports an asset and a liability on its balance sheet. On the income statement, the lessee reports depreciation expense and interest expense instead of rental expense.

For analytical purposes, an operating lease should be treated as a finance lease, increasing assets and liabilities by the present value of the remaining lease payments. Since assets and liabilities are initially increased by the same amount, stockholders' equity is not affected by this adjustment. Capitalizing an operating lease will increase financial leverage because of the increase in liabilities.

On the income statement, it is necessary to replace the rental expense (payment) for the operating lease with depreciation expense (on the lease asset) and interest expense (on the lease liability). Recall that in the early years of a finance lease, depreciation expense and interest expense will exceed the lease payment. As a result, net income will be lower in the early years for a finance lease compared to an operating lease. In addition, by recognizing interest expense in the lessee's income statement, the interest coverage ratio will likely decline (higher denominator).

Consider an example. Roadrunner, Inc., the lessee, reports an agreement to finance manufacturing equipment as an operating lease. The discounted present value of the lease payments is $9.1 million at an interest rate of 10%. The lease term is five years and the annual payment is $2.4 million.

Figure 19.19 illustrates the effect of analyst adjustments on selected leverage and interest coverage ratios.

Figure 19.19: The Effect of Operating Lease Adjustments on Selected Ratios

$ in Thousands	Reported	Adjustments	Pro Forma
Financial leverage			
$\frac{\text{total assets}}{\text{total equity}}$	$\frac{\$71,940}{\$50,190} = 1.43$	9,100[a] / —	$\frac{\$81,040}{\$50,190} = 1.61$
Total debt-to-equity			
$\frac{\text{total debt}}{\text{equity}}$	$\frac{\$21,750}{\$50,190} = 0.43$	9,100[a] / —	$\frac{\$30,850}{\$50,190} = 0.61$
Interest coverage			
$\frac{\text{EBIT}}{\text{interest expense}}$	$\frac{\$4,160}{\$1,400} = 3.0$	2,400[b] – 1,820[c] / 910[d]	$\frac{\$4,740}{\$2,310} = 2.1$

[a] Present value of lease payments

[b] Rent expense (payment)

[c] Depreciation expense: 9,100 / 5 years = 1,820

[d] Interest expense: 9,100 × 10% = 910

As a result of capitalizing the operating lease, financial leverage is increased and interest coverage is decreased.

PROFESSOR'S NOTE

Though not specifically discussed in this topic review, an analyst might also split the lease liability into a current portion (current liability) and non-current portion (long-term liability). This adjustment involves increasing current liabilities by the principal portion of the lease payment due within the next 12 months. The principal payment can be derived by subtracting the interest expense from the total lease payment. The non-current portion is simply equal to the difference in the total lease liability and the current portion. As a result of this adjustment, the current ratio decreases (higher denominator).

Other examples of off-balance-sheet financing techniques are debt guarantees, sales of receivables with recourse, and take-or-pay agreements. In each case, the analytical adjustment is similar to the operating lease adjustment; that is, increase assets and liabilities by the amount of the transaction that is off-balance-sheet.

LOS 19.d: Evaluate how a given change in accounting standards, methods, or assumptions affects financial statements and ratios.

CFA® Program Curriculum, Volume 2, page 388

Anticipating Changing Accounting Standards

Users must be aware of proposed changes in accounting standards because of the financial statement effects and the potential impact on a firm's valuation. Over the next few years, significant accounting changes are expected as U.S. GAAP and IFRS converge.

For example, in the United States, the Financial Accounting Standards Board (FASB) has generally eliminated the operating lease treatment in financial statements. In most cases, firms are now required to capitalize leases. This may significantly increase reported leverage. Lease capitalization will also affect the firm's compliance with its bond covenants based on financial leverage calculated in accordance with U.S. GAAP. To avoid the increase in leverage from capitalizing a lease, the firm could raise additional equity, which would dilute existing investors' ownership interests.

MODULE QUIZ 19.7

To best evaluate your performance, enter your quiz answers online.

1. Bledsoe Corporation is the lessee in a non-cancelable operating lease. Which of the following *best* describes the effect of adjusting Bledsoe's financial statements for analytical purposes?
   A. The current ratio would increase.
   B. The debt-to-equity ratio would decrease.
   C. Operating profit would increase.

KEY CONCEPTS

LOS 19.a

The basic financial analysis framework involves:

1. Establishing the objectives.
2. Collecting the data.
3. Processing the data.
4. Analyzing the data.
5. Developing and communicating the conclusions.
6. Following up.

LOS 19.b

Use the extended DuPont equation to examine the sources of earnings and performance. Remove equity income from associates and the investment account to eliminate any bias.

Examine the composition of the balance sheet over time.

Determine if the capital structure can support future obligations and strategic plans by analyzing the components of long-term capital. Some liabilities don't necessarily result in an outflow of cash.

Segment disclosures are valuable in identifying the contribution of revenue and profit by each segment, the relationship between capital expenditures and rates of return, and identifying segments that should be de-emphasized or eliminated.

LOS 19.c

The balance sheet should be adjusted for off-balance-sheet financing activities. Capitalize operating leases for analytical purposes by increasing assets and liabilities by the present value of the remaining lease payments. Also, adjust the income statement by replacing rent expense with depreciation expense on the lease asset and interest expense on the lease liability.

LOS 19.d

Users must be aware of the proposed changes in accounting standards because of the financial statement effects and the potential impact on a firm's valuation.

LOS 19.e

Earnings can be disaggregated into cash flow and accruals using a balance sheet approach and a cash flow statement approach. The lower the accruals ratio, the higher the earnings quality.

Earnings are considered higher quality when confirmed by cash flow. Cash flow can be compared to operating profit by adding back cash paid for interest and taxes to operating cash flow.

The standalone market value of a firm can be computed by eliminating the pro-rata market value of investment in associates.

An implied P/E multiple can be computed by dividing the standalone market value by earnings without regard to equity income from associates.

ANSWER KEY FOR MODULE QUIZZES

Module Quiz 19.1

1. **C** Common-size financial statements are created in the data processing step of the framework for financial analysis. (LOS 19.a)

2. **C** Communication with management, suppliers, customers, and competitors is an input during the data collection step. (LOS 19.a)

Module Quiz 19.2

1. **A** ROE = tax burden × interest burden × EBIT margin × asset turnover × financial leverage = (1 – 0.35) × 0.70 × 0.11 × 1.2 × 1.5 = 0.09

   tax burden = net income / earnings before tax = 1 – tax rate

   (LOS 19.b)

2. **B** (158,650 net income – 16,750 equity income) / 236,500 EBT = 60.0% (LOS 19.b)

3. **B** 848,000 revenue / [(2016 total assets of 468,000 – 2016 Creston investment of 56,400 + 2015 total assets of 363,600 – 2015 Creston investment of 42,100) / 2] = 848,000 / 366,550 = 2.31 (LOS 19.b)

4. **A** Rainbow may be overallocating resources to Red because Red has the lowest EBIT margin and a ratio of proportional capital expenditures to proportional assets that is greater than 1 (70% / 40% = 1.75). Green has highest EBIT margin and a ratio of proportional capital expenditures to proportional assets that is less than 1 (30% / 60% = 0.50). (LOS 19.b)

Module Quiz 19.3, 19.4, 19.5

1. **A** Cash flow accruals ratio = (NI – CFO – CFI) ÷ average NOA = [12,000 – 33,000 – (–30,000)] / 180,000 = 5%. (Module 19.5, LOS 19.e)

Module Quiz 19.6

1. **B** Pro-rata share of Small's market cap / Big's market cap = (€150,000 × 25% × 0.85) / £275,000 = 11.6%. (LOS 19.e)

2. **B** Big's implied value without Small is £243,125, or £275,000 Big market cap – £31,875 pro-rata share of Small market cap (€150,000 × 25% × 0.85 current exchange rate).

   Big's net income without Small is £14,800, or £16,000 Big net income – £1,200 pro-rata share of Small net income (€6,000 × 25% × 0.80 average exchange rate).

   Implied P/E = 16.4 (£243,125 Big's implied value without Small / £14,800 Big's net income without Small). (LOS 19.e)

Module Quiz 19.7

1. **C** When adjusting the income statement for an operating lease, the rent expense is added back to operating income and depreciation expense on the lease asset is subtracted. The rental payment will likely exceed the implied depreciation expense; thus, operating income will increase. Interest expense will also be increased by interest on the lease liability, but this will not affect operating income. The D/E ratio will increase. The current ratio will decrease because the current portion of the lease liability will increase current liabilities. (LOS 19.c)

TOPIC ASSESSMENT: FINANCIAL REPORTING AND ANALYSIS

You have now finished the Financial Reporting and Analysis topic section. The following topic assessment will provide immediate feedback on how effective your study of this material has been. The test is best taken timed; allow 3 minutes per subquestion (18 minutes per item set). This topic assessment is more exam-like than typical module quiz or QBank questions. A score less than 70% suggests that additional review of this topic is needed.

Use the following information to answer Questions 1 through 6.

Gotham Pharmaceuticals wants to increase its sales growth, which has sagged in recent quarters, by increasing its research and development budget and by purchasing a smaller company that lacks the resources to market its groundbreaking osteoporosis treatment. Operating cash flow alone will not provide the cash Gotham wants to spend, so the company has decided to sell some of its assets.

Below is a list of Gotham's financial assets, most of which the company has owned for a decade or more. Assume that U.S. GAAP applies.

Securities	Carrying Value at End of Most Recent Fiscal Year	Estimated Market Value Six Months Into Current Year
Corporate Bonds 6.25%	$75,000,000	$74,000,000
Treasury Bonds 6.75%	$125,000,000	$128,000,000
S&P 500 Index Fund	$35,000,000	$41,000,000
General Electric Preferred Stock	$13,000,000	$12,500,000
Package of Residential Mortgages	$42,000,000	$43,000,000

Frank Caper, Gotham's CFO, is unsure how to approach the security sales, so he assigns Julia Ward, director of the company's accounting division, to handle the recordkeeping. When Ward asks Caper which securities he plans to sell, Caper responds that he has not yet decided, but he expects the purchase of the smaller drug company will require between $190 million and $240 million.

Ward begins her review of Gotham's securities holdings and learns the following:

- The corporate bonds are classified as held-to-maturity.
- The preferred stock is classified as a trading security.
- The Treasury bonds, package of mortgages, and index fund are classified as available-for-sale.

A review of the balance sheet left Ward with several questions. She called Caper for clarification, who made the following statements:

- The fact is that, up until this point, we never had any real intent with regard to selling these securities.
- The package of mortgages is carried at cost because such securities are not commonly traded and no market value is available.
- We know the market price for the corporate bonds but record their value at amortized cost anyway.

- Wc intend to reclassify the Treasury bonds as trading securities because they mature in less than a year.
- Because the index fund has the most appreciation potential, we intend to reclassify it as held-to-maturity.

Confused by Caper's statements, Ward tries a new tactic and looks at the securities from an income-statement perspective. She prepares a table showing how the securities have performed over the last year and then reviews the income statement and balance sheet for the year to see how Gotham handled the accounting.

Securities	**Dividends/ Interest, Last Fiscal Year**	**Unrealized Gains/Losses, Last Fiscal Year**	**Realized Gains/Losses, Last Fiscal Year**
Corporate Bonds 6.25%	$4,500,000	$2,500,000	
Treasury Bonds 6.75%	$8,500,000	–$6,000,000	
S&P 500 Index Fund	$630,000	$4,000,000	$500,000
General Electric Preferred Stock	$740,000	$1,200,000	
Package of Residential Mortgages	$2,200,000	–$3,600,000	$3,000,000

After reviewing Gotham's accounting for its securities, Ward rcalizes she does not have enough information to recommend reclassification for the securities.

While preparing to call Caper for more information, Ward comes across one additional investment not included in the original list. Gotham owns 35% of the Klesten Research Center, a laboratory that provides preclinical testing services. That stake is not represented on the income statement and is carried on the balance sheet at original cost. Last year, Klesten Research Center lost $150 million, increased its debt load by $400 million to $2.1 billion, saw its market value fall by $100 million to $4.85 billion, and paid $40 million in dividends.

1. The effect of Gotham's investment portfolio on reported net income in the last fiscal year was *closest to* a gain of:
   A. $18,170,000.
   B. $19,270,000.
   C. $21,270,000.

2. Under Gotham's current accounting system, which of the following securities are *least accurately* classified?
   A. Preferred stock.
   B. Package of mortgages.
   C. Corporate bonds.

3. Caper has not provided enough information for Ward to reclassify the securities. She needs more details regarding:
   A. when the securities were originally purchased.
   B. how much Gotham intends to spend on the purchase.
   C. which securities Gotham plans to sell to raise the money.

4. Gotham, which purchased 35% of Klesten Research Center in 2013, restates the last three years of financial statements to account for the purchase. Gotham has not elected the fair value option. In the fiscal year ended December 2016, what is the *most likely* effect the Klesten investment would have on Gotham's financial statements?
   A. Decrease income and assets.
   B. Increase income and assets.
   C. Decrease income and increase assets.

5. Which of Caper's statements reflects the *best* understanding of security classification?
   A. The package of mortgages is carried at cost because such securities are not commonly traded, and no market value is available.
   B. We know the market price for the corporate bonds but record their value at amortized cost anyway.
   C. We intend to reclassify the Treasury bonds as trading securities because they mature in less than a year.

6. After reviewing Gotham's financial statements and reconsidering Caper's statements, Ward will *most likely* conclude that the proposed reclassification of the S&P 500 Index fund:
   A. is correct and will reduce ROE.
   B. is incorrect because it cannot be classified as held-to-maturity.
   C. will only be correct if Gotham can prove that it has the capability as well as the intent to hold-to-maturity.

Use the following information to answer Questions 7 through 12.

James Reed, CFA, a health care analyst for the Jacobs Independent Advisors Group (JIAG), is conducting a review of Two Bear Pharmaceutical, Inc. (Two Bear).

Reed reviews his initial report on Two Bear with Krista Reynolds, a Level I CFA candidate. During their discussion, Reynolds tells Reed that she is unclear about the basic characteristics of a defined benefit versus a defined contribution pension plan. Reed proceeds to discuss the pros and cons of defined benefit plans and defined contribution pension plans with Reynolds.

Reed and Reynolds continue their discussion by looking at Two Bear's defined benefit pension plan. Specifically, they review Two Bear's selection of discount rate, rate of compensation growth, and expected return on plan assets.

Reed enlists Reynolds's assistance in comparing and contrasting Two Bear's pension and other post-retirement health plan assumptions over the past few years and across similar pharmaceutical firms. Reynolds gathers historical and competitive data and has questions about the ultimate health care trend rate as well as the internal consistency of Two Bear's post-retirement benefit assumptions. Reynolds notes that Two Bear has replaced the compensation growth rate with a health care inflation rate. Later, she asks Reed what the assumptions underlying the estimate of the health care inflation rate are.

As part of his analysis of Two Bear's defined benefit pension plan, Reed would like to estimate the underlying economic liability (or asset) of the plan and prepare an adjusted income statement. Reed gathers the following data.

($ in Thousands)		Unadjusted Income Statement Items	
Beginning pension obligation	$4,545	Operating profit	$25,000
Beginning plan assets	$4,327	Interest expense	($1,300)
		Other income	$350
Service costs	$404	Income before taxes	$24,050
Interest costs	$275		
Loss due to change in actuarial assumptions during the year	$42		
Benefits paid	$560		
Expected return on plan assets	$200		
Actual return on plan assets	$176		
Contributions to plan	$895		

While reading through the annual reports for Two Bear, Reynolds notes that Two Bear has a share-based compensation plan in place. Being unaware of the accounting treatment of share-based compensation plans, Reynolds consults with Reed as to how they are treated.

7. In responding to Reynolds's question about the characteristics of a defined benefit pension plan, Reed would have *most accurately* told her that in a defined benefit plan:
   A. the employee's actual benefit will depend on the future value of the pension plan's assets.
   B. the amount of the future obligation is based on a plan formula and must be estimated in the current period.
   C. a firm's pension benefit obligation (PBO) is the actuarial present value of all future benefits earned to date based on present salary levels.

8. In explaining the compensation growth rate to Reynolds, Reed would have *most accurately* told her that reducing the compensation growth rate will:
   A. increase periodic pension cost in P&L.
   B. result in lower future pension payments, lower current service cost, and lower interest cost.
   C. reduce future pension payments, and the projected benefit obligation (PBO) will be higher.

9. What is the typical assumption regarding the ultimate health care trend rate?
   A. Inflation rate in health care costs will taper off to zero long term.
   B. Inflation rate in health care costs will decline over time to a lower, constant rate sometime in the future.
   C. Expected growth in health care costs causes the ultimate health care trend rate to increase over time and then become constant.

10. The balance sheet liability or asset of Two Bear's defined benefit pension fund for the end of period is *closest* to:
    A. an asset of $132.
    B. an asset of $174.
    C. a liability of $218.

11. After reclassifying operating and non-operating pension items appropriately, the adjusted operating profit is *closest* to:
    A. \$23,775.
    B. \$24,026.
    C. \$25,075.

12. The proper accounting treatment for the issuance and eventual exercise of employee stock options on 1,000 shares at \$15, granted and immediately vested on September 25, 2016, when the market value of the shares is \$18, and exercised on September 25, 2019, when the market value of the shares is \$27, is to:
    A. record no expense at the grant date and record an expense of \$9,000 at the exercise date.
    B. record an expense on the grant date equal to the options' value based on a model of option pricing.
    C. spread the expense for the options, equal to their option pricing model value on the grant date over the three-year period.

TOPIC ASSESSMENT ANSWERS: FINANCIAL REPORTING AND ANALYSIS

1. **C** To calculate the reported net income effect, we begin by looking at how each security is classified. The corporate bonds are classified as held-to-maturity; preferred stock is a trading security; the Treasury bonds, package of mortgages, and index fund are classified as available-for-sale. For trading securities, dividends, interest, and both realized and unrealized losses count toward income. For securities classified held-to-maturity or available-for-sale, only dividends, interest, and realized gains count toward income.

Securities	Dividends/ Interest	Unrealized Gains/Losses	Realized Gains/Losses	Accounting	Income Effect
Corporate Bonds 6.25%	$4,500,000	$2,500,000		Held-to-Maturity	$4,500,000
Treasury Bonds 6.75%	$8,500,000	–$6,000,000		Available-for-Sale	$8,500,000
S&P 500 Index Fund	$630,000	$4,000,000	$500,000	Available-for-Sale	$1,130,000
General Electric Preferred Stock	$740,000	$1,200,000		Trading	$1,940,000
Package of Residential Mortgages	$2,200,000	–$3,600,000	$3,000,000	Available-for-Sale	$5,200,000
Total					$21,270,000

(Study Session 5, Module 14.2, LOS 14.a)

2. **A** There is nothing wrong with how Gotham classifies the treasury bonds and mortgages, as the available-for-sale classification leaves plenty of flexibility. However, until recently, Gotham appeared to have no intention of selling securities. As such, no investments should have been classified as a trading security. (Study Session 5, Module 14.2, LOS 14.a)

3. **C** Ward must know which securities Gotham will sell so she can correctly classify the securities. The purchase date of the securities is irrelevant, and even if Ward knew how much Gotham intended to spend, it would not tell her which securities to reclassify. Return potential may have an effect on which securities the company chooses to sell, but that return information will not help Ward change the accounting policy. (Study Session 5, Module 14.3, LOS 14.a)

4. **A** The equity method appears to be the best way to account for Gotham's 35% stake in Klesten Research Center. Under the equity method, the proportional share of Klesten's operational loss is included in Gotham's income, which will decrease Gotham's total income. This decrease would also reduce the carrying value of the Klesten stake on the balance sheet, and the dividend would reduce it still further. Market value is irrelevant in this case, as is the increase in Klesten's debt level. (Study Session 5, Module 14.4, LOS 14.a)

5. **B** Securities held-to-maturity, like the corporate bonds, are supposed to be carried at amortized cost on the balance sheet even if a market price is available. The remaining statements reflect a lack of understanding. The mortgages are classified as available-for-sale and must be carried at market value. Gotham must either determine a market value for them or classify them as held-to-maturity. The maturity of a bond has nothing to do with its classification. Furthermore, the classification of a trading security has to do with intent to sell, not marketability. (Study Session 5, Module 14.2, LOS 14.a)

6. **B** The S&P 500 Index fund is an equity security, and equity securities cannot be held to maturity (they do not have a stated maturity). (Study Session 5, Module 14.2, LOS 14.a)

7. **B** In a defined benefit pension plan, the amount of the future obligation is based on a plan formula and has to be estimated in the current period. A *defined contribution plan* is dependent on the future value of the pension plan's assets. Under a defined benefit plan, the PBO is the actuarial present value of all future pension benefits earned to date based on *expected future* salary levels at an assumed future salary growth rate. (Study Session 5, Module 15.1, LOS 15.a)

8. **B** Reducing the compensation growth rate will reduce estimated future pension payments, thus reducing the projected benefit obligation (PBO) and improving the funded status of the plan. In addition, reducing the compensation growth rate will reduce current service cost, interest cost, and periodic pension cost in P&L. (Study Session 5, Module 15.5, LOS 15.d)

9. **B** The broadly held assumption is that health care costs, over time, will taper off to a lower, constant rate. This future inflation rate is defined as the ultimate health care trend rate. (Study Session 5, Module 15.5, LOS 15.d)

10. **A** The balance sheet asset for Two Bear is $132, calculated as follows:

($ in Thousands)	Beginning	Economic Expense		Benefits Paid/ Contributions		End of Period
Pension obligation	$4,545					**$4,706**
		Service costs	$404	Benefits paid	**–$560**	
		Interest costs	$275			
		Actuarial loss	$42			
		Total	**$721**			
Plan assets	$4,327					**$4,838**
		Actual return	**$176**	Contributions to plan	$895	
				Benefits paid	–$560	
				Total	**$335**	
Net funded position	–$218					**$132**

(Study Session 5, Module 15.4, LOS 15.c)

11. **C** The adjusted operating profit is $25,075, calculated as follows:

	Unadjusted	Adjustments	Adjusted
Operating profit	$25,000	($404 + $275 – $200) – $404 = +75	$25,075
Interest expense	–$1,300	–$275	–$1,575
Other income	$350	+$176	$526
Income before taxes	$24,050		**$24,026**

The adjustment to operating profit is to add back reported pension expense [calculated as service costs ($404) plus interest cost ($275) less expected return on assets ($200)], then subtract current service cost ($404). The adjustment to interest expense is to add interest cost ($275). The adjustment to other income is to add actual return on plan assets ($176).
(Study Session 5, Module 15.6, LOS 15.e)

12. **B** Under both U.S. GAAP and IFRS, the option expense for options that are fully vested on the grant date is equal to the value of the options using some option valuation model and is recorded on the grant date. (Study Session 5, Module 15.7, LOS 15.h)

The following is a review of the Corporate Finance (1) principles designed to address the learning outcome statements set forth by CFA Institute. Cross-Reference to CFA Institute Assigned Reading #20.

READING 20

Capital Budgeting

Study Session 7

EXAM FOCUS

This topic review covers various methods for evaluating capital projects and builds on the net present value (NPV) decision criterion that you learned at Level I. The first thing you need to know is that the relevant cash flows for evaluating a capital project are the incremental after-tax cash flows. Pay special attention to after-tax salvage value and the impact that depreciation has on determining cash flow. Once you have the cash flows down, it should be relatively easy to discount those cash flows and apply the proper NPV analysis for an expansion or replacement project, or decide between two mutually exclusive projects with different lives. Another concept to know is how various real options give managers flexibility with capital budgeting projects. Even if you are unsure how to handle the calculation of NPV involving real options, remember that the existence of options will always increase NPV. Finally, familiarize yourself with alternative concepts of calculating income, including economic income, economic profit, residual income, and claims analysis, and pay attention to the proper discount rate under each method. You'll see these concepts later in the Equity Valuation Study Sessions.

MODULE 20.1: CASH FLOW ESTIMATION

Video covering this content is available online.

Warm-Up: Basics of Capital Budgeting

The **capital budgeting process** is the process of identifying and evaluating capital projects; that is, projects where the cash flow to the firm will be received over a period longer than a year. Any corporate decisions with an impact on future earnings can be examined using this framework. Decisions about whether to buy a new machine, expand business in another geographic area, move the corporate headquarters to Cleveland, or replace a delivery truck, to name a few, can be examined using a capital budgeting analysis.

Categories of Capital Budgeting Projects

Capital budgeting projects may be divided into the following categories:

- *Replacement projects to maintain the business* are normally made without detailed analysis. The only issues are whether the existing operations should continue and, if so, whether existing procedures or processes should be maintained.
- *Replacement projects for cost reduction* determine whether equipment that is obsolete, but still usable, should be replaced. A fairly detailed analysis is necessary in this case.
- *Expansion projects* are taken on to expand the business and involve a complex decision-making process since they require an explicit forecast of future demand. A very detailed analysis is required.
- *New product or market* development also entails a complex decision-making process that will require a detailed analysis due to the large amount of uncertainty involved.
- *Mandatory projects* may be required by a governmental agency or insurance company and typically involve safety-related or environmental concerns. These projects typically generate little to no revenue, but they accompany new revenue-producing projects undertaken by the company.
- *Other projects*. Some projccts are not easily analyzed through the capital budgeting process. Such projects may include a pet project of senior management (e.g., corporate perks), or a high-risk endeavor that is difficult to analyze with typical capital budgeting assessment methods (e.g., research and development projects).

Principles of Capital Budgeting

The capital budgeting process involves five key principles:

1. *Decisions are based on cash flows, not accounting income*. The relevant cash flows to consider as part of the capital budgeting process are **incremental cash flows**, the changes in cash flows that will occur if the project is undertaken.

   Sunk costs are costs that cannot be avoided, even if the project is not undertaken. Since these costs are not affected by the accept/reject decision, they should not be included in the analysis. An example of a sunk cost is a consulting fee paid to a marketing research firm to estimate demand for a new product prior to a decision on the project.

   Externalities are the effects the acceptance of a project may have on other firm cash flows. The primary one is a negative externality called **cannibalization**, which occurs when a new project takes sales from an existing product. When considering externalities, the full implication of the new project (loss in sales of existing products) should be taken into account. An example of cannibalization is when a soft drink company introduces a diet version of an existing beverage. The analyst should subtract the lost sales of the existing beverage from the expected new sales of the diet version when estimating incremental project cash flows. A positive externality exists when doing the project would have a positive effect on sales of a firm's other project lines.

2. *Cash flows are based on opportunity costs.* **Opportunity costs** are cash flows that a firm will lose by undertaking the project under analysis. These are cash flows generated by an asset the firm already owns that would be forgone if the project under consideration is undertaken. Opportunity costs should be included in project costs. For example, when building a plant, even if the firm already owns the land, the cost of the land should be charged to the project since it could be sold or rented to an outside party if not used.
3. *The timing of cash flows is important.* Capital budgeting decisions account for the time value of money, which means that cash flows received earlier are worth more than cash flows to be received later.
4. *Cash flows are analyzed on an after-tax basis.* The impact of taxes must be considered when analyzing all capital budgeting projects. Firm value is based on cash flows they get to keep, not those they send to the government.
5. *Financing costs are reflected in the project's required rate of return.* The required rate of return is a function of its risk. Ordinarily, the level of risk is measured relative to the firm's overall risk and the required return relative to the firm's cost of capital. Only projects that are expected to return more than the cost of the capital needed to fund them will increase the value of the firm.

Modified Accelerated Cost Recovery System (MACRS)

The choice of depreciation method has important implications for the after-tax cash flows of a capital project. Most countries specify which depreciation methods are acceptable to use for tax purposes. In the United States, most companies use straight-line depreciation for financial reporting and the **modified accelerated cost recovery system** (MACRS) for tax purposes. For capital budgeting purposes, we should use the same depreciation method used for tax reporting since capital budgeting analysis is based on after-tax cash flows and not accounting income.

Under MACRS, assets are classified into 3-, 5-, 7-, or 10-year classes, and each year's depreciation is determined by the applicable recovery percentage given in Figure 20.1.

Figure 20.1: Recovery Allowance Percentage for Personal Property

Ownership Year	Class of Investment			
	3-Year	5-Year	7-Year	10-Year
1	33%	20%	14%	10%
2	45	32	25	18
3	15	19	17	14
4	7	12	13	12
5		11	9	9
6		6	9	7
7			9	7
8			4	7
9				7
10				6
11				3
	100%	100%	100%	100%

Buildings are 39-year assets: 1.3% in years 1 and 40 and 100 / 39 = 2.6% in the other years.

PROFESSOR'S NOTE

You do not need to memorize the MACRS tables, but you should be prepared to use MACRS or any other accelerated depreciation method if you need to compute incremental cash flows for a capital budgeting project.

The **half-year convention** under MACRS assumes that the asset is placed in service in the middle of the first year. The effect of this is to extend the recovery period of a 3-year class asset to four calendar years (33%, 45%, 15%, 7%) and a 5-year asset to six calendar years (20%, 32%, 19%, 12%, 11%, 6%).

The **depreciable basis** is equal to the purchase price plus any shipping or handling and installation costs. The basis is not adjusted for salvage value regardless of whether the accelerated or straight-line method is used (however, the formula for computing depreciation expense differs between straight-line and accelerated depreciation).

LOS 20.a: Calculate the yearly cash flows of expansion and replacement capital projects and evaluate how the choice of depreciation method affects those cash flows.

CFA® Program Curriculum, Volume 3, page 27

Generally, we can classify incremental cash flows for capital projects as (1) initial investment outlay, (2) operating cash flow over the project's life, and (3) terminal-year cash flow.

- **Initial investment outlay** is the up-front costs associated with the project. Components are price, which includes shipping and installation (FCInv) and **investment in net working capital** (NWCInv).

  outlay = FCInv + NWCInv

  The investment in NWC must be included in the capital budgeting decision. Whenever a firm undertakes a new operation, product, or service, additional inventories are usually needed to support increased sales, and the increased additional sales lead to increases in accounts receivable. Accounts payable and accruals will probably also increase proportionally.

  The investment in net working capital is defined as the difference between the changes in non-cash current assets and changes in non-cash current liabilities (i.e., those other than short-term debt). Cash is excluded because it is generally assumed not to be an operating asset.

  $$\begin{aligned}\text{NWCInv} &= \Delta\text{non-cash current assets} - \Delta\text{non-debt current liabilities} \\ &= \Delta\text{NWC}\end{aligned}$$

  If NWCInv is *positive*, additional financing is required and represents a cash outflow because cash must be used to fund the net investment in current assets. (If negative, the project frees up cash, creating a cash inflow.) Note that at the termination of the project, the firm will expect to receive an end-of-project cash inflow (or outflow) equal to initial NWC when the need for the additional working capital ends.

- **After-tax operating cash flows** (CF) are the incremental cash inflows over the capital asset's economic life. Operating cash flows are defined as:

  $$\begin{aligned}\text{CF} &= (\text{S} - \text{C} - \text{D})(1 - \text{T}) + \text{D} \\ &= (\text{S} - \text{C})(1 - \text{T}) + (\text{TD})\end{aligned}$$

  where:
  S = sales
  C = cash operating costs
  D = depreciation expense
  T = marginal tax rate

  Although **depreciation** is a non-cash operating expense, it is an important part of determining operating cash flow because it reduces the amount of taxes paid by the firm. We can account for depreciation either by adding it back to net income from the project (as in the first cash flow formula) or by adding the tax savings caused by depreciation back to the project's after-tax gross profit (as in the second formula). In general, a higher depreciation expense will result in greater tax savings and higher cash flows. This means that accelerated depreciation methods will create higher after-tax cash flows for the project earlier in the project's life as compared to the straight-line method, resulting in a higher net present value (NPV) for the project.

PROFESSOR'S NOTE

Interest is not included in operating cash flows for capital budgeting purposes because it is incorporated into the project's cost of capital.

- **Terminal year after-tax non-operating cash flows** (TNOCF). At the end of the asset's life, there are certain cash inflows that occur. These are the after-tax salvage value and the return of the net working capital.

$$TNOCF = Sal_T + NWCInv - T\,(Sal_T - B_T)$$

where:
Sal_T = pre-tax cash proceeds from sale of fixed capital
B_T = book value of the fixed capital sold

PROFESSOR'S NOTE

The notation for this formula is somewhat confusing because *T* is used in two different ways: (1) as the marginal tax rate and (2) as a time subscript indicating year *T*, the final year of the project. If *T* shows up in a formula, assume it refers to the marginal tax rate unless it is subscripted.

Expansion Project Analysis

An expansion project is an investment in a new asset to increase both the size and earnings of a business.

EXAMPLE: Expansion project analysis

Mayco, Inc. would like to set up a new plant (expand). Currently, Mayco has an option to buy an existing building at a cost of $24,000. Necessary equipment for the plant will cost $16,000, including installation costs. The equipment falls into a MACRS 5-year class. The building falls into a MACRS 39-year class. The project would also require an initial investment of $12,000 in net working capital. The initial working capital investment will be made at the time of the purchase of the building and equipment.

The project's estimated economic life is four years. At the end of that time, the building is expected to have a market value of $15,000 and a book value of $21,816, whereas the equipment is expected to have a market value of $4,000 and a book value of $2,720.

Annual sales will be $80,000. The production department has estimated that variable manufacturing costs will total 60% of sales and that fixed overhead costs, excluding depreciation, will be $10,000 a year [costs: (0.60)80,000 + 10,000 = 58,000]. Depreciation expense will be determined for the year in accordance with the MACRS rate.

Mayco's marginal federal-plus-state tax rate is 40%; its cost of capital is 12%; and, for capital budgeting purposes, the company's policy is to assume that operating cash flows occur at the end of each year. The plant will begin operations immediately after the investment is made, and the first operating cash flows will occur exactly one year later.

Under MACRS, the pre-tax depreciation for the building and equipment is:

Year 1 = \$3,512; Year 2 = \$5,744; Year 3 = \$3,664; Year 4 = \$2,544

Compute the initial investment outlay, operating cash flow over the project's life, and the terminal-year cash flows for Mayco's expansion project. Then determine whether the project should be accepted using NPV analysis.

Answer:

Initial outlay:

initial outlay = price of building + price of equipment + NWCInv
= \$24,000 + \$16,000 + \$12,000 = \$52,000

Operating cash flows:

$$CF = (S - C)(1 - T) + DT$$
$$CF_1 = [(\$80{,}000 - 58{,}000)(0.6)] + (3{,}512)(0.4) = \$14{,}605$$
$$CF_2 = 13{,}200 + (5{,}744)(0.4) = \$15{,}498$$
$$CF_3 = 13{,}200 + (3{,}664)(0.4) = \$14{,}666$$
$$CF_4 = 13{,}200 + (2{,}544)(0.4) = \$14{,}218$$

Terminal year after-tax non-operating cash flows:

There are two elements to the terminal year cash flow (TNOCF): (1) return of net working capital and (2) salvage value of both the building and the equipment.

First calculate the after-tax terminal cash flows associated with the building and the equipment separately:

CF for building = \$15,000 – 0.4(\$15,000 – \$21,816) = \$17,726

CF for equipment = \$4,000 – 0.4(\$4,000 – \$2,720) = \$3,488

Then include the return of NWCInv:

TNOCF = \$17,726 + \$3,488 + \$12,000 = \$33,214

Note in this example the investment in NWC was positive (a use of cash resulting in a cash outflow), so the terminal value effect will be a cash inflow. Had the project freed up working capital, the initial investment in NWC would be negative (a cash inflow) and the terminal value effect would be a cash outflow. Also notice that the building was sold for less than book value. The loss on the building reduces taxes and results in a positive incremental cash flow equal to the tax savings.

Using the expansion project's relevant after-tax cash flows and given that Mayco has a cost of capital of 12%, the NPV for the project can be computed as:

$$NPV = -52{,}000 + \frac{\$14{,}605}{1.12^1} + \frac{\$15{,}498}{1.12^2} + \frac{\$14{,}666}{1.12^3} + \frac{\$14{,}218}{1.12^4} + \frac{\$33{,}214}{1.12^4} = \$13{,}978$$

IRR (from financial calculator) = 21.9%

Decision: Since NPV > 0 and the IRR > 12%, Mayco should accept the expansion project.

Study Session 7

PROFESSOR'S NOTE

Remember that you can use the time value functions of your calculator to quickly calculate NPV and IRR.

The TI BA II Plus keystrokes to calculate the 21.9% IRR for Mayco's new plant project are: [CF] [2nd] [CLR WORK] 52000 [+/-] [ENTER] [↓] 14605 [ENTER] [↓][↓] 15498 [ENTER] [↓][↓] 14666 [ENTER] [↓][↓] 47432 [ENTER] [↓] [IRR] [CPT]

Other Presentation Formats

There are two other formats for presenting the analysis of a capital budgeting project with which you should be familiar: (1) table format with cash flows collected by year, and (2) table format with cash flows collected by type. Be prepared to analyze a project when the cash flows are presented in either of these formats on the exam.

Figure 20.2 presents the analysis of the Mayco capital budgeting project with cash flows collected by year.

Figure 20.2: Mayco Project: Cash Flows Collected by Year

Year	0	1	2	3	4
Initial outlay:					
FCInv	– $40,000				
WCInv	– $12,000				
	– $52,000				
After-tax operating CFs:					
Sales		$80,000	$80,000	$80,000	$80,000
Cash operating expenses		58,000	58,000	58,000	58,000
Depreciation		3,512	5,744	3,664	2,544
Oper. income before taxes		18,488	16,256	18,336	19,456
Taxes on oper. income		7,395	6,502	7,334	7,782
Oper. income after taxes		11,093	9,754	11,002	11,674
Add back: depreciation		3,512	5,744	3,664	2,544
After tax oper. CF		14,605	15,498	14,666	14,218
Terminal year after-tax non-oper. CF (TNOCF)					
After-tax salvage value					21,214
Return of NWC					12,000
TNOCF					33,214
Total after-tax CF	–$52,000	$14,605	$15,498	$14,666	$47,432
NPV(12%)	**$13,978**				
IRR	**21.9%**				

Figure 20.3 presents the analysis of the Mayco capital budgeting project with cash flows collected by type.

Figure 20.3: Mayco Project: Cash Flows Collected by Type

Time	Type of CF	Before-Tax CF	After-Tax CF	PV at 12%
0	FCInv	–$40,000	–$40,000	–$40,000
0	NWCInv	–12,000	–12,000	–12,000
1 – 4	Sales – cash expenses	22,000	22,000 (1 – 0.4) = 13,200	40,093
1	Depreciation tax savings*	None	3,512 (0.4) = 1,405	1,255
2	Depreciation tax savings*	None	5,744(0.4) = 2,298	1,832
3	Depreciation tax savings*	None	3,664(0.4) = 1,466	1,043
4	Depreciation tax savings*	None	2,544(0.4) = 1,018	647
4	After-tax salvage value	19,000 = 15,000 + 4,000	21,214 (from Figure 20.2)	13,482
4	Return of NWCInv	12,000	12,000	7,626
			NPV =	**$13,978**

*Note that if straight-line depreciation is used, the depreciation tax savings is an annuity and you can calculate the present value of that annuity directly, rather than summing the present values of the individual depreciation tax savings for each year.

Study Session 7

Replacement Project Analysis

Replacement project analysis occurs when a firm must decide whether to replace an existing asset with a newer or better asset. There are two key differences in the analysis of a replacement project versus an expansion project. In a replacement project analysis we have to:

1. Reflect the sale of the old asset in the calculation of the initial outlay:

$$\text{outlay} = \text{FCInv} + \text{NWCInv} - \text{Sal}_0 + \text{T}\,(\text{Sal}_0 - \text{B}_0)$$

2. Calculate the incremental operating cash flows as the cash flows from the new asset minus the cash flows from the old asset:

$$\Delta\text{CF} = (\Delta\text{S} - \Delta\text{C})(1 - \text{T}) + \Delta\text{DT}$$

3. Compute the terminal year non-operating cash flow:

$$\text{TNOCF} = (\text{Sal}_{\text{TNew}} - \text{Sal}_{\text{TOld}}) + \text{NWCInv} - \text{T}[(\text{Sal}_{\text{TNew}} - \text{B}_{\text{TNew}}) - (\text{Sal}_{\text{TOld}} - \text{B}_{\text{TOld}})]$$

EXAMPLE: Replacement project analysis

Suppose Mayco wants to replace an existing printer with a new high-speed copier. The existing printer was purchased ten years ago at a cost of $15,000. The printer is being depreciated using straight line basis assuming a useful life of 15 years and no salvage value (i.e., its annual depreciation is \$1,000). If the existing printer is not replaced, it will have zero market value at the end of its useful life.

The new high-speed copier can be purchased for \$24,000 (including freight and installation). Over its 5-year life, it will reduce labor and raw materials usage sufficiently to cut annual operating costs from \$14,000 to \$8,000.

It is estimated that the new copier can be sold for \$4,000 at the end of five years; this is its estimated salvage value. The old printer's current market value is \$2,000, which is below its \$5,000 book value. If the new copier is acquired, the old printer will be sold to another company.

The company's marginal federal-plus-state tax rate is 40%, and the replacement copier is of slightly below-average risk. Net working capital requirements will also increase by \$3,000 at the time of replacement. By an IRS ruling, the new copier falls into the 3-year MACRS class. The project's cost of capital is set at 11.5%.

Under the MACRS system, the pre-tax depreciation for the equipment is:

Year 1 = \$7,920; Year 2 = \$10,800; Year 3 = \$3,600; Year 4 = \$1,680;
Year 5 = \$0

Compute the initial investment outlay, operating cash flow over the project's life, and the terminal-year cash flows for Mayco's replacement project. Then determine whether the project should be accepted using NPV analysis.

Answer:

Initial investment outlay:

$$\begin{aligned}\text{initial outlay} &= \$24{,}000 + \$3{,}000 - \$2{,}000 + 0.4\,(\$2{,}000 - \$5{,}000)\\ &= \$23{,}800\end{aligned}$$

Operating cash flows:

$$\begin{aligned}
CF_t &= [(\Delta S - \Delta C)(1 - T)] + \Delta DT\\
\Delta S &= 0\\
\Delta C &= -6{,}000\\
\Delta DT &= (\text{MACRSD} - 1{,}000)(0.4)\\
CF_1 &= [0 - (-6{,}000)](1 - 0.4) + (7{,}920 - 1{,}000)(0.4) = \$6{,}368\\
CF_2 &= [0 - (-6{,}000)](1 - 0.4) + (10{,}800 - 1{,}000)(0.4) = \$7{,}520\\
CF_3 &= [0 - (-6{,}000)](1 - 0.4) + (3{,}600 - 1{,}000)(0.4) = \$4{,}640\\
CF_4 &= [0 - (-6{,}000)](1 - 0.4) + (1{,}680 - 1{,}000)(0.4) = \$3{,}872\\
CF_5 &= [0 - (-6{,}000)](1 - 0.4) + (0 - 1{,}000)(0.4) = \$3{,}200
\end{aligned}$$

PROFESSOR'S NOTE:

When calculating depreciation, we need to decrease the new printer depreciation expense by the depreciation that would have occurred with the old printer, which was \$1,000 per year.

Terminal year flow:

- Sal (new machine) = \$4,000
- Sal (old) = 0 (after five more years)—this is given in the first paragraph.
- NWCInv (given) = \$3,000
- profit on salvage of new = 4,000 – 0 (*book value*) = 4,000
- profit on salvage of old = 0
- Tax on (4,000 – 0) at 40% = 1,600

$$TNOCF = (Sal_{New} - Sal_{Old}) + NWCInv - T[(Sal_{TNew} - B_{TNew}) - (Sal_{TOld} - B_{TOld})]$$

$$TNOCF = (4,000 - 0) + 3,000 - 0.4[(4,000 - 0) - (0)] = \$5,400$$

Given Mayco's incremental cash flows and a cost of capital of 11.5%, net present value (NPV) for the project can be computed as:

$$NPV = -23,800 + \frac{6,368}{1.115^1} + \frac{7,520}{1.115^2} + \frac{4,640}{1.115^3} + \frac{3,872}{1.115^4} + \frac{3,200 + 5,400}{1.115^5}$$
$$= -\$1,197.28$$

$$IRR = 9.46\%$$

Decision: Since the NPV is negative and the IRR is less than the cost of capital, Mayco should not replace the printer with the new copier.

LOS 20.b: Explain how inflation affects capital budgeting analysis.

CFA® Program Curriculum, Volume 3, page 38

Inflation is a complication that must be considered as part of the capital budgeting process.

- **Analyzing nominal or real cash flows.** Nominal cash flows reflect the impact of inflation, while real cash flows are adjusted downward to remove inflation effects. Although either type of cash flow can be used in the capital budgeting process, it is important to match the type of cash flows with the discount rate. Nominal cash flows should be discounted at a nominal discount rate, while real cash flows should be discounted at a real discount rate.
- **Changes in inflation affect project profitability.** If inflation is higher than expected, future project cash flows are worth less, and the value of the project will be lower than expected. The opposite is also true, however. If inflation turns out to be lower than originally expected, future cash flows from the project will be worth more, effectively increasing the project's value.
- **Inflation reduces the tax savings from depreciation.** If inflation is higher than expected, the firm's real taxes paid to the government are effectively increased because the depreciation tax shelter is less valuable. This is because the depreciation charge, which is based upon the asset's purchase price, is less than it would be if recalculated at current (i.e., inflated) prices.
- **Inflation decreases the value of payments to bondholders.** Bondholders receive fixed payments that are effectively worth less as inflation increases. This means

that higher than expected inflation effectively shifts wealth to issuing firms at bondholders' expense.

- **Inflation may affect revenues and costs differently.** If prices of goods change at a different rate than the prices for inputs used to create those goods, the firm's after-tax cash flows may be better or worse than expected.

MODULE QUIZ 20.1

To best evaluate your performance, enter your quiz answers online.

1. Which of the following factors is a firm *least likely* to consider when appropriately evaluating a new project?
   A. The depreciation expense tax shield on the new project.
   B. The current market value of any equipment to be replaced.
   C. Previous expenditures associated with a market test to determine the feasibility of the project.

Use the following information to answer Questions 2 through 4.

- Mayco, Inc. is considering the purchase of a new machine for $60,000. The machine will reduce manufacturing costs by $5,000 annually.
- Mayco will use the modified accelerated cost recovery system (MACRS) accelerated method (5-year asset) to depreciate the machine and expects to sell the machine at the end of its 6-year operating life for $10,000. Use the MACRS table in Figure 1. (Remember, you don't have to memorize the MACRS tables!)
- The firm expects to be able to reduce net working capital by $15,000 when the machine is installed, but required working capital will return to the original level when the machine is sold after six years.
- Mayco's marginal tax rate is 40%, and it uses a 12% cost of capital to evaluate projects of this nature.

2. The first year's MACRS depreciation and the initial cash outlay are *closest* to:
   A. $10,000 depreciation and $60,000 initial outlay.
   B. $12,000 depreciation and $45,000 initial outlay.
   C. $12,000 depreciation and $60,000 initial outlay.
3. The first year's operating cash flow and terminal year's cash flow excluding the last year's operating cash flow are *closest* to:
   A. $4,800 OCF and –$4,000 CF.
   B. $7,800 OCF and –$4,000 CF.
   C. $7,800 OCF and –$9,000 CF.
4. Suppose for this question only that the machine is depreciated to zero over six years using the straight-line method and all other information is the same. The NPV of the project is *closest* to:
   A. –$20,780.
   B. –$18,753.
   C. –$17,125.

5. An analyst has collected the following information on a replacement project:

Purchase price of the new machine	$8,000
Shipping and installation charge	2,000
Sale price of old machine	6,000
Book value of old machine	2,000
Inventory increase if the new machine is installed	3,000
Accounts payable increase if the new machine is installed	1,000
Marginal tax rate	25%

The initial cash flow is *closest* to:
A. –$10,000.
B. –$7,000.
C. –$3,000.

6. Michael Eastman and David Mann are part of the management team responsible for evaluating capital projects at Anasi, Inc. The tax laws in the country where Anasi is located allow the company to choose the depreciation method for tax purposes. Eastman is trying to explain to Mann the importance of considering depreciation when making capital budgeting decisions. Eastman makes the following statements:

Statement 1: Depreciation is a non-cash expense; however, it is an important part of determining incremental cash flows because it reduces the interest expense paid by the firm.

Statement 2: If we use the double-declining balance method of depreciation for tax purposes, the NPV of the project we are considering should be higher than if we use the straight-line method.

Is Eastman *most likely* correct or incorrect with regards to the statements?
A. Both statements are correct.
B. Only one of the statements is correct.
C. Neither statement is correct.

7. Bruce Spang is teaching a finance class about the impact of inflation on capital budgeting analysis. Spang makes the following statements to his class:

Statement 1: Project cash flows should always be discounted at the real interest rate in order to avoid double counting inflation in the capital budgeting analysis.

Statement 2: Inflation tends to affect costs and revenues for a firm proportionally because firms are generally able to pass price increases of inputs along to consumers as price increases in the final product.

Is Spang *most likely* correct or incorrect with regards to the statements?
A. Both statements are correct.
B. Only one of the statements is correct.
C. Neither statement is correct.

Video covering this content is available online.

MODULE 20.2: EVALUATION OF PROJECTS AND DISCOUNT RATE ESTIMATION

LOS 20.c: Evaluate capital projects and determine the optimal capital project in situations of 1) mutually exclusive projects with unequal lives, using either the least common multiple of lives approach or the equivalent annual annuity approach, and 2) capital rationing.

CFA® Program Curriculum, Volume 3, page 38

Mutually Exclusive Projects With Different Lives

When two projects are *mutually exclusive*, the firm may choose one project or the other, but not both. If mutually exclusive projects have different lives, and the projects are expected to be replaced indefinitely as they wear out, an adjustment needs to be made in the decision-making process. There are two procedures to make this adjustment:

1. Least common multiple of lives approach.
2. Equivalent annual annuity (EAA) approach.

EXAMPLE: Projects with unequal lives

Mayco, Inc. is planning to modernize its production facilities. Mayco is considering the purchase of either (1) a book press with a useful life of six years *or* (2) an offset printer, which has a useful life of three years. The time lines presented in the following two figures show the cash flows, NPVs, and IRRs for both of these mutually exclusive projects.

Expected Cash Flows (in dollars) for Book Press

0	1	2	3	4	5	6
–20,000	4,000	7,000	6,500	6,000	5,500	5,000

NPV_{press} @ 12% = \$3,245.47; IRR = 17.5%.

Expected Cash Flows (in dollars) for the Offset Printer Project

0	1	2	3
–10,000	3,500	6,500	6,000

$NPV_{printer}$ @ 12% = \$2,577.44; IRR = 25.20%.

Evaluate these projects using both the least common multiple of lives approach, and the equivalent annual annuity approach, assuming whichever process is chosen will be repeated indefinitely.

Answer:

Least common multiple of lives method

The NPVs indicate the book press should be selected:

$$NPV_{press} = \$3,245.47 > NPV_{printer} = \$2,577.44$$

However, the IRRs recommend the opposite decision because the IRR of the offset printer is larger than the IRR of the book press. To make the comparison meaningful, we can find the NPVs for the two projects over the least common multiple of lives.

In this case, the least common multiple of lives is six years. This means that, for the printer, we will need to buy another 3-year printer in year 3 to make it comparable to the 6-year press. Assuming no changes in annual cash flows and a constant cost of capital of 12%, we can compute the NPV of the two back-to-back offset printers using the process illustrated in the next figure.

PROFESSOR'S NOTE:

A project where equipment will need to be replaced every few years is often called a replacement chain. The key is to analyze the entire chain and not just the first link in the chain.

Replacement Chain for Offset Printer

0	1	2	3	4	5	6
–10,000	3,500	6,500	6,000	3,500	6,500	6,000
			– 10,000			
			– 4,000			

$NPV_{\text{chained printers}}$ @ 12% = \$4,412.01; IRR = 25.2%.

Decision: The NPV of this extended printer project is \$4,412, and its IRR is 25.2%.

Since the \$4,412 extended NPV of two chained-together 3-year printers (six years total) is greater than the \$3,245.50 NPV of the offset press, the printer should be selected.

The next figure illustrates that the value of the cash flow streams of two consecutive printers can be summarized by two separate project NPVs: one at year 0 representing the value of the initial project and one at year 3 representing the value of the replication project.

Replacement Chain NPVs

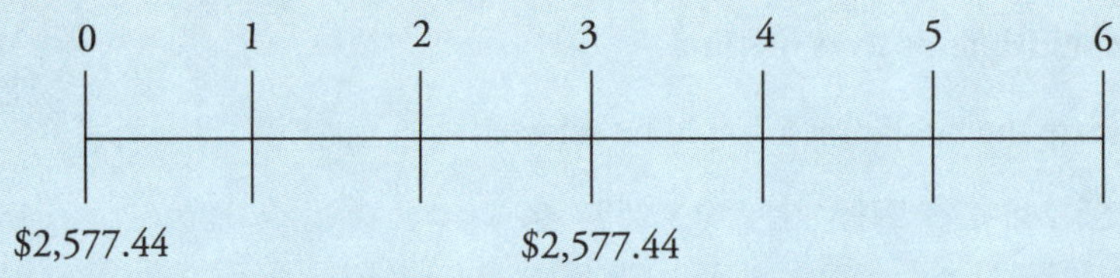

NPV @ 12% = $4,412.01 = 2,577.44 + (2,577.44/1.12^3)

The present value of these two cash flows, when discounted at 12%, is $4,412, so we again come to the conclusion that the printer should be selected.

Equivalent Annual Annuity (EAA) Approach

The EAA approach is a simpler approach to evaluating mutually exclusive projects with different lives. The EAA approach finds the sequence of equal annual payments with a present value that is equal to the project's NPV. The resulting calculation is an annual payment that allows for an "apples to apples" comparison of projects with different lives.

As demonstrated in the next example, there are three steps to the EAA approach.

EXAMPLE: EAA approach

Evaluate the offset printer and the book press from the preceding example using the EAA approach.

Answer:

Step 1: Find each project's NPV.

NPV_{press} = $3,245

$NPV_{printer}$ = $2,577

Step 2: Find an annuity (EAA) with a present value equal to the project's NPV over its individual life at the WACC.

EAA_{press}: PV = –3,245; FV = 0; N = 6; I = 12;

compute PMT = $789

$EAA_{printer}$: PV = –2,577; FV = 0; N = 3; I = 12;

compute PMT = $1,073

Note the negative sign in front of the PV value. This is for the calculator's sign convention and not to signify that the NPV is negative.

Step 3: Select the project with the highest EAA. In this example, the printer should be accepted because:

$EAA_{printer} > EAA_{press}$

PROFESSOR'S NOTE

As you can see, either of the two methods will lead to the same conclusion. However, per the LOS, you are expected to know both of them!

CAPITAL RATIONING

Ideally, firms will continue to invest in positive return NPV projects until the marginal returns equal the marginal cost of capital. Should a firm have insufficient capital to do this, it must ration its capital (allocate its funds) among the best possible combination of acceptable projects. **Capital rationing** is the allocation of a fixed amount of capital among the set of available projects that will maximize shareholder wealth. A firm with less capital than profitable (i.e., positive NPV) projects should choose the combination of projects it can afford to fund that has the greatest total NPV.

Note that capital rationing is not the optimal decision from the firm's perspective. More value would be created by investing in all positive NPV projects. Therefore, capital rationing violates market efficiency because society's resources are not allocated to their best use (i.e., to generate the highest return).

Hard capital rationing occurs when the funds allocated to managers under the capital budget cannot be increased. **Soft capital rationing** occurs when managers are allowed to increase their allocated capital budget if they can justify to senior management that the additional funds will create shareholder value.

EXAMPLE: Capital rationing (1)

Mayco has a $2,000 capital budget and has the opportunity to invest in five projects. The initial investment and NPV of the projects are described in the next figure. Determine in which projects Mayco should invest.

Projects Available to Mayco

	Investment Outlay	NPV
Project A	–$800	$300
Project B	–$500	$180
Project C	–$400	$100
Project D	–$350	$85
Project E	–$300	–$50

Answer:

Projects A, B, C, and D are all profitable. However, the cost of taking on all four projects would be $2,050, which would exceed the capital budget. Mayco should choose Projects A, B, and C, which have a total NPV of $580 and a total outlay of $1,700. These three projects maximize the NPV while not exceeding the capital budget constraint of $2,000. The remaining $300 in the capital budget could then be used elsewhere in the company. Note that Project E is not considered acceptable, regardless of the availability of capital, because of its negative NPV.

EXAMPLE: Capital rationing (2)

Mayco has a $2,000 capital budget and has the opportunity to invest in five different projects. The initial investment and NPV of the projects are described in the following figure. Determine in which projects Mayco should invest.

Projects Available to Mayco

	Investment Outlay	NPV
Project F	–$1,200	$500
Project G	–$1,000	$480
Project H	–$800	$300
Project I	–$450	$150
Project J	–$200	$40

Answer:

All of the projects are profitable, but with a capital budget of only $2,000, Mayco should choose Projects G, H, and J that have a combined NPV of $820.

Note that choosing Projects G, H, and J, means that Project F, which has the highest NPV, is not chosen. If Project F were chosen, the next best choice would be Project H, which would max out the capital budget with a combined NPV of only $800. Remember, the goal with capital rationing is to maximize the overall NPV within the capital budget, not necessarily to select the individual projects with the highest NPV.

LOS 20.d: Explain how sensitivity analysis, scenario analysis, and Monte Carlo simulation can be used to assess the stand-alone risk of a capital project.

CFA® Program Curriculum, Volume 3, page 42

Sensitivity analysis involves changing an input (independent) variable to see how sensitive the dependent variable is to the input variable. For example, by varying sales, we could determine how sensitive a project's NPV is to changes in sales, assuming that all other factors are held constant. The key to sensitivity analysis is to only change one variable at a time.

With sensitivity analysis, we start with the base-case scenario. Base case would be the NPV we determined by using the project's input estimates. Now we change one of the selected variables by a fixed percentage point above and below the base case, noting the effect this change has on the project's NPV. We could do this for all the variables used in the analysis.

EXAMPLE: Sensitivity analysis

Ferndale Inc. is analyzing a capital budgeting expansion project with the following cash flow forecasts:

- 3-year project
- Unit sales = 1,500 per year

- Price = $50.00
- Variable cost = $20.00 per unit
- Fixed cost = $5,000 per year
- FCInv = $60,000
- Depreciated straight-line over three years to book value of zero
- NWCInv = $15,000
- Salvage value at end of three years = $10,000
- Marginal tax rate = 40%
- Cost of capital = 15%

The base case NPV and IRR are $11,871 and 23.5%, respectively.

The following figure includes a sensitivity analysis of the key inputs assuming a 20% increase and decrease in each variable, holding the others constant. (We haven't provided the solutions here because we want to focus on sensitivity analysis, but feel free to check our answers!)

Ferndale Inc. Sensitivity Analysis

Input Estimate		Down 20%	Base Case	Up 20%
Unit sales	NPV	**–$458**	$11,871	**$24,200**
	IRR	**14.7%**	23.5%	**32.2%**
Price	NPV	**–$8,678**	$11,871	**$32,420**
	IRR	**8.6%**	23.5%	**37.8%**
Variable costs	NPV	**$20,091**	$11,871	**$3,651**
	IRR	**29.3%**	23.5%	**17.6%**
Fixed costs	NPV	**$13,241**	$11,871	**$10,501**
	IRR	**24.5%**	23.5%	**22.5%**
Salvage value	NPV	**$11,083**	$11,871	**$12,660**
	IRR	**23%**	23.5%	**24%**

To which inputs are the NPV and the IRR estimates (1) most sensitive and (2) least sensitive?

Answer:

The project's NPV and IRR are most sensitive to changes in price because when price drops by 20% the NPV goes from positive to negative. The project is also sensitive to changes in unit sales because a 20% drop in sales will generate a negative NPV. The project appears to be least sensitive to changes in the estimate of salvage value and fixed costs.

Scenario analysis is a risk analysis technique that considers both the sensitivity of some key output variable (e.g., NPV) to changes in a key input variable (e.g., sales) and the likely probability distribution of these variables. The key difference between scenario analysis and sensitivity analysis is that scenario analysis allows for changes in multiple input variables all at once. In scenario analysis, we study the different possible scenarios, such as *worst case*, *best case*, and *base case*.

A scenario analysis for the Ferndale capital budgeting project is shown in Figure 20.4. Notice that in the worst case scenario unit sales, price, and salvage value are down 20%, while fixed and variable costs are up 20%. In the best case scenario, unit sales, price, and salvage value are up 20%, while costs are down 20%. In fact, the worst case scenario is so bad that the IRR is negative.

Figure 20.4: Ferndale Inc. Scenario Analysis

	Worst Case	Base Case	Best Case
Unit sales	Down 20%	1,500	Up 20%
Price	Down 20%	$50	Up 20%
Variable costs	Up 20%	$20	Down 20%
Fixed costs	Up 20%	$5,000	Down 20%
Salvage value	Down 20%	$10,000	Up 20%
NPV	**–$25,632**	**$11,871**	**$60,882**
IRR	**–4.4%**	**23.5%**	**56.8%**

Simulation analysis (or **Monte Carlo simulation**) results in a probability distribution of project NPV outcomes, rather than just a limited number of outcomes as with sensitivity or scenario analysis (e.g., base case, best case, worst case). The steps in simulation analysis are as follows:

Step 1: Assume a specific probability distribution for each input variable. For example, we might assume that unit sales are normally distributed with a mean of 100,000 and a standard deviation of 15,000, unit prices are normally distributed with a mean of $40 and a standard deviation of $5, and so on for each input variable. We don't necessarily have to assume a normal distribution for each variable, however.

Step 2: Simulate a random draw from the assumed distribution of each input variable. That results in a single value for each of the inputs. For example, our first draw might be unit sales of 85,000, a unit price of $42.00, and so on.

Step 3: Given each of the inputs from Step 2, calculate the project NPV.

Step 4: Repeat Step 2 and Step 3 10,000 times.

Step 5: Calculate the mean NPV, the standard deviation of the NPV, and the correlation of NPV with each input variable.

Step 6: Graph the resulting 10,000 NPV outcomes as a probability distribution.

For example, our NPV probability distribution for a simulation analysis of the Ferndale expansion project might look like Figure 20.5. Notice that the probability distribution in Figure 20.5 is not symmetrical or necessarily perfectly normal. That will typically be the case, although with a large number of observations, the distribution is likely to be approximately normal.

Figure 20.5: Example of Simulation Analysis

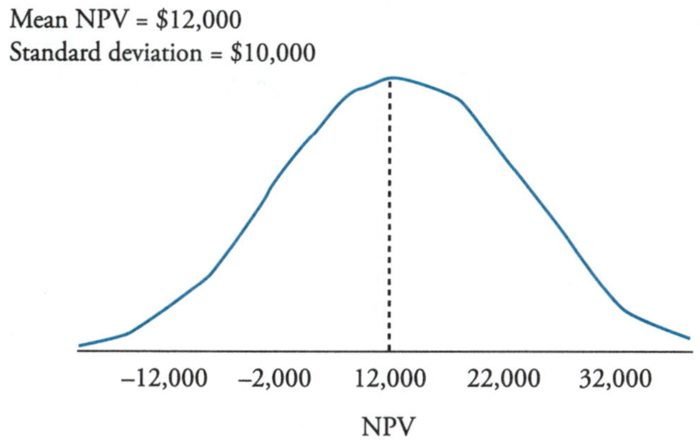

LOS 20.e: Explain and calculate the discount rate, based on market risk methods, to use in valuing a capital project.

CFA® Program Curriculum, Volume 3, page 49

In the capital asset pricing model (CAPM), risk is separated into systematic and unsystematic components. Unsystematic, or company-specific, risk can be diversified away, while systematic, or market, risk cannot be diversified away. A diversified investor is compensated for taking on systematic risk, but not unsystematic risk. In a capital budgeting context, beta, a systematic risk measure, is appropriate for measuring project or asset risk when a company is, or the company's investors are, diversified. The project's or asset's beta in conjunction with the CAPM can be used to determine the appropriate discount rate for the asset or project.

PROFESSOR'S NOTE

The CAPM is also covered in the Study Sessions covering Equity Valuation and Portfolio Management.

Beta risk is based on the equation of the CAPM, or the security market line (SML), which defines a project's required rate of return (discount rate) using the equation:

$$R_{project} = R_F + \beta_{project}\,[E(R_{MKT}) - R_F]$$

where

R_F = risk-free rate

$\beta_{project}$ = project beta

$E(R_{MKT}) - R_F$ = market risk premium

EXAMPLE: Using the SML to estimate the discount rate for a capital project

Compute the NPV for a 3-year project that has a beta of 1.2. The initial investment is $1,000, and the project will generate annual cash flows of $400. Use a risk-free interest rate of 8% and an expected market return of 13%.

Answer:

The appropriate discount rate for the project is:

$$R_{project} = R_F + \beta_{project} [E(R_{MKT}) - R_F] = 8\% + [1.2(13\% - 8\%)] = 14\%$$

The project's NPV at a cost of capital of 14% is –\$71.35. You can either calculate the NPV using the NPV function on your financial calculator or the following formula:

$$NPV = -\$1,000 + \frac{\$400}{1.14} + \frac{\$400}{1.14^2} + \frac{\$400}{1.14^3} = -\$71.35$$

Using a project's beta to determine discount rates is important when the risk of a project is different from the risk of the overall company. Such a project-specific discount rate is also called a **hurdle rate**. Hurdle rates vary from project to project. Simply using the company's weighted average cost of capital (WACC) will overstate the required return for a conservative (low beta) project and will understate the required return for an aggressive (high beta) project.

MODULE QUIZ 20.2

To best evaluate your performance, enter your quiz answers online.

1. Which of the following statements about capital budgeting is *most accurate*?
   - A. The capital budgeting analysis for expansion and replacement projects is the same.
   - B. If the fixed assets are sold for book value, terminal year after-tax non-operating cash flows equal the cash proceeds from the sale of fixed capital plus the recovery of net working capital.
   - C. The replacement decision involves an analysis of two independent projects where the relevant cash flows include the initial investment, additional depreciation, and the terminal value.

2. Mayco, Inc. wants to buy a new printer. Mayco is looking at two mutually exclusive projects: A and B.
   - Printer A costs \$100,000 and generates positive after-tax cash flows of \$75,000 at the end of each of the next two years.
   - Printer B also costs \$100,000 and has positive after-tax cash flows of \$50,000 at the end of each of the next four years.
   - Printer A can be replaced at the end of its life with the cash inflows and outflows remaining the same. It has no salvage value.
   - Both printers are expected to be replaced indefinitely with the same type at the end of their useful lives.

   Assuming a 4-year replacement chain and a 10% cost of capital, which of the following choices is *closest* to the net present value (NPV) of Printer A and Printer B?

	NPV (A)	NPV (B)
A.	\$63,996	\$56,884
B.	\$55,095	\$58,493
C.	\$75,221	\$3,786

3. Mayco, Inc. is evaluating two mutually exclusive investment projects. Assume both projects can be repeated indefinitely. Printer A has an NPV of $20,000 over a 3-year life, and Printer B has a NPV of $25,000 over a 5-year life. The project types are equally risky, and the firm's cost of capital is 12%. Which of the following choices is *closest* to the equivalent annual annuity (EAA) of project A and B?

	EAA (A)	EAA (B)
A.	$8,327	$6,935
B.	$3,567	$5,326
C.	$7,592	$7,592

4. Which of the following statements about replacement decisions is *least accurate*?
   A. Any loss on the sale of the old equipment is multiplied by the tax rate and is treated as an initial cash outflow.
   B. The present value of additional depreciation expense on the new equipment (as compared to depreciation on the old equipment) multiplied by the tax rate is treated as an operating inflow.
   C. The present value of the after-tax benefits of a cost reduction resulting from a new investment is treated as an operating inflow.
5. Elaine Smith has been given responsibility for developing General Pacific Company's capital budgeting policy manual. In a meeting with her team, she makes the following statements:

   Statement 1: The equivalent annual annuity approach assumes continuous replacements can and will be made each time the asset's life ends.

   Statement 2: In comparing mutually exclusive projects with unequal lives, you should always choose the project that has the highest NPV.

   Is Smith *most likely* correct or incorrect with regards to the statements?
   A. Both statements are correct.
   B. Only one of the statements is correct.
   C. Neither statement is correct.
6. Which of the following statements about Monte Carlo simulation is *least accurate*? Monte Carlo simulation:
   A. can be useful for estimating a project's stand-alone risk.
   B. is capable of using probability distributions for variables as input data.
   C. uses best- and worst-case scenarios to determine the most likely outcome.
7. Which of the following statements is *least accurate*?
   A. If a project is riskier than the firm's normal project, the firm should adjust the project's discount rate upward.
   B. In the absence of capital rationing, a firm should take all projects with a positive net present value.
   C. When capital is rationed, the projects with the highest IRRs should be selected.

8. Eldon Windows Inc. has an $80,000 capital budget and has the opportunity to invest in five different projects. The initial investment and NPV of the projects is shown in the table. In which combination of projects should Eldon Windows invest?

	Investment Outlay	NPV
Project 1	–$45,000	$18,000
Project 2	–$40,000	$16,000
Project 3	–$20,000	$9,000
Project 4	–$18,000	$8,000
Project 5	–$15,000	$4,000

A. Projects 1, 3, and 5.
B. Projects 2, 3, and 4.
C. Projects 1, 3, and 4.

9. Elaine Smith of General Pacific Company is analyzing a 5-year expansion project to increase manufacturing capacity. The project requires an investment in net working capital of $500,000 that will be recovered at the end of the project and has a cost of capital of 10%. In her analysis, Smith assumes that the two cash flows net out to zero over the life of the project, so she does not include a cash flow for net working capital at the beginning or the end of the project. Assuming she correctly analyzes all the other components of the project, Smith has *likely*:

A. overestimated the project's cash flow by approximately $310,000.
B. underestimated the project's net present value by approximately $310,000.
C. overestimated the project's net present value by approximately $190,000.

10. A company is analyzing two projects. Project A has a project beta of 1.2, and Project B has a beta of 0.6. The company's weighted average cost of capital is 10%. The risk-free rate is 5%, and the market risk premium is 9%. If the company incorrectly uses the company's weighted average cost of capital to calculate the NPV of both projects, will it overestimate or underestimate the NPV?

A. Overestimate NPV for both projects.
B. Underestimate NPV for both projects.
C. Overestimate one NPV, but not both projects.

Video covering this content is available online.

MODULE 20.3: REAL OPTIONS AND PITFALLS IN CAPITAL BUDGETING

LOS 20.f: Describe types of real options and evaluate a capital project using real options.

CFA® Program Curriculum, Volume 3, page 52

Real options allow managers to make future decisions that change the value of capital budgeting decisions made today. Real options are similar to financial call and put options in that they give the option holder the right, but not the obligation, to make a decision. The difference is that real options are based on real assets rather than financial assets and are contingent on future events. Real options offer managers flexibility that can improve the NPV estimates for individual projects.

Types of real options include the following:

- **Timing options** allow a company to delay making an investment with the hope of having better information in the future.
- **Abandonment options** are similar to put options. They allow management to abandon a project if the present value of the incremental cash flows from exiting a project exceeds the present value of the incremental cash flows from continuing a project.
- **Expansion options** are similar to call options. Expansion options allow a company to make additional investments in a project if doing so creates value.
- **Flexibility options** give managers choices regarding the operational aspects of a project. The two main forms are price-setting and production flexibility options.
  - *Price-setting* options allow the company to change the price of a product. For example, the company may raise prices if demand for a product is high in order to benefit from that demand without increasing production.
  - *Production-flexibility* options may include paying workers overtime, using different materials as inputs, or producing a different variety of product.
- **Fundamental options** are projects that are options themselves because the payoffs depend on the price of an underlying asset. For example, the payoff for a copper mine is dependent on the market price for copper. If copper prices are low, it may not make sense to open a copper mine, but if copper prices are high, opening the copper mine could be very profitable. The operator has the option to close the mine when prices are low and open it when prices are high.

A manager can use a number of different approaches for evaluating the profitability of an investment with real options. Examples of different approaches include the following:

- *Determine the NPV of the project without the option.* A real option adds value to a project, even if it is difficult to determine the monetary amount of that value. If the NPV of the project without the option is positive, the analyst knows that the project with the option must be even more valuable, and determining a specific value for the option is unnecessary.
- *Calculate the project NPV without the option and add the estimated value of the real option.* In equation form, this can be expressed as:

  overall NPV = project NPV (based on DCF) – option cost + option value

  Imagine that an analyst determines that the NPV of a project is –$100 million. If the analyst believes that the real option value net of its cost is at least $100 million, it makes sense to take on the project. This method effectively determines a "hurdle value" that the option must exceed in order for the project to add value.

- *Use decision trees*. This method does not determine a value for the option but may allow a manager to make a more informed choice by showing the sequence of decisions made.
- *Use option pricing models*. This method may require the use of complex equations or special consultants.

PROFESSOR'S NOTE

Option pricing models are discussed in Study Session 14.

EXAMPLE: Production-flexibility option

Black Pearl Yachts estimated that the NPV of the expected cash flows from a new production facility to produce Classic Yachts is negative \$8 million. Black Pearl's production manager is evaluating an additional investment of \$5 million in equipment that would give management the flexibility to switch between Classic, Deluxe, and Elite models of yachts depending on demand. The option to switch production among models of yachts is estimated to have a value of \$15 million. Evaluate the profitability of the project, including the real option.

Answer:

overall NPV = project NPV – option cost + option value

overall NPV = –\$8 million – \$5 million + \$15 million = \$2 million

Without the option, the NPV of the production facility is negative. However, the real option adds enough value to make the overall project profitable.

EXAMPLE: Abandonment option

Recall from an earlier example the 3-year project with a project cost of capital of 14%. The initial investment is \$1,000 and the expected cash flows are \$400. We determined previously that based on this discounted cash flow (DCF) analysis that the NPV was –\$71.35. The appropriate decision based on this analysis is to not undertake the project.

Suppose instead that we have more information on the expected cash flows. First, there is a 50% probability that the cash flows will be \$200 and a 50% probability that they will be \$600 (i.e., the expected cash flows are still \$400). In addition, at the end of the first year we will know whether the project is a success (cash flow is \$600) or a failure (\$200), and we have the option to abandon the project at the end of the first year and receive the salvage value of \$650.

First determine the optimal abandonment strategy. Then calculate the project's NPV and the value of the abandonment option using that strategy.

Answer:

By abandoning the project, we receive the salvage value of \$650 but give up the cash flows in years 2 and 3. Therefore, the optimal strategy is to abandon the project at the end of the first year if the present value of the remaining cash flows in years 2 and 3 is less than the salvage value of \$650.

If the project is a *success*, the cash flows will be \$600 in years 2 and 3, and the present value of those cash flows at the end of year 1 at 14% is \$988 (N = 2; I/Y = 14; PMT = \$600; CPT PV = \$988). This is larger than the salvage value of

$650, so the optimal strategy is to not abandon the project if we determine at the end of the first year that it is a success.

If the project is a *failure*, the cash flows in years 2 and 3 will only by $200. The present value drops to $329 (N = 2; I/Y = 14; PMT = $200; CPT PV = $329), which is less than the salvage value of $650, so if the project is a failure, the optimal strategy is to abandon the project.

If the project is a success (the probability of which is 50%), we will receive $600 at the end of each of the three years, and the NPV is:

$$\text{NPV} = -\$1{,}000 + \frac{\$600}{1.14} + \frac{\$600}{1.14^2} + \frac{\$600}{1.14^3} = \$393$$

If the project is a failure (a 50% probability), we will receive $200 at the end of the first year plus the salvage value of $650, and the NPV is:

$$\text{NPV} = -\$1{,}000 + \frac{\$200 + \$650}{1.14} = -\$254$$

The project's expected present value with the abandonment option is:

$$\text{NPV} = 0.5(\$393) + 0.5(-\$254) = \$69.50$$

The value of the option is:

$$\text{value of abandonment option} = \$69.50 - (-\$71.35) = \$140.85$$

The abandonment option has made the project viable; we should now accept it because the NPV is greater than 0.

LOS 20.g: Describe common capital budgeting pitfalls.

CFA® Program Curriculum, Volume 3, page 55

Common mistakes managers make when evaluating capital projects include the following:

- *Failing to incorporate economic responses into the analysis*. For example, if a profitable project is in an industry with low barriers to entry, competitors may undertake a similar project, lowering profitability.
- *Misusing standardized templates*. Since managers may evaluate hundreds of projects in a given year, they often create templates to streamline the analysis process. However, the template may not be an exact match for the project, resulting in estimation errors.
- *Pet projects of senior management*. Projects that have the personal backing of influential members of senior management may contain overly optimistic projections that make the project appear more profitable than it really is. In addition, the project may not be subjected to the same level of analysis as other projects.
- *Basing investment decisions on EPS or ROE*. Managers whose incentive compensation is tied to increasing EPS or ROE may avoid positive long-term NPV investments that have the short-run effect of reducing EPS or ROE.

Study Session 7

- *Using the IRR criterion for project decisions.* Using IRR may result in conflicts with the NPV approach for mutually exclusive projects. The NPV criterion is economically sound, accurately reflects the goal of maximizing shareholder wealth, and should drive the project accept/reject decision when IRR and NPV are in conflict.
- *Poor cash flow estimation.* For a complex project, it is easy to double count or fail to include certain cash flows in the analysis. For example, the effects of inflation must be properly accounted for.
- *Misestimation of overhead costs.* The cost of a project should include only the incremental overhead costs related to management time and information technology support. These costs are often difficult to quantify, and over or underestimation can lead to incorrect investment decisions.
- *Using the incorrect discount rate.* The required rate of return on the project should reflect the project's risk. Simply using the company's WACC as a discount rate without adjusting it for the risk of the project may lead to significant errors when estimating the NPV of a project.
- *Politics involved with spending the entire capital budget.* Many managers try to spend their entire capital budget each year and ask for an increase for the following year. In a company with a culture of maximizing shareholder value, managers will return excess funds whenever there is a lack of positive NPV projects and make a case for expanding the budget when there are multiple positive NPV opportunities.
- *Failure to generate alternative investment ideas.* Generating investment ideas is the most important step of the capital budgeting process. However, once a manager comes up with a "good" idea, they may go with it rather than coming up with an idea that is "better."
- *Improper handling of sunk and opportunity costs.* Managers should not consider sunk costs in the evaluation of a project because they are not incremental cash flows. Managers should always consider opportunity costs because they are incremental. However, in reality, many managers do this incorrectly.

LOS 20.h: Calculate and interpret accounting income and economic income in the context of capital budgeting.

CFA® Program Curriculum, Volume 3, page 58

Accounting and economic income measures are alternatives to the basic discounted incremental cash flow approach used in the standard capital budgeting model.

A project's **economic income** is equal to the after-tax cash flow plus the change in the investment's market value. As with the basic capital budgeting model, interest is ignored for cash flow calculations and is instead included as a component of the discount rate.

economic income = cash flow + (ending market value – beginning market value)

or

economic income = cash flow – economic depreciation

where:

economic depreciation = (beginning market value – ending market value)

A project's **accounting income** is the reported net income on a company's financial statements that results from an investment in a project. Accounting income will differ from economic income because:

- Accounting depreciation is based on the original cost (not market value) of the investment.
- Financing costs (e.g., interest expense) are considered as a separate line item and subtracted out to arrive at net income. In the basic capital budgeting model, financing costs are reflected in the WACC.

PROFESSOR'S NOTE

Knowing how to calculate accounting income is nothing more than knowing how to construct the firm's income statement.

These concepts are best illustrated with an example.

EXAMPLE: Economic and accounting income

Blue Wave is a startup company that uses a brushless machine to wash cars. Suppose Blue Wave makes an initial investment in equipment of $400,000. The equipment is depreciated on a straight-line basis over four years to a zero book value. At the end of four years, the equipment will have a salvage value of $10,000. Blue Wave's marginal tax rate is 30%. The company is financed with 50% debt and 50% equity. The debt carries an interest rate of 6%, and the cost of equity is 19.8%. Blue Wave only expects to operate for the four year duration of the project, so all income is distributed to bondholders and stockholders. The company plans to maintain a 50% debt to value ratio.

Blue Wave expects to have sales, expenses, and cash flows for the next four years as shown in the following figure.

Sales, Expenses, and Cash Flows for Blue Wave

	Year 1	Year 2	Year 3	Year 4
Sales	$400,000	$450,000	$450,000	$400,000
Variable expenses	(150,000)	(175,000)	(175,000)	(150,000)
Fixed expenses	(40,000)	(40,000)	(40,000)	(40,000)
Depreciation	(100,000)	(100,000)	(100,000)	(100,000)
Operating income (EBIT)	110,000	135,000	135,000	110,000
Taxes at 30%	(33,000)	(40,500)	(40,500)	(33,000)
Operating income after taxes	77,000	94,500	94,500	77,000
Add back depreciation	100,000	100,000	100,000	100,000
After-tax operating cash flow	177,000	194,500	194,500	177,000
Salvage value				10,000
Tax on salvage value				(3,000)
After tax salvage value				7,000
Total after-tax cash flow	**$177,000**	**$194,500**	**$194,500**	**$184,000**

The project's required rate of return (i.e., its cost of capital) is the WACC. Calculate the project's NPV, economic income, accounting income, and discuss the differences between the various income measures.

Answer:

Calculate WACC:

$$\begin{aligned}\text{WACC} &= (0.198)(0.5) + (0.06)(1 - 0.3)(0.5) \\ &= 0.12\text{, or } 12\%\end{aligned}$$

Calculate NPV:

$$\text{NPV} = -\$400{,}000 + \frac{\$177{,}000}{1.12^1} + \frac{\$194{,}500}{1.12^2} + \frac{\$194{,}500}{1.12^3} + \frac{\$184{,}000}{1.12^4} = \$168{,}467$$

Calculate economic income:

The cash flows for Blue Wave's project are already determined in the next figure. The beginning market value at any point is the present value of the remaining after-tax cash flows discounted at the 12% WACC. Beginning market value for Year 1 is the value at time 0 or PV of cash flows for periods 1 through 4 or $568,467. The economic income for years 1 through 4 are shown in the following figure.

Economic Income for Blue Wave

	Year 1	Year 2	Year 3	Year 4
Beginning market value	$568,467	$459,682	$320,344	$164,286
Ending market value	459,682	320,344	164,286	0
Change in market value	–108,785	–139,338	–156,058	–164,286
After-tax cash flow	177,000	194,500	194,500	184,000
Economic income	**$68,215**	**$55,162**	**$38,442**	**$19,714**
Economic rate of return	12%	12%	12%	12%

For year 1:

$$\text{ending market value} = \frac{\$194,500}{1.12^1} + \frac{\$194,500}{1.12^2} + \frac{\$184,000}{1.12^3} = \$459,682$$

economic income = \$177,000 – \$108,785 = \$68,215

economic rate of return = \$68,215 / \$568,467 = 12%

The economic income rate of return for each year is precisely equal to the project's WACC. This makes sense because the WACC is the discount rate used to determine the value of the company.

Calculate accounting income:

Accounting Income for Blue Wave

	Year 1	Year 2	Year 3	Year 4
Sales	$400,000	$450,000	$450,000	$400,000
Variable expenses	(150,000)	(175,000)	(175,000)	(150,000)
Fixed expenses	(40,000)	(40,000)	(40,000)	(40,000)
Depreciation	(100,000)	(100,000)	(100,000)	(100,000)
Operating income (EBIT)	110,000	135,000	135,000	110,000
Interest expense (50% of company value at 6% rate)	(17,054)	(13,790)	(9,610)	(4,928)
Earnings before tax (EBT)	92,946	121,210	125,390	105,072
Taxes at 30%	(27,884)	(36,363)	(37,617)	(31,522)
Net income before salvage	65,062	84,847	87,773	73,550
After tax salvage value				7,000
Net (Accounting) Income	**$65,062**	**$84,847**	**$87,773**	**$80,550**

Study Session 7

Interest expense is calculated by assuming that Blue Wave finances 50% of the project's market value with debt at a pre-tax cost of debt of 6%. Each year, interest expense is equal to 6% of beginning market value times 0.5. For example, year 2 interest expense is 6% of ($459,682 × 0.5), or $13,790.

The accounting income differs from the economic income for two reasons.

1. Accounting depreciation is based on the original cost of the investment, while economic depreciation (beginning – ending value) is based on the market value of the asset. The economic depreciation for the project is much larger than the accounting depreciation, resulting in an economic income amount that is much smaller than accounting income.
2. Interest expense is deducted from the accounting income figure. Interest expense is ignored when computing economic income because it is reflected in the WACC.

LOS 20.i: Distinguish among the economic profit, residual income, and claims valuation models for capital budgeting and evaluate a capital project using each.

CFA® Program Curriculum, Volume 3, page 61

Economic profit is a measure of profit in excess of the dollar cost of capital invested in a project. It is calculated as:

EP = NOPAT – $WACC

where:
NOPAT = net operating profit after tax = EBIT (1 – tax rate)
$WACC = dollar cost of capital = WACC × capital
Capital = dollar amount of investment

PROFESSOR'S NOTE

Make sure you can distinguish between economic income and economic profit. They sound like they refer to the same concept ("income" and "profit") but in fact, the calculations are very different. Also, economic income in the capital budgeting context is not the same as economic income used in the equity valuation context.

EXAMPLE: Calculating economic profit

Using the data from our previous example, calculate the economic profit for Blue Wave in years 1 through 4.

Answer:

Economic Profit for Blue Wave

	Year 1	**Year 2**	**Year 3**	**Year 4**
Capital	$400,000	$300,000	$200,000	$100,000
NOPAT	77,000	94,500	94,500	84,000*
$WACC	48,000	36,000	24,000	12,000
Economic profit	**$29,000**	**$58,500**	**$70,500**	**$72,000**

*Year 4 NOPAT of $84,000 includes the after-tax gain from the sale.

PROFESSOR'S NOTE

Capital is simply the $400,000 initial investment reduced by depreciation of $100,000 each year.

Once the economic profit is determined, it is easily applied to the valuation of an asset. The NPV based on economic profit is called the **market value added** (MVA) and is calculated as:

$$\text{NPV} = \text{MVA} = \sum_{t=1}^{\infty} \frac{\text{EP}_t}{(1 + \text{WACC})^t}$$

The economic profit approach focuses on returns to all suppliers of capital, which includes both debt and equity holders, and therefore the appropriate discount rate is the WACC.

Discounting the four years of economic profit for Blue Wave gives an MVA of:

$$\text{MVA} = \frac{\$29,000}{1.12^1} + \frac{\$58,500}{1.12^2} + \frac{\$70,500}{1.12^3} + \frac{\$72,000}{1.12^4} = \$168,467$$

Notice that the MVA is identical to the NPV calculated in the original Blue Wave example. The valuation using economic profit is the same as the valuation using the basic NPV approach. No matter which method is used for determining income, if it is applied correctly, the resulting NPV should be the same.

The value of the company is the NPV of the project plus the initial investment:

company value = $168,467 + $400,000 = $568,467

Residual income focuses on returns on equity and is determined by subtracting an equity charge from the accounting net income. The equity charge is found by multiplying the required return on equity by the beginning book value of equity.

The calculation for residual income is:

residual income = net income − equity charge

or

$RI_t = NI_t - r_e B_{t-1}$

where:
RI_t = residual income in period t
NI_t = net income in period t
r_e = required return on equity
B_{t-1} = beginning of period book value of equity

Like other capital budgeting methods, discounting the residual income at the required rate of return on equity will give the NPV of the investment.

$$NPV = \sum_{t=1}^{\infty} \frac{RI_t}{(1 + r_e)^t}$$

The residual income approach focuses only on returns to equityholders; therefore, the appropriate discount rate is the required return on equity.

EXAMPLE: Residual income method applied to Blue Wave

Recall that the WACC for the Blue Wave project is 12%, and the required return on equity is 19.8%. Beginning book value of assets on the balance sheet is equal to the initial outlay in the project of $400,000. The book value is depreciated straight-line to zero over four years, so assets decline by $100,000 each year. Liabilities each year are equal to 50% of the market value of the project. Balance sheet data is provided in the following table.

Blue Wave Balance Sheet

Year	0	1	2	3	4
Assets	$400,000	$300,000	$200,000	$100,000	$0
Liabilities	$284,233	$229,841	$160,172	$82,143	$0
Net worth	$115,767	$70,159	$39,828	$17,857	$0

Calculate the NPV of the Blue Wave project and the company using the residual income method.

Answer:

First calculate residual income in each year. Residual income is equal to net income minus the charge for equity, which is equal to beginning net worth times the required return on equity.

Year	1	2	3	4
Net income	$65,062	$84,847	$87,773	$80,550
$r_e B_{t-1} = 0.198 B_{t-1}$*	$22,922	$13,891	$7,886	$3,536
Residual income	$42,140	$70,956	$79,887	$77,014

* For year 1, the B_0 = net worth at time 0 = 115,767.

The present value of the residual income stream (at the required return on equity of 19.8%) is $168,467. Therefore, the NPV of the project is $168,467, which is the same value calculated from applying the previous valuation methods.

The value of the company is the sum of the present value of the residual income plus the equity investment (net worth in year 0) plus the value of debt:

company value = $168,467 + $115,767 + $284,233 = $568,467

PROFESSOR'S NOTE

Residual income is covered comprehensively in the Equity Valuation portion of the curriculum.

The **claims valuation approach** divides operating cash flows based on the claims of debt and equityholders that provide capital to the company. These debt and equity cash flows are valued separately and then added together to determine the value of the company.

PROFESSOR'S NOTE

The claims valuation method calculates the value of the company, not the project. This is different from the economic profit and residual income approaches, which calculate both project and company value.

The claims valuation approach is based on the balance sheet concept that assets equal liabilities plus equity. Every asset is financed by some combination of debt and equity, and the claims valuation approach merely separates the cash flows provided by the asset into the proportionate debt and equity components.

- The *cash flows to debtholders* consist of interest and principal payments and are discounted at the cost of debt.
- The *cash flows to equityholders* are dividends and share repurchases and are discounted at the cost of equity.

The sum of the present value of each stream of cash flows will equal the value of the company.

We can demonstrate the claims valuation method using the Blue Wave information.

Cash flow to bondholders is equal to principal repayments (the change in liabilities from the balance sheet) plus interest expense, as shown in the Figure 20.6.

Figure 20.6: Cash Flow to Blue Wave Bondholders

Year	1	2	3	4
Principal payments	$54,392	$69,669	$78,029	$82,143
Interest expense	17,054	13,790	9,610	4,928
Cash flow to bondholders	$71,446	$83,459	$87,639	$87,071

You can verify that the present value of these cash flows at the cost of debt (6%) is $284,233, which is the market value of the debt.

The cash flow to shareholders is equal to operating cash flow (net income plus depreciation) minus the principal payments to bondholders (interest expense is already deducted in the computation of net income), as shown in the following figure.

Figure 20.7: Cash Flow to Blue Wave Shareholders

Year	1	2	3	4
Net income	$65,062	$84,847	$87,773	$80,550
Plus: Depreciation	100,000	100,000	100,000	100,000
Operating cash flow	165,062	184,847	187,773	180,550
Less: Principal payments	54,392	69,669	78,029	82,143
Dividends	$110,670	$115,178	$109,744	$98,407

You can verify that the present value of these cash flows at the cost of equity (19.8%) is $284,234, which is the market value of the equity.

The value of the company is the sum of the market value of the debt and equity:

company value = $284,233 + $284,234 = $568,467

This is the same company value we calculated using the economic profit and the residual income methods. Note that the value of debt is equal to the value of equity in this example (allowing for rounding) because the company is financed with 50% debt and 50% equity, so the debt to equity ratio is 1:1.

Whether the economic profit, residual income, or claims valuation method for determining income is used, the key is that in theory, any of the three methods should result in the same value for the company. In practice, however, accounting complications, such as pension adjustments, goodwill, and deferred taxes, may complicate the calculation of income, leading some analysts to prefer a particular method.

PROFESSOR'S NOTE

These accounting complications are addressed in exhaustive detail in the Study Sessions covering Financial Reporting and Analysis.

MODULE QUIZ 20.3

To best evaluate your performance, enter your quiz answers online.

1. Which of the following statements about cash flow analysis is *least accurate*?
   A. Financing cash flows are considered in the incremental cash flow analysis.
   B. If two projects are independent, the fact that they have unequal lives does not affect the analysis.
   C. An incremental cash flow represents the change in the firm's total cash flow that occurs as a direct result of taking a project.

2. Albert Duffy, Project Manager at Crane Plastics, is considering taking on a new capital project. When presenting the project, Duffy shows members of Crane's executive management team that the project is marginally profitable, but because the company has the ability to use various materials interchangeably through the production process, the project makes sense. The project Duffy is taking on would be *best* described as having a:
   A. fundamental option.
   B. expansion option.
   C. flexibility option.

Use the following information to answer Questions 3 and 4.

McCool Air Conditioning Systems is considering a capital project with the following characteristics:

- The initial investment outlay is $500,000.
- The project life is three years.
- Annual operating cash flows have a 50% probability of being $100,000 for three years and a 50% probability of being $280,000 for three years.
- The required rate of return on the project is 10%.
- There is zero salvage value at project termination.
- In one year, after realizing the first cash flow, the company has the opportunity to abandon the project and receive a cash flow of $250,000.

3. Assuming that there is no abandonment option, the project's NPV is *closest* to:
   A. –$27,498.
   B. $12,545.
   C. $22,622.

4. Assuming that McCool follows the optimal abandonment strategy, the NPV of the project, inclusive of the abandonment option, is *closest* to:
   A. –$12,545.
   B. $7,250.
   C. $12,545.

5. Steven Munn and David Hu are discussing potential capital projects for the Tryon Corporation. Hu is concerned about making capital budgeting mistakes, and he tells Munn that he wants to avoid such mistakes. Munn tells Hu not to worry and makes two statements:

Statement 1: Although we use templates for streamlining the evaluation of capital budgeting projects, the employees inputting the data in the template are highly trained to adjust the numbers that are put into the template for the specific project, which virtually eliminates template errors.

Statement 2: All projects we consider use Tryon Corp.'s weighted average cost of capital for the discount rate with an adjustment up or down reflecting the project's risk. By adjusting the discount rate for the risk of the project, we get a more accurate representation of the project's risk/reward tradeoff.

Should Hu say that Munn's statements are correct or incorrect?
A. Both statements are correct.
B. Only one of the statements is correct.
C. Neither statement is correct.

Use the following information for Question 6 and 7.

Olympic Orthotics is investing in a €200 million capital project that is being depreciated on a straight-line basis to zero over the project's short 2-year life. The project will generate operating earnings before interest and taxes of €140 million for both years, and at the end of the project's 2-year life, the project will have a zero salvage value. Olympic Orthotics' WACC and cost of capital for the project is 15%, and the tax rate is 40%.

6. The economic income for Olympic Orthotics for years 1 and 2 is *closest* to:
A. €45 million in year 1 and €69 million in year 2.
B. €45 million in year 1 and €24 million in year 2.
C. €54 million in year 1 and €69 million in year 2.

7. The economic profit for Olympic Orthotics in years 1 and 2 is *closest* to:
A. €45 million in year 1 and €69 million in year 2.
B. €45 million in year 1 and €24 million in year 2.
C. €54 million in year 1 and €69 million in year 2.

8. Marybeth Krause has been asked by her employer to evaluate different valuation models for capital projects. Krause's report makes the following two comments:

Comment 1: The present value of future economic profit will be the same as the NPV found by discounted cash flow analysis in the basic capital budgeting approach if the WACC is used as the economic profit discount rate.

Comment 2: The residual income approach focuses only on returns to equity investors, and the proper discount rate to use for finding the NPV of the project based on this approach is the cost of equity.

Are Krause's two comments correct or incorrect?
A. Both comments are correct.
B. Only one of the comments is correct.
C. Neither comment is correct.

KEY CONCEPTS

LOS 20.a

For an expansion project:

- Initial outlay = FCInv + WCInv
- CF = (S – C – D)(1 – T) + D = (S – C)(1 – T) + DT
- TNOCF = Sal_T + NWCInv – T(Sal_T – B_T)

For a replacement project, the cash flows are the same as the above except:

- Current after-tax salvage value of the old assets reduces the initial outlay.
- Depreciation is the change in depreciation if the project is accepted compared to the depreciation on the old machine.

Depreciation schedules affect capital budgeting decisions because they affect after-tax cash flows. In general, accelerated depreciation methods lead to higher after-tax cash flows and a higher project NPV.

LOS 20.b

Inflation is a complication that must be considered as part of the capital budgeting process:

- Nominal cash flows must be discounted at the nominal interest rate, and real cash flows must be discounted at the real interest rate.
- Unexpected changes in inflation affect project profitability.
- Inflation reduces the real tax savings from depreciation.
- Inflation decreases the value of fixed payments to bondholders.
- Inflation affects costs and revenues differently.

LOS 20.c

There are two methods to compare projects with unequal lives that are expected to be repeated indefinitely:

- The least common multiple of lives approach extends the lives of the projects so that the lives divide equally into the chosen time horizon. It is assumed that the projects are repeated over the time horizon, and the NPV over this horizon is used as the decision criterion.
- The equivalent annual annuity of each project is the annuity payment each project year that has a present value (discounted at the WACC) equal to the NPV of the project.

Capital rationing is the allocation of a fixed amount of capital among the set of available projects that will maximize shareholder wealth. A firm with less capital than profitable (positive NPV) projects should choose the combination of projects it can afford to fund that has the greatest total NPV.

LOS 20.d

Risk analysis techniques include:

- Sensitivity analysis involves varying an independent variable to see how much the dependent variable changes, all other things held constant.
- Scenario analysis considers the sensitivity of the dependent variable to simultaneous changes in all of the independent variables.
- Simulation analysis uses repeated random draws from the assumed probability distributions of each input variable to generate a simulated distribution of NPV.

LOS 20.e

The CAPM can be used to determine the appropriate discount rate for a project based on risk. The project beta, β, is used as a measure of the systematic risk of the project, and the security market line (SML) estimates the required return as:

$$R_{project} = R_f + \beta_{project}[E(R_M) - R_f]$$

LOS 20.f

Real options allow managers to make future decisions that change the value of capital budgeting decisions made today.

- Timing options allow a company to delay making an investment.
- Abandonment options allow management to abandon a project if the PV of the incremental CFs from exiting a project exceeds the PV value of the incremental CFs from continuing a project.
- Expansion options allow a company to make additional investments in a project if doing so creates value.
- Flexibility options give managers choices regarding the operational aspects of a project. The two main forms are price-setting and production flexibility options.
- Fundamental options are projects that are options themselves because the payoffs depend on the price of an underlying asset.

Approaches to evaluating a capital project using real options include: determining the NPV of the project without the option; calculating the project NPV without the option and adding the estimated value of the real option; using decision trees; and using option pricing models.

LOS 20.g

Common mistakes in the capital budgeting process include:

- Failing to incorporate economic responses into the analysis.
- Misusing standardized project evaluation templates.
- Having overly optimistic assumptions for pet projects of senior management.
- Basing long-term investment decisions on short-term EPS or ROE considerations.
- Using the IRR criterion for project decisions.
- Poor cash flow estimation.

- Misestimation of overhead costs.
- Using a discount rate that does not accurately reflect the project's risk.
- Politics involved with spending the entire capital budget.
- Failure to generate alternative investment ideas.
- Improper handling of sunk and opportunity costs.

LOS 20.h

Economic income is equal to the after-tax cash flow plus the change in the project's market value. Accounting income is equal to the revenues minus costs of the project.

There are two key factors that account for the differences between economic and accounting income:

- Accounting depreciation is based on the original cost of the investment, while economic depreciation is based on the change in market value of the investment.
- The after-tax cost of debt (interest expense) is subtracted from net income, while financing costs for determining economic income are reflected in the discount rate.

LOS 20.i

Alternative forms of determining income should theoretically lead to the same calculated NPV if applied correctly.

- Economic profit is calculated as NOPAT – $WACC. Economic profit reflects the income earned by all capital holders and is therefore discounted at the WACC to determine the market value added (MVA) or NPV of the investment.
- Residual income is focused on returns to equity holders and is calculated as net income – equity charge. Residual income reflects the income to equityholders only and is discounted at the required return on equity to determine NPV.
- Claims valuation separates cash flows based on the claims that equityholders and debtholders have on the asset. Cash flows to debt holders are discounted at the cost of debt and cash flows to equity holders are discounted at the cost of equity. The present value of each set of cash flows is added together to determine the value of the company.

ANSWER KEY FOR MODULE QUIZZES

Module Quiz 20.1

1. **C** Previous expenditures associated with a market test would be a sunk cost and should not be included. (LOS 20.a)

2. **B** First-year depreciation = (\$60,000)(0.2) = \$12,000. Initial cash outlay = \$60,000 cost – \$15,000 NWC inflow = \$45,000 net outlay. (LOS 20.a)

3. **C** Year 1 operating cash flow = [net income impact × (1 – t)] + (depreciation × t) = (\$5,000)(0.6) + (\$60,000)(0.2)(0.4) = \$7,800. Terminal year cash flow (excluding that year's operating cash flow) = after-tax proceeds from sale of the new machine less working capital return = \$10,000 – [(\$10,000)(0.4)] – \$15,000 = –\$9,000. (LOS 20.a)

4. **A** initial net investment = –\$60,000 + \$15,000 = –\$45,000

   annual depreciation = \$60,000 / 6 = \$10,000

   CF(years 1 through 6) = \$5,000(1 – 0.4) + \$10,000(0.4) = \$7,000

   TNOCF(year 6) = \$10,000 – [\$10,000(0.4)] – \$15,000 = –\$9,000

   $NPV = -\$45,000 + \$7,000 / 1.12 + \$7,000 / 1.12^2 + \$7,000 / 1.12^3 + \$7,000 / 1.12^4 + \$7,000 / 1.12^5 + (\$7,000 - \$9,000) / 1.12^6 = -\$20,780$ (LOS 20.a)

5. **B** Initial cash outlay

   $= FCInv + NWCInv - Sal_0 + T(Sal_0 - B_0)$

   $= 10,000 + (3,000 - 1,000) - 6,000 + 0.25(6,000 - 2,000)$

   $= 7,000$

   This indicates an initial cash flow of –\$7,000. (LOS 20.a)

6. **B** Statement 1 is incorrect. Depreciation reduces cash taxes paid, not interest expense. Statement 2 is correct. Accelerated depreciation methods applied for tax purposes result in higher tax savings and higher cash flows early in a project's life, which will serve to increase the project's NPV. (LOS 20.a)

7. **C** Spang is incorrect with respect to both statements. All projects should *not* be discounted at the real interest rate. Discount rates should be matched up with cash flows so that real cash flows are discounted at the real interest rate and nominal cash flows are discounted at the nominal interest rate. The second statement is incorrect because it is rare for inflation to affect revenues and costs uniformly. The profits for a company will be better or worse than expected depending on how sales outputs or cost inputs are affected by inflation. Also, contracting with customers, suppliers, employees, and capital providers can all become more complicated as inflation rises. (LOS 20.b)

Module Quiz 20.2

1. **B** Capital budgeting analysis for expansion and replacement projects are not the same; change in working capital can be positive or negative; and replacement projects are mutually exclusive—B is the only correct statement. (LOS 20.c)

2. **B** Using the least common multiple of lives approach:

   NPV Project A = –100,000 + (75,000 / 1.10) + (75,000 – 100,000) / 1.10^2 + 75,000 / 1.10^3 + 75,000 / 1.10^4 = \$55,095.

   NPV Project B = –100,000 + 50,000 / 1.10 + 50,000 / 1.10^2 + 50,000 / 1.10^3 + 50,000 /1.10^4 = \$58,493.

   (LOS 20.c)

3. **A** EAA_A: PV=20,000; N = 3; I/Y = 12; CPT PMT → \$8,327. EAA_B: PV = 25,000; N = 5; I/Y = 12; CPT PMT → \$6,935. Note: take the highest EAA. (LOS 20.c)

4. **A** The tax shield from the loss on the sale of the old equipment is equal to the loss times the marginal tax rate. The tax shield is treated as an initial cash *inflow*. Answer B describes a cash inflow (a tax savings). (LOS 20.c)

5. **B** Statement 2 is incorrect because the analyst should use either the least common multiple of lives or equivalent annual annuity methods to analyze mutually exclusive projects with unequal lives. Statement 1 is correct: the "equivalent annual annuity" approach is one method of comparing mutually exclusive projects in a replacement chain (where it is assumed that company assets will be replaced as they wear out.) (LOS 20.c)

6. **C** Scenario analysis uses best and worst case scenarios to determine the most likely outcome. The other statements are true. (LOS 20.d)

7. **C** The combination of projects with the highest total NPV should be selected, subject to the constraint that the total investment required not exceed the allocated capital budget. (LOS 20.c)

8. **B** Since the capital budget is only \$80,000, this is an example of capital rationing since Eldon has more profitable projects than it has capital. The objective here is to maximize the NPV within the budget, which means that Projects 2, 3, and 4 should be taken for a combined NPV of \$33,000. Note that even though money is left over with this combination, it has the highest total NPV of the answer choices listed. Choosing Projects 1, 3, and 5 uses the entire capital budget but results in a total NPV of only \$31,000. Choosing Projects 1, 3, and 4 would exceed the capital budget. (LOS 20.c)

9. **C** By ignoring the initial \$500,000 cash outflow, she has overestimated project NPV by \$500,000. By ignoring the terminal cash inflow of \$500,000, she has underestimated project NPV by $\frac{\$500,000}{1.10^5} \approx \$310,000$.

   The net effect is to overestimate NPV by \$500,000 – \$310,000 = \$190,000. (LOS 20.c)

Study Session 7

10. **A** $R_{\text{project A}} = 5\% + 1.2(9\%) = 15.80\%$
$R_{\text{project B}} = 5\% + 0.6(9\%) = 10.40\%$
If the company uses the overall WACC of 10%, it will overestimate the value of both projects because the WACC is too low to reflect the higher risk of each project. (LOS 20.e)

Module Quiz 20.3

1. **A** Financing costs or cost of debt is reflected in the cost of capital. The other statements are accurate. (Module 20.3, LOS 20.h)

2. **C** The project described has a production-flexibility option, which includes overtime for workers, producing a different product, or using different inputs. In any case, the use of real options offers flexibility that can improve the NPV estimates for individual projects. (Module 20.3, LOS 20.f)

3. **A** The expected annual after-tax operating cash flow is 0.50($100,000) + 0.50($280,000) = $190,000. The cash flows discounted at the 10% cost of capital for the project give an NPV of:

$$NPV = -\$500{,}000 + \sum_{t=1}^{3} \frac{\$190{,}000}{1.10^t} = -\$27{,}498$$

(Module 20.1, 20.3, LOS 20.a, 20.h)

4. **B** The optimal abandonment strategy would be to abandon the project in one year if the subsequent cash flows are worth less than the abandonment value. If at the end of the first year the low cash flow occurs, McCool can abandon the project, receive $250,000 instead of $173,554 (present value of $100,000 over the next two years). If the high cash flow occurs, the present value of the cash flow for the remaining two years is $485,950, so McCool would not want to abandon the project.

If the high cash flow occurs, the total present value of the project would be:

$$NPV = -\$500{,}000 + \sum_{t=1}^{3} \frac{\$280{,}000}{1.10^t} = \$196{,}319$$

If the low cash flow occurs, McCool would receive the first year cash flow and the abandon value, and no further cash flows. In that case, the NPV would be:

$$NPV = -\$500{,}000 + \frac{\$100{,}000 + \$250{,}000}{1.10} = -\$181{,}818$$

With the abandonment option, the expected NPV is 0.50($196,319) + 0.50 (–$181,818) = $7,250. Note that the NPV was negative without the option but positive when the option is included in the analysis. (Module 20.3, LOS 20.f)

5. **B** Simply adjusting the numbers input into templates does not eliminate the possibility that the templates themselves may be incorrectly applied. Statement 1 is incorrect. Statement 2 is correct because a methodology is used that adjusts the discount rate for the risk of the project and does not simply use a single discount rate for all projects. (Module 20.3, LOS 20.g)

6. **B** First, determine the after-tax cash flow for years 1 and 2 as:

$$\text{CF} = (\text{S} - \text{C} - \text{D})(1 - \text{T}) + \text{D} = €140\ (1 - 0.40) + €100 = €184$$

Note that EBIT is equal to (S – C – D).

Next, determine the current market value of the project today and at the end of year 1 as:

$$\text{value today} = \frac{€184}{1.15} + \frac{€184}{1.15^2} = €299, \text{value after year 1} = \frac{€184}{1.15} = €160$$

The economic income for years 1 and 2 are €45 million and €24 million respectively, as shown in the following table.

(all figures in millions)	**Year 1**	**Year 2**
Beginning market value	€299	€160
Ending market value	160	0
Change in market value	–139	–160
After-tax cash flow	184	184
Economic income	**€45**	**€24**
Economic rate of return	15%	15%

(Module 20.3, LOS 20.h)

7. **C** Economic profit is calculated as NOPAT – \$WACC = EBIT(1 – T) – \$WACC

economic profit (year 1) = €140 million(1 – 0.4) – 0.15(€200 million) = €54 million

economic profit (year 2) = €140 million(1 – 0.4) – 0.15(€100 million) = €69 million

(Module 20.3, LOS 20.i)

8. **A** Both of Krause's comments are correct statements. (Module 20.3, LOS 20.i)

Study Session 7

The following is a review of the Corporate Finance (1) principles designed to address the learning outcome statements set forth by CFA Institute. Cross-Reference to CFA Institute Assigned Reading #21.

READING 21 Capital Structure

Study Session 7

EXAM FOCUS

This topic review explores various theories related to how a firm chooses its proportions of debt and equity financing. You should be able to discuss the impact of leverage on a firm's risk, return on equity, and share price. You should know the concepts underlying MM's propositions, the pecking order theory, and the static trade-off theory. You should also know what factors cause differences in capital structures across countries.

MODULE 21.1: THEORIES OF CAPITAL STRUCTURE

Video covering this content is available online.

CAPITAL STRUCTURE THEORY

Warm-Up: Overview of the Capital Structure Theories

As you read through the capital structure theory material, observe that the progression is from MM 1958 (no taxes, no costs of financial distress) to MM 1963 (with taxes, no costs of financial distress) to the static trade-off theory (with taxes and with costs of financial distress). Candidates often wonder, "Why do we need to know MM?" because the assumptions of no taxes and no financial distress costs are so clearly at variance with reality.

The answer is that by starting with MM 1958, we are laying the foundation that explains the fundamental relationship between capital structure and cost of equity. In moving to MM 1963, we are able to see how introducing taxes affects the cost of capital and firm value. Without this prior knowledge, it would not be possible to understand the static trade-off theory, which is built on the foundation provided by the MM theory, and is a realistic explanation of the relationship between capital structure and firm value. Remember, the goal of managers in a capital structure decision is to minimize the weighted average cost of capital (and thereby maximize the value of the company).

LOS 21.a: Explain the Modigliani–Miller propositions regarding capital structure, including the effects of leverage, taxes, financial distress, agency costs, and asymmetric information on a company's cost of equity, cost of capital, and optimal capital structure.

CFA® Program Curriculum, Volume 3, page 94

MM Proposition I (No Taxes): The Capital Structure Irrelevance Proposition

In 1958, Professors Franco Modigliani and Merton Miller (MM) published their seminal work on capital structure theory. Under a very restrictive set of assumptions, *MM proved that the value of a firm is unaffected by its capital structure*. To summarize, MM's results suggest that in a perfect world, it does not matter how a firm finances its operations. Thus, capital structure is irrelevant. MM's study is based on the following simplifying assumptions:

- *Capital markets are perfectly competitive*: there are no transactions costs, taxes, or bankruptcy costs.
- *Investors have homogeneous expectations*: they have the same expectations with respect to cash flows generated by the firm.
- *Riskless borrowing and lending*: investors can borrow/lend at the risk-free rate.
- *No agency costs*: no conflict of interest between managers and shareholders.
- *Investment decisions are unaffected by financing decisions*: operating income is independent of how assets are financed.

In the MM no-tax world, the value of a company is not affected by its capital structure. We can explain MM's capital structure irrelevance proposition in terms of a pie. That is, the size (value) of the pie (firm) depends not on how it is sliced (the capital structure), but rather on the size of the pie pan (the firm's asset base). So with a pie pan of a certain size, the value of a firm's assets will be the same, no matter how a firm finances (slices) it. This idea is illustrated in Figure 21.1.

Figure 21.1: MM Capital Structure Irrelevance Proposition

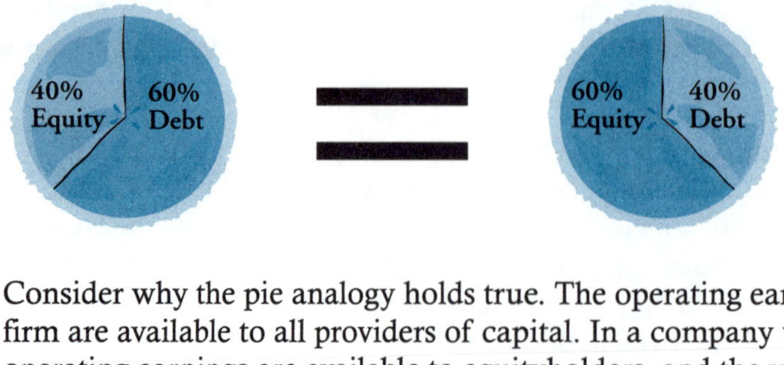

Consider why the pie analogy holds true. The operating earnings (EBIT) of a firm are available to all providers of capital. In a company with no debt, all of the operating earnings are available to equityholders, and the value of the company is

the discounted present value of these earnings. If a company is partially financed by debt, operating earnings are split between debtholders and equityholders. Under the assumption of perfect markets, the sum of a firm's debt and equity should equal the value of the all-equity company so the value of the company is unchanged. Another way of stating this is that the value of the company with leverage is equal to the value of the company without leverage:

$$V_L = V_U$$

where:
V_L = value of levered firm
V_U = value of unlevered firm

Given our assumptions, an investor can have homemade leverage. He can substitute his own leverage (in addition to owning stock) for company's leverage. As this process is assumed to be costless, a company's capital structure is irrelevant in the presence of perfect capital markets.

MM Proposition II (No Taxes): Cost of Equity and Leverage Proposition

MM's second proposition with no taxes states that *the cost of equity increases linearly as a company increases its proportion of debt financing*. Again, MM assume a perfect market where there are no taxes, no cost of bankruptcy, and homogeneous expectations. According to their proposition, debtholders have a priority claim on assets and income, which makes the cost of debt lower than the cost of equity. However, as companies increase their use of debt, the risk to equityholders increases, which in turn increases the cost of equity. Therefore, the benefits of using a larger proportion of debt as a cheaper source of financing are offset by the rise in the cost of equity, resulting in no change in the firm's weighted average cost of capital (WACC).

We can see this by using the WACC formula (assuming the marginal tax rate is zero) and solving for the cost of equity.

$$r_e = r_0 + \frac{D}{E}(r_0 - r_d)$$

where:
r_e = required rate of return on equity, or cost of equity
r_0 = company unlevered cost of capital (i.e., assume no leverage)
r_d = required rate of return on borrowings, or cost of debt
$\frac{D}{E}$ = debt-to-equity ratio

As leverage increases (i.e., the debt-to-equity ratio rises), the cost of equity increases, but WACC and the cost of debt are unchanged.

PROFESSOR'S NOTE

In this framework, WACC is also called the return on assets and denoted r_a.

This concept is illustrated in Figure 21.2.

Figure 21.2: MM Proposition II (No Taxes)

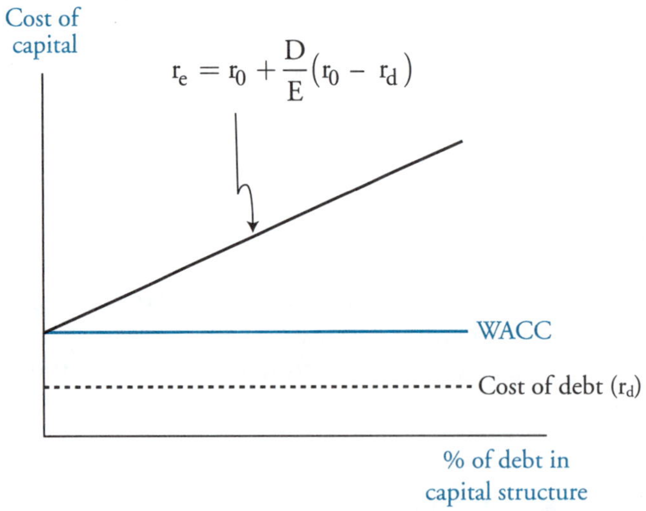

MM's second proposition supports their first proposition. Because the benefits of lower cost debt are offset by the increased cost of equity, the relative amount of debt versus equity in the firm's capital structure does not affect the overall value of the firm.

MM Proposition I (With Taxes): Value Is Maximized at 100% Debt

Tax shield provided by debt. Removing MM's assumption that there are no taxes changes the result of their propositions regarding capital structure irrelevance. Under the tax code of most countries, interest payments are a pretax expense and are therefore tax deductible, while dividends are paid on an after-tax basis. The differential tax treatment encourages firms to use debt financing because debt provides a **tax shield** that adds to the value of the company. The tax shield is equal to the marginal tax rate multiplied by the amount of debt in the capital structure. In other words, the value of a levered firm is equal to the value of an unlevered firm plus the tax shield.

$$V_L = V_U + (t \times d)$$

where:
V_L = value of levered firm
V_U = value of unlevered firm
t = marginal tax rate
d = value of debt in capital structure

If we maintain MM's other assumptions (i.e., no cost of bankruptcy), the value of the company increases with increasing levels of debt, *and the optimal capital structure is 100% debt*.

MM Proposition II (With Taxes): WACC Is Minimized at 100% Debt

If we assume the marginal tax rate is not zero and then use the WACC formula to solve for return on equity, we get MM Proposition II (With Taxes):

$$r_E = r_0 + \frac{D}{E}(r_0 - r_D)(1 - T_C)$$

where:
T_C = tax rate

Figure 21.3 shows that the tax shield provided by debt causes the WACC to decline as leverage increases. The value of the firm is maximized at the point where the WACC is minimized, which is 100% debt.

Figure 21.3: MM Proposition II (With Taxes)

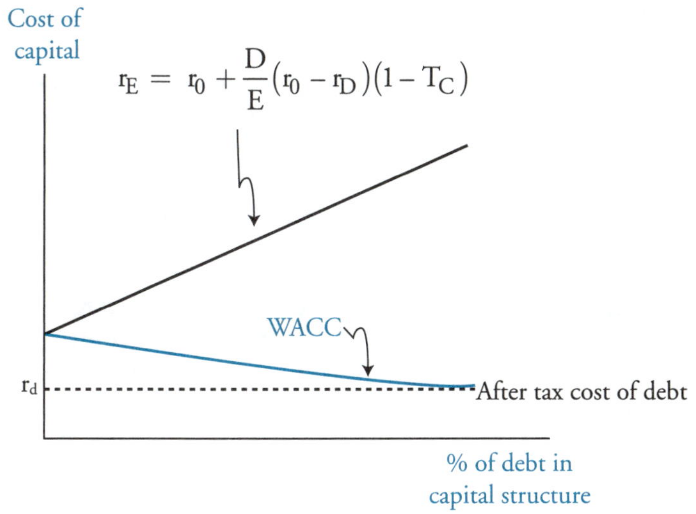

Study Session 7

MODULE QUIZ 21.1

To best evaluate your performance, enter your quiz answers online.

1. The optimal capital structure:
   A. maximizes firm value and minimizes the weighted average cost of capital.
   B. minimizes the interest rate on debt and maximizes expected earnings per share.
   C. maximizes expected earnings per share and maximizes the price per share of common stock.
2. Which of the following statements regarding Modigliani and Miller's propositions (assuming perfect capital markets and homogenous expectations) is *most accurate*?
   A. Firm value is maximized with a capital structure consisting of 100% equity.
   B. The cost of equity increases as the firm increases its financial leverage.
   C. The use of debt financing increases the firm's weighted average cost of capital.

Video covering this content is available online.

MODULE 21.2: FACTORS AFFECTING CAPITAL STRUCTURE

Costs and Their Potential Effect on the Capital Structure

Costs of financial distress are the increased costs a company faces when earnings decline and the firm has trouble paying its fixed financing costs (i.e., interest on debt). The *expected* costs of financial distress for a firm have two components:

- *Costs of financial distress and bankruptcy* can be direct or indirect. Direct costs of financial distress include the cash expenses associated with the bankruptcy, such as legal fees and administrative fees. Indirect costs include foregone investment opportunities and the costs that result from losing the trust of customers, creditors, suppliers, and employees.
- *Probability of financial distress* is related to the firm's use of operating and financial leverage. In general, higher amounts of leverage result in a higher probability of financial distress. Other factors to consider include the quality of a firm's management and the company's corporate governance structure; lower quality management and corporate governance lead to a higher probability of financial distress.

Higher expected costs of financial distress tend to discourage companies from using large amounts of debt in their capital structure, all else equal.

Agency costs of equity refer to the costs associated with the conflicts of interest between managers and owners. Managers who do not have a stake in the company do not bear the costs associated with excessive compensation or taking on too much (or too little) risk. Because shareholders are aware of this conflict, they will take steps to minimize these costs, and the net result is called the **net agency cost of equity**. Net agency costs of equity have three components:

- *Monitoring costs* are the costs associated with supervising management and include the expenses associated with making reports to shareholders and paying the board of directors. Note that strong corporate governance systems will reduce monitoring costs.
- *Bonding costs* are assumed by management to assure shareholders that the managers are working in the shareholders' best interest. Examples of bonding costs include the premiums for insurance to guarantee performance and implicit costs associated with non-compete agreements.
- *Residual losses* may occur even with adequate monitoring and bonding provisions because such provisions do not provide a perfect guarantee.

According to agency theory, the use of debt forces managers to be disciplined with regard to how they spend cash because they have less free cash flow to use for their own benefit. It follows that greater amounts of financial leverage tend to reduce agency costs.

PROFESSOR'S NOTE

Agency relationships are discussed in depth in the Corporate Governance topic review.

Costs of asymmetric information refer to costs resulting from the fact that managers typically have more information about a company's prospects and future performance than owners or creditors. Firms with complex products or little transparency in financial statements tend to have higher costs of asymmetric information, which results in higher required returns on debt and equity capital.

Because shareholders and creditors are aware that the asymmetric information problems exist, these investors will look for management behavior that "signals" what knowledge management may have. Specifically, management's choice of debt or equity financing may provide a signal regarding management's opinion of the firm's future prospects.

- Taking on the commitment to make fixed interest payments through debt financing sends a signal that management has confidence in the firm's ability to make these payments in the future.
- Issuing equity is typically viewed as a negative signal that managers believe a firm's stock is overvalued.

The cost of asymmetric information increases as the proportion of equity in the capital structure increases.

Pecking order theory, based on asymmetric information, is related to the *signals* management sends to investors through its financing choices. According to pecking order theory, managers prefer to make financing choices that are least likely to send signals to investors. Financing choices under pecking order theory follow a hierarchy based on visibility to investors with internally generated capital being the most preferred, debt being the next best choice, and external equity being the least preferred financing option.

In other words, the pecking order (from most favored to least favored) is:

- Internally generated equity (i.e., retained earnings).
- Debt.
- External equity (i.e., newly issued shares).

Therefore, the pecking order theory predicts that the capital structure is a by-product of the individual financing decisions.

Static Trade-Off Theory

The **static trade-off theory** seeks to balance the costs of financial distress with the tax shield benefits from using debt. Under the static trade-off theory, there is an optimal capital structure that has an optimal proportion of debt.

If we remove the assumption that there are no costs of financial distress, there comes a point where the additional value added from the debt tax shield is exceeded by the value-reducing costs of financial distress from the additional borrowing. This point represents the optimal capital structure for a firm where the WACC is minimized and the value of the firm is maximized.

Accounting for the costs of financial distress, the expression for the value of a levered firm becomes:

$$V_L = V_U + (t \times d) - PV(\text{costs of financial distress})$$

Figure 21.4 shows that the after-tax cost of debt has an upward slope due to the increasing costs of financial distress that come with additional leverage. As the cost of debt increases, the cost of equity also increases because some of the costs of financial distress are effectively borne by equityholders. The optimal proportion of debt is reached at the point when the marginal benefit provided by the tax shield of taking on additional debt is equal to the marginal costs of financial distress incurred from the additional debt. This point also represents the firm's optimal capital structure because it is the point that minimizes the firm's WACC and therefore maximizes the value of the firm.

Figure 21.4: Static Trade-Off Theory: Cost of Capital vs. Capital Structure

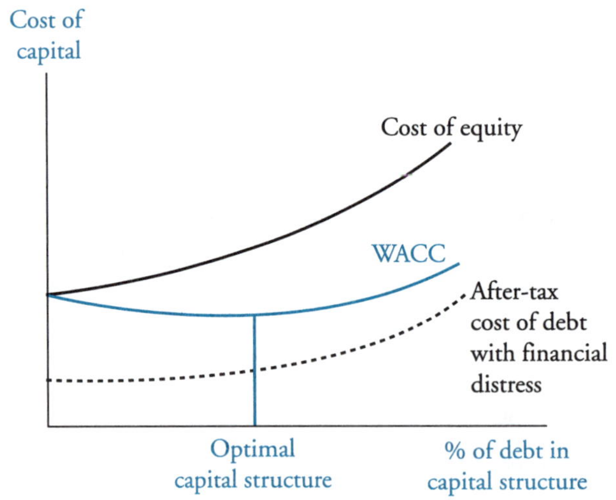

Figure 21.5 illustrates the theory as the trade-off between firm value and capital structure.

Figure 21.5: Static Trade-Off Theory: Firm Value vs. Capital Structure

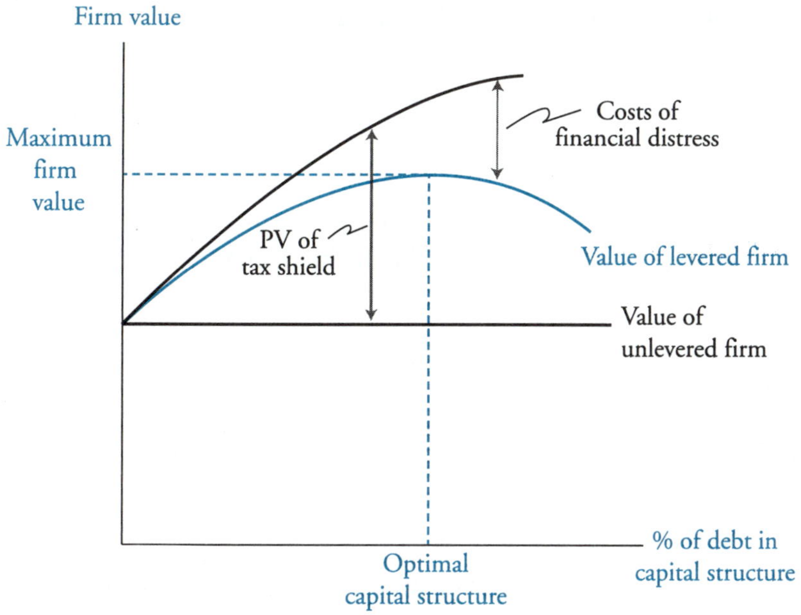

Note that every firm will have a different optimal capital structure that depends on each firm's operating risk, sales risk, tax situation, corporate governance, industry influences, and other factors.

Implications for Managerial Decision Making

MM's propositions with no taxes follow a restrictive set of assumptions in that there are no taxes and no costs associated with financial distress. MM's first proposition says that the capital structure of a company is irrelevant because the value of the company is determined by the discounted present value of its operating earnings. MM's second proposition states that increasing the use of cheaper debt financing will increase the firm's cost of equity, resulting in a zero net change in the firm's WACC. The implication for managers' decisions regarding capital structure under both propositions is that capital structure is irrelevant.

MM's propositions with taxes say that the tax shield provided by interest expense makes borrowing valuable, and that the WACC is minimized (and the value of the firm maximized) at 100% debt.

Static trade-off theory recognizes that there are tax benefits associated with issuing debt because interest expense is tax deductible, but increasing the use of debt also increases the costs of financial distress. At some point, the costs of financial distress will exceed the tax benefits of debt. Managers following the static trade-off approach will seek to balance the benefits of debt with the costs of financial distress and identify an optimal capital structure.

LOS 21.b: Describe target capital structure and explain why a company's actual capital structure may fluctuate around its target.

CFA® Program Curriculum, Volume 3, page 107

The **target capital structure** is the structure that the firm uses over time when making decisions about how to raise additional capital. Management's use of a target capital structure reflects the knowledge that the firm has an optimal capital structure. For managers trying to maximize the value of the firm, the target capital structure will be the same as the optimal capital structure.

In practice, the firm's actual capital structure tends to fluctuate around the target capital structure for two reasons:

- *Management may choose to exploit opportunities in a specific financing source.* For example, a temporary rise in the firm's stock price may create a good opportunity to issue additional equity, which would result in a higher percentage of equity than the target.
- *Market value fluctuations will occur.* Changes in stock and bond markets will cause fluctuations in the firm's stock and bond prices. Because capital structure weights are determined by market values, market fluctuations may cause the firm's actual capital structure to vary from the target.

LOS 21.c: Describe the role of debt ratings in capital structure policy.

CFA® Program Curriculum, Volume 3, page 109

Debt ratings from ratings agencies such as Standard & Poor's and Moody's reflect the creditworthiness of a company's debt. The agencies perform an extensive analysis of a company's ability to make interest and principal payments and assign a rating based on the bond's default risk. Lower debt ratings denote higher levels of default risk for both shareholders and bondholders, who in turn demand higher returns on their capital.

Because the cost of capital is tied to debt ratings, many managers have goals for maintaining certain minimum debt ratings when determining their capital structure policies. Managers prefer to have the highest rating possible because higher ratings mean cheaper financing costs. If a bond rating drops from investment grade to speculative grade, the cost of debt increases considerably. Historically, the difference in yield between a AAA-rated bond and a BBB-rated bond (the highest and lowest investment grade categories) has averaged 100 basis points, although this spread can be higher or lower depending on economic conditions and investor willingness to take on risk.

The rating categories for Moody's and Standard & Poor's are shown in Figure 21.6.

Figure 21.6: Bond Ratings from Moody's and Standard & Poor's

	Moody's	Standard & Poor's	Grade
Highest quality	Aaa	AAA	Investment grade
High quality	Aa	AA	
Upper medium grade	A	A	
Medium grade	Baa	BBB	
Speculative	Ba	BB	Speculative grade
Highly speculative	B	B	
Substantial risk	Caa	CCC	
Extremely speculative	Ca		
Possibly in default	C		
Default		D	

LOS 21.d: Explain factors an analyst should consider in evaluating the effect of capital structure policy on valuation.

CFA® Program Curriculum, Volume 3, page 110

When evaluating a company's capital structure, the analyst should consider the following factors:

- Changes in the company's capital structure over time.
- Capital structure of competitors with similar business risk.
- Company-specific factors (e.g., quality of corporate governance). Recall that better corporate governance systems will reduce agency costs.

Scenario analysis is a useful tool to determine whether management's current capital structure policy is maximizing the value of the firm. Starting with the firm's current capital structure, an analyst can assess how changes in the firm's debt ratio may reduce the WACC and then evaluate what happens to the firm's value if the company moves toward its optimal capital structure.

LOS 21.e: Describe international differences in the use of financial leverage, factors that explain these differences, and implications of these differences for investment analysis.

CFA® Program Curriculum, Volume 3, page 111

For international firms, country-specific factors may have a significant impact on a firm's capital structure policy. Observations regarding international differences in financial leverage include the following:

- *Total debt.* Companies in Japan, Italy, and France tend to have more total debt in their capital structure than firms in the United States and the U.K.

- *Debt maturity*. Companies in North America tend to use longer maturity debt than companies in Japan.
- *Emerging market differences*. Companies in developed countries tend to use more total debt and use longer maturity debt than firms in emerging markets.

The factors that explain the majority of the differences in capital structure across countries fall into three broad categories: institutional and legal factors, financial markets and banking system factors, and macroeconomic factors.

Institutional and Legal Factors

- *Strength of legal system*. Firms operating in countries with weak legal systems tend to have greater agency costs due to the lack of legal protection for investors. These firms tend to use more leverage in their capital structure and have a greater reliance on short-term debt. By contrast, firms operating in countries with strong legal systems tend to use less debt overall, and the debt used tends to have longer maturities.
- *Information asymmetry*. A high level of information asymmetry between managers and investors encourages greater use of debt (especially short-term debt) in the capital structure. This is so because of greater enforceability of clearly defined debt contracts as opposed to less clearly defined stockholder rights. In countries where auditors and financial analysts have a greater presence, information asymmetries are reduced. Increased transparency tends to result in lower financial leverage.
- *Taxes*. The tax shield provided by debt encourages the use of debt financing; however, this relationship changes somewhat if dividends are taxed at a more favorable rate than interest income. A favorable tax rate for dividends should reduce the return that investors require on equity capital, thus reducing the cost of equity for the firm. The lower cost of equity will cause firms operating in countries with lower tax rates on dividend income to have less debt in their capital structure.

Financial Markets and Banking System Factors

- *Liquidity of capital markets*. Companies operating in countries with larger and more liquid capital markets tend to use longer maturity debt than firms in countries with less liquid capital markets.
- *Reliance on banking system*. Companies operating in countries that are more reliant on the banking system than corporate bond markets as a source of corporate borrowing tend to be more highly leveraged.
- *Institutional investor presence*. A greater prevalence of large institutional investors in a country may affect firms' capital structure as well. Institutional investors may have preferred maturity ranges for their debt investments (preferred habitat). For example, life insurance companies and pension plans may exhibit a preference for long-term debt securities relative to short-term debt. There is some evidence that firms in countries with active institutional investors issue relatively more long-term debt compared to short-term debt. We may also observe marginally lower debt-to-equity ratios in these countries.

PROFESSOR'S NOTE

The concept of institutional investors preferring longer maturity debt is similar to the preferred habitat theory for the shape of the yield curve discussed in the Study Sessions covering Fixed Income.

Macroeconomic Factors

- *Inflation*. Higher inflation reduces the value to investors of fixed interest payments. As a result, firms operating in countries with high inflation tend to use less debt financing, and the debt used has a shorter maturity.
- *GDP growth*. Firms operating in countries with higher GDP growth tend to use longer maturity debt.

The impact of country-specific factors on leverage is summarized in Figure 21.7.

Figure 21.7: Impact of Country-Specific Factors on Capital Structure

Country-Specific Factor	Use of Total Debt	Maturity of Debt
Institutional and Legal Factors		
Strong legal system	Lower	Longer
Less information asymmetry	Lower	Longer
Favorable tax rates on dividends	Lower	N/A
Common law as opposed to civil law	Lower	Longer
Financial Market Factors		
More liquid stock and bond markets	N/A	Longer
Greater reliance on banking system	Higher	N/A
Greater institutional investor presence	Lower	Longer
Macroeconomic Factors		
Higher inflation	Lower	Shorter
Higher GDP growth	Lower	Longer

MODULE QUIZ 21.2

To best evaluate your performance, enter your quiz answers online.

1. Which of the following is *least likely* to be a component of a firm's expected cost of financial distress?
   A. Legal and administrative fees associated with bankruptcy.
   B. Cost of insurance premiums to guarantee management performance.
   C. Loss of trust from customers.

Use the following information to answer Questions 2 through 4.

Darren Munn recently came back from a conference titled Capital Structure Theory and was extremely excited about what he learned concerning Modigliani and Miller's capital structure propositions. Munn has been trying to choose between three potential capital structures for his firm, MunnMart, and believes that Modigliani and Miller's work may guide him in the right direction. The capital structures Munn is considering are:

- 100% equity.
- 50% equity and 50% debt.
- 100% debt.

2. If Munn uses Modigliani and Miller's propositions and includes all of their assumptions including the assumption of no taxes, which capital structure is Munn *most likely* to choose?
   A. 100% equity.
   B. 100% debt.
   C. It does not matter which structure he chooses.
3. If Munn uses Modigliani and Miller's propositions assuming the firm pays taxes, which capital structure is Munn *most likely* to choose?
   A. 100% equity.
   B. 100% debt.
   C. It does not matter which structure he chooses.
4. At the conference, Munn also learned about the static trade-off theory. If Munn uses the static trade-off approach, which capital structure is Munn *most likely* to choose?
   A. Either 100% equity or 100% debt.
   B. 50% equity and 50% debt.
   C. It does not matter which structure he chooses.

Use the following information to answer Questions 5 and 6.

Firms operating in the countries of Remus and Romulus have very different capital structures. Firms operating in Remus have low levels of leverage, and the debt they do have in their capital structure tends to have a long maturity. Firms operating in Romulus have high debt-to-capital ratios with shorter maturity debt.

5. Remus *most likely* has:
   A. a small institutional investor presence.
   B. a strong legal system.
   C. relatively illiquid stock and bond markets.
6. Romulus *most likely* has:
   A. few analysts and auditors working in the country.
   B. a low reliance on the banking system for raising debt capital.
   C. favorable tax rates on dividends.

Use the following information to answer Questions 7 and 8.

Garry Bartolet, the Chief Financial Officer for the Gendron Corporation, is leading a meeting to discuss financing options for the firm. At the meeting, Mary Iwinski, a project manager with Gendron, makes the following statements:

Statement 1: Raising additional debt capital is likely to be more beneficial for our firm than issuing new equity because issuing debt would give a signal to our shareholders that we have confidence in our firm's ability to make future debt service payments.

Statement 2: We need to conduct a careful analysis to decide how much debt to issue because increasing our financial leverage could either increase or decrease Gendron's value.

Statement 3: If our corporate tax rate increases from 25% to 30%, our weighted average cost of capital is likely to decline.

Statement 4: What is happening in the stock or bond markets is irrelevant to our decisions for how to raise capital. We should always seek to raise capital in the exact proportions called for by our optimal capital structure.

7. Iwinski's Statements 1 and 2, respectively, correspond *most closely* to which of the following theories regarding capital structure?

	Statement 1	Statement 2
A.	MM's propositions	Pecking order theory
B.	Static trade-off theory	MM's propositions
C.	Pecking order theory	Static trade-off theory

8. Are Iwinski's Statements 3 and 4 correct or incorrect?
   A. Both statements are correct.
   B. Only one of the statements is correct.
   C. Neither statement is correct.

9. Barney Flint, CFA, is the CFO of Bee Heaven, a publicly traded chain of flower shops. Bee Heaven is currently rated A but is likely to drop to BBB once the disappointing results of an ill-considered merger are released to the public. Flint receives the following quote of credit spreads:

Treasuries	6.00%
AAA	14bp
AA	29bp
A	63bp
BBB	108bp
BB	197bp
B	305bp

Flint is concerned that the $10 million annual pay 20-year bonds Bee Heaven expects to issue next month will now be more expensive. The consequences of more expensive credit are *least likely* to:

A. eliminate several planned expansion projects.
B. invalidate existing bond covenants.
C. increase the weighted average cost of capital.

10. A bond analyst is interested in Bee Heaven's upcoming bond offering; when considering capital structure policy, she should consider each of the following except:

A. changes in the company's capital structure over time.
B. factors affecting agency costs, such as quality of corporate governance.
C. management's mandatory scenario analysis disclosure in the annual report.

KEY CONCEPTS

LOS 21.a

Under the assumptions of no taxes, transaction costs, or bankruptcy costs, the value of the firm is unaffected by leverage changes. MM Proposition I (No Taxes) says capital structure is irrelevant.

MM Proposition II (No Taxes) concerning the cost of equity and leverage says that increasing the use of cheaper debt financing serves to increase the cost of equity, resulting in a zero net change in the company's WACC. Again, the implication is that capital structure is irrelevant.

According to MM Proposition I (With Taxes), the tax deductibility of interest payments creates a tax shield that adds value to the firm, and the optimal capital structure is achieved with 100% debt. MM Proposition II (With Taxes) says that WACC is minimized at 100% debt.

Costs of financial distress are the increased costs companies face when earnings decline and the company has trouble paying its fixed costs. Higher amounts of leverage result in greater expected costs of financial distress.

The net agency costs of equity are the costs associated with the conflict of interest between a company's managers and owners and consist of three components:

- Monitoring costs.
- Bonding costs.
- Residual losses.

Costs of asymmetric information result from managers having more information about a firm than investors. The cost of asymmetric information increases as more equity is used in capital structure. Hence the pecking order theory. Pecking order theory states that managers prefer financing choices that send the least visible signal to investors, with internal capital being most preferred, debt being next, and raising equity externally the least preferred method of financing.

The static trade-off theory seeks to balance the costs of financial distress with the tax shield benefits from using debt and states that there is an optimal capital structure that has an optimal proportion of debt. Removing both MM's assumptions of no taxes and no costs of financial distress, there comes a point where the incremental value added by the tax shield is exceeded by the additional expected costs of financial distress, and this point represents the optimal capital structure.

LOS 21.b

The target capital structure is the structure that the firm uses over time when making capital structure decisions. In practice, the actual capital structure will fluctuate around the target due to management's exploitation of market opportunities and market value fluctuations.

LOS 21.c

Managers typically have goals to maintain a certain minimum credit rating when determining their capital structure policies because the cost of capital is tied to debt ratings; lower ratings translate into higher costs of capital.

LOS 21.d

Factors an analyst should consider when evaluating a firm's capital structure include:

- Changes in the firm's capital structure over time.
- Capital structure of competitors with similar business risk.
- Factors affecting agency costs such as the quality of corporate governance.

LOS 21.e

Major factors that influence international differences in financial leverage include:

- Institutional, legal, and taxation factors.
- Financial market and banking system factors.
- Macroeconomic factors.

ANSWER KEY FOR MODULE QUIZZES

Module Quiz 21.1

1. **A** The optimal capital structure minimizes the firm's WACC and maximizes the firm's value (stock price). (LOS 21.a)

2. **B** MM's Proposition I (No Taxes) states that the cost of equity increases linearly as a company increases its proportion of debt financing. Because debt is cheaper than equity, the net result is a zero change in the firm's WACC. The other statements are incorrect. Under MM's Proposition I (No Taxes), capital structure is irrelevant because value is based on operating cash flows. Note that we are not told whether to assume a world with taxation or without. The most appropriate answer choice is one that applies to either scenario. (LOS 21.a)

Module Quiz 21.2

1. **B** The cost of insurance premiums to guarantee management performance is an example of a bonding cost associated with the net agency cost of equity. The expected costs of financial distress for a firm are based on direct costs such as fees associated with bankruptcy, indirect costs such as loss of trust from customers and suppliers, and the probability of financial distress associated with operating and financial leverage. (Module 21.2, LOS 21.a)

2. **C** Modigliani and Miller's original study was based on the assumption of perfect markets with no taxes and no costs of financial distress. Their conclusion [MM Proposition I (No Taxes)] was that under such assumptions, capital structure has no impact on firm value. (Module 21.1, LOS 21.a)

3. **B** MM Proposition I with taxes concludes that the optimal capital structure is 100% debt. This is because the tax deductibility of interest payments provides a tax shield that adds value to the firm, and the value of the tax shield is maximized with 100% debt. (Module 21.1, LOS 21.a)

4. **B** The static trade-off theory seeks to balance the costs of financial distress with the tax benefits provided by debt and states that there is some optimal capital structure with an optimal proportion of debt. Given Munn's choices, the 50% debt, 50% equity choice is most likely to provide this balance. (Module 21.2, LOS 21.a)

5. **B** Countries where companies have low levels of debt with long maturities in their capital structures tend to have a strong legal system. A small institutional investor presence, illiquid capital markets, and high inflation tend to be associated with either higher leverage or shorter maturity debt. (Module 21.2, LOS 21.e)

6. **A** A lack of analysts and auditors tends to increase information asymmetry, which leads to higher debt usage and shorter debt maturities. Note that a low reliance on the banking system, favorable dividend tax rates, and high GDP growth tend to be associated with either lower debt ratios or the use of longer maturity debt. (Module 21.2, LOS 21.e)

7. **C** Iwinski's Statement 1 is indicative of the pecking order theory, which states that managers prefer financing choices that send the least visible signal to investors, with internal capital being most preferred, debt being next, and raising external equity the least preferred method of financing.

   Iwinski's Statement 2 is indicative of the static trade-off theory. Additional leverage could increase or decrease the value of the firm depending on the relationship between the additional tax benefits of debt and the additional costs of financial distress. The key to static trade-off theory is to find the point where the marginal costs and benefits of additional debt balance, which is the optimal capital structure. (Module 21.2, LOS 21.a)

8. **B** Statement 3 is correct. The cost of debt is measured on an after-tax basis, and the higher the tax rate, the greater the tax shield benefits from using debt. Therefore, the WACC will decrease and firm value will increase, all else equal.

   Statement 4 is incorrect. A firm's target capital structure is best described as a *moving target* where the actual capital structure will fluctuate around the optimal structure. One of the reasons why the actual capital structure may not match the target capital structure is that the financial markets may offer an opportunity to raise cheap debt or equity capital, in which case it makes sense to deviate slightly from the target. (Module 21.2, LOS 21.b)

9. **B** The drop in the bond rating may impact bond covenants but will not invalidate them. Bond covenants are discussed further in the debt securities topic reviews. Higher interest costs will increase WACC, making some borderline projects unviable. Higher debt costs would increase the firm's weighted average cost of capital. (Module 21.2, LOS 21.c)

10. **C** Management is not required to perform or disclose a scenario analysis of capital structure. The analyst may, however, find this tool useful. A capital structure policy evaluation should consider changes in the company's capital structure over time, capital structure of competitors with similar business risk, and factors affecting agency costs, such as quality of corporate governance. (Module 21.2, LOS 21.d)

The following is a review of the Corporate Finance (1) principles designed to address the learning outcome statements set forth by CFA Institute. Cross-Reference to CFA Institute Assigned Reading #22.

READING 22

Dividends and Share Repurchases: Analysis

Study Session 7

EXAM FOCUS

The focus of the Level II exam is valuation, so pay close attention to the theories that explain how dividend policy affects company value and the signals investors get from dividend changes. Payout policy is broader than dividend policy as it includes other means (e.g., special dividends, stock repurchases, etc.) by which companies can pay out cash to stockholders. In recent years, firms have announced plans to repurchase record numbers of shares, making this an important and timely topic. You should have a basic understanding of the factors that affect a firm's payout policy and be able to analyze the sustainability of dividends using coverage ratios.

MODULE 22.1: THEORIES OF DIVIDEND POLICY

Video covering this content is available online.

LOS 22.a: Describe the expected effect of regular cash dividends, extra dividends, liquidating dividends, stock dividends, stock splits, and reverse stock splits on shareholders' wealth and a company's financial ratios.

CFA® Program Curriculum, Volume 3, page 127

Types of dividends include the following:

1. **Regular cash dividends:** Periodic dividend payments made in cash are known as regular cash dividends. Generally, companies strive for stability in their regular dividends—increasing them slowly and refraining from any reductions. Stable or increasing dividends paid regularly are perceived as a sign of consistent (and growing) profitability.

   In some countries, companies can have dividend reinvestment plans (DRPs) that, at shareholders' requests, automatically reinvest all or part of the regular cash dividend by purchasing additional shares. The additional shares can be purchased in the open market (**open market DRP**) or can be newly issued (as in a **new issue DRP**, or **scrip dividend scheme** in the U.K.) by the company.

For the company, a DRP promotes a diverse shareholder base because DRPs provide a cost effective opportunity for small shareholders to accumulate shares. DRPs also promote long-term investment. New issue DRPs allow companies to raise additional capital without the floatation cost of a secondary offering.

DRPs offer shareholders a number of potential advantages. First, DRPs generally allow for purchase of additional shares with no transaction costs. Second, DRPs allow shareholders to benefit from cost averaging. And third, the shares are sometimes offered to DRP participants at a discount to market price.

One disadvantage of DRPs is that shareholders may have to cope with additional record keeping for tax purposes. Dividends reinvested at a market price higher than the original purchase price increase the average cost basis. Additionally, dividends are fully taxed in the year they are paid—even if they are reinvested. Therefore, it makes sense to hold DRPs in tax-sheltered accounts (e.g., retirement accounts).

2. **Extra or special (irregular) dividends:** A cash dividend supplementing regular dividends, or a dividend of a company that normally does not pay dividends, is known as a special dividend. Special dividends are paid under unusual circumstances (e.g., when the company sells off a division) under the expectation that the dividend is not recurring. Extra dividends may be paid if the company had an especially profitable year but does not want to commit to a higher *ongoing* regular dividend payment.
3. **Liquidating dividend:** This is paid by a company when the whole firm or part of the firm is sold, or when dividends in excess of cumulative retained earnings are paid (resulting in a reduction of stated capital). A liquidating dividend is considered to be a return *of* capital as opposed to a return *on* capital.
4. **Stock dividend:** A non-cash dividend paid in the form of additional shares is known as a stock dividend. After payment of a stock dividend, shareholders have more shares and the cost per share will be lower (while the total cost basis remains the same). Shareholders' proportionate ownership of the company does not change, because every shareholder receives the same percentage stock dividend. Shareholders are usually not taxed on stock dividends. Because the market value of the company is unchanged, the market price per share declines, leaving the shareholders with no net gain.

   Imagine a company earning $100,000 annually that has 100,000 shares outstanding with a market price per share of $10. Current EPS and P/E are then $1.00 and 10 respectively. Suppose that this company then declares a 10% stock dividend; the company now has 110,000 shares outstanding and earnings per share (EPS) of $0.90909. Applying the original P/E multiple of 10, the stock price should now be $9.091. Hence, a holder of 110 shares should have holdings valued at $1000—the same as before the stock dividend.

   Companies consider stock dividends desirable because they encourage long-term investing and, hence, may reduce the cost of equity capital. Stock dividends also help increase a stock's float, and therefore, its liquidity. Stock dividends may also be used to decrease the market price of a stock to a desirable trading range that attracts more investors (high stock prices coupled with a minimum order size tend to limit ownership by small retail investors). Companies that continue to pay the same regular cash dividend per share following a stock dividend have effectively increased their cash dividend. However, companies that pay out the same total *amount* of cash dividends as before (i.e., the same payout ratio) effectively *decrease* the dividend per share (though the dividend yield would be unchanged, because dividends and price decrease by same percentage following the stock dividend).

The popularity of stock dividends varies by market. For example, stock dividends are very popular in China.

5. **Stock splits:** These are similar to stock dividends (non-cash) but generally larger in size. A two-for-one stock split is the same as a 100% stock dividend. Reverse stock splits (much less common) reduce the number of shares outstanding and increase the price per share. The intent of a reverse stock split is similar to that of a regular stock split—to bring the market price of the stock within a desirable range, but in this case the firm is trying to attract institutional investors and mutual funds that shun low-priced stocks. Reverse stock splits are less common in Asia (e.g., reverse stock splits were illegal in Japan until 2001).

Accounting Issues

Cash dividend payments reduce cash as well as stockholders' equity. This results in a lower quick ratio and current ratio, and higher leverage (e.g., debt-to-equity and debt-to-asset) ratios. Conversely, stock dividends (and stock splits) leave a company's capital structure unchanged and do not affect any of these ratios. In the case of a stock dividend, a decrease in retained earnings (corresponding to the value of the stock dividend) is offset by an increase in contributed capital, leaving the value of total equity unchanged.

LOS 22.b: Compare theories of dividend policy and explain implications of each for share value given a description of a corporate dividend action.

CFA® Program Curriculum, Volume 3, page 134

Dividend irrelevance. Merton Miller and Franco Modigliani (MM) maintain that *dividend policy* is irrelevant, as it has no effect on the price of a firm's stock or its cost of capital. MM's argument of dividend irrelevance is based on their concept of *homemade dividends*. Assume, for example, that you are a stockholder and you don't like the firm's dividend policy. If the firm's cash dividend is too big, you can just take the excess cash received and use it to buy more of the firm's stock. If the cash dividend you received was too small, you can sell a little bit of your stock in the firm to get the cash flow you want. In either case, the combination of the value of your investment in the firm and your cash in hand will be the same.

You should note that the dividend irrelevance theory holds only in a perfect world with no taxes, no brokerage costs, and infinitely divisible shares. You should also note that the MM discussion pertains to the firm's total *payout policy* (rather than to the narrower *dividend policy*).

Bird-in-hand (dividend preference theory) argument for dividend policy. When MM conclude that dividends are irrelevant, they mean that investors don't care about the firm's dividend policy since they can create their own. If they don't care, the firm's dividend policy will not affect the firm's stock price and, consequently, dividend policy will not affect the firm's required rate of return on equity capital (r_s). Myron Gordon and John Lintner, however, argue that r_s decreases as the dividend payout increases. Why? Because investors are less certain of receiving future capital gains from the reinvested retained earnings than they are of receiving current (and therefore certain) dividend payments. The main argument of Gordon and Lintner is that investors place a higher value on a dollar of dividends that they are certain to receive than on a dollar of *expected* capital gains. They base this argument on the fact that, when measuring total return, the dividend yield component, D_1 / P_0, has less risk than the growth component g.

PROFESSOR'S NOTE

The Gordon/Lintner argument is called the bird-in-the-hand-theory based on the old expression: a "bird in the hand" (dividends) is worth two in the bush (expected capital gains).

Tax aversion. In many countries, dividends have historically been taxed at higher rates than capital gains. In the 1970s, U.S. tax rates on dividend income were as high as 70%, while the taxes on capital gains were 35%. In the late 1990s, the rates were much lower, but the same general relationship was still in place: dividends were taxed as ordinary income with rates as high as 39.1%, while long-term capital gains were taxed at 20%. Under such a situation, according to the tax-aversion theory, investors will prefer to *not* receive dividends due to their higher tax rates. Taken to the extreme, the tax-aversion theory implies that investors would want companies to have a zero dividend payout ratio so that they will not be burdened with higher tax rates.

In the real world, tax laws often prevent companies from accumulating excess earnings, making dividend payments necessary. Also note that in 2003, tax laws in the United States changed so that dividends and long-term capital gains are both taxed at the same 15% rate.

Conclusions from the three theories. The results of empirical tests are unclear as to which of these theories best explains the empirical observations of dividend policy. Research suggests that higher tax rates do result in lower dividend payouts. In the United States, however, the change in tax law that put dividends and capital gains on common ground is likely to make the tax aversion theory irrelevant. There is empirical support for the "bird-in-the-hand" theory as some companies that pay dividends are perceived as less risky and specific groups of investors do prefer dividend paying stocks. MM counter this argument by saying that different dividend policies appeal to different clienteles, and that since all types of clients are active in the marketplace, dividend policy has no effect on company value if all clienteles are satisfied.

LOS 22.c: Describe types of information (signals) that dividend initiations, increases, decreases, and omissions may convey.

CFA® Program Curriculum, Volume 3, page 141

Information asymmetry refers to differences in information available to a company's board and management (insiders) as compared to the investors (outsiders). Dividends convey more credible information to the investors as compared to plain statements. This is so because dividends entail actual cash flow and are expected to be "sticky" (i.e., continue in the future). Companies refrain from increasing dividends unless they expect to continue to pay out the higher levels in the future. Similarly, companies loathe cutting dividends unless they expect that the lower levels of dividends reflect long-run poorer prospects of the company in the future.

The information conveyed by **dividend initiation** is ambiguous. On one hand, a dividend initiation could mean that a company is optimistic about the future and is sharing its wealth with stockholders—a positive signal. On the other hand, initiating a dividend could mean that a company has a lack of profitable reinvestment opportunities—a negative signal.

An **unexpected dividend increase** can signal to investors that a company's future business prospects are strong and that managers will share the success with shareholders. Studies have found that companies with a long history of dividend increases, such as GE and Exxon Mobil, are dominant in their industries and have high returns on assets and low debt ratios.

Unexpected dividend decreases or **omissions** are typically negative signals that the business is in trouble and that management does not believe that the current dividend payment can be maintained. In rare instances, however, a dividend decrease or omission could be a positive sign. Management may believe that profitable investment opportunities are available and that shareholders would ultimately receive a greater benefit by having earnings reinvested in the company rather than being paid out as dividends.

LOS 22.d: Explain how clientele effects and agency costs may affect a company's payout policy.

CFA® Program Curriculum, Volume 3, page 137

OTHER DIVIDEND POLICY THEORIES

Clientele effect. This refers to the varying dividend preferences of different groups of investors, such as individuals, institutions, and corporations. The dividend clientele effect states that different groups desire different levels of dividends. Rationales for the existence of the clientele effect include:

- *Tax considerations.* High-tax-bracket investors (like some individuals) tend to prefer low dividend payouts, while low-tax-bracket investors (like corporations and pension funds) may prefer high dividend payouts.

  In the presence of differential tax rates on dividends (T_D) and capital gains (T_{CG}), investors would be indifferent between receiving: \$D in dividends or \$D $(1 - T_D) / (1 - T_{CG})$ in capital gains.

Study Session 7

In other words, when the stock goes ex-dividend:

$$\Delta P = \frac{D(1-T_D)}{(1-T_{CG})}$$

where:

ΔP = change in price when the stock goes from with dividend to ex-dividend

EXAMPLE: Dividends vs. capital gains

1. Consider a firm that is planning to declare €12 in dividends. The tax rates for a marginal investor are: T_{CG} = 15% and T_D = 30%. Compute the expected drop in share price when the stock goes ex-dividend.
2. Suppose the tax rate on capital gains T_{CG} = 25%. If the stock price of a company falls by 85% of the dividend amount on average when the stock goes ex-dividend, what is the tax rate on dividends for a marginal investor in that stock?

Answer:

1. Expected drop in stock price = 12 × (1 – 0.30) / (1 – 0.15) = €9.88. In other words, investors would be indifferent between €12 in dividends and €9.88 in capital gains. Note that since the tax rate on dividends is higher, investors would prefer capital gains over dividends. Hence, a €1 dividend is worth less than a €1 capital gain.
2. $\Delta P = D(1 - T_D) / (1 - T_{CG})$

   $0.85 = 1(1 - T_D) / (1 - 0.25)$

   $T_D = 0.3625$

- Requirements of institutional investors. For legal or strategic reasons, some institutional investors will invest only in companies that pay a dividend or have a dividend yield above some target threshold. Examples are dividend-focused mutual funds and some trusts that are required to hold dividend-paying stocks.
- *Individual investor preferences*. Some investors prefer to buy stocks so they can spend the dividends while preserving the principal.

It should be noted that the existence of dividend clienteles does not contradict dividend irrelevance theory. A firm's dividend policy would attract a certain clientele. After that, changes in the policy would have no impact as the firm would be simply swapping one clientele for other.

Agency Costs

Between shareholders and managers: Agency costs reflect the inefficiencies due to divergence of interests between managers and stockholders. One aspect of agency issue is that managers may have an incentive to overinvest ("empire building"). This may lead to investment in some negative NPV projects, which reduces stockholder wealth. One way to reduce agency cost is to increase the payout of free cash flow as dividends. Generally, it makes sense for growing firms to retain a larger proportion of their earnings. However, mature firms in relatively non-cyclical industries do not need to hoard cash. In such cases, a higher dividend payout would be welcomed by the investors resulting in increases in stock value.

Between shareholders and bondholders: For firms financed by debt as well as equity, there may be an agency conflict between shareholders and bondholders. When there is risky debt outstanding, shareholders can pay themselves a large dividend, leaving the bondholders with a lower asset base as collateral. This way, there could be a transfer of wealth from bondholders to stockholders. Typically, agency conflict between stockholders and bondholders is resolved via provisions in the bond indenture. These provisions may include restrictions on dividend payment, maintenance of certain balance sheet ratios, and so on.

LOS 22.e: Explain factors that affect dividend policy in practice.

CFA® Program Curriculum, Volume 3, page 147

A company's dividend payout policy is the approach a company follows in determining the amount and timing of dividend payments to shareholders. Six primary factors affect a company's dividend payout policy:

1. **Investment opportunities.** Availability of positive NPV investment opportunities and the speed with which the firm must react to the opportunities determines the amount of cash the firm must keep on hand. If a firm faces many profitable investment opportunities and has to react quickly to capitalize on the opportunities (i.e., it does not have time to raise external capital), the dividend payout may be low.
2. **Expected volatility of future earnings.** Firms tie their target payout ratio to long-run sustainable earnings and are reluctant to increase dividends unless reversal is not expected in the near future. Hence, when earnings are volatile, firms are more cautious in *changing* dividend payout.
3. **Financial flexibility.** Firms with excess cash and a desire to maintain financial flexibility may resort to stock repurchases instead of dividends as a way to pay out excess cash. Since stock repurchase plans are not considered sticky (i.e., there is no implicit expectation by the market of an ongoing repurchase program), they don't entail reduction in financial flexibility going forward. Having cash on hand affords companies flexibility to meet unforeseen operating needs and investment opportunities. Financial flexibility is especially important during times of crisis when liquidity dries up and credit may be hard to obtain.
4. **Tax considerations.** Investors are concerned about after-tax returns. Investment income is taxed by most countries; however, the ways that dividends are taxed vary widely from country to country. The method and amount of tax applied to a dividend payment can have a significant impact on a firm's dividend policy. Generally, in countries where capital gains are taxed at a favorable rate compared to dividends, high-tax-bracket investors (like some individuals) prefer low dividend payouts, and low-tax-bracket investors (like corporations and pension funds) prefer high dividend payouts.

   A lower tax rate for dividends compared to capital gains does not necessarily mean companies will raise their dividend payouts. Stockholders may not prefer a higher dividend payout, even if the tax rate on dividends is more favorable, for multiple reasons:

- Taxes on dividends are paid when the dividend is received, while capital gains taxes are paid only when shares are sold.
- The cost basis of shares may receive a step-up in valuation at the shareholder's death. This means that taxes on capital gains may not have to be paid at all.
- Tax-exempt institutions, such as pension funds and endowments, will be indifferent between dividends or capital gains.

5. **Flotation costs.** When a company issues new shares of common stock, a *flotation cost* of 3% to 7% is taken from the amount of capital raised to pay for investment bankers and other costs associated with issuing the new stock. Since retained earnings have no such fee, the cost of new equity capital is always higher than the cost of retained earnings. Larger companies typically have lower flotation costs as compared to smaller companies. Generally, the higher the floatation costs, the lower the dividend payout, given the need for equity capital in positive NPV projects.
6. **Contractual and legal restrictions**. Companies may be restricted from paying dividends either by legal requirements or by implicit restrictions caused by cash needs of the business. Common legal and contractual restrictions on dividend payments include:
   - The **impairment of capital rule.** A legal requirement in some countries mandates that dividends paid cannot be in excess of retained earnings.
   - **Debt covenants.** These are designed to protect bondholders and dictate things a company must or must not do. Many covenants require a firm to meet or exceed a certain target for liquidity ratios (e.g., current ratio) and coverage ratios (e.g., interest coverage ratio) before they can pay a dividend.

LOS 22.f: Calculate and interpret the effective tax rate on a given currency unit of corporate earnings under double taxation, dividend imputation, and split-rate tax systems.

CFA® Program Curriculum, Volume 3, page 149

Dividends paid in the United States are taxed according to what is called a **double-taxation system**. Earnings are taxed at the corporate level regardless of whether they are distributed as dividends, and dividends are taxed again at the shareholder level. In 2003, new tax legislation was passed in the United States that reduced the maximum tax rate on dividends at the individual shareholder level from 39.6% to 15%.

Since a dollar of earnings distributed as dividends is first taxed at the corporate level, with the after-corporate-tax amount taxed at the individual level, we can calculate the total effective tax rate as:

effective tax rate
= corporate tax rate + (1 − corporate tax rate)(individual tax rate)

EXAMPLE: Effective tax rate under a double taxation system

A U.S. company's annual earnings are $300, and the corporate tax rate is 35%. Assume that the company pays out 100% of its earnings as dividends. Calculate the effective tax rate on a dollar of corporate earnings paid out as dividends assuming a 15% tax rate on dividend income.

Answer:

Earnings	$300.00
(–) Tax @ 35%	(105.00)
Earnings after tax	195.00
Dividends (100% payout)	195.00
Tax on dividends (@ 15%)	(29.25)
After tax dividend to investor	165.75

Effective (double) tax rate = (300 – 165.75) / 300 = 44.75%

or

0.35 + (1 – 0.35)(0.15) = 0.4475 or 44.75%.

A **split-rate** corporate tax system taxes earnings distributed as dividends at a lower rate than earnings that are retained. The effect is to offset the higher (double) tax rate applied to dividends at the individual level. Germany had a split-rate system until 2009. The calculation of the effective tax rate under a split rate system is similar to the computation of the effective tax rate under double taxation except that the corporate tax rate applicable would be the corporate tax rate for distributed income.

EXAMPLE: Effective tax rate under a split-rate system

A German company's annual pretax earnings are €300. The corporate tax rate on retained earnings is 35%, and the corporate tax rate that applies to earnings paid out as dividends is 20%. Assuming that the company pays out 50% of its earnings as dividends, and the individual tax rate that applies to dividends is 30%, calculate the effective tax rate on one euro of corporate earnings paid out as a dividend.

Answer:

effective tax rate on income distributed as dividends
= 20% + [(1 – 20%) × 30%] = 44%

Note that under a split-rate system, earnings that are distributed as dividends are still taxed twice, but at a lower corporate tax rate (the corporate rate for distributed income).

Under an **imputation tax system**, taxes are paid at the corporate level but are attributed to the shareholder, so that *all taxes are effectively paid at the shareholder rate*. Shareholders deduct their portion of the taxes paid by the corporation from their tax return. If the shareholder tax bracket is lower than the company rate, the shareholder would receive a tax credit equal to the difference between the two rates.

If the shareholder's tax bracket is higher than the company's rate, the shareholder pays the difference between the two rates.

EXAMPLE: Effective tax rate under an imputation system

Phil Cornelius and Ian Todd both own 100 shares of stock in a British corporation that makes £1.00 per share in pretax income. The corporation pays out all of its income as dividends. Cornelius is in the 20% individual tax bracket, while Todd is in the 40% individual tax bracket. The tax rate applicable to the corporation is 30%. Calculate the effective tax rate on the dividend for each shareholder.

Answer:

Effective Tax Rate Under an Imputation System

	Cornelius: 20% Rate	Todd: 40% Rate
Pretax income	£100	£100
Taxes at 30% corporate tax rate	£30	£30
Net income after tax	£70	£70
Dividend assuming 100% payout	£70	£70
Shareholder taxes	£20	£40
Less tax credit for corporate payment	£30	£30
Tax due from shareholder	(£10)	£10
Effective tax rate on dividend	20 / 100 = 20%	40 / 100 = 40%

Under an imputation system, the effective tax rate on the dividend is simply the shareholder's marginal tax rate.

MODULE QUIZ 22.1

To best evaluate your performance, enter your quiz answers online.

1. In a country where capital gains are taxed favorably compared to dividends, when a share goes ex-dividend, the share's price is *most likely* to drop by:
   A. less than the amount of the dividend.
   B. more than the amount of the dividend.
   C. the same amount as the dividend.

Use the following information to answer Questions 2 through 4.

Klaatu is a country that taxes dividends based on a double-taxation system. The corporate tax rate on company profits is 35%. Barada is a country that taxes dividends based on a split-rate tax system. The corporate tax rate applied to retained earnings is 36%, while the corporate tax rate applied to earnings paid out as dividends is 20%. Nikto is a country that taxes dividends based on an imputation tax system. The corporate tax rate on earnings is 38%.

2. An investor living in Klaatu holds 100 shares of stock in the Lucas Corporation. Lucas's pretax earnings for the current year are $2.00 per share, and the company has a payout ratio of 100%. The investor's individual tax rate on dividends is 30%. The effective tax rate on a dollar of funds to be paid out as dividends is *closest* to:
   A. 35.0%.
   B. 54.5%.
   C. 62.3%.
3. An investor living in Barada holds 100 shares of Prowse, Inc. Prowse's pretax earnings in the current year are $1.00 per share, and Prowse pays dividends based on a target payout ratio of 40%. The individual tax rate that applies to dividends is 28%, and the individual tax rate that applies to capital gains is 15%. The effective tax rate on earnings distributed as dividends is:
   A. 20.0%.
   B. 42.4%.
   C. 53.9%.
4. Jenni White and Janet Langhals are each shareholders that live in Nikto, and each owns 100 shares of OCP, Inc., which has €1.00 per share in net income. OCP pays out 100% of its earnings as dividends. White is in the 25% tax bracket, while Langhals is in the 42% tax bracket. The effective tax rate on earnings paid out as dividends is:
   A. 28.0% for White and 42.0% for Langhals.
   B. 53.5% for White and 64.0% for Langhals.
   C. 25.0% for White and 42.0% for Langhals.
5. Which of the following factors would encourage a company to maintain a high dividend payout ratio?
   A. The double-taxation system is in place in the company's home country.
   B. Most of the shares in the company are held by income-oriented mutual funds.
   C. The company's debt covenants require an interest coverage ratio of at least 2.0x.
6. The bird-in-hand argument for dividend policy is based on the idea that:
   A. $r_s = D_1 / P_0 + g$ is constant for any dividend policy.
   B. a decrease in current dividends signals that future earnings will fall.
   C. because of perceived differences in risk, investors value a dollar of dividends more highly than a dollar of expected capital gains.

Study Session 7

Video covering this content is available online.

MODULE 22.2: STOCK BUYBACKS

LOS 22.g: Compare stable dividend, constant dividend payout ratio, and residual dividend payout policies, and calculate the dividend under each policy.

CFA® Program Curriculum, Volume 3, page 155

Stable Dividend Policy

The **stable dividend policy** focuses on a steady dividend payout, even though earnings may be volatile from year to year. Companies that use a stable dividend policy typically look at a forecast of their long-run earnings to determine the appropriate level for the stable dividend. This typically means aligning the company's dividend growth rate with the company's long-term earnings growth rate.

A stable dividend policy could be gradually moving towards a target dividend payout ratio. A model of gradual adjustment is called a **target payout adjustment model**.

Target Payout Adjustment Model

If company earnings are expected to increase and the current payout ratio is below the target payout ratio, an investor can estimate future dividends through the following formula:

expected increase in dividends = [(expected earnings × target payout ratio) – previous dividend] × adjustment factor

where:

adjustment factor = 1 / number of years over which the adjustment in dividends will take place

EXAMPLE: Expected dividend based on a target payout adjustment approach

Last year, Buckeye, Inc., had earnings of \$3.50 per share and paid a dividend of \$0.70. In the current year, the company expects to earn \$4.50 per share. The company has a 35% target payout ratio and plans to bring its dividend up to the target payout ratio over a 5-year period. Calculate the expected dividend for the current year using the target payout adjustment model.

Answer:

expected increase in dividends

= [(expected earnings × target payout ratio) – previous dividend] × adjustment factor

= [(\$4.50 × 35%) – \$0.70] × 0.2 = \$0.175

expected dividend for the current year

= previous dividend + expected increase in dividends

= \$0.70 + \$0.175 = \$0.875

PROFESSOR'S NOTE

Notice that the payout ratio actually *falls* from 20% to 19.4%. This is counterintuitive and seems to contradict the concept of the target payout ratio approach, which suggests that the firm should always be moving toward its target payout ratio (which in this case is 35%). Level II candidates are always troubled by the apparent inconsistency in the target payout adjustment approach. However, we can assure you that this example correctly applies the method and answers the LOS accurately. The target payout adjustment approach is expected to work in the long-run, even though year-to-year results may defy the logic behind it.

Constant Dividend Payout Ratio Policy

A payout ratio is the percentage of total earnings paid out as dividends. The constant payout ratio represents the proportion of earnings that a company plans to pay out to shareholders. A strict interpretation of the constant payout ratio method means that a company would pay out a specific percentage of its earnings each year as dividends, and the amount of those dividends would vary directly with earnings. This practice is seldom used.

Residual Dividend Model

In the **residual dividend model**, dividends are based on earnings less funds the firm retains to finance the equity portion of its capital budget. The model is based on the firm's (1) investment opportunity schedule (IOS), (2) target capital structure, and (3) access to and cost of external capital.

The following steps are followed to determine the target payout ratio (dividends per share / earnings per share):

Step 1: Identify the optimal capital budget.

Step 2: Determine the amount of equity needed to finance that capital budget for a given capital structure.

Step 3: Meet equity requirements to the maximum extent possible with retained earnings.

Step 4: Pay dividends with the "residual" earnings that are available after the needs of the optimal capital budget are supported. In other words, the residual policy implies that dividends are paid out of leftover earnings.

EXAMPLE: Dividends under the residual dividend model

Suppose that the Larson Company has $1,000 in earnings and $900 in planned capital spending (representing positive NPV projects). Larson has a target debt-to-equity ratio of 0.5. Calculate the company's dividend under a residual dividend policy.

Study Session 7

Answer:

Larson has a target debt-to-equity ratio of 0.5. This implies a capital structure of one-third debt and two-thirds equity. (If D is $1.00, equity, E, must be $2.00 since D/E = 0.5 = 1/2. This means that assets, A, are $3.00 = $1.00 + $2.00, so the capital structure is D/A = 1/3 and E/A = 2/3).

If planned capital spending is less than the total amount of capital available, the firm can pay dividends. To maintain the target capital structure, the $900 capital spending will be financed with [(1/3)($900)] = $300 of debt and [(2/3)($900)] = $600 of equity. The residual amount is ($1,000 – $600) = $400, so dividends under the residual method would be $400.

Advantages of the residual dividend model:

- The model is simple to use. The company uses the funds necessary to invest in profitable projects and then gives what is left over to the shareholders.
- The model allows management to pursue profitable investment opportunities without being constrained by dividend considerations.

Disadvantages of the residual dividend model:

- If a firm follows the residual dividend policy, its dividend payments may be unstable. Investment opportunities and earnings often vary from year to year. This means that dividends will fluctuate if a firm strictly adheres to a residual dividend policy.

Long-term residual dividend. Some companies try to mitigate the disadvantages of the residual dividend approach by forecasting their capital budget over a longer time frame (e.g., five to ten years). The leftover earnings over this longer time frame are allocated as dividends and are paid out in relatively equal amounts each year. Any excess cash flows are distributed through share repurchases.

Now that we have discussed various dividend policy approaches, it is important to point out that a share repurchase program can be an important part of a company's payout policy. A share repurchase is a transaction in which a company buys back its own common stock. Because shares are bought using a company's own cash, a share repurchase can be considered an alternative to a cash dividend.

LOS 22.h: Compare share repurchase methods.

CFA® Program Curriculum, Volume 3, page 162

Four common methods are used for share buybacks, though due to varying rules, some markets may not allow all methods. Outside the United States and Canada, method 1 is used almost exclusively.

1. **Open market transactions** are the most flexible approach, allowing a company to buy back its shares in the open market at the most favorable terms. There is no obligation on the part of the company to complete an announced buyback program. Unlike their European counterparts, American companies do not need shareholder approval for open market transactions.

2. **Fixed price tender offer** is an approach where the firm buys a predetermined number of shares at a fixed price, typically at a premium over the current market price. Although the company forgoes flexibility (the firm cannot execute its purchases at an exact opportune time), it allows a company to buy back its shares rather quickly. If more than the desired number of shares are tendered in response to the offer, the company will typically buy back a prorated number of shares from each shareholder responding to the offer.
3. **Dutch auction** is a tender offer in which the company specifies not a single fixed price but rather a range of prices. Dutch auctions identify the minimum clearing price for the desired number of shares that need to be repurchased. Each participating shareholder indicates the price and the number of shares tendered. Bids are accepted based on lowest price first until the desired quantity is filled. The price of the last offer accepted (i.e., the highest accepted bid price) will however be the price paid for all shares tendered. Hence, a shareholder can increase the chance of having their tender accepted by offering shares at a low price. Dutch auctions also can be accomplished rather quickly, though not as quickly as tender offers.
4. **Repurchase by direct negotiation** entails purchasing shares from a major shareholder, often at a premium over market price. This method is often used in a greenmail scenario (where a hostile bidder is offered a premium to go away) to the detriment of the remaining shareholders. A negotiated purchase can also occur when a company wants to remove a large overhang in the market that is dampening the share price. Surprisingly, many negotiated transactions occur at a discount to market price, indicating that urgent liquidity needs of the seller motivated the transaction.

LOS 22.i: Calculate and compare the effect of a share repurchase on earnings per share when 1) the repurchase is financed with the company's surplus cash and 2) the company uses debt to finance the repurchase.

CFA® Program Curriculum, Volume 3, page 164

Repurchases made using a company's surplus cash will lower cash and shareholders' equity and, therefore, increase the firm's leverage (i.e., the debt-to-asset and debt-to-equity ratios). After the repurchase, earnings per share may increase (depending on the amount of cash used) because there will be fewer shares outstanding. If the repurchase was financed with additional debt offerings, the reduction in net income from the (after-tax) cost of the borrowed funds must also be factored in to determine the new impact on earnings per share.

> **EXAMPLE: Methods of financing a stock repurchase and their effect on EPS**
>
> JetFun Inc. has 10 million shares outstanding and has just reported net income of $50 million. Because the company has $100 million of excess cash currently earning no return, JetFun's directors are considering repurchasing 2 million JetFun shares at a premium of 25% over the current market price of $40. Calculate and compare the effect of repurchase on EPS when the repurchase is (1) financed using the existing surplus cash, or (2) financed using new debt borrowed at an after-tax interest rate of 3%.

Answer:

Current EPS = \$50 million / 10 million shares = \$5

Repurchase price = \$40 + 25% premium = 40(1.25) = \$50 per share

Total cost of repurchase = \$50 × 2 million shares = \$100 million

Number of shares outstanding after buyback = 10 – 2 = 8 million shares

1. Using surplus cash:

   foregone income = \$0

   new EPS = \$50 million / 8 million shares = \$6.25 (*an increase of 25% from \$5*)

2. Using new debt:

   after-tax cost of funds = 3% of \$100 million or \$3 million

   earnings after deducting the cost of funds = 50 – 3 = \$47 million

   new EPS = \$47 million / 8 million shares = \$5.875 (*an increase of 17.5% from \$5*)

Note: Earnings yield before repurchase = EPS / price paid per share = 5/50 = 10%. When earnings yield is greater than the after-tax cost of debt (as is the case in both funding scenarios here), EPS will increase due to the repurchase.

From the previous example, we see that EPS will increase when the after-tax funding cost is less than the earnings yield. However, the firm will then also have higher leverage and, therefore, a higher cost of capital. Accordingly, an increase in EPS should not automatically lead to an increase in share price or in shareholder wealth.

LOS 22.j: Calculate the effect of a share repurchase on book value per share.

CFA® Program Curriculum, Volume 3, page 166

After a stock repurchase, the number of outstanding shares will decrease and the book value per share (BVPS) is likely to change as well. If the price paid is higher (lower) than the pre-repurchase BVPS, the BVPS will decrease (increase).

EXAMPLE: Impact of share repurchase on book value per share

Consider two companies, Alpha and Beta, which are both considering the repurchase of \$5 million worth of shares. Additional details are given below.

	Alpha	Beta
Stock price	\$20	\$20
Number of shares outstanding	1 million	1 million
Book value	\$15 million	\$25 million

Calculate the impact of the repurchase transactions on BVPS.

Answer:

	Alpha	Beta
BVPS (before buyback)	15 / 1 = $15	25 / 1 = $25
Number of shares repurchased	$5 million / $20 = 250,000	$5 million / $20 = 250,000
Number of shares outstanding (after buyback)	1,000,000 – 250,000 = 750,000	1,000,000 – 250,000 = 750,000
Book value (after buyback)	15 – 5 = $10 million	25 – 5 = $20 million
BVPS (after buyback)	$10 million / 750,000 = $13.33	$20 million / 750,000 = $26.67

Alpha's BVPS of $15.00 was less than the $20.00 stock price, so after the buyback, Alpha's BVPS decreased to $13.33. Beta's BVPS increased from $25.00 to $26.67 after the buyback because the BVPS was greater than the $20.00 stock price.

LOS 22.k: Explain the choice between paying cash dividends and repurchasing shares.

CFA® Program Curriculum, Volume 3, page 167

There are five common rationales for share repurchases (versus dividends):

1. **Potential tax advantages.** When the tax rate on capital gains is lower than the tax rate on dividend income, share repurchases have a tax advantage over cash dividends.

2. **Share price support/signaling.** Companies may purchase their own stock, thereby signaling to the market that the company views its own stock as a good investment. Signaling is important in the presence of asymmetric information (where corporate insiders have access to better information about the company's prospects than outside investors). Management can send a signal to investors that the future outlook for the company is good. This tactic is often used when a share price is declining and management wants to convey confidence in the company's future to investors.

3. **Added flexibility.** A company could declare a regular cash dividend and periodically repurchase shares as a supplement to the dividend. Unlike dividends, share repurchases are not a long-term commitment. Since paying a cash dividend and repurchasing shares are economically equivalent, a company could declare a small stable dividend and then repurchase shares with the company's leftover earnings to effectively implement a residual dividend policy without the negative impact that fluctuating cash dividends may have on the share price. Additionally, managers have discretion with respect to "market timing" their repurchases.

4. **Offsetting dilution from employee stock options.** Repurchases offset EPS dilution that results from the exercise of employee stock options.
5. **Increasing financial leverage.** When funded by new debt, share repurchases increase leverage. Management can change the company's capital structure (and perhaps move toward the company's optimal capital structure) by decreasing the percentage of equity.

EXAMPLE: Impact of share repurchase and cash dividend of equal amounts

Spencer Pharmaceuticals, Inc. (SPI) has 20,000,000 shares outstanding with a current market value of $50 per share. SPI made $100 million in profits for the recent quarter, and since only 70% of these profits will be reinvested back into the company, SPI's Board of Directors is considering two alternatives for distributing the remaining 30% to shareholders:

- Pay a cash dividend of $30,000,000 / 20,000,000 shares = $1.50 per share.
- Repurchase $30,000,000 worth of common stock.

Suppose that dividends are received when the shares go ex-dividend, the stock can be repurchased at the market price of $50 per share, and there are no differences in tax treatment between the two alternatives. How would the wealth of an SPI shareholder be affected by the board's chosen method of distribution?

Answer:

(1) Cash dividend

After the shares go ex-dividend, a shareholder of a single share would have $1.50 in cash and a share worth $50 – $1.50 = $48.50.

The ex-dividend value of $48.50 can also be calculated as the market value of equity after the distribution of the $30 million, divided by the number of shares outstanding after the dividend payment.

$$\frac{(20{,}000{,}000)(\$50)\ -\ \$30{,}000{,}000}{20{,}000{,}000} = \$48.50$$

Total wealth from the ownership of one share = $48.50 + $1.50 = $50.

(2) Share repurchase

With $30,000,000, SPI could repurchase $30,000,000 / $50 = 600,000 shares of common stock. The share price after the repurchase is calculated as the market value of equity after the $30,000,000 repurchase divided by the shares outstanding after the repurchase:

$$\frac{(20{,}000{,}000)\ (\$50)\ -\ \$30{,}000{,}000}{20{,}000{,}000\ -\ 600{,}000} = \frac{\$970{,}000{,}000}{19{,}400{,}000} = \$50$$

Total wealth from the ownership of one share = $50.

This demonstrates that, assuming the tax treatment of the two alternatives is the same, a share repurchase has the same impact on shareholder wealth as a cash dividend payment of an equal amount.

In the previous example, we assumed that the company used cash to repurchase its stock. What if the company borrows funds to buy back the stock?

EXAMPLE: Share repurchase when the after-tax cost of debt is less than the earnings yield

Spencer Pharmaceuticals, Inc. (SPI) plans to borrow $30 million that it will use to repurchase shares. SPI's chief financial officer has compiled the following information:

- Share price at the time of buyback = $50.
- Shares outstanding before buyback = 20,000,000.
- EPS before buyback = $5.00.
- Earnings yield = $5.00 / $50 = 10%.
- After-tax cost of borrowing = 8%.
- Planned buyback = 600,000 shares.

Calculate the EPS after the buyback.

Answer:

total earnings = $5.00 × 20,000,000 = $100,000,000

$$\text{EPS after buyback} = \frac{\text{total earnings} - \text{after-tax cost of funds}}{\text{shares outstanding after buyback}}$$

$$= \frac{\$100{,}000{,}000 - (600{,}000 \text{ shares} \times \$50 \times 0.08)}{(20{,}000{,}000 - 600{,}000) \text{ shares}}$$

$$= \frac{\$100{,}000{,}000 - \$2{,}400{,}000}{19{,}400{,}000 \text{ shares}}$$

$$= \frac{\$97{,}600{,}000}{19{,}400{,}000 \text{ shares}}$$

= $5.03 per share

Since the after-tax cost of borrowing of 8% is less than the 10% earnings yield (E/P) of the shares, the share repurchase will increase the company's EPS.

EXAMPLE: Share repurchase with borrowed funds, where the after-tax cost of debt *exceeds* the earnings yield

Spencer Pharmaceuticals, Inc. (SPI) plans to borrow $30 million that it will use to repurchase shares; however, creditors perceive the company to be a significant credit risk, and the after-tax cost of borrowing has jumped to 15%. Using the other information from the previous example, calculate the EPS after the buyback.

Answer:

$$\text{EPS after buyback} = \frac{\text{total earnings} - \text{after-tax cost of funds}}{\text{shares outstanding after buyback}}$$

$$= \frac{\$100{,}000{,}000 - (600{,}000 \text{ shares} \times \$50 \times 0.15)}{(20{,}000{,}000 - 600{,}000) \text{ shares}}$$

$$= \frac{\$100{,}000{,}000 - \$4{,}500{,}000}{19{,}400{,}000 \text{ shares}}$$

$$= \frac{\$95{,}500{,}000}{19{,}400{,}000 \text{ shares}}$$

$$= \$4.92 \text{ per share}$$

Because the after-tax cost of borrowing of 15% exceeds the earnings yield of 10%, the added interest paid reduces earnings, and the EPS after the buyback is less than the original $5.00.

The conclusion is that a share repurchase using borrowed funds will increase EPS if the after-tax cost of debt used to buy back shares is less than the earnings yield of the shares before the repurchase. It will decrease EPS if the cost of debt is greater than the earnings yield, and it will not change EPS if the two are equal.

LOS 22.1: Describe broad trends in corporate payout policies.

CFA® Program Curriculum, Volume 3, page 177

Dividend policy has been seen to have differences across countries and over time. This is probably to accommodate differences in investor preferences globally as well as changing investor preferences over time. The following generalizations can be made with respect to global trends in corporate payout policies:

1. A lower proportion of U.S. companies pay dividends compared to their European counterparts.
2. Globally, in developed markets, the proportion of companies paying cash dividends has trended downwards over the long term.
3. The percentage of companies making stock repurchases has been trending upwards in the United States since the 1980s and in the United Kingdom and continental Europe since the 1990s.

LOS 22.m: Calculate and interpret dividend coverage ratios based on 1) net income and 2) free cash flow.

LOS 22.n: Identify characteristics of companies that may not be able to sustain their cash dividend.

CFA® Program Curriculum, Volume 3, page 179 and 182

Dividend safety is the metric used to evaluate the probability of dividends continuing at the current rate for a company. Traditional ratios, such as **dividend payout ratio** (dividends/net income) or its inverse **dividend coverage ratio** (net income/dividends), are typically used for this purpose. A higher than normal dividend payout ratio (and lower than normal dividend coverage ratio) tends to typically indicate a higher probability of a dividend cut (or a lower probability of dividend sustainability).

In analyzing these ratios, we should compare the computed ratio to the average ratio for the industry and market within which a company operates. In making a qualitative judgment about a company, stable or increasing dividends are looked upon favorably, whereas companies that have cut their dividends in the past are looked upon unfavorably.

Another ratio considers free cash flow to equity (FCFE). FCFE is the cash flow available for distribution to stockholders after working capital and fixed capital needs are accounted for.

PROFESSOR'S NOTE

FCFE is discussed extensively in the Equity Valuation portion of the curriculum.

FCFE coverage ratio = FCFE / (dividends + share repurchases)

Note that unlike the dividend payout ratio, the FCFE coverage ratio considers not only dividends but also share repurchases.

A FCFE coverage ratio significantly less than one is considered unsustainable. In such a situation, the company is drawing down its cash reserves for dividends and repurchases.

Study Session 7

EXAMPLE: Dividend sustainability analysis

Chevron Corp. (NYSE: CVX) is a San Ramon, CA based global integrated energy company. Selected financial data for the years ending December 31, 2008 and 2009 is provided below:

Year Ending 31 December (US $ Millions)	2009	2008
Net income	$10,483	$23,931
Cash flow from operations	$19,373	$29,632
Capital expenditures (FCInv)	$19,843	$19,666
Net borrowing	$1,659	$1,682
Dividends paid	$5,373	$5,261
Stock repurchases	$(168)	$6,821

Source: Yahoo! Finance website. July 27, 2010.

1. Using the information provided, calculate:
   A. Dividend payout ratio.
   B. Dividend coverage ratio.
   C. FCFE coverage ratio.
2. Discuss the trend in dividend coverage ratio and compare it to FCFE coverage ratio.
3. Is Chevron's dividend sustainable?

Answer:

1.
   a. Dividend payout ratio = dividend / net income.
   2008: 5,261 / 23,931 = 0.22 or 22%
   2009: 5,373 / 10,483 = 0.51 or 51%
   b. Dividend coverage ratio = net income / dividend
   2008: 23,931 / 5,261 = 4.55
   2009: 10,483 / 5,373 = 1.95
   c. FCFE = cash flow from operations – FcInv + net borrowings
   2008: FCFE = 29,632 – 19,666 + 1,682 = 11,648
   2009: FCFE = 19,373 – 19,843 + 1,659 = 1,189
   FCFE coverage ratio = FCFE / (dividends + share repurchases)
   FCFE coverage ratio:
   2008: 11,648 / (5,261 + 6,821) = 0.96
   2009: 1,189 / [5,373 + (–168)] = 0.23
2. The dividend coverage ratio has decreased considerably from 4.55 in 2008 to 1.95 in 2009. The FCFE coverage ratio has also decreased significantly from 0.96 to 0.23. It appears that Chevron's dividend sustainability is lower in 2009 compared to 2008.
3. Chevron's dividend coverage has decreased significantly from 2008 to 2009. Still, even with this decrease, Chevron's dividend coverage is almost 2 times. Chevron's FCFE coverage ratio has also decreased dramatically from 2008 to 2009. This is despite the fact that the company stopped its share repurchase

plan in 2009 (in fact it issued additional stock—most likely to provide shares for exercise of employee stock options). Additionally, even if we consider 2009 to be a bad year due to a downturn in oil prices, the 2008 ratio is still below one. FCFE coverage ratio analysis therefore suggests that Chevron's payout policy is unsustainable for the long run.

MODULE QUIZ 22.2

To best evaluate your performance, enter your quiz answers online.

1. Over the past 25 years, in the developed markets including the United States, the United Kingdom, and the European Union, the fraction of companies that:
   A. pay out cash dividends has increased.
   B. repurchase shares has increased.
   C. use particular dividend policies has been consistent over time and across countries.
2. Which of the following is *most likely* to be sustainable?
   A. A FCFE coverage ratio of 0.5.
   B. A dividend payout ratio of 0.5.
   C. A dividend coverage ratio of 0.5.
3. Nick Adams is recommending to the board of directors that they share the profits from an excellent year (totaling $56 million) with shareholders by either declaring a special cash dividend of $20 million, or using the $20 million to repurchase shares of Volksberger common stock in the open market. Selected financial information about the firm is shown below.

Shares outstanding:	40 million
Current stock price:	$28.00
52-week trading range:	$20.00 to $36.00
Book value of equity:	$880 million
After-tax cost of borrowing:	5.5%

Adams drafts a memo to the board of directors detailing the financial impact of declaring a special cash dividend versus repurchasing shares. His memo includes the following two statements:

1. The total shareholder wealth resulting from owning one share of stock with the special dividend option will increase to $28.50.
2. Our company's P/E ratio after the share buyback will remain the same as before the buyback.

Which of Adams's statements are correct?

A. Both statements are correct.
B. Only one of the statements is correct.
C. Neither statement is correct.

4. Which of the following would not be a good reason for a company to repurchase shares of its own stock? Management:
   A. believes a stable cash dividend is in the best interests of shareholders.
   B. believes its stock is overvalued.
   C. wants to increase the amount of leverage in its capital structure.

5. Firms that use a residual dividend model are *least likely* to:
   A. determine their optimal capital budgets.
   B. issue common stock to maintain the dividend payout schedule.
   C. determine the amount of equity needed to meet the capital budget.

6. If a firm follows a residual dividend policy and has an optimal capital budget that will require the use of all this year's earnings, the firm would *most likely* pay:
   A. no dividends to common stockholders.
   B. dividends financed by borrowing the money.
   C. dividends but only out of past retained earnings.

7. An analyst gathered the following information about a company's investment plan:
   - Capital budget of $5,000.
   - Target capital structure is 70% debt and 30% equity.
   - Net income is $4,500.

   If the company follows a residual dividend policy, the portion of its net income it will pay out as dividends this year is *closest* to:
   A. 50%.
   B. 60%.
   C. 67%.

8. An analyst gathered the following information about a company's investment budget:
   - Expected net income of $800,000 during the next year.
   - Target and current capital structure is 40% debt and 60% common equity.
   - Optimal capital budget for next year is $1.2 million.

   If the company uses the residual dividend model to determine next year's dividend payout, the company payout is *closest* to:
   A. $0.
   B. $80,000.
   C. $720,000.

9. Last year, Wolverine Shoes and Boots had earnings of $4.00 per share and paid a dividend of $0.20. In the current year, the company expects to earn $4.40 per share. The company has a 30% target payout ratio and plans to bring its dividend up to the target payout ratio over an 8-year period. Next year's expected dividend is *closest* to:
   A. $0.14.
   B. $0.24.
   C. $0.34.

10. A company has provided the following financial data:
    - Target capital structure is 50% debt and 50% equity.
    - After-tax cost of debt is 8%.
    - Cost of retained earnings is estimated to be 13.5%.
    - Cost of equity is estimated to be 14.5% if the company issues new common stock.
    - Net income is $2,500.

    The company is considering the following investment projects:

Project	Size of project	IRR of project
Project A	$1,000	12.0%
Project B	$1,200	11.5%
Project C	$1,200	11.0%
Project D	$1,200	10.5%
Project E	$1,000	10.0%

If the company follows a residual dividend policy, its payout ratio will be *closest* to:

A. 32%.
B. 54%.
C. 66%.

KEY CONCEPTS

LOS 22.a

Cash dividend payments reduce cash as well as stockholders' equity. This results in a lower quick ratio and current ratio, and higher leverage (e.g., debt-to-equity and debt-to-asset) ratios. Stock dividends (and stock splits) leave a company's capital structure unchanged and do not affect any of these ratios. In the case of a stock dividend, a decrease in retained earnings (corresponding to the value of the stock dividend) is offset by an increase in contributed capital, leaving the value of total equity unchanged.

LOS 22.b

Following are the three theories of investor preference:

- MM's dividend irrelevance theory holds that in a no-tax/no-fees world, dividend policy is irrelevant since it has no effect on the price of a firm's stock or its cost of capital, because individual investors can create their own homemade dividend.
- Dividend preference theory says investors prefer the certainty of current cash to future capital gains.
- Tax aversion theory states that investors are tax averse to dividends and would prefer companies instead buy back shares, especially when the tax rate on dividends is higher than the tax rate on capital gains.

LOS 22.c

The signaling effect of dividend changes is based on the idea that dividends convey information about future earnings from management to investors (who have less information about a firm's prospects than management). In general, unexpected increases are good news and unexpected decreases are bad news as seen by U.S. investors.

LOS 22.d

Clientele effect refers to the varying preferences for dividends of different groups of investors, such as individuals, institutions, and corporations. Companies structure their dividend policies consistent with preferences of their clienteles. Miller and Modigliani, however, note that once all the clienteles are satisfied, changing the dividend policy would only entail changing clienteles and would not affect firm value.

Two types of agency costs affect dividend payout policies:

- Agency conflict between shareholders and managers can be reduced by paying out a higher proportion of the firm's free cash flow to equity so as to discourage investment in negative NPV projects.
- Agency conflict between shareholders and bondholders occurs when shareholders can expropriate bondholder wealth by paying themselves a large dividend (and leaving a lower asset base for outstanding bonds as collateral). Agency conflict between bondholders and stockholders is typically resolved via provisions in bond indenture.

LOS 22.e

Six primary factors affect a company's dividend payout policy:

1. Investment opportunities: affects the residual income available to pay as dividends.
2. Expected volatility of future earnings: firms are more cautious in changing dividend payout in the presence of high earnings volatility.
3. Financial flexibility: Firms may not increase dividends (even in presence of significant free cash flow) so as not to be forced to continue paying those dividends in the future and losing financial flexibility. Instead, firms can choose to pay out excess cash via stock repurchases.
4. Tax considerations: In the presence of differential tax rate on capital gains versus dividends, companies may structure their dividend policy to maximize investors' after-tax income.
5. Flotation costs: Flotation cost increases the cost of external equity as compared to retained earnings. Hence, higher flotation cost would motivate firms to have a lower dividend payout.
6. Contractual and legal restrictions: Dividend policy may be affected by debt covenants that the firm has to adhere to. Legal restrictions in some jurisdictions limit the dividend payout of a firm.

LOS 22.f

Effective rate under double taxation
= corporate tax rate + (1 – corporate tax rate) × (individual tax rate)

A split-rate system has different corporate tax rates on retained earnings and earnings that are paid out in dividends (distributed income). Under split-rate system, effective tax rate is computed the same way as double taxation but we use the corporate tax rate for distributed income as the relevant corporate tax rate in the double taxation formula.

Under a tax imputation system, taxes are paid at the corporate level but are used as credits by the stockholders. Hence, all taxes are effectively paid at the shareholder's marginal tax rate.

LOS 22.g

Stable dividend policy: A company tries to align its dividend growth rate with the company's long-term earnings growth rate to provide a steady dividend. A firm with a stable dividend policy could use a target payout adjustment model to gradually move towards its target payout.

expected increase in dividends = [(expected earnings × target payout ratio) – previous dividend] × adjustment factor

where:
adjustment factor = 1 / number of years over which the adjustment in dividends will take place

Constant payout ratio: Company defines a proportion of earnings that it plans to pay out to shareholders regardless of volatility in earnings (and consequently in dividends).

Study Session 7

Residual dividend approach: Dividends are based on earnings less funds the firm retains to finance the equity portion of its capital budget.

Advantages: (1) easy for the company to use; (2) maximizes allocation of earnings to investment.

Disadvantages: (1) dividend fluctuates with investment opportunities and earnings; (2) uncertainty causes higher required return and lower valuation.

Longer-term residual dividend: Company forecasts its capital budget over a longer time frame and attempts to pay out the residual in steady dividend payments.

LOS 22.h

Share repurchase methods:

1. Open market transactions: The firm buys back its shares in the open market.
2. Fixed price tender offer: The firm buys a predetermined number of shares at a fixed price, typically at a premium over the current market price.
3. Dutch auction: A tender offer where the company specifies a range of prices rather than a fixed price. Bids are accepted (lowest price first) until the desired quantity is filled. All accepted bids are then filled at the (higher) price of the last accepted bid.
4. Repurchase by direct negotiation: Purchasing shares from a major shareholder, often at a premium over market price. This method may be used in a greenmail scenario, or when a company wants to remove a large overhang in the market.

LOS 22.i

Repurchases made using a company's surplus cash will lower cash and shareholders' equity and, therefore, increase the firm's leverage. Earnings per share may increase because there will be fewer shares outstanding.

When the company uses debt to finance the repurchase, EPS will increase if the after-tax funding cost is less than the earnings yield. However, the firm will then also have higher leverage and, therefore, a higher cost of capital, so an increase in EPS will not automatically lead to an increase in share price or in shareholder wealth.

LOS 22.j

After a stock repurchase, the number of outstanding shares will decrease and the book value per share (BVPS) is likely to change as well. If the price paid is higher (lower) than the pre-repurchase BVPS, the BVPS will decrease (increase).

LOS 22.k

There are five common rationales for share repurchases (versus dividends):

1. Potential tax advantages: When capital gains are taxed favorably as compared to dividends.
2. Share price support/signaling: Management wants to signal better prospects for the firm.
3. Added flexibility: Reduces the need for "sticky" dividends in the future.

4. Offsets dilution from employee stock options.
5. Increases financial leverage by reducing equity in the balance sheet.

LOS 22.l

Global trends in corporate payout policies:

1. A lower proportion of U.S. companies pay dividends as compared to their European counterparts.
2. Globally, the proportion of companies paying cash dividends has trended downwards.
3. Stock repurchases have been trending upwards in the United States since the 1980s and in the United Kingdom and continental Europe since the 1990s.

LOS 22.m

Dividend coverage ratio = net income / dividends

FCFE coverage ratio = FCFE / (dividends + share repurchases)

LOS 22.n

For both dividend and FCFE coverage, ratios that are below industry averages or trending downwards over time indicate problems for dividend sustainability.

ANSWER KEY FOR MODULE QUIZZES

Module Quiz 22.1

1. **A** If most investors' marginal tax rates on capital gains are lower than their marginal tax rates on dividends, the share's price is most likely to drop by *less* than the amount of the dividend when the share goes ex-dividend. The amount of the price decrease is described by the equation $D \times (1 - T_D) / (1 - T_{CG})$. If T_D is greater than T_{CG}, then the price decrease should be less than D. (LOS 22.d)

2. **B** The effective tax rate on earnings distributed as dividends is 0.35 + (1 – 0.35)(0.30) = 0.545 = 54.5%. (LOS 22.f)

3. **B** The effective tax rate on earnings distributed as dividends is 0.20 + (1 – 0.20)(0.28) = 0.424 = 42.4%. (LOS 22.f)

4. **C** Under an imputation tax system, the effective tax rate on earnings distributed as dividends is the tax rate of the shareholder receiving the dividends. (LOS 22.f)

5. **B** Institutional investors such as income-oriented mutual funds would invest in companies that pay a high dividend. The clientele effect suggests a company should maintain its current dividend payout policy. A company in the early stage of its life cycle typically does not pay a dividend. Double taxation of dividends and debt covenants both encourage low dividend payout ratios. (LOS 22.d)

6. **C** The bird-in-hand argument for dividend policy is based on the fact that a dividend payment is more certain than future capital gains. (LOS 22.b)

Module Quiz 22.2

1. **B** Over the past decades, it has been observed that the percentage of companies engaging in share repurchases has increased over time. At the same time, the fraction of companies paying cash dividends has decreased. In addition to changing over time, dividend policies have been noted to differ between countries. (LOS 22.l)

2. **B** An FCFE coverage ratio or dividend coverage ratio much less than one is not sustainable because the company is drawing on cash and marketable securities to make payments. A dividend payout ratio less than one indicates that the company is paying out less in dividends than it is earning, which is the normal (and desirable) situation. (LOS 22.n)

3. **C** Adams is incorrect with respect to Statement 1. If the firm pays its special dividend of \$20 million, both the assets and equity of the firm will drop by \$20 million. The total wealth from owning one share will be [(40 million)(\$28) – \$20 million] / 40 million = \$27.50, plus \$20 million / 40 million = \$0.50 per share as a dividend, so the total shareholder wealth resulting from

owning one share of stock is \$28. Note that the total shareholder wealth of \$28 is the same whether the cash dividend or share repurchase option is chosen. Adams is also incorrect with respect to Statement 2. The current EPS is \$56 million / 40 million = \$1.40, so the current P/E ratio is \$28 / \$1.40 = 20 times earnings. The price per share will remain the same. Share buyback = \$20 million / 28 = 714,286 shares. New price = [(40 million × \$28/share) – \$20 million] / (40 million – 714,286) = \$28/share. EPS will increase. \$56 million / 39,285,714 = \$1.43. Since the price is the same, and EPS increases, the P/E ratio will fall slightly after the repurchase. (LOS 22.i)

4. **B** Management would repurchase shares of its own stock if it believed the shares were undervalued, not overvalued. (LOS 22.k)

5. **B** Under the residual dividend model, the firm pays dividends only if earnings are available to support the optimal capital budget. The firm would not take on additional equity to pay dividends. (LOS 22.g)

6. **A** If all earnings are used under a residual dividend policy, the firm would not pay any dividends. (LOS 22.g)

7. **C** 30% of \$5,000 or \$1,500 is equity. \$4,500 – \$1,500 is \$3,000, which as a percent is \$3,000 / \$4,500 = 67%. (LOS 22.g)

8. **B** 60% of \$1,200,000 is \$720,000. \$800,000 – \$720,000 is \$80,000. (LOS 22.g)

9. **C** expected increase in dividends

   = [(expected earnings × target payout ratio) – previous dividend] × adjustment factor

   = [(\$4.40 × 30%) – \$0.20] × (1 / 8)

   = \$0.14

   expected dividend for the current year

   = previous dividend + expected increase in dividends

   = \$0.20 + \$0.14

   = \$0.34

   (LOS 22.g)

10. **A** The cost of new equity capital is always higher than the cost of retained earnings. Under pecking order, internally generated equity (i.e., retained earnings) is most favored and external equity (i.e., newly issued shares) is least favored. In this case, the equity half of these projects can be financed using retained earnings, so new equity does not need to be issued. The cost of retained earnings is thus the appropriate rate to use. First, determine the WACC. WACC = $w_d \times r_d(1 - t) + w_e \times r_s$ where r_s is the required return on retained earnings. WACC = (0.5)(8) + (0.5)(13.5) = 10.75. Second, decide to accept projects A, B, and C since they all have an IRR greater than WACC. This results in a total capital budget of \$1,000 + \$1,200 + \$1,200 = \$3,400. The equity portion is (0.5)(\$3,400) = \$1,700. Net income = \$2,500 – \$1,700 is the amount used for the capital budget. \$800 remains. \$800 / \$2,500 = 0.32 = 32%. (LOS 22.g)

Study Session 7

The following is a review of the Corporate Finance (2) principles designed to address the learning outcome statements set forth by CFA Institute. Cross-Reference to CFA Institute Assigned Reading #23.

READING 23 Corporate Performance, Governance, and Business Ethics

Study Session 8

EXAM FOCUS

This topic review discusses the various stakeholders who have an interest in the well-being of a corporate entity as well as the principal-agent problem that can potentially lead to ethical violations. Additionally, the concept of conflict of interests among stake holders is discussed. Finally, the theories of ethical decision making are explained; these theories are highly testable.

MODULE 23.1: CORPORATE PERFORMANCE, GOVERNANCE, AND BUSINESS ETHICS

Video covering this content is available online.

ETHICAL DILEMMAS

Given the inherent conflict of interest not only between shareholders and managers, but also between other stakeholders in a business, the issue of ethical decision making and balancing the interests of different stakeholders becomes important in a corporate governance context.

LOS 23.a: Compare interests of key stakeholder groups and explain the purpose of a stakeholder impact analysis.

CFA® Program Curriculum, Volume 3, page 202

Stakeholders

Stakeholders are groups with an interest or claim in a company. The stakeholders can be internal or external to the company, and make differing contributions to the company. The company must consider the divergent nature of stakeholder interests and offer inducements to receive their continued support.

Key internal stakeholders:

- **Stockholders** are a unique group of stakeholders, and arguably the most important because they supply the risk capital necessary for business.
- **Employees** look to the company for compensation in exchange for their labor and skills. They seek immediate compensation as well as stability and growth in compensation.
- **Managers** are also employees but they enjoy a substantial, asymmetric information advantage that can lead to significant problems in the principal-agent relationship. At the executive level there is considerable opportunity for managers to enrich their own self-interest at the expense of the company and other stakeholders (more to come on this issue).
- **Members of the board of directors** are supposed to monitor and evaluate the performance of the senior managers of the company and look out for the best interests of the shareholders. Directors also enjoy asymmetric information advantage and risk becoming too close to managers, which can lead to favoring the interests of the managers they should be supervising. (This should sound familiar as the principal-agent problem covered throughout the CFA curriculum.)

External stakeholders:

- **Customers** buy company products, prefer a variety of products, and seek a stable, dependable relationship with the company they are buying these products from. But they also seek lower prices. The desire for an ongoing relationship is consistent with the company's desire for profits but the lower price goal is not. If dissatisfied, the customers can stop buying.
- **Suppliers** also seek stable, long-term relationships, but also want higher prices from the company, which will reduce company profits. If dissatisfied, suppliers can stop supplying the company.
- **Creditors** are essentially another supplier, but one which supplies debt capital and is paid in interest. Creditors value stability or improvement in the company's credit quality.
- **Unions** are viewed as an external stakeholder representing internal employees. They generally seek higher wages and compensation for their members, with potentially negative implications for short-run profits and long-run survivability for the company. The power to strike can be very disruptive.
- **Governments** provide rules and regulation and they expect compliance.
- **Local communities** provide infrastructure and expect good citizenship.
- The **general public** also provides national infrastructure to the firm in exchange for an increased quality of life due to the existence of the firm.

RECONCILING INTERESTS AND THE STAKEHOLDER ANALYSIS

While all stakeholders should be interested in the profitability (and survival) of a company, these stakeholders' interests often diverge. Customers are generally not averse to the company earning a profit, but these customers also do not want to overpay.

The purpose of the stakeholder impact analysis (SIA) is to force the company to identify which stakeholder groups are most critical to the company. The SIA should:

1. Identify the relevant stakeholders.
2. Identify the interests and concerns of each group.
3. Identify the demands of each group on the company.
4. Prioritize the importance of various stakeholders to the company.
5. Identify the strategic challenges these conflicting demands pose.

Stockholders are unique stakeholders who supply the risk capital that supports the business. They seek immediate return in the form of dividends and growth to supply increasing dividends and stock price. Return on invested capital (ROIC) and growth in profits are arguably the best tools with which to measure the ability of the company to satisfy shareholders and the other stakeholders' demands. Of course return and growth must be maximized while in compliance with laws and regulations; illegal activities will have severe consequences for the company.

The dual goals related to ROIC and growth also involve tradeoffs. Excess attention to growth would lead to investment in less-attractive business lines and lower ROIC. However, excess attention to maximizing ROIC could lead to ignoring growth opportunities that would produce future profits. Firms should choose a middle ground between highest and lowest growth that maximizes shareholder and stakeholder value.

Stakeholders are not always in conflict. Many stakeholders are also shareholders. The general public can be shareholders, as are many employees. Employee stock ownership programs (ESOPs) in the U.S. have increased the ownership by employees in their employer's stock. Even when there is conflict between stakeholders, in the long term, the twin strategies of maximizing ROIC and growth maximizes the funds available for division among the stakeholders. While not minimizing the real conflicts among stakeholders, all are served by a dual focus on ROIC and growth.

THE PRINCIPAL-AGENT RELATIONSHIP

LOS 23.b: Discuss problems that can arise in principal–agent relationships and mechanisms that may mitigate such problems.

CFA® Program Curriculum, Volume 3, page 206

The principal-agent relationship (PAR) arises when one group delegates decision making or control to another group. PAR can create problems because the group receiving the power (the agent) generally has an asymmetric information advantage over the group making the delegation (the principal). The PAR problem arises if the agent uses the information advantage for their own interests to the detriment of the interests of the principal. This problem is compounded because the asymmetric information makes it difficult for the principal to know enough to detect the problem and evaluate the agent's actions.

In corporate form of business, shareholders (principals) delegate authority to run the business to executive officers of the company (agents). The board of directors is intended to oversee the executives and look out for the interests of the shareholders.

The PAR problem between shareholders and executives compounds when senior executive officers delegate authority to additional officers who report to them. At each level of delegation, additional layers of information asymmetry occur with the potential for more PAR problems. In each case, the agent has incentives to exploit the information for improper personal gain. To illustrate:

- CEOs can enjoy on-the-job consumption in the form of lavish offices or travel that is passed off as a necessary business expense.
- CEOs can manipulate the board of directors to extract excessive compensation packages. A Business Week survey in the U.S. showed that in 1980 the average CEO earned 42 times more than what the average blue-collar worker earned. By 2006 this had increased to the average CEO earning more than 350 times the average blue-collar worker's pay. Unfortunately, the studies do not link rising compensation levels to improving company performance.
- Executives seek status by expanding the business (empire building) through acquisitions that may not benefit the existing shareholders. Company size has been strongly linked to executive compensation.

CONTROLLING PAR PROBLEMS

Principals should develop corporate governance procedures that:

- Guide the behavior of agents by setting goals and principles of behavior.
- Reduce the asymmetry of information.
- Lead to the removal of agents who misbehave and violate ethical principles.

ETHICS AND STRATEGY

Common examples of unethical behavior include:

- *Self-dealing* when agents misappropriate corporate assets for personal use.
- *Information manipulation* such as misleading financial information or hiding a health risk created by the company.
- *Anticompetitive behavior* in pursuit of monopoly power. Even if legal, it is unethical.
- *Opportunistic exploitation* of suppliers or distributors in violation of negotiated terms when it is believed they will not have the power to resist.
- *Substandard working conditions* imposed on employees.
- *Environmental degradation* of society's resources through pollution or improper use of resources.
- *Corruption* such as using bribery to gain illegal advantage.

LOS 23.c: Discuss roots of unethical behavior and how managers might ensure that ethical issues are considered in business decision making.

CFA® Program Curriculum, Volume 3, page 213

ROOTS OF UNETHICAL BEHAVIOR

Unethical behavior arises from:

- Agents whose personal ethics are flawed. Such agents are more likely to violate business ethics. Strong personal ethics are likely to lead to good business ethics.
- A failure to realize that an issue may lead to an ethics violation. Asking whether each decision has ethical implications will encourage business ethics.
- A culture focused only on profit and growth. Asking if it is ethical and profitable will encourage ethical business practices.
- A flawed business culture where top management sets unrealistic goals leads to ethics violations. Management must communicate that ethical behavior is expected.
- Unethical leadership that sets the tone for acceptable behavior. Ethical leadership formulates and communicates expectations that include sound ethical behavior.

Good business ethics and governance are important: managers who act unethically and illegally can harm or destroy the company. Unethical behavior, even if legal, can harm the business. Nike came under severe criticism from the public and customers for outsourcing production to independent suppliers who were alleged to have subjected employees to poor and dangerous working conditions. All of Nike's actions, and often those of the independent suppliers, were legal in their respective countries, but Nike took steps to develop and enforce ethical standards applicable to both Nike and the suppliers in order to protect the value of Nike's business.

Various stakeholders have rights that the company must respect. Stockholders are entitled to timely, accurate reporting, as are governments. Suppliers, including employees, should expect contractual obligations to be met. Society can expect adherence to environmental and other regulations. Others argue that business ethics must extend beyond these basics to encompass *noblesse oblige*. This term encompasses the notion that those who benefit most from society, in this case successful businesses, have an obligation to make contributions back to society.

PHILOSOPHIES UNDERLYING BUSINESS ETHICS

LOS 23.d: Compare the Friedman doctrine, Utilitarianism, Kantian Ethics, and Rights and Justice Theories as approaches to ethical decision making.

CFA® Program Curriculum, Volume 3, page 214

Through the **Friedman Doctrine**, Milton Friedman has added to the modern debate on business ethics. He narrowly addresses the social responsibility of business (not business ethics) and concludes that the only social responsibility of a business is to increase profits "within the rules of the game," meaning through "open and fair competition without deception or fraud." While Friedman wanted to avoid getting into business ethics, critics have argued that the inclusion of a caveat to follow rules of the game moves the doctrine into the realm of business ethics. Critics have pointed out that when law, regulation, and the rules of the game are poorly defined (such as Nike's use of off-shore suppliers with poor working conditions) ethical behavior entails a lot more than making profits.

Other philosophies that precede the Friedman doctrine include the following.

Utilitarianism argues that business must weigh the consequences to society of each of their actions and seek to produce the highest good for the largest number of people. Utilitarianism entails maximization of positive (good) outcomes and minimization of negative (bad) outcomes such that collective utility is maximized. Modern cost-benefit analysis is an application of this principal. The flaws of this philosophy include that many costs and benefits of actions are difficult to measure. In addition, utilitarianism fails to consider the injustice that occurs when the greatest good for the many could come at the expense of a smaller subgroup.

Kantian ethics argue that people are different from other factors of production; they are more than just an economic input and deserve dignity and respect. This argument is widely accepted but not sufficient to be a complete philosophy.

Rights theories argue that all individuals have fundamental rights and privileges, and that the pursuit of the utilitarianism's greatest good does not trump these fundamental rights. Managers should recognize their obligation to safeguard the fundamental human rights of others.

Justice theories focus on a just distribution of economic output. John Rawls argued that justice is met if all participants would agree the rules are fair if the results would be acceptable when decided under a "veil of ignorance." In other words, fair rules are decided ahead of time by participants who don't know their own particular individual characteristics.

Justice theories begin with political liberty, encompassing the right of free speech and to vote, and extend to issues of society's division of wealth and income. They recognize that unequal divisions of wealth and income may be acceptable under the *differencing principal*, which holds the unequal division must benefit the least-advantaged members of society. Consider the earlier discussion of production outsourced to independent suppliers. Substandard conditions for the workers of those suppliers can be argued as being just, if it is an improvement in those workers' standard of living. The veil of ignorance would be an appropriate test of whether the actions are ethical. Under this standard it is difficult to conceive that members of society would argue in favor of displacing existing domestic jobs into foreign jobs with dangerous and toxic conditions knowing they would not want to work in those jobs themselves.

The veil of ignorance does appear to be a useful tool for managers who must make ethical decisions requiring difficult tradeoffs.

ACTIONS IN PURSUIT OF ETHICAL BEHAVIOR

Managers can pursue seven steps to further ethical behavior:

Step 1: Hire and promote those with strong personal and business ethics (a sound moral compass). Psychological testing and careful review of past employment can help identify these individuals.

Step 2: Build an organization and culture that value ethical behavior highly. This must include: explicitly stating that ethical behavior is required, employing leaders who continually emphasize the necessity of highly ethical behavior, and promote those who act ethically and sanction those who do not.

Step 3: Select leaders who will implement step 2.

Step 4: Establish a systematic decision process that incorporates a moral compass, rights theory, and Rawls's theory of justice. Then turn this process into a series of yes or no decision tools such as:

- Does this decision meet our code of ethics and standards?
- Am I willing to have this decision widely reported to stakeholders and the press?
- Would others whose opinion I value and respect approve of this decision?

Step 5: Appoint ethics officers who articulate, propose, train, monitor, and revise a code and behavior.

Step 6: Establish strong corporate governance procedures that include:

- A majority of the board of directors are independent, outside, knowledgeable members of high integrity.
- The chairman and CEO positions are held by separate individuals with the chairman an independent, outside director.

- The compensation committee is made up exclusively of independent, outside directors.
- The board should retain outside auditors with no conflicts of interest (such as also providing consulting services to the company).

Step 7: Show moral courage by supporting managers who make tough decisions consistent with good business ethics, even at the expense of short-term profits.

Acting ethically is not simple or easy, but it is good business.

MODULE QUIZ 23.1

To best evaluate your performance, enter your quiz answers online.

1. The purpose of the stakeholder impact analysis can *best* be described as determining who the stakeholders are and:
   A. the best way to address their needs.
   B. meeting the needs of the most important stakeholders.
   C. operating the firm to meet all stakeholder needs in a profitable manner.
2. Which of the following is *least likely* to mitigate principal-agent problems?
   A. Shape the behavior of agents to align them with the goals of other agents.
   B. Reduce business information asymmetry between principals and agents.
   C. Remove agents that violate ethical standards.
3. Which of the following is *least likely* a root cause of unethical behavior observed in businesses?
   A. Agents whose personal ethics are flawed.
   B. A culture focused only on profit and growth.
   C. A business culture where top management sets a profitability goal.
4. Maximization of collective good is emphasized under:
   A. Justice theories.
   B. Rights theories.
   C. Utilitarianism.

KEY CONCEPTS

LOS 23.a

Key internal stakeholders: shareholders, managers, employees, and board of directors.

Key external stakeholders: customers, suppliers, creditors, union, government, local community, and general public.

The purpose of the stakeholder impact analysis (SIA) is to force the company to identify which groups are most critical to the company. The SIA should:

- Identify the relevant stakeholders.
- Identify the critical interests and desires of each group.
- Identify the demands of each group on the company.
- Prioritize the importance of various stakeholders to the company.
- Provide a business strategy to meet the critical demands.

LOS 23.b

The principal-agent relationship (PAR) arises when one group delegates decision making or control to another group. PAR can create problems because the group receiving the power (the agent) generally has an asymmetric information advantage over the group making the delegation (the principal). The PAR problem begins if the agent uses the information advantage to further their own interests to the detriment of the interests of the principal. Modern corporations are built on shareholders (principals) who delegate authority to run the business to executive officers of the company (agents). The Board of Directors is intended to oversee the executives and look out for the interests of the shareholders.

Principals should develop corporate governance procedures that:

- Affect the behavior of agents by setting goals and principals of behavior.
- Reduce the asymmetry of information.
- Remove agents who misbehave and violate ethics.

LOS 23.c

Unethical behavior arises from:

- Agents whose personal ethics are flawed are more likely to violate business ethics. Strong personal ethics will likely lead to good business ethics.
- A simple failure to realize an issue may lead to an ethics violation. Asking whether each decision has ethical implications will encourage business ethics.
- A culture focused only on profit and growth. Asking if it is ethical and profitable will encourage business ethics.

- A flawed business culture where top management sets unrealistic goals leads to ethics violations. Management must communicate that ethical behavior is expected.
- Unethical leadership will set the tone and lead to violations. Ethical leadership formulates and communicates expectations that include sound ethical behavior.

LOS 23.d

The **Friedman Doctrine** narrowly addresses the social responsibility of business (not business ethics) and concludes that the only social responsibility is to increase profits "within the rules of the game," meaning through "open and fair competition without deception or fraud."

Utilitarianism argues business must weigh the consequences to society of each of their actions and seek to produce the highest good for the largest number of people.

Kantian ethics argues that people are different from other factors of production; they are more than just an economic input and deserve dignity and respect.

Rights theories argue that all individuals have fundamental rights and privileges. The greatest good of utilitarianism cannot come in violation of these fundamental rights of others.

Justice theories focus on a just distribution of economic output. John Rawls argued that justice is met if all participants would agree the rules are fair if the results would be acceptable when decided under a "veil of ignorance."

ANSWER KEY FOR MODULE QUIZ

Module Quiz 23.1

1. **B** The purpose of the stakeholder impact analysis (SIA) is to force the company to identify which groups are most critical to the company and make choices among the stakeholders. Answer A is not wrong but it is very vague. C is incorrect because it is not reasonable to expect to meet all needs; priorities must be set. (LOS 23.a)

2. **A** Ways to mitigate the principal-agent problem are: (1) shape the behavior of agents so their actions are in alignment with the goals of the principals, (2) reduce the asymmetry of information between the agents who have more information about the business and the *principals* who have less information, and (3) implement methods to be able to remove and replace agents who violate the ethical standards of the company. (LOS 23.b)

3. **C** A and B are root causes of unethical behavior. A management goal of earning a reasonable profit is fundamental to any for-profit business. An excessive and unrealistic focus on profit that encourages employees to "cut corners" would be a root cause. (LOS 23.c)

4. **C** Utilitarianism focuses on maximization of collective good. (LOS 23.d)

The following is a review of the Corporate Finance (2) principles designed to address the learning outcome statements set forth by CFA Institute. Cross-Reference to CFA Institute Assigned Reading #24.

READING 24 Corporate Governance

Study Session 8

EXAM FOCUS

You should know the potential conflicts of interest that create the need for corporate governance as well as the responsibilities of a corporate board of directors. Be prepared for an exam question that asks you to assess whether or not a particular practice is indicative of sound corporate governance. This is a topic that could easily relate to other areas in the Level II curriculum, such as ethics and financial statement analysis, so be prepared for corporate governance material to show up anywhere on the exam.

MODULE 24.1: CORPORATE GOVERNANCE

Video covering this content is available online.

WARM-UP: CONFLICTS OF INTEREST IN A CORPORATION

A public corporation typically has multiple owners who often play little or no role in business decisions. Instead, decisions are delegated to professional managers who determine how assets are used and how the business is run. This separation between business owners and management creates the potential for conflicts where management may put their own interests ahead of those of shareholders. Other potential conflicts of interest in a corporation may involve directors, creditors, and other stakeholders, such as employees and customers. The goal of corporate governance is to minimize these conflicts of interest through the application of practical measures and policies.

LOS 24.a: Describe objectives and core attributes of an effective corporate governance system and evaluate whether a company's corporate governance has those attributes.

CFA® Program Curriculum, Volume 3, page 225

McEnally and Kim[1] define **corporate governance** as "the system of principles, policies, procedures, and clearly defined responsibilities and accountabilities used by stakeholders to overcome conflicts of interest inherent in the corporate form." A company that does not have a sound system of corporate governance in place is taking on a major risk. Recent examples, such as Enron (bankruptcy filing in 2001) and Adelphia (bankruptcy filing in 2002), show that the lack of an effective corporate governance system can threaten a company's very existence. Recently enacted laws and regulations, such as Sarbanes-Oxley in the United States, reflect the fact that a strong system of corporate governance is essential for companies and financial markets to operate efficiently.

Corporate governance has two major objectives:

1. *Eliminate or reduce conflicts of interest.* Although many conflicts of interest exist in a corporation, most corporate governance systems focus on the conflict between management and shareholders.
2. *Use the company's assets in a manner consistent with the best interests of investors and other stakeholders.*

Corporate governance systems will differ according to the legal environment, culture, and industry in which a firm operates; however, there are core attributes that all effective corporate governance systems share. An effective corporate governance system will:

- Define the rights of shareholders and other important stakeholders.
- Define and communicate to stakeholders the oversight responsibilities of managers and directors.
- Provide for fair and equitable treatment in all dealings between managers, directors, and shareholders.
- Have complete transparency and accuracy in disclosures regarding operations, performance, risk, and financial position.

LOS 24.b: Compare major business forms and describe the conflicts of interest associated with each.

CFA® Program Curriculum, Volume 3, page 225

Sole proprietorships are businesses owned and operated by a single individual. Setting up a sole proprietorship is relatively easy and has few legal requirements, thus making it the most common form of business found in the world. Such businesses are usually small-scale operations; examples include hairdressers, restaurants, and dry cleaners. From a legal standpoint, there is no distinction

1. Rebecca Todd McEnally and Kenneth Kim, "Corporate Governance," *CFA® Program Readings*, (Boston: Pearson, 2007), 5–51.

between the business and its owner, resulting in liability for the owner that is potentially unlimited.

Conflict of interest concerns. Since the owner and manager of a sole proprietorship is the same person, conflicts between management and owners do not exist. Conflicts of interest for a sole proprietorship typically involve creditors and suppliers.

Partnerships are composed of two or more owners/managers, but are otherwise similar to a sole proprietorship in that there is no legal distinction between the business and its owners. Liability is unlimited, but is shared among the partners. The primary advantage of a partnership structure is that partners can pool knowledge and capital, as well as share in business risks. Law firms, real estate firms, and advertising agencies are often organized as partnerships.

Conflict of interest concerns. The conflicts for partnerships are similar to those of sole proprietorships, involving creditors and suppliers. Potential conflicts between partners are typically addressed by creating partnership contracts that delineate the roles and responsibilities of each partner.

Corporations are distinct legal entities that have rights similar to those of an individual person. The top managers of a corporation are empowered to act as agents of the company and control all corporate activities, including signing contracts, on behalf of the business. In the United States, corporations represent less than 20% of all businesses, but generate over 90% of business revenues.[2]

Compared to sole proprietorships or partnerships, corporations have several advantages:

- It is much easier to raise large amounts of capital. A corporation can raise capital by issuing common stock to the public, selling ownership interests to private investors in exchange for cash, or borrowing money from creditors.
- There is no need for owners to be industry experts. Any individual with sufficient capital can become a shareholder.
- Ownership stakes are easily transferable, which allows a corporation to have an unlimited life.
- Corporate shareholders have limited liability. Since there is a legal distinction between a corporation and its shareholders, the most a shareholder can lose is the amount invested, nothing more.

Conflict of interest concerns. Corporate shareholders typically have no input in day-to-day management of the firm and usually have difficulty monitoring a firm's operations and the actions of management. Separation of ownership and control creates the potential for conflicts between management and shareholders.

PROFESSOR'S NOTE

Corporate governance is designed to address the conflicts of interest that occur in a corporation. The primary conflicts of interest and how they are addressed are covered in the next LOS.

2. William J. Megginson, *Corporate Finance Theory* (Reading, MA: Addison Wesley, 1997).

LOS 24.c: Explain conflicts that arise in agency relationships, including manager–shareholder conflicts and director–shareholder conflicts.

CFA® Program Curriculum, Volume 3, page 228

An **agency relationship** occurs when an individual, who is referred to as the agent, acts on behalf of another individual, who is referred to as the *principal*. Such a relationship creates the potential for a **principal-agent problem** where the agent may act for his own well being rather than that of the principal. Corporate governance systems are primarily concerned with potential principal-agent problems in two areas: (1) between managers and shareholders, and (2) between directors and shareholders.

Managers and shareholders. The managers (the agents) make the day-to-day business decisions on behalf of the shareholders (the principals). Therefore, managers are effectively trustees of the capital belonging to the shareholders who, in turn, rely on management to use the funds efficiently to generate profits. Shareholders want management to make decisions that maximize shareholder wealth, but managers, left on their own, may well make decisions that maximize their own wealth. Examples of ways that management may act for their own interests rather than those of shareholders include:

- *Using funds to expand the size of the firm*. A larger firm may increase the managers' job security, power, and compensation without benefiting the shareholders.
- *Granting excessive compensation and perquisites*. Managers may give themselves high salaries and perquisites, such as corporate jets and lavish apartments that are expensed as normal business expenses, forcing shareholders to bear the costs.
- *Investing in risky ventures*. This is one of the key criticisms leveled against the excessive use of executive stock options. By virtue of the nature of their position, managers often stand to reap huge benefits if the risky venture succeeds, but do not share in losses if the venture fails.
- *Not taking enough risk*. Conversely, extremely risk-averse managers who have the bulk of their wealth tied to a firm's stock may only invest in conservative projects to protect that wealth and avoid potentially risky projects that would do a better job of maximizing value for shareholders.

Effective corporate governance systems are designed to monitor management's activities, reward good performance, and discipline managers who do not act in the best interests of shareholders.

Directors and shareholders. The purpose of the board of directors of a corporation is to serve as an intermediary between shareholders and management to help ensure that management is acting in the shareholders' best interest. The conflict between directors and shareholders occurs when directors align more with management interests rather than those of shareholders. The following factors may cause directors to align more closely with managers than shareholders:

- *Lack of independence*. Board members that are tied to the company or that may themselves be managers are less likely to identify with shareholder concerns.

- *Board members have personal relationships with management.* Board members may be asked to join the board because of a friendship or family ties with senior management.
- *Board members have consulting or other business agreements with the firm.* Business agreements may give the board member a dual responsibility of answering to management as a consultant while also supervising management as a board member.
- *Interlinked boards.* Senior managers of Firm A may serve as directors in Firm B, while Firm B's senior managers are on the board of Firm A.
- *Directors are overcompensated.* The goal of maintaining their excessive compensation may cause directors to accommodate management wishes rather than protect the best interests of shareholders.

LOS 24.d: Describe responsibilities of the board of directors and explain qualifications and core competencies that an investment analyst should look for in the board of directors.

LOS 24.e: Explain effective corporate governance practice as it relates to the board of directors and evaluate strengths and weaknesses of a company's corporate governance practice.

CFA® Program Curriculum, Volume 3, page 233

The Board of Directors

PROFESSOR'S NOTE

We will address these two LOS together. The first LOS asks you to know board attributes, while the second asks you to evaluate if the way a company is addressing the attribute illustrates strong or weak corporate governance. Pay attention to the "best practices" described in the attributes section below—whether or not a company's board is adhering to corporate governance best practices is a likely source of exam questions.

The board of directors of a corporation is a crucial part of an effective corporate governance system that provides a check and balance between management and shareholders. The board of directors for a corporation has the responsibility to:

- *Institute corporate values* and corporate governance mechanisms that will ensure business is conducted in a proficient, ethical, and fair manner.
- Ensure that the firm meets and *complies with all legal and regulatory requirements* in a timely manner.
- *Create long-term strategic objectives* for the company that are consistent with the shareholders' best interests.
- *Determine management's responsibilities* and how managers will be held accountable. Performance should be measured in all areas of a company's operations.

Study Session 8

- Hire, appropriately compensate, and regularly *evaluate the performance of the chief executive officer (CEO).*
- *Require management to supply the board with complete and accurate information* in order for the board to make decisions for which it is responsible and adequately monitor company management.
- *Meet regularly* to conduct its normal business, and attend extraordinary sessions when necessary.
- *Ensure board members are adequately trained* to perform board functions.

In order to determine the effectiveness of a board of directors, investors or investment analysts must assess:

- *The composition of the board of directors and whether or not directors are independent.* In order to assure that directors are serving shareholders, global best practice recommends that at least three-quarters of board members should be independent.
- *Whether the board has an independent chairman.* Many companies have a single individual serve the dual role of CEO and Chairman of the Board. Some arguments support the dual role as providing the board with in-depth knowledge and experience regarding company strategy and operations. However, others claim that having the CEO chairing board meetings allows the CEO to control the board's agenda and diminishes the role of independent board members, particularly when determining management compensation. For the exam, remember that having the CEO and Chairman as separate positions is considered a strong corporate governance practice.
- *Qualifications of directors.* Directors should bring skills and experience that will assure they will fulfill their fiduciary responsibilities to stakeholders. Corporate governance best practice is for board members to have the requisite industry, strategic planning, and risk management knowledge, not serve on more than two or three boards, and show a commitment to investor interests and ethical management and investing principles.
- *How the board is elected.* All board members may stand for election annually, or staggered elections may take place in which only a portion of the directors are up for election each year. Proponents of staggered elections say that they ensure board continuity. However, strong corporate governance practice says that staggered elections limits the power of shareholders and doesn't allow changes to the board composition to occur quickly. Annual elections force directors to make more careful decisions and be more attentive to shareholders because they can cast a vote to keep or eliminate a director each year.
- *Board self-assessment practices.* Boards should evaluate and assess their effectiveness at least annually. The focus of the self-assessment should be on member participation, committee activities, and future needs of the board. The compensation committee should consist of only independent directors.
- *Frequency of separate sessions for independent directors.* Best practice requires independent board members to meet at least annually, preferably quarterly, in separate sessions without management in attendance. Such meetings allow the independent directors to engage in an open discussion about policies, management, and compensation without concerns about management influence.

- *Audit committee and audit oversight*. The audit committee has the responsibility to oversee a company's financial reporting, non-financial corporate disclosure, and internal control systems. The internal audit staff of the firm should report directly to the audit committee. Best practice mandates that the audit committee consists only of independent directors, has expertise in financial and accounting matters, has full access to and the cooperation of management, and meets with auditors at least once annually.
- *Nominating committee*. The nominating committee is responsible for establishing criteria for identifying and evaluating candidates for the board of directors as well as senior management. Corporate governance best practice requires that the nominating committee consists only of independent directors.
- *Compensation committee and the compensation awarded to management*. The directors should use compensation to attract, retain, and motivate talented managers on behalf of shareholders. Compensation should focus on long-term goals and should not be excessive. A common industry practice that is considered poor corporate governance is to use the salary at other companies as a reference point rather than company performance. Another poor practice is the repricing of stock options, which allows management to recoup losses after a stock price decline. Best practice would have base salary and perquisites as a small percentage of compensation, with bonuses, stock options, and grants of restricted stock awarded for exceeding performance goals making up the majority of a senior manager's income.
- *Use of independent or expert legal counsel*. The board of directors should hire expert legal counsel as needed to fulfill its fiduciary duties and assess the company's compliance with regulatory requirements. A common practice is for internal corporate counsel to advise the board of directors, but this is considered weak governance, because of the potential for conflict of interest. Corporate governance best practice is for the board to use independent, outside counsel whenever legal counsel is required.
- *Statement of governance policies*. Statements provided in shareholder materials about corporate governance policies, and how those policies change over time, can be a great tool for analysts and investors in evaluating a firm's corporate governance system.

PROFESSOR'S NOTE

Details regarding the various components of a statement of governance policies are included in the next LOS.

- *Disclosure and transparency*. The purpose of accounting and disclosure is to fairly and accurately present a company's financial situation. Since investors depend on timely, complete, and accurate financial statements to value securities, providing inaccurate financial data can result in mispriced securities, thus reducing the efficiency of financial markets. In general, best practice supports the conclusion that more disclosure is better. A company should provide information about organization structure, corporate strategy, insider transactions, compensation policies, and changes to governance structures.

PROFESSOR'S NOTE

Financial statement disclosure and quality financial reporting practices are discussed in the Financial Reporting and Analysis section of the curriculum.

- *Insider or related-party transactions*. A recent financial scandal involved a CEO who borrowed millions of company dollars through an employee loan program, and then used his authority as CEO to "forgive" the loan. Best practice for any related-party transaction is to have the transaction approved by the board of directors.
- *Responsiveness to shareholder proxy votes*. Management's response to shareholder proxy matters is a sign of how seriously management takes its fiduciary duties. If an important matter such as executive compensation, a merger, or a governance issue is put to a shareholder vote and management ignores the result of the vote, it is obvious that management is not motivated by shareholder opinion as to what is in the best interest of the shareholders.

LOS 24.f: Describe elements of a company's statement of corporate governance policies that investment analysts should assess.

CFA® Program Curriculum, Volume 3, page 243

Companies that wish to present a commitment to effective corporate governance to the public often supply a statement of corporate governance policies in their regulatory filings or in materials provided to investors. Investors and analysts should assess the following policies of corporate governance:

- *Codes of ethics*. A corporate code of ethics articulates the values, responsibilities, and ethical conduct of an organization.
- *Directors' oversight, monitoring, and review responsibilities*. These include statements regarding internal controls, risk management, audit and accounting disclosure policies, regulatory compliance, nominations, and compensation.
- *Management's responsibility to the board*. These include management's responsibility to provide complete and timely information to board members, and to provide directors with direct access to the company's control and compliance functions.
- *Reports of directors' oversight and review of management*.
- *Board self assessments*.
- *Management performance assessments*.
- *Director training*. Includes training that is provided to directors before they join the board as well as ongoing training.

LOS 24.g: Describe environmental, social, and governance risk exposures.

CFA® Program Curriculum, Volume 3, page 258

ENVIRONMENTAL, SOCIAL, AND GOVERNANCE FACTORS

When considering the factors that could impact a firm's long-term sustainability, in addition to traditional business risk exposures, there are "ESG" risk factors that must be considered to get a full picture of the company's long-term risks.

The ESG factors are:

- **Environmental risk:** For example, related to greenhouse gas emissions that may cause climate change.
- **Social risk:** Such as labor rights or occupational safety.
- **Governance risk:** The effectiveness of the firm's governance structure.

The risks from these ESG factors can be categorized as follows:

Legislative and Regulatory Risk

This is the risk that new laws or regulations will negatively impact a firm's profitability or business model. Examples of this kind of risk include new standards that restrict automotive emissions: any manufacturer that fails to meet these standards will suffer a negative impact on sales. It is important to consider legislative and regulatory risk when analyzing investments since a company that has invested in cleaner or safer technologies is less likely to suffer from new legislation than their competitors.

Legal Risk

Legal risk is the potential for lawsuits resulting from management's failure to adequately address one of the ESG factors. Such lawsuits could originate from employees, shareholders, or the government. The potential value of such judgments could have a material impact on a company.

To evaluate the level of legal risk that a specific company is exposed to, an analyst should examine the company's regulatory filings, such as form 10-K, which requires companies to disclose possible legal risk exposures. Additionally, an analyst should consider the industry in which the firm operates, as well as its specific operations, in order to evaluate the magnitude of legal risk exposure.

Reputational Risk

Reputational risk is increasingly important as investors come to see this factor as a major source of risk and thus an important input in valuation.

Companies with management that has been seen in the past to show insufficient regard for environmental, social, and corporate governance issues will be valued at a lower market value compared to companies that manage these risk exposures suitably.

Operating Risk

Operating risk refers to the possibility that a firm will be forced to modify an operation, or shut it down altogether, due to impact of ESG factors. The use of refrigerant products containing chlorofluorocarbons is one example of operating risk: when the U.S. Environmental Protection Agency essentially banned it, several industries, including appliance and automobile manufacturers, were negatively impacted.

Financial Risk

Financial risk is simply the risk that the ESG risk factors will result in a monetary cost to the firm or shareholders. Because of this potential financial cost, analysts should be sure to examine all possible sources of ESG risk when analyzing a company and include these potential risk impacts in the valuation.

LOS 24.h: Explain the valuation implications of corporate governance.

CFA® Program Curriculum, Volume 3, page 260

The strength and effectiveness of a corporate governance system has a direct and significant impact on the value of a company.

Strong/effective corporate governance system. U.S. and international companies with effective corporate governance systems have been shown to have higher measures of profitability and generate higher returns for shareholders.

- In a joint study conducted by Institutional Shareholder Services and Georgia State University, the best governed companies generated a return on equity (ROE) that was 23.8% higher than firms with poor corporate governance.[3]
- Portfolios of companies with strong shareholder-rights protections were found to outperform portfolios of companies with weaker protections by 8.5% annually.[4]
- A study of 100 emerging market companies that ranked companies based on seven governance criteria found that companies with the best governance practices generated a cumulative 5-year return 542% greater than firms that had poor governance.[5]

---

3. Lawrence D.Brown and Marcus Caylor, "Corporate Governance Study: The Correlation Between Corporate Governance and Company Performance," (Institutional Shareholder Services, 2004).
4. Paul A. Gompers, Joy L. Ishti, and Andrew Metrick, "Corporate Governance and Equity Prices," Quarterly Journal of Economics, 118, no. 1, (February 2003), 107–155.
5. Amar Gill, "Corporate Governance in Emerging Markets – Saints and Sinners: Who's Got Religion?" CLSA Emerging Markets, (April 2001).

Weak or ineffective corporate governance system. The lack of an effective corporate governance system increases the risk to an investor, thus reducing the value of the company. In extreme cases (e.g., Enron, 2001), deficient governance could cause a company to go bankrupt. Risks of an ineffective corporate governance system include:

- *Financial disclosure risk*. Information and disclosures that investors use as a basis for financial decisions are incomplete, misleading, or materially misstated.
- *Asset risk*. Managers and directors may use company assets inappropriately. Examples include excessive compensation and "perks."
- *Liability risk*. Management may enter into off-balance-sheet obligations that reduce the value of the shareholders' stake in the company.
- *Strategic policy risk*. Management may enter into transactions that may not be in the best interests of shareholders, but will provide benefits for management. Examples include acquisitions that may increase the size of the firm and improve management's prestige and perhaps its pay, but ultimately destroy shareholder value.

MODULE QUIZ 24.1

To best evaluate your performance, enter your quiz answers online.

1. Which of the following is *least likely* to be a core attribute of an effective corporate governance system?
   A. There is clear and measurable accountability for managers and directors in assuming their responsibilities.
   B. Company management receives compensation that is fair and reflective of job performance.
   C. Disclosures regarding operations and financial position are made with complete transparency and accuracy.
2. Charlene Harmon is meeting with her supervisor, Cipriano Bernal, about the implementation of a new corporate governance structure at their business. Bernal tells Harmon that there are two primary objectives of corporate governance:

Objective 1:	Eliminate or reduce conflicts of interest that are inherent with the corporate business form.
Objective 2:	Clearly define the responsibilities that managers and directors have to shareholders and other company stakeholders.

   Are Objectives 1 and 2 appropriate objectives of corporate governance?
   A. Only Objective 1 is correct.
   B. Only Objective 2 is correct.
   C. Both are correct.

Study Session 8

3. Which of the following situations is the *best* example of the principal-agent problem?
   A. The senior management team of a supplier of condiments to the restaurant industry purchases a supplier of cups and napkins. The merger increases the size of the business by 50% and is immediately accretive to earnings per share.
   B. Directors of a corporation for a large industrial company are required to sign an agreement that they will not serve as a director for any other firm.
   C. The senior managers of a small biotechnology company consistently invest in drug processes that have small chances of success, but have the potential to generate huge profits if they do succeed. The bulk of management compensation comes in the form of executive stock options.

Use the following information to answer Questions 4 and 5.

The Brinley Corporation's Board of Directors recently engaged in an annual self-assessment. The written report of the self-assessment included the following four observations:

Observation 1:	The independent directors meet in separate session without management on an as-needed basis.
Observation 2:	Two of Brinley's ten directors are senior managers of the corporation.
Observation 3:	Board members are elected on a staggered basis in which two directors are up for election each year.
Observation 4:	Corporate counsel is always available for the Board of Directors to answer any legal questions that may arise.

4. Are observations 1 and 2 *likely* to be consistent with corporate governance best practice?
   A. Both observations are correct.
   B. Only one of the observations is correct.
   C. Neither observation is correct.
5. Are observations 3 and 4 *likely* to be consistent with corporate governance best practice?
   A. Both observations are correct.
   B. Only one of the observations is correct.
   C. Neither observation is correct.
6. Which of the following is *least likely* to be useful in evaluating a company's corporate governance system for the purpose of investment analysis?
   A. Quarterly conference calls with analysts after earnings announcements.
   B. Performance self-assessments from individual committees on the Board of Directors.
   C. Statement of management's responsibilities to directors.

7. Which of the following statements concerning having a CEO serve as chairman of the board is *most accurate*? Having a CEO also serve as chairman is considered:
   A. good corporate governance practice as the CEO is the best person to provide the board with information about the company's strategy and operations.
   B. poor corporate governance practice as having the CEO serve as chairman is an inherent conflict when determining management compensation.
   C. poor corporate governance practice as having the CEO and chairman serve as separate positions ensures a properly-functioning board.

8. The nontraditional ESG factors that must be considered to get a full picture of a company's long-term risks are *most accurately* described as:
   A. exchange, sales, and general risk.
   B. earnings, systematic, and governmental risk.
   C. environmental, social, and governance risk.

9. Benjamin Myers is an analyst for Hanover Capital Management, an equity manager specializing in large capitalization growth stocks. Myers believes that investment results for the firm could be improved if a corporate governance assessment were included as part of the criteria for analyzing investment opportunities. In a memo used to convince his colleagues of the implications for corporate governance in company valuation, Myers makes two statements to support his claim that corporate governance is important for valuing a company:

Statement 1:	The lack of a corporate governance structure increases the risk that financial statements will be materially misstated, and also increases the risk that company assets will be used for management's benefit.
Statement 2:	Studies indicate that companies with effective corporate governance structures in place generate a higher return on equity than companies without a strong corporate governance system.

   Do Myer's statements provide appropriate support for his claim?
   A. Both statements are correct.
   B. Only one of the statements is correct.
   C. Neither statement is correct.

Study Session 8

Use the following information to answer Questions 10 and 11.

Regan Albright-Williams is the CEO for Karazim, a company that provides an Internet auction marketplace. Karazim was a private company for eight years, but recently had an IPO and became publicly traded. Albright-Williams has been with Karazim since it was founded. She is new to corporate governance requirements as this is her first time running a public company.

Albright-Williams' first task in setting up a corporate governance system is to formalize the structure for the board of directors. Karazim had an ad hoc board as a private company that consisted of five members of the Williams family. Two of these family members have worked for Karazim for the last eight years. She decides to invite all five of them to be on the new board. In order to meet a recommendation she read about in an article on corporate governance best practices, Albright-Williams also recruits ten independent board members who are not family members. She decides it would be best to have board members who are knowledgeable about both finance and the Internet auction business, so she decides to ask four bankers that have acted as ongoing lenders to Karazim over the past ten years to serve as board members. She also sends letters to six people she knows that serve on boards of other public companies who have a reputation for being respected business leaders. In her letter asking these individuals to serve on the board, Albright-Williams tells them that their commitment to the board will be for at least two years because members of the board of directors will be elected in even-numbered years.

Two of Karazim's Executive Vice Presidents were asked to make preparations for the first board meeting. Mark Davidson states, "we should send out a letter to investors introducing the new board members before the first meeting is convened." Jeff Pyle replies, "I think we should have a training session for the board members so they can perform their responsibilities to the board."

The primary task at the first board meeting is to finalize the board's committee structure. In the first order of business, Albright-Williams is appointed Chairman of the board. The nominating committee is formed with four directors, each of whom is independent. Finally, the audit committee is formed, with the company's CFO chairing the committee, and bankers who are lenders to the company taking the other four positions on the committee.

10. Which of the following pairs of concerns *most accurately* describes the problems with the structure that Albright-Williams has put together for the board of directors?
    A. Five family members on the board does not meet the best practices concerning the proportion of independent board members, and lenders to the company cannot be classified as independent.
    B. Two former employees on the board does not meet the best practices concerning the proportion of independent board members, and individuals that serve on boards for other companies cannot be classified as independent.
    C. Two former employees on the board does not meet the best practices concerning the proportion of independent board members, and lenders to the company cannot be classified as independent.

11. Whose statements are *most* consistent with corporate governance best practice?
    A. Albright-Williams' letter.
    B. Davidson's statement.
    C. Pyle's statement.
12. Activist shareholders are pressuring Yellow Frond, Inc., for a change in senior management after six consecutive quarters of poor earnings and a declining share price. The Board of Yellow Frond votes to enact a series of aggressive anti-takeover provisions with all independent directors dissenting, then resigning. This situation *most likely* indicates Yellow Frond has a:
    A. principal-agent problem.
    B. disclosure assessment problem.
    C. exogenous change problem.

KEY CONCEPTS

LOS 24.a

McEnally and Kim define corporate governance as "the system of principles, policies, procedures, and clearly defined responsibilities and accountabilities used by stakeholders to overcome conflicts of interest inherent in the corporate form." The lack of an effective corporate governance system could threaten the existence of a corporation and weaken the trust and confidence that is essential for effective financial markets.

The objectives of corporate governance are to:

- Eliminate or reduce conflicts of interest.
- Use the company's assets in a manner consistent with the best interests of investors and other stakeholders.

An effective corporate governance system will:

- Define the rights of shareholders and other important stakeholders.
- Define and communicate to stakeholders the oversight responsibilities of managers and directors.
- Provide clear and measurable accountability for managers and directors in assuming their responsibilities.
- Provide for fair and equitable treatment in all dealings between managers, directors, and shareholders.
- Have complete transparency and accuracy in disclosures regarding operations, performance, risk, and financial position.

LOS 24.b

There are three major business forms:

- Sole proprietorship.
- Partnership.
- Corporation.

Corporations differ from sole proprietorships and partnerships in that the corporation is a separate legal entity from its owners.

LOS 24.c

An agency relationship creates the potential for a principal-agent problem where the agent may act for his own well-being rather than that of the principal. There are two potential areas of conflict.

- Managers and shareholders: Shareholders want management to make decisions that maximize shareholder wealth, but managers, left on their own, may well make decisions that maximize their own wealth. Examples of ways that management may act for their own interests include using funds to expand the size of the firm, granting excessive compensation and perquisites, investing in risky ventures, or not taking enough risk.

- Directors and shareholders: The conflict between directors and shareholders occurs when directors align more with management interests rather than those of shareholders. The following factors may cause this to occur: lack of independence, board members have personal relationships with management, board members have consulting or other business agreements with the firm, interlinked boards, or directors are overcompensated.

LOS 24.d

The board of directors for a corporation has the responsibility to:

- Institute corporate values and corporate governance mechanisms that will ensure business is conducted in a proficient, ethical, and fair manner.
- Ensure firm compliance with all legal and regulatory requirements in a timely manner.
- Create long-term strategic objectives for the company that are consistent with the shareholders' best interests.
- Determine management's responsibilities and how they will be held accountable. Performance should be measured in all areas of a company's operations.
- Evaluate the performance of the chief executive officer (CEO).
- Require management to supply the board with complete and accurate information in order for the board to make decisions for which it is responsible.
- Meet regularly to conduct its normal business, and meet in extraordinary session if necessary.
- Ensure that board members are adequately trained.

LOS 24.e

Corporate governance best practices includes the following:

- 75% independent board members.
- CEO and Chairman are separate positions.
- Directors knowledgeable/experienced, serve on only two or three boards.
- Annual elections (not staggered).
- Evaluate/assess board annually.
- Meet annually without management.
- Independent directors with finance expertise on audit committee; meet auditors annually.
- Independent directors on nominating committee.
- Most senior manager pay is tied to performance.
- Board use independent/outside counsel.
- Board approves related-party transactions.

LOS 24.f

Investors and analysts should assess the following policies of corporate governance:

- Codes of ethics.
- Directors' oversight, monitoring, and review responsibilities.
- Management's responsibility to the board.
- Reports of directors' oversight and review of management.
- Board self-assessments.
- Management performance assessments.
- Director training.

LOS 24.g

In addition to traditional business risk exposures, there are three additional risk factors that must be considered to get a full picture of a firm's long-term risks:

- Environmental risk: For example, related to greenhouse gas emissions that may cause climate change.
- Social risk: Such as labour rights or occupational safety.
- Governance risk: The effectiveness of the firm's governance structure.

The risks from these ESG factors can be categorized as follows:

- Legislative and regulatory risk: Risk that the government will pass new laws or regulations (e.g., emissions standards).
- Legal risk: Potential for lawsuits resulting from management's failure to adequately deal with one of the ESG factors.
- Reputational risk: Valuation impact of management's insufficient past attention to ESG factors.
- Operating risk: Possibility that a firm's operations will be negatively impacted by ESG factors.
- Financial risk: Risk of incurring a monetary cost due to ESG risk factors.

LOS 24.h

Studies have shown that strong corporate governance increases profitability and returns to shareholders. Weak corporate governance systems decrease the value of a company by increasing financial disclosure risk, asset risk, liability risk, or strategic policy risk.

ANSWER KEY FOR MODULE QUIZ

Module Quiz 24.1

1. **B** Although fair compensation for management that is reflective of job performance may result from an effective corporate governance system, it is not considered one of the core attributes. (LOS 24.a)

2. **A** The objectives of corporate governance are to (1) eliminate or reduce conflicts of interest, particularly those between managers and shareholders, that are inherent with the corporate form of doing business, and (2) ensure that company assets are used in a manner consistent with the best interests of investors and other stakeholders. (LOS 24.a)

3. **C** The principal-agent problem in a corporation refers to a situation where agents, such as management or directors, act in their own best interests rather than those of the principal (i.e., the shareholders). The best example of the principal-agent problem is the biotech company whose management generates big payoffs from their stock options if a risky project succeeds, but has little downside risk if the project fails. The condiment supplier to the restaurant industry seems to be engaging in a vertical merger that makes sense for shareholders. Having directors that are paid in stock is a way to align director interests with those of shareholders, and having directors only serve on one board is a means of having directors focus their energies on one firm. (LOS 24.c)

4. **B** Observation 1 is not consistent because meetings of the independent directors should be held at least annually. Meeting on an as-needed basis is too vague. Best practice dictates that 75% of directors should be independent. In the case of Brinley, it appears 80% are independent, so Observation 2 is consistent. (LOS 24.d)

5. **C** Observation 3 is not consistent because best practice calls for annual elections. Observation 4 is not consistent—boards should use independent counsel rather than corporate counsel for legal issues. (LOS 24.e)

6. **A** Quarterly conference calls may be useful to learn about operations and management's assessment of the business environment, but of the choices listed, they are the least likely to provide information about a company's corporate governance practices. (LOS 24.f)

7. **B** Having an individual serve the dual role of CEO and Chairman is considered a poor corporate governance practice. Not only does it cause a conflict of interest when determining management compensation, there is a concern that the CEO/Chairman could drive the board agenda and influence the boardroom culture, diminishing the independence of independent directors. Note that while separating the CEO and Chairman positions reduces potential questions about the board's commitment to shareholders, it does not guarantee the board will function properly. (LOS 24.e)

8. **C** The nontraditional ESG business factors that should be considered when analyzing a firm are a company's environmental, social, and governance risk exposures. (LOS 24.g)

9. **A** Both of Myers' statements about the valuation characteristics of corporate governance support his claim. The lack of corporate governance structure increases accounting risk and asset risk, which are both described in his statement, as well as liability risk and strategic policy risk. Companies with strong corporate governance systems have been shown in studies to have higher profitability measures such as ROE. (LOS 24.h)

10. **A** The board structure that Karazim has proposed would consist of 15 board members. Former employees would not be considered independent, but having only two former employees on the board would be a ratio of 2:15, which would meet the best practice that at least 75% of the board members are independent. A bigger concern would be having five family members on the board, which would be one-third of the directors. In general, there is no problem with having directors that serve on other boards, however, if an individual serves on more than two or three boards, it raises the question of how much time they have to devote to each board. Another big concern would be having lenders serve on the board. If the lenders have an ongoing relationship with the company, they cannot be classified as independent. (LOS 24.e)

11. **C** The statement in Albright-Williams' letter is inconsistent with corporate governance best practice. Although it is admirable that elections will not be staggered, best practice would have elections take place annually. Davidson's suggestion is a nice gesture, but it is incomplete—shareholders should be able to vote on the board members before the first meeting. Pyle's statement is most consistent with best practice—board members should be trained so they can adequately perform board functions. (LOS 24.e)

12. **A** The internal board appears to be protecting management at the expense of shareholders; this is a principal-agent problem. "Disclosure assessment" has little or no meaning in this context. An "exogenous change" (i.e., an SEC investigation) could help or hurt Yellow Frond shareholders, but has nothing to do with this topic review. (LOS 24.e)

The following is a review of the Corporate Finance (2) principles designed to address the learning outcome statements set forth by CFA Institute. Cross-Reference to CFA Institute Assigned Reading #25.

READING 25 Mergers and Acquisitions

Study Session 8

EXAM FOCUS

This topic review is a corporate finance treatment of mergers and acquisitions, an important Level II topic. As you study this material, focus on how these concepts can be applied to the valuation process from the point of view of the analyst. When analysts analyze proposed mergers, they ask questions like the following: "Does this merger add value?"; "Does the justification for the merger proposed by management make sense?"; "Which company (the acquirer or the target) captures the value (if any) created by the merger?"; "How will the takeover defenses employed by the target firm affect the likelihood of the merger succeeding?" Pay particular attention to the three methods for valuing an M&A transaction and make sure you know how to evaluate a merger bid. These topics have important links to other places in the Level II curriculum, particularly the equity valuation material, and are therefore likely exam topics.

MODULE 25.1: MERGER MOTIVATIONS

Video covering this content is available online.

WARM-UP: BACKGROUND ON MERGERS AND ACQUISITIONS

The term mergers and acquisitions, or M&A for short, generally refers to two businesses combining in some manner. Many companies use M&A activities as a way to achieve growth, while others may use M&A to diversify their businesses. In any case, M&A activities are one of the most controversial topics in finance and are associated with complex legal, tax, and synergistic issues. A casual reading of the headlines indicates that mergers and acquisitions take a variety of forms (e.g., friendly or hostile), but almost always someone is left unhappy (usually the managers that are removed, or workers that will be laid off).

Although "M&A" is often used as a generic term that refers to any business combination, we can differentiate between mergers and acquisitions. An **acquisition** refers to one company buying only part of another company. A typical acquisition transaction may involve the purchase of assets or a distinct business segment (e.g., subsidiary) from another company. If the acquirer absorbs the entire target company, the transaction is considered a **merger**. Once a merger is completed, only one company will remain, and the other will cease to exist. Whether a transaction is called a merger or an acquisition, the initiator of the venture is referred to as the bidder, or **acquirer**, while the opposite side of the transaction is known as the **target**.

LOS 25.a: Classify merger and acquisition (M&A) activities based on forms of integration and relatedness of business activities.

CFA® Program Curriculum, Volume 3, page 278

There are a variety of ways to classify merger and acquisition activities. For the exam, you should be able to classify M&A activities based on how the companies physically come together (i.e., forms of integration) and on how the companies' business activities relate to one another (i.e., types of mergers).

Forms of Integration

In a **statutory merger**, the acquiring company acquires all of the target's assets and liabilities. As a result, the target company ceases to exist as a separate entity. Note that in a statutory merger, the target company is usually smaller than the purchaser, but this is not always the case.

In a **subsidiary merger**, the target company becomes a subsidiary of the purchaser. Most subsidiary mergers typically occur when the target has a well-known brand that the acquirer wants to retain (e.g., Proctor and Gamble buying Gillette).

With a **consolidation**, both companies cease to exist in their prior form, and they come together to form a completely new company. Consolidations are common in mergers when both companies are of a similar size.

Types of Mergers

In a **horizontal merger**, the two businesses operate in the same or similar industries, and may often be competitors. Therefore, if BurgerWorld and World of Burgers were to merge, the basic operations of the new firm would be very similar to those of the separate entities.

In a **vertical merger**, the acquiring company seeks to move up or down the product supply chain. For example, an ice cream manufacturer decides to acquire a restaurant chain so it can have an outlet for its products and not rely on supermarkets or other restaurants. This is an example of *forward integration*, where the acquirer is moving up the supply chain toward the ultimate consumer. If the same ice cream manufacturer purchases a farm so it can supply its own milk and cream for its products, it is called *backward integration* because the company is moving down the supply chain toward the raw material inputs.

In a **conglomerate merger**, the two companies operate in completely separate industries. As such, there are expected to be few, if any, synergies from combining the two companies. For example, BurgerWorld's decision to venture into the oil exploration business via acquisition represents a conglomerate merger because there are no apparent benefits (other than perhaps feeding hungry workers).

LOS 25.b: Explain common motivations behind M&A activity.

CFA® Program Curriculum, Volume 3, page 281

Managers often cite a variety of reasons for mergers and acquisitions. Some of these explanations make economic sense (i.e., they create synergies and are a source of added value) and some do not. Analysts and investors should carefully evaluate the motivation for a merger, keeping in mind there may be several motives and that some motives may be interrelated.

Synergies. The most common motivation for a merger is the idea that it will create synergies in which the combined company will be worth more than the two companies would be worth if operating separately. Usually, synergy results from either reducing costs or increasing revenues. Cost synergies are exactly the strategy behind a pure horizontal merger. On the surface, who can argue with increasing economies of scale? This is one of the basic principles of microeconomics. Imagine this scenario: two firms plan to combine even though there is no expected increase in sales. If the new entity can reduce the combined fixed costs (via elimination of duplicate functions), the average cost per unit will decrease by spreading the now lower fixed costs over the same number of units. Of course, it is easier said than done to eliminate duplicate functions and integrate the remaining business functions. Revenue synergies are typically created by cross-selling products, increasing market share, or raising prices to take advantage of reduced competition.

Achieving more rapid growth. External growth via M&A activity is usually a much faster way for managers to increase revenues than making investments internally (i.e., organic growth). Growth through M&A is especially common in mature industries where organic growth opportunities are limited. In addition, it is typically a less risky way to generate growth by acquiring resources through a merger with another company rather than developing them internally.

Increased market power. When a horizontal merger occurs in an industry with few competitors, the newly combined company will typically come away with increased market share and a greater ability to influence market prices. Vertical mergers may also increase market power by reducing dependence on outside suppliers. For example, if a company acquires a key supplier of raw materials, it can guarantee that materials will be available in its own production process and potentially lock out competing firms who may rely on the same raw materials. By controlling critical supply inputs, the firm can influence industry output and market prices. Regulators closely scrutinize both horizontal and vertical mergers to make sure the combined company does not gain too much market power, which could potentially harm consumers.

PROFESSOR'S NOTE

The Herfindahl-Hirschman Index is often used as a measure of market power resulting from a merger. This index is discussed in a later LOS.

Gaining access to unique capabilities. If a company is lacking a specific capability or resource (e.g., research and development or intellectual capital), it can either try to develop it internally or seek to acquire something that already exists. M&A activity can be a cost effective way to acquire proven capabilities or resources.

Diversification. Managers may cite the need to diversify the firm's cash flows as grounds for a merger. This makes no sense for shareholders but may be rational for the managers. It is much easier and cheaper for the shareholders to diversify simply by investing in the shares of unrelated companies themselves rather than having one company go through the long, expensive process of acquiring and merging the two firms' operations and corporate cultures. In fact, research has revealed that conglomerates trade at a discount relative to the sum of the value of individual businesses. In this case, the whole is *less* than the sum of the individual parts. This finding demonstrates that mergers are not likely to increase value purely for diversification reasons.

Bootstrapping EPS. Another motivation for mergers is the bootstrapping effect on earnings per share that sometimes results from a stock deal. Bootstrapping is discussed in the next LOS.

Personal benefits for managers. Studies concerning executive compensation find there is a high correlation between the size of a company and how much a manager is paid. This means that there is a strong financial incentive for managers to maximize the size of the firm rather than shareholder value. In addition, being part of the executive team for a larger company implies greater power and prestige and is probably good for managerial egos.

PROFESSOR'S NOTE

The tendency of managers to maximize their own wealth rather than shareholders' wealth is an example of an agency problem, discussed in an earlier topic review of Corporate Governance.

Tax benefits. Consider the case of two companies where one has large amounts of taxable income and the other has accumulated large tax loss carryforwards. By merging with the company that has tax losses, the acquirer can use the losses to lower its tax liability. Regulators typically do not approve mergers that are undertaken purely for tax reasons, but with the many potential motivations to enter into a merger, proving that tax reasons are the key factor is difficult.

Unlocking hidden value. When a company has struggled for an extended period of time, an acquirer may believe it can pay a lower price to buy the company and unlock hidden value by improving management, adding resources, or improving the organizational structure. In some cases, a merger may occur because the acquirer believes it is purchasing assets for less than their replacement cost. For example, a manufacturing company may be able to acquire an existing production process for less than it would cost to develop the process on its own.

Achieving international business goals. Since the 1990s, international M&A deals have become an important way for multinational companies to achieve cross-border business goals. Many of these goals reflect the same motivations behind domestic mergers, such as extending global market power or gaining access to unique capabilities. However, there are a number of factors driving international M&A that are specific to international business:

- *Taking advantage of market inefficiencies.* Acquiring a manufacturing plant in a country where labor costs are less expensive is a prime example of gaining an advantage from an inefficient global marketplace.
- *Working around disadvantageous government policies.* International M&A is a potential way to overcome barriers to free trade, such as tariffs or quotas.
- *Use technology in new markets.* A company with an exciting new technology may acquire companies in other countries in order to gain access to new markets where the technology can be marketed.
- *Product differentiation.* Buying foreign companies can help firms with a unique line of products expand their competitive advantage.
- *Provide support to existing multinational clients.* Companies may wish to gain a presence overseas in order to maintain or expand an existing relationship with a client who has multinational operations.

LOS 25.c: Explain bootstrapping of earnings per share (EPS) and calculate a company's post-merger EPS.

CFA® Program Curriculum, Volume 3, page 282

PROFESSOR'S NOTE

The term "bootstrapping" as used here is not the same as the fixed income topic of bootstrapping forward rates or spot rates.

Bootstrapping is a way of packaging the combined earnings from two companies after a merger so that the merger generates an increase in the earnings per share of the acquirer, even when no real economic gains have been achieved.

The "bootstrap effect" occurs when a high P/E firm (generally a firm with high growth prospects) acquires a low P/E firm (generally a firm with low growth prospects) in a stock transaction. Post-merger, the earnings of the combined firm are simply the sum of the respective earnings prior to the merger. However, by purchasing the firm with a lower P/E, the acquiring firm is essentially exchanging higher-priced shares for lower-priced shares. As a result, the number of shares outstanding for the acquiring firm increases, but at a ratio that is less than 1-for-1. When we compute the EPS for the combined firm, the numerator (total earnings) is equal to the sum of the combined firms, but the denominator (total shares outstanding) is less than the sum of the combined firms. The result is a higher reported EPS, even when the merger creates no additional synergistic value.

EXAMPLE: Bootstrapping earnings per share

Fastgro, Inc., is planning to acquire Slowgro, Inc., in a merger transaction. Financial information for the two companies both prior to and after the merger are shown in the following table. Calculate Fastgro's post-merger EPS and determine whether the merger created economic gains.

Financial Information for Fastgro and Slowgro

	Fastgro, Inc.	Slowgro, Inc.	Fastgro–Post Merger
Stock Price	$80.00	$40.00	$80.00
EPS	$3.00	$2.00	
P/E Ratio	26.7	20.0	
Total shares outstanding	200,000	100,000	250,000
Total earnings	$600,000	$200,000	$800,000
Market capitalization	$16,000,000	$4,000,000	$20,000,000

Answer:

Given Fastgro's stock price of $80, it can issue 50,000 new shares and use the proceeds to buy Slowgro ($4,000,000 / $80 = 50,000 shares). The total shares outstanding for the post-merger Fastgro will be 250,000, which consists of Fastgro's original 200,000 shares and the newly issued 50,000 shares. If we divide the post-merger combined earnings of $800,000 by the 250,000 shares outstanding, we compute Fastgro's post-merger EPS as $3.20, which is $0.20 higher per share than Fastgro would have reported before the merger.

However, no economic value was created by the merger because the market capitalization of Fastgro post-merger is equal to the sum of the two companies' values prior to the merger ($16 + $4 = $20 million).

The apparent growth in EPS through bootstrapping was not the result of growth in earnings through capital investment, increased corporate efficiency, or synergistic gains, but rather from the accounting involved in a stock merger with a low-growth firm. In an efficient market, the post-merger P/E should adjust to the weighted average of the two companies' contributions to the post-merger company's total earnings. In our example, this would mean that the post-merger P/E would be about 25, which would imply that Fastgro's stock price would remain at $80 after the merger.

In practice, the market tends to recognize the bootstrapping effect and post-merger P/E's adjust accordingly. However, there have been periods in history, such as the technology bubble in the late 1990s, where bootstrapping helped high P/E companies show EPS growth, even in cases where the mergers created no value for shareholders.

LOS 25.d: Explain, based on industry life cycles, the relation between merger motivations and types of mergers.

CFA® Program Curriculum, Volume 3, page 285

The industry life cycle recognizes that industries go through certain phases based on their rates of growth. The motivations that a company may have for entering into a merger and the type of merger can depend a great deal on what phase of the industry life cycle the company is in.

Pioneer/development phase. In the pioneer phase, it is generally still uncertain whether consumers will accept a firm's product or service. The industry typically has large capital needs to fund development, but is not generating profits. In this stage, younger, smaller companies may seek to sell themselves to larger, more mature companies that have ample resources and want to find a new growth opportunity, or they may merge with a similar firm that will allow both companies to share management talents and financial resources. As a result, the common types of mergers seen in this stage are conglomerate mergers and horizontal mergers.

Rapid growth phase. The rapid growth phase is characterized by high profit margins and accelerating sales and earnings. The product or service provided by the company is accepted by consumers, but there is little competition in the industry. Merger motivations in this stage are usually driven by capital requirements as companies look for more resources to finance their expansion. The common types of mergers seen in this stage are conglomerates, as larger, more mature companies are able to provide capital, and horizontal mergers as similar firms combine resources to finance further growth.

Mature growth phase. In the mature phase, new competition has reduced industry profit margins, but the potential still exists for above-average growth. Merger motivations are generally focused on operational efficiencies as companies seek to generate economies of scale to reduce costs to keep profit margins high. As a result, horizontal and vertical mergers that provide synergies and expand market power are most common in this phase.

Stabilization phase. In the stabilization phase, competition has eliminated most of the growth potential in the industry, and the rate of growth is in line with that of the overall economy. Companies in this phase seek mergers to generate economies of scale in order to compete with a lower cost structure. They may also acquire smaller companies that can provide stronger management and a wider financial base. In this phase, horizontal mergers are the most common as the strongest companies acquire the weaker companies to consolidate market share and reduce costs.

Decline phase. The decline phase is characterized by overcapacity, declining profit margins, and lower demand as tastes may have changed and consumers seek new technologies. In this stage, all three types of mergers are common. A company may seek a horizontal merger simply to survive, vertical mergers may be used to increase efficiencies and increase profit margins, and conglomerate mergers may occur as companies acquire smaller companies in different industries to try to find new growth opportunities. Figure 25.1 summarizes this discussion.

Figure 25.1: Merger Motivations in the Industry Life Cycle

Industry Life Cycle Stage	Industry Characteristics	Merger Motivations	Common Types of Mergers
Pioneer/ development	■ Unsure of product acceptance ■ Large capital requirements and low profit margins	■ Gain access to capital from more mature businesses ■ Share management talent	■ Conglomerate ■ Horizontal
Rapid growth	■ High profit margins ■ Accelerating sales and earnings ■ Competition still low	■ Gain access to capital ■ Expand capacity to grow	■ Conglomerate ■ Horizontal
Mature growth	■ Lots of new competition ■ Still opportunities for above-average growth	■ Increase operational efficiencies ■ Economies of scale/synergies	■ Horizontal ■ Vertical
Stabilization	■ Competition has reduced growth potential ■ Capacity constraints	■ Economies of scale/reduce costs ■ Improve management	■ Horizontal
Decline	■ Consumer tastes have shifted ■ Overcapacity/ shrinking profit margins	■ Survival ■ Operational efficiencies ■ Acquire new growth opportunities	■ Horizontal ■ Vertical ■ Conglomerate

MODULE QUIZ 25.1

To best evaluate your performance, enter your quiz answers online.

1. Uritus Pharmaceuticals, a maker of flu vaccines and cancer drugs, is acquiring Troup Healthcare Systems, a distributor of branded and generic drugs to hospitals and retail customers. After the merger, a press release is made by the companies announcing that a new company called Sovereign Health is being formed from the assets of the combined companies. The form of integration and type of merger in this transaction would be *best* described as:
   A. horizontal statutory merger.
   B. vertical consolidation.
   C. bilateral statutory consolidation.

2. The management team of Acme Machinery wants to acquire Viera Equipment. Which of the following is *least likely* to be a motivation for the merger?
   A. Acme's management team believes that external growth will increase revenues faster than organic growth.
   B. Acme has large accumulated tax losses on its balance sheet, which could offset gains at Viera.
   C. Viera has struggled for a long period of time and Acme believes it can buy the company and change the organizational structure.
3. Bootstrapping occurs when a:
   A. high P/E firm acquires a low P/E firm for cash.
   B. low P/E firm acquires a high P/E firm for stock.
   C. high P/E firm acquires a low P/E firm for stock.
4. Gusto Technologies, a semiconductor manufacturer with high profit margins, is seeking to merge with Hexelon, Inc., a maker of aerospace materials, in a conglomerate merger in order to gain access to Hexelon's large capital base. Gusto is *most likely* in the:
   A. rapid growth stage.
   B. mature growth stage.
   C. stabilization stage.

MODULE 25.2: DEFENSE MECHANISMS AND ANTITRUST

Video covering this content is available online.

LOS 25.e: Contrast merger transaction characteristics by form of acquisition, method of payment, and attitude of target management.

CFA® Program Curriculum, Volume 3, page 286

The characteristics of a merger transaction are important because they largely determine how the transaction will take place, how it will be valued, and what regulatory and tax rules will apply.

Forms of Acquisition

The two basic forms of acquisition are a stock purchase or an asset purchase.

In a **stock purchase**, the acquirer gives the target firm's shareholders cash and/or securities in exchange for shares of the target company's stock. There are several important issues regarding stock purchases of which you should be aware.

- With a stock purchase, it is the shareholders that receive compensation, not the company itself. As a result, shareholders must approve the transaction with at least a majority shareholder vote (sometimes it's more than a majority, depending on the law where the merger takes place). Winning shareholder approval can be time consuming; but if the merger is hostile, dealing directly with shareholders is a way to avoid negotiations with management.
- Also, shareholders will bear any tax consequences associated with the transaction. Shareholders must pay tax on gains, but there are no taxes at the

corporate level. If the target company has accumulated tax losses, a stock purchase benefits the shareholders because under U.S. rules, the use of a target's tax losses is allowable for stock purchases, but not for asset purchases.

- Finally, most stock purchases involve purchasing the entire company and not just a portion of it. This means that not only will the acquirer gain the target company's assets, but it will also assume the target's liabilities.

In an **asset purchase**, the acquirer purchases the target company's assets, and payment is made directly to the target company.

- Unless the assets are substantial (e.g., more than 50% of the company), shareholder approval is generally not required.
- Also, because payment is made to the company, there are no direct tax consequences for the shareholder. The target company will pay any capital gains taxes associated with the transaction at the corporate level.
- Asset purchase acquisitions usually focus on specific parts of the company that are of particular interest to the acquirer, rather than the entire company, which means that the acquirer generally avoids assuming any of the target company's liabilities. However, an asset purchase for the sole purpose of avoiding the assumption of liabilities is generally not allowed from a legal standpoint. Figure 25.2 summarizes the key differences between stock purchase and an asset purchase.

Figure 25.2: Key Differences Between Forms of Acquisition

	Stock Purchase	**Asset Purchase**
Payment	Made directly to target company shareholders in exchange for their shares	Made directly to target company
Approval	Majority shareholder approval required	No shareholder approval needed unless asset sale is substantial
Corporate taxes	None	Target company pays capital gains taxes
Shareholder taxes	Shareholders pay capital gains tax	None
Liabilities	Acquirer assumes liabilities of target	Acquirer usually avoids assumption of target's liabilities

Method of Payment

The two basic methods of payment are a securities offering and a cash offering. We will discuss these two methods of payment separately; but you should know that in many cases, mergers will use a combination of the two, which is referred to a mixed offering.

In a **securities offering**, the target shareholders receive shares of the acquirer's common stock in exchange for their shares in the target company. The number of the acquirer's shares received for each target company share is based on the *exchange ratio*. For example, shareholders in the target company may receive 1.3 shares of the acquirer's stock for every one share they own in the target company. In practice, exchange ratios are negotiated in advance of a merger due to the daily fluctuations that can occur in stock prices. The total compensation ultimately paid by the acquirer in a stock offering is based on three factors: the exchange ratio, the number of shares outstanding of the target company, and the value of the acquirer's stock on the day the deal is completed.

Cash offers are straightforward in that the acquirer simply pays an agreed upon amount of cash for the target company's shares.

When an acquirer is negotiating with a target over the method of payment, there are three main factors that should be considered:

1. *Distribution between risk and reward for the acquirer and target shareholders.* In a stock offering, since the target company's shareholders receive new shares in the post-merger company, they share in the risk related to the ultimate value that is realized from the merger. In a cash offering, all of the risk related to the value of the post-merger company is borne by the acquirer. As a result, when the acquirer is highly confident in the synergies and value that will be created by the merger, it is more inclined to push for a cash offering.
2. *Relative valuations of companies involved.* If the acquirer's shares are considered overvalued by the market, the acquirer is likely to want to use its overpriced shares as currency in the merger transaction. In fact, investors sometimes interpret a stock offering as a signal that the acquirer's shares may be overvalued.
3. *Changes in capital structure.* Different payment structures have an impact on the acquiring firm's capital structure. If the acquirer borrows money to raise cash for a cash offering, the associated debt will increase the acquirer's financial leverage and risk. Issuing new stock for a securities offering can dilute the ownership interest for the acquirer's existing shareholders.

Attitude of Target Management

A merger offer will be viewed as either friendly or hostile by the target company's management. Management's attitude toward the merger offer is important because it shapes how the merger is completed and the process that is followed.

Friendly merger offers usually begin with the acquirer directly approaching the target's management. If both parties like the idea of a potential deal, they will negotiate the method of payment and the terms of the transaction. At this point, each party to the merger will conduct due diligence on the other party by examining financial statements and other records. The goal of the due diligence process is for each party to protect its shareholders by confirming the accuracy of assertions made during negotiations. The acquirer will want to make sure the target's assets truly exist, while the target will want to make sure the acquirer has the financial capacity to pay for the transaction. Once the negotiation and due diligence process is complete, attorneys draft a *definitive merger agreement* that outlines the terms of the transaction and the rights of each party.

So far, the entire process for the merger has been kept secret from the general public in order to avoid violating securities laws related to material insider information. Only when each party signs the definitive merger agreement is the transaction announced to the public. In a friendly merger, the announcement is accompanied by an endorsement of the merger from the target's management and board of directors to encourage target shareholders to vote for the deal. The target company's shareholders are then given a proxy statement that outlines all of the pertinent facts of the transaction. Once it has been approved by shareholders and regulators, payment is made, and the deal is complete.

Hostile merger offers typically follow a much different process than friendly mergers. If the target company's management does not support the deal, the acquirer submits a merger proposal directly to the target's board of directors in a process called a *bear hug*.

If the bear hug is unsuccessful, the next step is to appeal directly to the target's shareholders using one of two methods—a tender offer or a proxy battle.

- In a *tender offer*, the acquirer offers to buy the shares directly from the target shareholders, and each individual shareholder either accepts or rejects the offer.
- In a *proxy battle*, the acquirer seeks to control the target by having shareholders approve a new "acquirer approved" board of directors. A proxy solicitation is approved by regulators and then sent to the target's shareholders. If the shareholders elect the acquirer's slate of directors, the new board may replace the target's management and the merger offer may become friendly.

LOS 25.f: Distinguish among pre-offer and post-offer takeover defense mechanisms.

CFA® Program Curriculum, Volume 3, page 291

Managers can be very creative when it comes to employing defensive measures to resist a hostile takeover. These measures can be divided into two classes: (1) pre-offer defenses and (2) post-offer defenses. As the terms imply, defensive measures can be taken either before or after a hostile offer takes place, but most M&A legal experts recommend that defenses are set up before an offer occurs, because pre-offer defenses tend to face less scrutiny in court.

Pre-Offer Defense Mechanisms

Poison pill. Poison pills are extremely effective anti-takeover devices and were the subject of many legal battles in their infancy. In its most basic form, a poison pill gives current shareholders the right to purchase additional shares of stock at extremely attractive prices (i.e., at a discount to current market value), which causes dilution and effectively increases the cost to the potential acquirer. The pills are usually triggered when a shareholder's equity stake exceeds some threshold level (e.g., 10%). Specific forms of a poison pill are a *flip-in pill*, where the target company's shareholders have the right to buy the target's shares at a discount, and a *flip-over pill*, where the target's shareholders have the right to buy the acquirer's shares at a discount. In case of a friendly merger offer, most poison pill plans give the board of directors the right to redeem the pill prior to a triggering event.

Poison put. This anti-takeover device is different from the others, as it focuses on bondholders. These puts give bondholders the option to demand immediate repayment of their bonds if there is a hostile takeover. This additional cash burden may fend off a would-be acquirer.

Restrictive takeover laws. Companies in the United States are incorporated in specific states, and the rules of that state apply to the corporation. Some states are more *target friendly* than others when it comes to having rules to protect against hostile takeover attempts. Companies that want to avoid a potential hostile merger offer may seek to reincorporate in a state that has enacted strict anti-takeover laws. Historically, Ohio and Pennsylvania have been considered to provide target companies with the most protection.

Staggered board. In this strategy, the board of directors is split into roughly three equal-sized groups. Each group is elected for a 3-year term in a staggered system: in the first year the first group is elected, the following year the next group is elected, and in the final year the third group is elected. The implications are straight-forward. In any particular year, a bidder can win at most one-third of the board seats. It would take a potential acquirer at least two years to gain majority control of the board since the terms are overlapping for the remaining board members. This is usually longer than a bidder would want to wait and can deter a potential acquirer.

Restricted voting rights. Equity ownership above some threshold level (e.g., 15% or 20%) triggers a loss of voting rights unless approved by the board of directors. This greatly reduces the effectiveness of a tender offer and forces the bidder to negotiate with the board of directors directly.

Supermajority voting provision for mergers. A supermajority provision in the corporate charter requires shareholder support in excess of a simple majority. For example, a supermajority provision may require 66.7%, 75%, or 80% of votes in favor of a merger. Therefore, a simple majority shareholder vote of 51% would still fail under these supermajority limits.

Fair price amendment. A fair price amendment restricts a merger offer unless a *fair* price is offered to current shareholders. This fair price is usually determined by some formula or independent appraisal.

Golden parachutes. Golden parachutes are compensation agreements between the target and its senior management that give the managers lucrative cash payouts if they leave the target company after a merger. In practice, payouts to managers are generally not big enough to stop a large merger deal, but they do ease the target management's concern about losing their jobs.

PROFESSOR'S NOTE

In many cases, these pre-offer defenses are used in combination with each other. A hostile takeover attempt of a company that has restricted voting rights and a supermajority provision means that an acquirer could lose voting rights while acquiring shares, but still need an 80% approval for the merger to go through.

Post-Offer Defense Mechanisms

"Just say no" defense. The first step in avoiding a hostile takeover offer is to simply say no. If the potential acquirer goes directly to shareholders with a tender offer or a proxy fight, the target can make a public case to the shareholders concerning why the acquirer's offer is not in the shareholder's best interests.

Litigation. The basic idea is to file a lawsuit against the acquirer that will require expensive and time-consuming legal efforts to fight. The typical process is to attack the merger on anti-trust grounds or for some violation of securities law. The courts may disallow the merger or provide a temporary injunction delaying the merger, giving managers more time to load up their defense or seek a friendly offer from a *white knight*, as discussed later in this LOS.

Greenmail. Essentially, greenmail is a payoff to the potential acquirer to terminate the hostile takeover attempt. Greenmail is an agreement that allows the target to repurchase its shares from the acquiring company at a premium to the market price. The agreement is usually accompanied by a second agreement that the acquirer will not make another takeover attempt for a defined period of time. Greenmail used to be popular in the United States in the 1980s, but it has been rarely used after a 1986 change in tax laws added a 50% tax on profits realized by acquirers through greenmail.

Share repurchase. The target company can submit a tender offer for its own shares. This forces the acquirer to raise its bid in order to stay competitive with the target's offer and also increases the use of leverage in the target's capital structure (less equity increases the debt/equity ratio), which can make the target a less attractive takeover candidate.

Leveraged recapitalization. In a leveraged recapitalization, the target assumes a large amount of debt that is used to finance share repurchases. Like the share repurchase, the effect is to create a significant change in capital structure that makes the target less attractive while delivering value to shareholders.

Crown jewel defense. After a hostile takeover offer, a target may decide to sell a subsidiary or major asset to a neutral third party. If the hostile acquirer views this asset as essential to the deal (i.e., a *crown jewel*), then it may abandon the takeover attempt. The risk here is that courts may declare the strategy illegal if a significant asset sale is made after the hostile bid is announced.

Pac-Man® defense. In the video game Pac-Man, electronic ghosts would try to eat the main character, but after eating a power pill, Pac-Man would turn around and try to eat the ghosts. The analogy applies here. After a hostile takeover offer, the target can defend itself by making a counteroffer to acquire the acquirer. In practice, the Pac-Man defense is rarely used because it means a smaller company would have to acquire a larger company, and the target may also lose the use of other defense tactics as a result of its counteroffer.

White knight defense. A white knight is a friendly third party that comes to the rescue of the target company. The target will usually seek out a third party with a good strategic fit with the target that can justify a higher price than the hostile acquirer. In many cases, the white knight defense can start a bidding war between the hostile acquirer and the third party, resulting in the target receiving a very good price when a deal is ultimately completed. This tendency for the winner to overpay in a competitive bidding situation is called the *winner's curse*.

White squire defense. In medieval times, a squire was a *junior knight*. In today's M&A world, the squire analogy means that the target seeks a friendly third party that buys a minority stake in the target without buying the entire company. The idea is for the minority stake to be big enough to block the hostile acquirer from gaining enough shares to complete the merger. In practice, the white squire defense involves a high risk of litigation, depending on the details of the transaction, especially if the third party acquires shares directly from the company and the target's shareholders do not receive any compensation.

LOS 25.g: Calculate and interpret the Herfindahl–Hirschman Index and evaluate the likelihood of an antitrust challenge for a given business combination.

CFA® Program Curriculum, Volume 3, page 298

In 1982, the **Herfindahl-Hirschman Index** (HHI) replaced market share as the key measure of market power for determining potential antitrust violations. The HHI is calculated as the sum of the squared market shares for all firms within an industry.

$$HHI = \sum_{i=1}^{n} (MS_i \times 100)^2$$

where:

MS_i = market share of firm i

n = number of firms in the industry

Regulators initially focus on what the HHI would be *after the merger takes place*. If the post-merger HHI is less than 1,000, the industry is considered competitive and an antitrust challenge is unlikely. A post-merger HHI value between 1,000 and 1,800 will place the industry in the *moderately concentrated* category. In this case, regulators will compare the pre-merger and post-merger HHI. If the change is greater than 100 points, the merger is likely to be challenged on antitrust grounds. A post-merger HHI value greater than 1,800 implies a highly concentrated industry. Regulators will again compare the pre-merger and post-merger HHI calculations, but in this case, if the change is greater than 50, the merger is likely to be challenged. The guidelines for determining the likelihood of an antitrust challenge are summarized in Figure 25.3.

Figure 25.3: HHI Concentration Level and Likelihood of Antitrust Action

Post-Merger HHI	Industry Concentration	Change in Pre- and Post-Merger HHI	Antitrust Action
Less than 1,000	Not concentrated	Any amount	No action
Between 1,000 and 1,800	Moderately concentrated	100 or more	Possible antitrust challenge
Greater than 1,800	Highly concentrated	50 or more	Antitrust challenge virtually certain

EXAMPLE: Herfindahl-Hirschman Index in a competitive market

Suppose that there are 20 firms in the industry, each with a 5% market share. Also imagine that firms 19 and 20 decide to merge. Calculate the pre-merger and post-merger Herfindahl-Hirschman Index and discuss the likelihood of an antitrust challenge of the merger.

Answer:

$$\text{Pre-merger HHI} = (0.05 \times 100)^2 \times 20 = 500$$

$$\text{Post-merger HHI} = [(0.05 \times 100)^2 \times 18] + (0.10 \times 100)^2 = 550$$

Since the post-merger HHI < 1,000, the market is not considered to be concentrated and an antitrust challenge is unlikely. Note that since the post-merger HHI is lower than the 1,000 threshold, there is no need to consider the pre-merger HHI and the change between the two values.

EXAMPLE: Herfindahl-Hirschman Index in a concentrated market

Imagine that there are five firms in the industry, each with a 20% market share. Also suppose that firms 4 and 5 decide to merge. Calculate the pre-merger and post-merger Herfindahl-Hirschman Index and discuss the likelihood of an antitrust challenge for the merger.

Answer:

$$\text{Pre-merger HHI} = (0.20 \times 100)^2 \times 5 = 2{,}000$$

$$\text{Post-merger HHI} = [(0.20 \times 100)^2 \times 3] + (0.40 \times 100)^2 = 2{,}800$$

Since the post-merger HHI > 1,800, the market is considered concentrated and an anti-trust challenge is likely. Also, the difference between the pre-merger and post-merger HHI is much greater than the threshold of 50, making an antitrust challenge virtually certain.

Valuing a Target Company

The three basic methods that analysts use to value target companies in an M&A transaction are: (1) discounted cash flow analysis, (2) comparable company analysis, and (3) comparable transaction analysis. In the following discussion, we will explain how each method works, and then compare the three methods.

MODULE QUIZ 25.2

To best evaluate your performance, enter your quiz answers online.

1. Which of the following is a typical characteristic of an asset purchase of less than 50% of the target's assets?
   A. Majority shareholder approval is typically required.
   B. The target company is responsible for any capital gains taxes associated with the deal.
   C. The acquirer takes on a portion of the target firm's liabilities.
2. Which of the following merger defense mechanisms is likely to receive the *most* scrutiny in court after a hostile takeover attempt?
   A. Restricted voting rights.
   B. Supermajority voting provisions.
   C. Crown jewel defense.

3. Spears Financial is seeking to merge with the Cyrus Capital Group, but the managers of Spears are concerned that regulators may consider the merger an antitrust violation. The market consists of nine competitors. The largest company has a 20% market share and the second largest company has an 18% market share. Spears Financial and Cyrus Capital Group are the third and fourth largest competitors with a 12% and 10% market share, respectively. The remaining five competitors each have an 8% market share. What would be the increase in the Herfindahl-Hirschman Index (HHI) as a result of the merger and the *most likely* reaction by regulators to the merger?

Increase in the HHI	Probable response by regulators
A. 60	No antitrust challenge
B. 240	Potential antitrust challenge
C. 240	No antitrust challenge

MODULE 25.3: TARGET COMPANY VALUATION

Video covering this content is available online.

LOS 25.i: Calculate free cash flows for a target company and estimate the company's intrinsic value based on discounted cash flow analysis.

CFA® Program Curriculum, Volume 3, page 301

Discounted cash flow (DCF) analysis in the M&A context is very similar to the free cash flow to the firm (FCFF) approach discussed in Study Session 11. First, we want to determine the expected future free cash flows available to all investors after making necessary expenditures (e.g., working capital, capex) for the firm to continue as a going concern. From there, we want to discount these cash flows back to the present at the appropriate discount rate.

To calculate **free cash flow** (FCF) for a target company and estimate its value using DCF analysis, we can use the following steps:

Step 1: Determine which free cash flow model to use for the analysis. Basic free cash flow models come in two-stage or three-stage varieties. To make things easy for our discussion here, we will use a two-stage model that estimates the company's cash flows during a high growth phase and a stable growth phase.

Step 2: Develop pro forma financial estimates. These projected financial statements form the estimates that are the basis for our analysis.

Step 3: *Calculate free cash flows using the pro forma data*. Starting with net income, we can calculate free cash flows as:

net income
+ net interest after tax
= unlevered net income
± change in deferred taxes
= net operating profit less adjusted taxes (NOPLAT)
+ net noncash charges
– change in net working capital
– capital enditures capex
= free cash flow FCF

where:

net working capital = current assets (excluding cash and equivalents) – current liabilities (excluding short-term debt)

net interest after tax = (interest expense – interest income)(1 – marginal tax rate)

Note that unlevered net income also equals earnings before interest and taxes multiplied by 1 minus the tax rate and that you may be required to *back into* the tax rate by dividing taxes by net income before tax.

PROFESSOR'S NOTE

We will present a different version of free cash flow valuation in Study Session 11. You can work the corporate finance problems using the formula in Study Session 11 if you are provided the inputs that allow you to do so. However, if you encounter a corporate finance question on the exam, it is likely you will be provided with data using the terms from this topic review (e.g., unlevered net income, NOPLAT, etc.). In that case it will probably be easier to use the formula presented here.

Refer to the FCFF formula in the Study Sessions covering Equity:

$$FCFF = NI + NCC + [Int \times (1 - \text{tax rate})] - FCInv - WCInv$$

where:
NI = net income
NCC = non cash charges (e.g., depreciation and change in deferred taxes)
Int = interest expense
FCInv = fixed capital investment (capital expenditures)
WCInv = working capital investment

Step 4: *Discount free cash flows back to the present at the appropriate discount rate*. Usually, this discount rate is simply the target's weighted average cost of capital (WACC), but in the context of evaluating a potential merger target, we want to adjust the target's WACC to reflect any changes in the target's risk or capital structure that may result from the merger ($WACC_{adjusted}$).

Step 5: *Determine the terminal value and discount it back to the present*. The terminal value can be determined in two ways. The first is to use a constant growth model that assumes the company grows in perpetuity at a constant rate. The constant growth formula can be used when the terminal growth rate is less than the discount rate:

$$\text{terminal value}_T = \frac{FCF_T(1 + g)}{\left(WACC_{adjusted} - g\right)}$$

The second method applies a market multiple that the analyst believes that the firm will trade at the end of the first stage (e.g., a projected price/free cash flow ratio):

$$\text{terminal value}_T = FCF_T \times (P/FCF)$$

Step 6: Add the discounted FCF values for the first stage and the terminal value to determine the value of the target firm.

PROFESSOR'S NOTE

In a corporate finance problem, you may see the term enterprise value (EV) used to describe the sum of the FCF values for the first stage and the terminal value. EV is discussed later in this topic review, as well as in Study Session 11.

EXAMPLE: Valuing a merger target using discounted cash flow analysis

Goliath Manufacturing is considering acquiring Slingshot Systems, a software development company. Goliath's analysts have determined that a two-stage FCFF model is appropriate for their analysis, and have developed the pro forma income statement and other financial data shown in the follow table. Calculate Slingshot's free cash flows and estimate Slingshot's value as of January 2017 using DCF analysis. The WACC for Slingshot is 9.75%. If the merger is completed, Goliath plans to add debt to the capital structure that reduces the post-merger weighted average cost of capital, thus making the appropriate discount rate 9.50%.

Pro Forma Income Statement and Other Financial Data for Slingshot Systems

Income Statement (in thousands)	**2017**	**2018**	**2019**	**2020**	**2021**
Revenues	$12,000	$12,960	$14,126	$15,397	$16,783
Cost of Goods Sold	7,200	7,776	8,475	9,238	10,069
Gross Profit	4,800	5,184	5,651	6,159	6,714
Selling, general and administrative	1,344	1,452	1,582	1,725	1,880
Depreciation	420	454	494	539	587
Earnings before interest and taxes (EBIT)	3,036	3,279	3,574	3,896	4,247
Net interest expense	556	528	502	477	453
Earnings before taxes (EBT)	2,480	2,751	3,072	3,419	3,794
Income tax	868	963	1,075	1,197	1,328
Net income	1,612	1,788	1,997	2,222	2,466
Other Financial Data					
Change in net working capital	$384	$415	$452	$493	$537
Change in deferred tax liability	$17	$19	$22	$25	$27
Capital expenditures	$1,104	$1,192	$1,300	$1,417	$1,544

Tax rate = 35.0%

WACC = 9.75%

$WACC_{adjusted}$ = 9.50%

Terminal growth rate = 6.00%

Answer:

Steps 1 and 2 are complete. We are using a two-stage FCF model and have computed the pro forma financials.

Step 3: Calculate free cash flows using the pro forma data.

Free Cash Flow for Slingshot Systems	**2017**	**2018**	**2019**	**2020**	**2021**
Net income	$1,612	$1,788	$1,997	$2,222	$2,466
Add: Net interest after tax	361	343	326	310	294
Unlevered net income	1,973	2,131	2,323	2,532	2,760
Add: Change in deferred taxes	17	19	22	25	27
NOPLAT	1,990	2,150	2,345	2,557	2,787
Add: Depreciation	420	454	494	539	587
Subtract: Change in net working capital	384	415	452	493	537
Subtract: Capital expenditures	1,104	1,192	1,300	1,417	1,544
Free cash flow	$922	$997	$1,087	$1,186	$1,293

PROFESSOR'S NOTE:

Using the formula from Study Session 11, the calculations are as follows:

FCFF = NI + NCC + [Int × (1 – tax rate)] – FCInv – WCInv

2017 FCFF = $1,612 + 420 + 17 + [556 × (1 – 0.35)] – 1,104 – 384
= $922

2018 FCFF = $1,788 + 454 + 19 + [528 × (1 – 0.35)] – 1,192 – 415
= $997

2019 FCFF = $1,997 + 494 + 22 + [502 × (1 – 0.35)] – 1,300 – 452
= $1,087

2020 FCFF = $2,222 + 539 + 25 + [477 × (1 – 0.35)] – 1,417 – 493
= $1,186

2021 FCFF = $2,466 + 587 + 27 + [453 × (1 – 0.35)] – 1,544 – 537
= $1,293

Step 4: Discount free cash flows back to the present at the appropriate discount rate.

We discount the FCFs for the first five years at the adjusted WACC of 9.50%.

$$\text{discounted FCF} = \frac{\$922}{1.095} + \frac{\$997}{1.095^2} + \frac{\$1,087}{1.095^3} + \frac{\$1,186}{1.095^4} + \frac{\$1,293}{1.095^5} = \$4,148$$

Step 5: Determine the terminal value and discount it back to the present.

To calculate the terminal value, we assume that Slingshot's future free cash flows will grow in perpetuity at a constant rate of 6%.

$$\text{terminal value}_5 = \frac{FCF_5(1+g)}{\left(WACC_{adjusted} - g\right)} = \frac{\$1,293(1+0.06)}{(0.095-0.06)} = \$39,159$$

$$\text{terminal value}_0 = \frac{\$39,159}{1.095^5} = \$24,875$$

Step 6: Add the discounted FCF values for the first stage and the terminal value to determine the value of the target firm.

Adding the present value of the free cash flows and the terminal value gives our estimated value for the target (as of January 2017).

target value = \$4,148 + \$24,875 = \$29,023 = \$29.023 million

LOS 25.j: Estimate the value of a target company using comparable company and comparable transaction analyses.

CFA® Program Curriculum, Volume 3, page 307

Comparable company analysis uses relative valuation metrics for similar firms to estimate market value and then adds a takeover premium to determine a fair price for the acquirer to pay for the target.

Comparable company analysis involves the following steps:

Step 1: Identify the set of comparable firms. Comparable company analysis involves identifying a set of other companies that are similar to the target firm. Ideally, the sample of other companies will come from the same industry as the target and have a similar size and capital structure.

Step 2: Calculate various relative value measures based on the current market prices of companies in the sample. Some analysts use relative value measures based on enterprise value (EV), which is the market value of the firm's debt and equity minus the value of cash and investments. These include EV to free cash flow, EV to EBITDA, and EV to sales. Other relative value measures use equity multiples such as price to earnings (P/E), price to book (P/B), and price to sales (P/S). Depending on what industry the target firm is in, some industry specific multiples may also be appropriate.

Step 3: Calculate descriptive statistics for the relative value metrics and apply those measures to the target firm. Analysts will typically calculate the mean, median, and range for the chosen relative value measures and apply those to the estimates for the target to determine the target's value. Value is equal to the multiple times the appropriate variable; for example, using the P/E ratio:

value = EPS × (P/E)

Ideally, the different relative value measures will produce similar estimates for the target's value in order to give the analyst confidence in the valuation estimate. If the valuation estimates are significantly different when using different metrics, the analyst will have to make a judgment about which estimates are most accurate.

Step 4: Estimate a takeover premium. A takeover premium is the amount that the takeover price of each of the target's shares must exceed the market price in order to persuade the target shareholders to approve the merger deal. This premium is usually expressed as a percentage of the target's stock price and is calculated as:

$$TP = \frac{DP - SP}{SP}$$

where:
TP = takeover premium
DP = deal price per share
SP = target company's stock price

To estimate an appropriate takeover premium, analysts usually look at premiums paid in recent takeovers of companies most similar to the target firm. SP should be the price of the target stock before any market speculation causes the target's stock price to jump; this typically occurs during the early stages of the process when the target company is first identified by the market as being a potential takeover opportunity.

Step 5: Calculate the estimated takeover price for the target as the sum of estimated stock value based on comparables and the takeover premium. The estimated takeover price is considered a *fair price* to pay for control of the target company. Once the takeover price is computed, the acquirer should compare it to the estimated synergies from the merger to make sure the price makes economic sense.

EXAMPLE: Valuing a merger target using comparable company analysis

Mia Yost, an investment banker, has been retained by the Gracico Corporation to estimate the price that should be paid to acquire Albert Garage Systems, Inc. (AGSI). Yost decides to use comparable company analysis to value AGSI and has gathered information on comparable firms and recent acquisitions shown in the following figures to help with her analysis. Calculate the appropriate valuation metrics and using the mean of those metrics, estimate the price that Gracico should pay for AGSI.

Comparable Company Data

Company Statistics	AGSI	Comparable Firm 1	Comparable Firm 2	Comparable Firm 3
Current stock price		$25.00	$33.00	$19.00
Earnings per share (EPS) ($)	2.95	1.50	2.25	1.20
Book value per share ($)	15.20	8.80	10.50	6.00
Cash flow per share ($)	3.80	2.00	2.90	1.80
Sales per share ($)	46.00	21.60	28.70	19.50

Study Session 8

Takeover Prices in Recent M&A Transactions

Target Company	Stock Price Prior to Takeover	Takeover Price
Target 1	$22.00	$27.25
Target 2	$18.25	$21.00
Target 3	$108.90	$130.00
Target 4	$48.50	$57.00

Answer:

Step 1: Identify the set of comparable firms.

We can check off Step 1 as complete with the first table "Comparable Company Data."

Step 2: Calculate various relative value measures based on the current market prices of companies in the sample.

Using the data from the table "Comparable Company Data," the appropriate relative value measures for each firm are calculated in the following table.

Relative Value Measures for Comparable Firms

Relative Value Measure	Comparable Firm 1	Comparable Firm 2	Comparable Firm 3
Current stock price	$25.00	$33.00	$19.00
P/E	$25 / 1.50 = 16.67	$33 / 2.25 = 14.67	$19 / 1.20 = 15.83
P/B	$25 / 8.80 = 2.84	$33 / 10.50 = 3.14	$19 / 6.00 = 3.17
P/CF	$25 / 2.00 = 12.50	$33 / 2.90 = 11.38	$19 / 1.80 = 10.56
P/Sales	$25 / 21.60 = 1.16	$33 / 28.70 = 1.15	$19 / 19.50 = 0.97

Step 3: Calculate descriptive statistics for the relative value metrics and apply those measures to the target firm.

The following figure shows the calculation for the average for each of the four valuation metrics.

Mean Relative Value Measures

Relative Value Measure	Firm 1 (a)	Firm 2 (b)	Firm 3 (c)	Mean (average) Relative Value Measure (a + b + c) / 3
P/E	16.67	14.67	15.83	15.72
P/B	2.84	3.14	3.17	3.05
P/CF	12.50	11.38	10.56	11.48
P/Sales	1.16	1.15	0.97	1.09

The next figure applies these mean values to the statistics for AGSI. Since the four relative value metrics all produce estimates that are relatively close, it is appropriate to use an average of the four estimates as the estimated value for AGSI.

Estimated Stock Value for AGSI

Target Company Statistics	AGSI Statistics (a)	Relative Value Measure	Mean Relative Value Measure (b)	Estimated Stock Value Based on Comparables (a × b)
Earnings per share (EPS) ($)	2.95	P/E	15.72	$46.37
Book value per share ($)	15.20	P/B	3.05	$46.36
Cash flow per share ($)	3.80	P/CF	11.48	$43.62
Sales per share ($)	46.00	P/Sales	1.09	$50.14
		Mean Estimated Stock Value: = $46.62		

Step 4: Estimate a takeover premium.

The takeover premium is calculated for recent deals most similar to Gracico's proposed acquisition of AGSI. Since the four takeover premiums are relatively close, it is appropriate to use an average of the four estimates to apply to AGSI.

Calculation of Takeover Premium

Target Company	Target Stock Price Prior to Takeover (a)	Deal Price (b)	Takeover Premium [(b) – (a)] / (a)
Target 1	$22.00	$27.25	23.9%
Target 2	$18.25	$21.00	15.1%
Target 3	$108.90	$130.00	19.4%
Target 4	$48.50	$57.00	17.5%
		Mean premium: 19.0%	

Step 5: Calculate the estimated takeover price for the target as the sum of estimated stock value based on comparables and the takeover premium.

Estimated stock value based on comparable firms: $46.62

Estimated takeover premium: 19.0%

Estimated takeover price for AGSI = $46.62 × 1.19 = $55.48

ESTIMATING THE VALUE OF A MERGER TARGET USING COMPARABLE TRANSACTION ANALYSIS

Comparable transaction analysis uses details from recent takeover transactions of similar companies to estimate the target's takeover value. The methodology behind the approach is very similar to the comparable company approach we just showed you, except that all of the comparables are firms that have recently been taken over. The biggest challenge is finding enough relevant takeover transactions for firms that are similar to the target being analyzed. However, using recent transaction data means that the takeover premium is already included in the price, so there is no need to calculate it separately. Comparable transaction analysis involves the following steps:

Step 1: Identify a set of recent takeover transactions. Ideally, all of the takeovers will involve firms in the same industry as the target and have a similar capital structure. These sorts of deals can be difficult to find, so the analyst will have to use some judgment as to what recent merger deals are most applicable to the analysis.

Step 2: Calculate various relative value measures based on completed deal prices for the companies in the sample. The measures used here are the same as those used in comparable company analysis (e.g., P/E, P/CF), but they are based on prices for completed M&A deals rather than current market prices.

Step 3: Calculate descriptive statistics for the relative value metrics and apply those measures to the target firm. Again, analysts will typically calculate the mean, median, and range for the chosen relative value measures and apply those to the firm statistics for the target to determine the target's value.

EXAMPLE: Valuing a merger target using comparable transaction analysis

Ken Lloyd, an investment banker, has been retained by the Gase Equipment Company to estimate a fair price for the proposed acquisition of the Peerless Saw Company. Lloyd decides to use comparable transaction analysis to value Peerless and has gathered information concerning recent M&A transactions in the industrial equipment industry, which is shown in the following figure. Calculate the appropriate valuation metrics and using the mean of those metrics, and estimate the price that Gase Equipment should pay for the Peerless Saw Company.

Comparable Transaction Data

Company Statistics	Peerless Saw	Acquired Company 1	Acquired Company 2	Acquired Company 3
Deal price per share ($)		$42.00	$21.50	$90.00
Earnings per share (EPS) ($)	3.25	1.80	0.85	4.65
Book value per share ($)	18.50	9.75	5.25	22.25
Cash flow per share ($)	4.10	2.10	1.10	5.05
Sales per share ($)	33.00	18.20	9.75	38.90

Answer:

Step 1: Identify a set of recent takeover transactions.

Recent takeover transactions in the industrial equipment industry are shown in the preceding figure.

Step 2: Calculate various relative value measures based on completed deal prices for the companies in the sample.

The relative value measures are computed by dividing the deal price for each acquired company by the appropriate valuation statistic from the following figure.

Relative Value Measures Based on Completed Deal Prices

Relative Value Measure	Acquired Company 1	Acquired Company 2	Acquired Company 3
P/E	23.33	25.29	19.35
P/B	4.31	4.10	4.04
P/CF	20.00	19.55	17.82
P/Sales	2.31	2.21	2.31

Step 3: Calculate descriptive statistics for the relative value metrics and apply those measures to the target firm.

The following figure shows the calculation for the arithmetic mean for each of the four valuation metrics.

Mean Relative Value Measures

Relative Value Measure	Acquired Company 1 (a)	Acquired Company 2 (b)	Acquired Company 3 (c)	Mean (average) Relative Value Measure (a + b + c) / 3
P/E Ratio	23.33	25.29	19.35	22.66
P/B Ratio	4.31	4.10	4.04	4.15
P/CF Ratio	20.00	19.55	17.82	19.12
P/Sales Ratio	2.31	2.21	2.31	2.28

The next figure applies those mean values to the statistics for Peerless Saw. Since the four relative value metrics all produce estimates that are relatively close, it is appropriate to use an average of the four estimates as the estimated value for Peerless Saw.

Estimated Target Value for Peerless Saw Company

Target Company Statistics	Peerless Saw Company Statistics (a)	Relative Value Measure	Mean Relative Value Measure (b)	Estimated Stock Value Based on Comparables (a × b)
Earnings per share (EPS) ($)	3.25	P/E	22.66	$73.65
Book value per share ($)	18.50	P/B	4.15	$76.78
Cash flow per share ($)	4.10	P/CF	19.12	$78.39
Sales per share ($)	33.00	P/Sales	2.28	$75.24
		Mean Estimated Target Value: = $76.02		

The estimated target value of $76.02 is considered a *fair price* to pay for control of Peerless Saw. Note that since we used deal prices from actual M&A transactions as the basis for our analysis, there is no need to calculate a separate transaction premium because it is already incorporated into the price.

LOS 25.h: Compare the discounted cash flow, comparable company, and comparable transaction analyses for valuing a target company, including the advantages and disadvantages of each.

CFA® Program Curriculum, Volume 3, page 301

Discounted cash flow analysis is based on a pro forma forecast of the target firm's expected future free cash flows, discounted back to the present.

Advantages:

- It is relatively easy to model any changes in the target company's cash flow resulting from operating synergies or changes in cost structure that may occur after the merger.
- The estimate of company value is based on forecasts of fundamental conditions in the future rather than on current data.
- The model is easy to customize.

Disadvantages:

- The model is difficult to apply when free cash flows are negative. For example, a target company experiencing rapid growth may have negative free cash flows due to large capital expenditures.
- Estimates of cash flows and earnings are highly subject to error, especially when those estimates are for time periods far in the future.
- Discount rate changes over time can have a large impact on the valuation estimate.
- Estimation error is a major concern since the majority of the estimated value for the target is based on the terminal value, which is highly sensitive to estimates used for the constant growth rate and discount rate.

Comparable company analysis uses market data from similar firms plus a takeover premium to derive an estimated value for the target.

Advantages:

- Data for comparable companies is easy to access.
- Assumption that similar assets should have similar values is fundamentally sound.
- Estimates of value are derived directly from the market rather than assumptions and estimates about the future.

Disadvantages:

- The approach implicitly assumes that the market's valuation of the comparable companies is accurate.
- Using comparable companies provides an estimate of a fair stock price, but not a fair takeover price. An appropriate takeover premium must be determined separately.
- It is difficult to incorporate merger synergies or changing capital structures into the analysis.
- Historical data used to estimate a takeover premium may not be timely, and therefore may not reflect current conditions in the M&A market.

Comparable transaction analysis uses details from completed M&A deals for companies similar to the target being analyzed to calculate an estimated value for the target.

Advantages:

- Since the approach uses data from actual transactions, there is no need to estimate a separate takeover premium.
- Estimates of value are derived directly from recent prices for actual deals completed in the marketplace rather than from assumptions and estimates about the future.
- Use of prices established by recent transactions reduces the risk that the target's shareholders could file a lawsuit against the target's managers and board of directors for mispricing the deal.

Disadvantages:

- The approach implicitly assumes that the M&A market valued past transactions accurately. If past transactions were over or underpriced, the mispricings will be carried over to the estimated value for the target.
- There may not be enough comparable transactions to develop a reliable data set for use in calculating the estimated target value. If the analyst isn't able to find enough similar companies, she may try to use M&A deals from other industries that are not similar enough to the deal being considered.
- It is difficult to incorporate merger synergies or changing capital structures into the analysis.

MODULE QUIZ 25.3

To best evaluate your performance, enter your quiz answers online.

1. Naomi Hirauye and Michael Klinkenfus, financial analysts with Mintier Textiles, are discussing potential ways to value a target firm that Mintier is considering acquiring. As they are discussing which valuation method to use, Klinkenfus makes two statements:
   - "One of the advantages to the DCF method is that it makes it easy to model changes in the target company's cash flow resulting from changes in operating synergies that may occur after the merger."
   - "Since the comparable transaction approach uses actual transaction data, there is no need to calculate a takeover premium."

   How should Hirauye respond to Klinkenfus's statements?

   A. Agree with both statements.
   B. Disagree with both statements.
   C. Agree with only one statement.

Use the following information to answer Questions 2 through 6.

Gretsch Industries is considering acquiring Flueger Systems. Although Flueger has said it is not for sale, Gretsch is considering a hostile takeover by making a tender offer directly to Flueger's shareholders. Meghan Doyle, a financial analyst with Gretsch, has been assigned the task of estimating a fair acquisition price for the tender offer. Doyle plans to use three different valuation methods to estimate the acquisition price and has collected the necessary financial data for this purpose.

Flueger Systems has 20 million shares outstanding. Doyle has estimated that at the end of each of the next four years, Flueger will have free cash flow to equity (FCFE) (in millions) of $24, $27, $32, and $36. After the fourth year, Doyle expects Flueger's FCFE to grow at a constant rate of 6% per year. She also determines that Flueger's cost of equity of 10.5% is the appropriate discount rate to use for the analysis.

Doyle has also found three companies that are in the same industry as Flueger and have a similar capital structure—Behar Corporation, Walters Inc., and Hasselbeck Dynamics. In addition, Doyle has identified data for three takeover transactions with characteristics similar to Flueger—Bullseye, Dart Industries, and Arrow Corp. Data for both sets of firms are shown in the following figure.

Company Statistics	Flueger Systems	Behar Corporation	Walters Inc.	Hasselbeck Dynamics
Current stock price	$32.00	$54.00	$36.50	$108.20
Earnings per share (EPS) ($)	1.75	2.80	2.10	6.50
Book value per share ($)	9.75	17.25	12.10	35.75
Sales per share ($)	29.75	52.75	37.80	105.00

Company Statistics	Bullseye	Dart Industries	Arrow Corp.
Stock price pre-takeover	$18.25	$27.80	$43.00
Acquisition stock price	$22.00	$35.00	$52.00
Earnings per share (EPS) ($)	0.95	1.65	2.50
Book value per share ($)	6.10	9.85	14.20
Sales per share ($)	17.60	26.75	39.75

Lily Tyler, the CEO of Flueger Systems, was not happy when she heard the rumor that Gretsch Industries may try to take over Flueger in a hostile takeover. Tyler asked two of her executive vice presidents for suggestions on what her firm could do. Jordan Collier said, "If the Gretsch does make a hostile takeover offer, we could implement a fair price amendment to make sure a fair price is offered to our shareholders. Another EVP, Kyle Baldwin stated, "One option is to use a white knight defense and sell a minority stake to a third party that could help block Gretsch from making a deal."

2. The value per share of Flueger stock using the discounted cash flow approach is *closest* to:
   A. $27.50.
   B. $29.78.
   C. $33.02.
3. The average stock price of Flueger Systems under the comparable company approach for the three relative valuation ratios, assuming it is traded at the mean of the three valuations, is *closest* to:
   A. $27.50.
   B. $30.33.
   C. $32.00.
4. Using the comparable company approach, the mean takeover premium and the estimate of the fair acquisition price for Flueger Systems are *closest* to a:
   A. 22.4% premium and a $37.12 acquisition price.
   B. 22.4% premium and a $40.28 acquisition price.
   C. 15.6% premium and a $37.12 acquisition price.
5. The fair acquisition price for Flueger Systems using the comparable transaction approach is *closest* to:
   A. $30.33.
   B. $32.50.
   C. $37.20.
6. Are Collier and Baldwin correct in regard to their suggestions to Tyler about potential courses of action if there is a hostile takeover?
   A. Both are correct.
   B. Both are incorrect.
   C. Only one is correct.

MODULE 25.4: BID EVALUATION

Video covering this content is available online.

LOS 25.k: Evaluate a takeover bid and calculate the estimated post-acquisition value of an acquirer and the gains accrued to the target shareholders versus the acquirer shareholders.

CFA® Program Curriculum, Volume 3, page 312

Post-Merger Value of an Acquirer

In any merger that makes economic sense, the combined firm will be worth more than the sum of the two separate firms. This difference is the *gain*, which is a function of synergies created by the merger and any cash paid to shareholders as part of the transaction.

In equation form, we can denote the post-merger value of the combined company as:

$$V_{AT} = V_A + V_T + S - C$$

where:
V_A = post-merger value of the combined company (acquirer + target)
V_A = pre-merger value of acquirer
V_T = pre-merger value of target
S = synergies created by the merger
C = cash paid to target shareholders

Once again, remember that the pre-merger value of the target should be the price of the target stock before any market speculation causes the target's stock price to jump.

Gains Accrued to the Target

In most merger transactions, acquirers must pay a takeover premium to entice the target's shareholders to approve the merger. The target company's management will try to negotiate the highest possible premium relative to the value of the target company. From the target's perspective, the takeover premium is the amount of compensation received in excess of the pre-merger value of the target's shares, or:

$$Gain_T = TP = P_T - V_T$$

where:
$Gain_T$ = gains accrued to target shareholders
TP = takeover premium
P_T = price paid for target
V_T = pre-merger value of target

Gains Accrued to the Acquirer

Acquirers are willing to pay a takeover premium because they expect to generate their own gains from any synergies created by the transaction. The acquirer's gain is therefore equal to the synergies received less the premium paid to the target's shareholders, or:

$$Gain_A = S - TP = S - (P_T - V_T)$$

where:
$Gain_A$ = gains accrued to the acquirer's shareholders

Note that in a cash deal the cash paid to the target shareholders (C) is equal to the price paid for the target (P_T).

PROFESSOR'S NOTE

The gains for the acquirer and the gains for the target leave us with S, or the synergies from the deal. It's the gain resulting from the estimated value of cost reduction synergies or revenue enhancement synergies that the acquirer and the target are dividing.

Cash Payment vs. Stock Payment

In addition to the price paid, the ultimate gain to the acquirer or the target is also affected by the choice of payment method. Mergers can be either financed through cash or through an exchange of shares of the combined firm. The chosen payment method typically reflects how confident both parties are about the estimated value of the synergies resulting from the merger. This is because different methods of payment will give the acquirer and the target different risk exposures with respect to misestimating the value of synergies.

Let's think about the intuition before we go through any examples. With a cash offer, the target firm's shareholders will profit by the amount paid over its current share price (i.e., the takeover premium). However, this gain is capped at that amount.

With a stock offer, the gains will be determined in part by the value of the combined firm, because the target firm's shareholders do not receive cash and just walk away, but rather retain ownership in the new firm. Accordingly, for a stock deal we must adjust our formula for the price of the target:

$$P_T = (N \times P_{AT})$$

where:
N = number of new shares the target receives
P_{AT} = price per share of combined firm after the merger announcement

PROFESSOR'S NOTE

Note the use of P_{AT} (market price of AT) and not V_{AT} (value of AT in the formula).

EXAMPLE: Evaluating a merger bid

Giant Foods and Kazmaier's Grocery are negotiating a friendly acquisition of Kazmaier's by Giant Foods. The management teams at both companies have tentatively agreed upon a transaction value of about $27 per share for Kazmaier's stock, but are presently negotiating alternative methods of payment. Jennifer Nagy, CFA, works for Kozlowski Inc, the investment banking firm representing Giant Foods. Nagy has compiled the data in the following figure to analyze the transaction.

Merger Evaluation Inputs

	Giant Foods	Kazmaier's Grocery
Pre-merger stock price	$36	$24
Number of shares outstanding (millions)	50	24
Pre-merger market value (millions)	$1,800	$576
Estimated NPV of cost reduction synergies	$120 million	

Calculate the post-merger value of the combined firm, gains accrued to the target, and gains accrued to the acquirer under the following scenarios:

- Case 1: Cash offer of $27 per share for Kazmaier's stock.
- Case 2: Stock offer of 0.75 shares of Giant Foods stock per share of Kazmaier's.

Answer Case 1 – Cash Offer:

A cash offer is the method of payment that is most straight-forward and easiest to evaluate.

Post merger value of the combined firm: $V_{AT} = V_A + V_T + S - C$

V_A = $1,800

V_T = $576

S = $120

C = cash price offered × number of shares = $27 × 24 = $648

The value of the combined firm is V_{AT} = $1,800 + $576 + $120 – $648 = $1,848.

Gain to target: Kazmaier's gain in the merger as the target = $Gain_T$ = TP = $P_T - V_T$ = $648 – $576 = $72. This represents the takeover premium in the transaction.

Gain to acquirer: Giant Foods' gain in the merger as the acquirer = $S - (P_T - V_T)$ = $120 – ($648 – $576) = $48. This equals the value of synergies in the deal less the takeover premium paid to Kazmaier's shareholders.

Answer Case 2 – Stock Offer:

A stock offer is much more complex and more difficult to evaluate. In this case, the stock offer of 0.75 shares for each share of Kazmaier's is equal to (0.75 × $36) = $27, so it appears to be equivalent to the cash offer. However, the results are different because there is dilution when Giant Foods issues new stock to Kazmaier's shareholders. Since there are 24 million shares of Kazmaier's outstanding, Giant Foods must issue 24 million × 0.75 = 18 million new shares.

Post merger value of the combined firm: $V_{AT} = V_A + V_T + S - C$

V_A = $1,800

V_T = $576

S = $120

C = $0 because no cash is changing hands

The value of the combined firm is V_{AT} = \$1,800 + \$576 + \$120 – 0 = \$2,496.

Gain to target: To account for the dilution and find the price per share for the combined firm, P_{AT}, divide the post-merger value by the post-merger number of shares outstanding. Since 18 million new shares were issued, the total shares outstanding for Giant Foods is (50 + 18) = 68 million.

$$P_{AT} = \frac{\$2,496}{68} = \$36.70$$

This means the actual value of each share given to Kazmaier's shareholders is \$36.70, and the actual price paid for the target is:

$$P_T = (N \times P_{AT}) = (18 \times \$36.70) = \$660.60$$

Kazmaier's gain in the merger as the target is:

$$Gain_T = TP = P_T - V_T = \$660.60 - \$576 = \$84.60$$

This represents the takeover premium in the transaction.

Gain to acquirer: Giant Foods' gain in the merger as the acquirer is:

$$Gain_A = S - TP = S - (P_T - V_T) = \$120 - (\$660.60 - \$576) = \$35.4 \text{ million}$$

This equals the value of synergies in the deal less the takeover premium paid to Kazmaier's shareholders.

The examples show that the gain to Giant Foods' shareholders was \$48 million in the all cash deal, but only \$35.4 million in the stock deal. The dilution from the stock offer effectively reduced the acquirer's gains because the target was able to share in the risk and reward of the deal as a result of receiving shares.

LOS 25.1: Explain how price and payment method affect the distribution of risks and benefits in M&A transactions.

CFA® Program Curriculum, Volume 3, page 313

Effect of Price

With any merger deal, the acquirer and the target are on opposite sides of the table because both parties want to extract as much value as possible for themselves out of the deal. This means that the *acquirer will want to pay the lowest possible price* (the pre-merger value of the target, V_T), while the *target wants to receive the highest possible price* (the pre-merger value of the target plus the expected synergies, $V_T + S$).

Effect of Payment Method

Cash offer. In a cash offer, the acquirer assumes the risk and receives the potential reward from the merger, while the gain for the target shareholders is limited to the takeover premium. If an acquirer makes a cash offer in a deal, but the synergies realized are greater than expected, the takeover premium for the target would remain unchanged while the acquirer reaps the additional reward. Likewise, if synergies were less than expected, the target would still receive the same takeover premium, but the acquirer's gain may evaporate.

Stock offer. In a stock offer, some of the risks and potential rewards from the merger shift to the target firm. When the target receives stock as payment, the target's shareholders become a part owner of the acquiring company. This means that if estimates of the potential synergies are wrong, the target will share in the upside if the actual synergies exceed expectations, but will also share in the downside if the actual synergies are below expectations.

The main factor that affects the method of payment decision is confidence in the estimate of merger synergies. The more confident both parties are that synergies will be realized, the more the acquirer will prefer to pay cash and the more the target will prefer to receive stock. Conversely, if estimates of synergies are uncertain, the acquirer may be willing to shift some of the risk (and potential reward) to the target by paying for the merger with stock, but the target may prefer the guaranteed gain that comes from a cash deal.

LOS 25.m: Describe characteristics of M&A transactions that create value.

CFA® Program Curriculum, Volume 3, page 316

Short-term performance studies that look at stock returns before and after merger announcement dates conclude that targets gain approximately 30%, while acquirers lose stock value of between 1% and 3%.[1] Some believe that the high premiums received by target firms are the result of acquiring firms suffering from a *winner's curse*, in which the competitive bidding process is won by the firm who overpays the most. Managers also may overestimate the synergies and expected benefits of the merger. This tendency is called *managerial hubris*.

Longer term performance studies of post-merger companies show that acquirers tend to underperform their peers. Average returns for acquirers three years after a merger are –4% with over 60% of acquiring firms lagging their peer group.[2] Some believe that these results are due to a failure to capture promised synergies after a merger is completed.

However, some mergers do enhance value for the acquirer. Acquirers are likely to earn positive returns on a deal characterized by:

- **Strong buyer:** Acquirers that have exhibited strong performance (in terms of earnings and stock price growth) in the prior three years.
- **Low premium:** The acquirer pays a low takeover premium.
- **Few bidders:** The lower the number of bidders, the greater the acquirer's future returns.
- **Favorable market reaction:** Positive market price reaction to the acquisition announcement is a favorable indicator for the acquirer.

1. J. Fred Weston and Samuel C. Weaver, *Mergers & Acquisitions* (New York: McGraw-Hill, 2001), 93–116.
2. T. Koller, M. Goedhart, and D. Wessels, *Valuation: Measuring and Managing the Value of Companies*, 4th ed. (Hoboken, NJ: John Wiley and Sons, 2005), 439, footnotes 3 and 4.

LOS 25.n: Distinguish among equity carve-outs, spin-offs, split-offs, and liquidation.

CFA® Program Curriculum, Volume 3, page 318

In this section, we discuss ways a firm can reduce its size. Divestitures, equity carve-outs, spin-offs, split-offs, and liquidation are all methods by which a firm separates a portion of its operations from the parent company.

Divestitures refer to a company selling, liquidating, or spinning off a division or subsidiary. Most divestitures involve a direct sale of a portion of a firm to an outside buyer. The selling firm is typically paid in cash and gives up control of the portion of the firm sold.

PROFESSOR'S NOTE

Divestiture is often used as a generic term for a disposing of assets, so a carve-out, spin-off, or liquidation may also be considered a divestiture.

Equity carve-outs create a new, independent company by giving an equity interest in a subsidiary to outside shareholders. Shares of the subsidiary are issued in a public offering of stock, and the subsidiary becomes a new legal entity whose management team and operations are separate from the parent company.

Spin-offs are like carve-outs in that they create a new independent company that is distinct from the parent company. The primary difference is that shares are not issued to the public, but are instead distributed proportionately to the parent company's shareholders. This means that the shareholder base of the spin-off will be the same as that of the parent company, but the management team and operations are completely separate. Since shares of the new company are simply distributed to existing shareholders, the parent company does not receive any cash in the transaction.

Split-offs allow shareholders to receive new shares of a division of the parent company *in exchange for* a portion of their shares in the parent company. The key here is that shareholders are giving up a portion of their ownership in the parent company to receive the new shares of stock in the division.

Liquidations break up the firm and sell its asset piece by piece. Most liquidations are associated with bankruptcy.

LOS 25.o: Explain common reasons for restructuring.

CFA® Program Curriculum, Volume 3, page 318

Division no longer fits into management's long-term strategy. The parent may feel that it will be unable to make a profit with a particular division, or that the division is no longer a strategic fit with the long-term direction of the company. In this case, to focus on its core business, the parent can sell the assets to another firm that can utilize the assets more effectively.

Lack of profitability. The return on a division could be less than the firm's cost of capital, causing economic losses for the company. A poorly performing division could be caused by management making a bad choice to enter the division in the first place, or because the attractiveness of the division declines over time due to rising cost structures or changing consumer tastes.

Individual parts are worth more than the whole. One of major reasons cited for M&A deals is *synergy*, which is the concept that a combined entity is worth more than the sum of the parts. In the same line of thinking, *reverse synergy*, the concept that the individual parts are worth more than the whole, is a common justification for divestitures. A parent company may decide that it can unlock more value from a division by selling it to an outside bidder rather than keeping it.

Infusion of cash. Selling a division can create a significant cash inflow for the parent company. If the parent company is experiencing financing difficulty, selling a division can be a quick way to raise cash and reduce debt.

MODULE QUIZ 25.4

To best evaluate your performance, enter your quiz answers online.

1. Andrew Barton is an intern with the Gilmore Capital Group. Barton's supervisor, Barbara Clemens, asks him to compile information about academic studies concerning the distribution of benefits in a merger. After a week, Barton sends Clemens an e-mail with the following statements:
   - "Studies show that immediately after a merger announcement, target firm shareholders gain approximately 30%, while acquirers' stock prices tend to fall."
   - "Longer term performance studies of post-merger companies show that they outperform their peers, indicating that merger synergies often exceed expectations."

   Are Barton's statements correct?
   A. Both statements are correct.
   B. Neither statement is correct.
   C. Only one statement is correct.

2. Vinova Corporation is seeking to acquire JJK Systems, Inc. The management teams of both JJK and Vinova feel confident that estimates of synergies resulting from the merger and the valuation of JJK are extremely precise. Given the confidence of both firms, which method of payment would each firm prefer in the merger?

Vinova corporation	JJK Systems, Inc.
A. Stock offer	Stock offer
B. Stock offer	Cash offer
C. Cash offer	Stock offer

Study Session 8

3. Vona Whatley, an analyst for Discovery Electronics, is considering alternatives for divesting the company's personal computer (PC) business. Whatley believes that the PC industry offers a high degree of competition and few growth opportunities, so Whatley wants to explore Discovery's options for using the assets more efficiently. In a conversation with Marquis Stone, the CFO for Discovery, Whatley makes the following statements:
   - "I think it would be best if we created a new, independent company out of the PC business and generate a cash infusion for our remaining core business by issuing shares of the new company in a public stock offering."
   - "Another alternative would be to give current shareholders a choice of what business they want to own, and allow them to exchange shares of Discovery Electronics for shares in the new PC company."

   Which forms of corporate restructuring *most closely* reflect Whatley's proposals to:

	Issue shares in an IPO?	Exchange shares?
A.	Carve-out	Split-off
B.	Split-off	Spin-off
C.	Carve-out	Spin-off

4. Which of the following is *least likely* to be a reason for making a divestiture?
   A. Management feels that they would have greater access to capital markets as part of a more focused company.
   B. A division is making significant profits as part of a high growth industry.
   C. Management believes that the parts of a company are worth more individually than the company as a whole.

Use the following information to answer Questions 5 through 7.

Madura Publishing, a publisher of academic textbooks, has made an offer to acquire Dorman-Gladwell, a publisher of children's books. The management teams at both companies have tentatively agreed upon a transaction value of $56 per share for Dorman-Gladwell, but are presently negotiating alternative methods of payment. Data used for the analysis of the transaction is given below.

	Madura Publishing	Dorman-Gladwell
Pre-merger stock price	$80	$48
Number of shares outstanding (millions)	30	20
Pre-merger market value (millions)	$2,400	$960

Once the merger is completed, Dominic Culp, the CEO of Madura Publishing, plans for Madura to take on all of Dorman-Gladwell's assets and liabilities, and the combined company will continue to operate under the Madura Publishing name. Culp estimates that cost reduction synergies as a result of the merger will total approximately $180 million.

5. The form of integration and type of merger in this transaction would be *best* described as:
   A. statutory vertical.
   B. statutory horizontal.
   C. subsidiary horizontal.
6. If the deal is completed as a cash transaction, the amount of the gain for Dorman-Gladwell's shareholders is *closest* to:
   A. $90 million.
   B. $112 million.
   C. $160 million.
7. If the deal is completed as a stock transaction with an exchange ratio of 0.7, the amount of the gain for Madura Publishing's shareholders is *closest* to:
   A. $9.6 million.
   B. $13.7 million.
   C. $20.0 million

Study Session 8

KEY CONCEPTS

LOS 25.a

Mergers can be classified according to the form of acquisition.

- In a statutory merger, the target ceases to exist and all assets and liabilities become part of the acquirer.
- In a subsidiary merger, the target company becomes a subsidiary of the acquirer.
- With consolidations, both companies cease to exist in their prior form and come together to form a new company.

Mergers can also be classified by type:

- Horizontal mergers, where firms in similar lines of business combine.
- Vertical mergers, which combine firms either further up or down the supply chain.
- Conglomerate mergers, which combine firms in unrelated businesses.

LOS 25.b

Common motivations behind M&A activity include achieving synergies, more rapid growth, increasing market power, gaining access to unique capabilities, diversification, personal benefits for managers, tax benefits, unlocking hidden value for a struggling company, achieving international business goals, and bootstrapping earnings.

LOS 25.c

Bootstrapping is a technique whereby a high P/E firm acquires a low P/E firm in an exchange of stock. The total earnings of the combined firm are unchanged, but the total shares outstanding are less than the two separate entities. The result is higher reported earnings per share, even though there may be no economic gains.

LOS 25.d

Companies tend to focus on different motivations for mergers depending on what stage of the industry life cycle they are in.

- In the pioneer and rapid growth phases, companies look to mergers to provide additional capital or capacity for growth; conglomerate and horizontal mergers are common.
- In the mature growth and stabilization phases, firms are looking for synergies to reduce costs; horizontal and vertical mergers are common.
- In the decline phase companies are typically looking for new growth opportunities to survive; all three merger types are common.

LOS 25.e

A merger transaction may take the form of a stock purchase or an asset purchase.

- In a stock purchase, the target's shareholders receive cash or shares of the acquiring company's stock in exchange for their shares of the target.
- In an asset purchase, payment is made directly to the target company in return for specific assets.

The method of payment in a merger transaction may be cash, stock, or a combination of the two. Cash offerings are straight forward, but in a stock offering, the exchange ratio determines the number of the acquirer's shares that each target company shareholder will receive.

The target company's management will either view a merger as being friendly or hostile.

- In a friendly merger, the acquirer and target work together to perform due diligence and sign a definitive merger agreement before submitting the merger proposal to the target's shareholders.
- In a hostile merger, the acquirer seeks to avoid the target's management through a tender offer or proxy battle.

LOS 25.f

Pre-offer defense mechanisms to avoid a hostile takeover include poison pills, poison puts, reincorporating in a state with restrictive takeover laws, staggered board elections, restricted voting rights, supermajority voting, fair price amendments, and golden parachutes.

Post-offer defense mechanisms to avoid a hostile takeover include the "just say no" defense, litigation, greenmail, share repurchases, leveraged recapitalizations, the crown jewel defense, the Pac man defense, and finding a white knight or white squire.

LOS 25.g

The Herfindahl-Hirschman Index (HHI) measures market power based on the sum of the squared market shares for all firms within an industry. High or increasing HHI values means that regulators are more likely to challenge a merger based on anti-trust grounds.

LOS 25.h

The three basic methods for determining the value of a target in an M&A transaction are:

- Discounted cash flow method.
- Comparable company analysis.
- Comparable transaction analysis.

Discounted cash flow analysis

Advantages:

- Easy to model changes in cash flow from synergies or changes in cost structure.
- Based on forecasts of fundamental conditions.
- Easy to customize.

Disadvantages:

- Difficult with negative FCF.
- Estimates highly subject to error, especially for the distant future.
- Discount rate changes over time can have a large impact on the estimate.
- Heavily dependent on terminal value, growth rate, and discount rate.

Comparable company analysis

Advantages:

- Data for comparable companies is easy to access.
- Fundamental valuation assumptions are sound.
- Current market-based estimates of value, not guesses about the future.

Disadvantages:

- Assumes the market's valuation of the comparable companies is accurate.
- Estimate is a fair stock price, not a fair takeover price. An appropriate takeover premium must be determined separately.
- Difficult to include synergies or changing capital structures into the analysis.
- Historical data may not reflect current conditions in the M&A market.

Comparable transaction analysis

Advantages:

- Based on actual transactions: no need to estimate a takeover premium.
- Uses recent market prices from actual deals rather than assumptions and estimates about the future.
- Easily justified to target's shareholders, managers, and board.

Disadvantages:

- Assumes that the M&A market valued past transactions accurately; mispricings will be carried over to the estimated value for the target.
- Truly comparable transactions are rare. The analyst may be forced to use dissimilar M&A deals from other industries.
- Difficult to incorporate synergies or changing capital structures into the analysis.

LOS 25.i

The process for valuing a target company with discounted cash flow analysis requires the following steps:

- Determine which free cash flow model to use for the analysis.
- Develop pro forma financial estimates.
- Calculate free cash flows using the pro forma data.
- Discount free cash flows back to the present.
- Determine the terminal value and discount it back to the present.
- Add the discounted FCF values to the discounted terminal value.

LOS 25.j

The process for valuing a target company with comparable company analysis requires the following steps:

- Identify the set of comparable firms.
- Calculate various relative value measures based on the current market prices of companies in the sample.
- Calculate descriptive statistics for the relative value metrics and apply those measures to the target firm.
- Estimate a takeover premium.
- Calculate the estimated takeover price for the target as the sum of estimated stock value based on comparables and the takeover premium.

The process for valuing a target company with comparable transaction analysis requires the following steps:

- Identify a set of recent takeover transactions.
- Calculate various relative value measures based on completed deal prices for the companies in the sample.
- Calculate descriptive statistics for the relative value metrics and apply those measures to the target firm.

LOS 25.k

The value of the combined firm after a merger deal is a function of synergies created by the merger and any cash paid to shareholders as part of the transaction, or $V_{AT} = V_A + V_T + S - C$.

In a merger transaction, target shareholders capture the takeover premium, which is the amount that the price paid exceeds the target's value: $\text{Gain}_T = TP = P_T - V_T$.

The acquirer in a merger transaction captures the value of any synergies created in the merger less the premium paid to the target, or $\text{Gain}_A = S - TP = S - (P_T - V_T)$.

LOS 25.l

In a cash offer, the acquirer assumes the risk and receives the potential reward from the merger synergies, but in a stock offer, some of the risks and potential rewards from the merger shift to the target firm.

Study Session 8

LOS 25.m

Empirical evidence shows that targets receive the majority of benefits in a merger deal. In the years following a deal, acquirers tend to underperform their peers, which suggests that estimated synergies are not realized.

Acquirers are likely to earn positive returns on a deal characterized by:

- **Strong buyer:** Acquirers that have exhibited strong performance in the prior three years.
- **Low premium:** The acquirer pays a low takeover premium.
- **Few bidders:** The lower the number of bidders, the greater the acquirer's future returns.
- **Favorable market reaction:** Positive market price reaction is a favorable indicator for the acquirer.

LOS 25.n

When a firm separates a portion of its operations from a parent company it is called a divestiture. Four common forms of divestitures include equity carve-outs, spin-offs, split-offs, and liquidations.

- **Equity carve-out:** Creates a new, independent company by giving an equity interest in a subsidiary to outside shareholders. The subsidiary becomes a new legal entity whose management team and operations are separate from the parent company.
- **Spin-off:** Creates a new, independent company that is distinct from the parent company, but unlike in carve-outs, shares are not issued to the public but are instead distributed proportionately to the parent company's shareholders.
- **Split-off:** Allows shareholders to receive new shares of a division of the parent company in exchange for a portion of their shares in the parent company.
- **Liquidation:** Breaks up a firm and sells its assets piece by piece. Most liquidations are associated with bankruptcy.

LOS 25.o

Reasons why a company may divest assets include:

- A division no longer fitting into management's strategy.
- Poor profitability for a division.
- Reverse synergy.
- To receive an infusion of cash.

ANSWER KEY FOR MODULE QUIZZES

Module Quiz 25.1

1. **B** Since the two companies will cease to exist in their prior form and a new company will be formed, the form of integration is a consolidation. Also, Uritus Pharmaceuticals, a drug manufacturer, is moving up the supply chain by acquiring Troup Healthcare Systems, a distributor, which is an example of a vertical merger. (LOS 25.a)

2. **B** Achieving more rapid growth by external acquisition, gaining access to unique capabilities, and unlocking hidden value are all potential motivations for mergers. Tax benefits are also a potential motivation for a merger, but the acquirer would want the target to have tax losses, not the other way around. (LOS 25.b)

3. **C** Bootstrapping occurs when the high P/E firm purchases the low P/E firm in exchange for stock. By purchasing the firm with a lower P/E, the acquiring firm is essentially exchanging higher priced shares for lower priced shares. As a result, the number of shares outstanding for the acquiring firm increases, but at a ratio that is less than 1-for-1. When we compute the EPS for the combined firm, the numerator (total earnings) is equal to the sum of the combined firms, but the denominator (total shares outstanding) is less than the sum of the combined firms, resulting in the appearance of EPS growth. (LOS 25.b)

4. **A** A firm with high profit margins that is looking for a conglomerate merger with the goal of gaining access to capital to finance growth is most likely in the rapid growth stage of the industry life cycle. (LOS 25.d)

Module Quiz 25.2

1. **B** In an asset purchase, payment is made directly to the target company, no shareholder approval is needed (unless the asset sale is more than 50% of the company), the acquirer avoids the assumption of the target's liabilities, and the target is responsible for any capital gains taxes, not the shareholder. (LOS 25.e)

2. **C** Pre-offer merger defense mechanisms are usually easier to defend in court than a post-merger defense mechanisms once a hostile takeover has been announced. Poison pills, restricted voting rights, and supermajority voting provisions are all examples of pre-merger defense mechanisms. The crown jewel defense is a post-merger defense mechanism in which the target tries to sell valuable assets to a neutral third party in order to cause the acquirer to call off the merger. (LOS 25.f)

3. **B** The industry the firms operate in is considered moderately concentrated because the post-merger HHI falls between 1,000 and 1,800. With a change in HHI greater than 100, a challenge is possible. (LOS 25.g)

$$\text{pre-merger HHI} = (0.20 \times 100)^2 + (0.18 \times 100)^2 + (0.12 \times 100)^2 + (0.10 \times 100)^2 + [(0.08 \times 100)^2 \times 5] = 1{,}288$$

$$\text{post-merger HHI} = (0.20 \times 100)^2 + (0.18 \times 100)^2 + (0.22 \times 100)^2 + [(0.08 \times 100)^2 \times 5] = 1{,}528$$

change in HHI = 1,528 – 1,288 = 240

(LOS 25.g)

Module Quiz 25.3

1. **A** Hirauye should agree with both of Klinkenfus's statements. One of the key advantages to using the discounted cash flow method to value a target firm is that it makes it easy to model any changes that may result from operating synergies or changes in cash flow from the merger. One of the key advantages to the comparable transaction approach is that there is no need to compute a separate takeover premium as there is in the comparable company approach. (LOS 25.i)

2. **C**

$$\text{Discounted FCFE} = \frac{\$24}{1.105} + \frac{\$27}{1.105^2} + \frac{\$32}{1.105^3} + \frac{\$36}{1.105^4} = \$91.69 \text{ million}$$

$$\text{Terminal value}_4 = \frac{\text{FCFE}_4(1+g)}{(k_e - g)} = \frac{\$36(1+0.06)}{(0.105-0.06)} = \$848.0 \text{ million}$$

$$\text{Terminal value}_0 = \frac{\$848.0}{1.105^4} = \$568.78 \text{ million}$$

estimated value for Flueger = (\$91.69 million + \$568.78 million) / 20 million shares = \$33.02

(LOS 25.i)

3. **B** The calculation for the relative value valuation is shown in the following figures:

Company Statistics	Behar Corporation	Walters Inc.	Hasselbeck Dynamics	Mean
Current stock price	\$54.00	\$36.50	\$108.20	
P/E Ratio	\$54.00 / 2.80 = 19.29	\$36.50 / 2.10 = 17.38	\$108.20 / 6.50 = 16.65	17.77
P/B Ratio	\$54.00 / 17.25 = 3.13	\$36.50 / 12.10 = 3.02	\$108.20 / 35.75 = 3.03	3.06
P/S Ratio	\$54.00 / 52.75 = 1.02	\$36.50 / 37.80 = 0.97	\$108.20 / 105.00 = 1.03	1.01

Multiple	Mean	Flueger Systems Statistics	Flueger Systems Valuation
P/E Ratio	17.77	1.75	$31.10
P/B Ratio	3.06	9.75	$29.84
P/S Ratio	1.01	29.75	$30.05
Mean value for Flueger Systems using comparable firms: $30.33			

(LOS 25.j)

4. **A** The calculation for the mean takeover premium is:

Company Statistics	Bullseye	Dart Industries	Arrow Corp.	Mean Takeover Premium
Stock price pre-takeover	$18.25	$27.80	$43.00	
Acquisition stock price	$22.00	$35.00	$52.00	
Takeover premium = (DP – SP) / SP	20.5%	25.9%	20.9%	**22.4%**

Applying this value to the mean comparable company valuation calculated in the previous question gives us: $30.33 × 1.224 = $37.12. (LOS 25.j)

5. **C** The calculation for the fair acquisition price under the comparable transaction approach is shown in the following figures:

Company Statistics	Bullseye	Dart Industries	Arrow Corp.	Mean
Takeover price	$22.00	$35.00	$52.00	
P/E Ratio	$22.00 / 0.95 = 23.16	$35.00 / 1.65 = 21.21	$52.00 / 2.50 = 20.80	21.72
P/B Ratio	$22.00 / 6.10 = 3.61	$35.00 / 9.85 = 3.55	$52.00 / 14.20 = 3.66	3.61
P/S Ratio	$22.00 / 17.60 = 1.25	$35.00 / 26.75 = 1.31	$52.00 / 39.75 = 1.31	1.29

Company Statistics	Mean	Flueger Systems Statistics	Flueger Systems Valuation
P/E Ratio	21.72	1.75	$38.01
P/B Ratio	3.61	9.75	$35.20
P/S Ratio	1.29	29.75	$38.38
Fair acquisition value using the comparable transaction approach: $37.20			

(LOS 25.j)

6. **B** Both Collier's statement and Baldwin's statement are incorrect. Collier suggests using a fair price amendment after the takeover is announced; however, a fair price amendment is a pre-offer defense, not a post-offer defense. Baldwin's statement is incorrect because he is actually describing a white squire defense, not a white knight defense. (LOS 25.f)

Module Quiz 25.4

1. **C** Barton's first statement is correct. Empirical evidence shows that the majority of gains from a merger go to the target: target firm stock prices increased 30% on average, while acquiring firm stock prices declined. Barton's second statement is incorrect. Longer-term studies of post-merger firms show that most have negative stock performance three years after a merger, and they lag their peer group. This indicates that there may be a failure to capture promised synergies from the merger. (LOS 25.m)

2. **C** Both the acquirer and the target are confident about the estimate of merger synergies. In this scenario, Vinova Corporation's shareholders, as the acquirer, would prefer to make a cash offer because it would allow Vinova to keep more of the gain from the merger synergies and limit JJK's gain to the takeover premium. JJK's shareholders would want to share in the rewards as well, so they would prefer to receive a stock offer that would give them ownership in the combined company and enable them to profit from the potential synergies. (LOS 25.l)

3. **A** Statement 1 reflects a carve-out. In a carve-out, a new independent company is created by issuing shares in a public offering of stock. Statement 2 reflects a split-off. Split-offs allow shareholders to receive new shares of a division in exchange for a portion of their shares in the parent company. (LOS 25.n)

4. **B** A declining, low growth division is more likely to be part of a divestiture than a division that is making significant profits as part of a high-growth industry. Other common reasons for making a divestiture include greater access to capital markets, reverse synergy, or lack of profitability. (LOS 25.o)

5. **B** The form of integration in this transaction is a statutory merger because Dorman-Gladwell's assets and liabilities will be absorbed by Madura, and Dorman-Gladwell will cease to exist. Since both companies are in the publishing business, this is a horizontal merger. (LOS 25.a)

6. **C** *Gain to target:* Dorman-Gladwell's gain in the merger as the target =

   $\text{Gain}_T = TP = P_T - V_T = (\$56 \times 20) - \$960 = \$160$ million. This represents the takeover premium in the transaction. (LOS 25.j)

7. **B** First, calculate the post-merger value of the combined firm as:

$V_{AT} = V_A + V_T + S - C$

where:

$V_A = \$2{,}400$

$V_T = \$960$

$S = \$180$

$C = \$0$ because no cash is changing hands

The value of the combined firm is:

$V_{AT} = \$2{,}400 + \$960 + \$180 - 0 = \$3{,}540$

Next, to account for dilution and find the price per share of the combined firm, divide the post-merger value by the post-merger shares outstanding. Since the exchange ratio is 0.7, Madura will need to issue 14 million new shares to acquire the 20 million shares of Dorman-Gladwell. Adding 14 million new shares to the 30 million shares of Madura already outstanding means the post-merger shares outstanding is 44 million.

$$P_{AT} = \frac{\$3{,}540}{44} = \$80.45$$

This means that the actual value of each share given to Dorman-Gladwell's shareholders is \$80.45, and that the actual price paid for the target is:

$P_T = (N \times P_{AT}) = (14 \times \$80.45) = \$1{,}126.3$ million

Madura Publishing's gain in the merger as the acquirer is:

$Gain_A = S - TP = S - (P_T - V_T) = \$180 - (\$1{,}126.3 - \$960) = \$13.7$ million (LOS 25.k)

TOPIC ASSESSMENT: CORPORATE FINANCE

You have now finished the Corporate Finance topic section. The following topic assessment will provide immediate feedback on how effective your study of this material has been. The test is best taken timed; allow 3 minutes per subquestion (18 minutes per item set). This topic assessment is more exam-like than typical module quiz or QBank questions. A score less than 70% suggests that additional review of this topic is needed.

Use the following information for Questions 1 through 6.

The CEO of Edgington Enterprises, Nicole Johnson, is conferring with her finance staff regarding the plans for capital projects during the upcoming year. Like most firms, Edgington is capital constrained, and Johnson wants to make the most out of what is available. During the meeting, several issues are raised.

While inflation has recently been low, some evidence is present in the commodities markets to suggest that it could become a concern during the life of even a medium-term project. Johnson knows that inflation can have a significant impact on project selection. The staff is asked how an increase in the rate of inflation might affect the capital budgeting process.

The following data pertains to two capital projects currently under consideration. The cost of both projects is $30 million.

	Net Present Value	Life in Years
Project Andover	$35,000,000	8
Project Baltimore	$25,000,000	5

Johnson informs the staff that it appears that the firm will have only $30 million available for investment during the upcoming year, so a choice will have to be made. The finance staff estimates that the firm's after-tax WACC is 7.5%.

In recent months, there has been a vigorous discussion in the financial press about the need to manage risk. During this past November, Johnson attended a three-day seminar on risk management at the University of Chicago. One of the key points made by seminar faculty was that reducing risk, even if there is a cost incurred to do so, can increase firm value. Johnson has asked the finance team how project risk is evaluated, and what type of risk is being measured during the capital budgeting process.

Another key point made during the seminar was that some projects are not well evaluated with traditional capital budgeting methods, such as NPV. These are projects that require management to make critical decisions after the commitment to undertake the project has been made, and at least part of the project's capital has been invested. She wonders if the finance staff is familiar with the evaluation of such projects.

As the meeting was coming to a close, Marques Wilson, CFA, suggested to the staff that it may be useful to try to connect project performance with incremental changes in firm value. To this end, he suggests that it may be useful to attempt to measure a project's economic profits. These can be used to infer how the project is affecting overall firm value.

Johnson charged the staff with giving consideration to the matters raised during the meeting before they reconvene at the end of the week.

After work, Johnson heads out to teach a CFA review course for her local society. The topic for that evening coincides with her work in corporate finance, but focuses more on mergers and acquisitions. She presents the class with the following case study:

> Toulouse Tempered Steel Industries (TTS) is weighing its strategic options following a wave of mergers in the industry across Europe and worldwide. Pascal LaPage, managing director of TTS is wondering whether it makes sense for the firm to position itself as a standalone entity, or if the firm should be pursuing a merger/acquisition of another firm that would provide a good strategic fit. Lyon Bank has been the firm's primary lender for many years, and Alaine Clamon, CFA, from Lyon's corporate finance department is due to meet with LaPage and other members of the firm's finance group to discuss some strategic options.
>
> Clamon begins his presentation with the underlying rationale for even considering a merger or acquisition as a strategic alternative. Some reasons cited by Clamon that can be used to justify a merger are the pursuit of economies of scale, the elimination of operating inefficiencies, and diversification of the firm's assets. In general, the underlying rationale helps to determine what type of merger the firm will be undertaking. LaPage asks his staff to keep these in mind as they seek suitable candidates for evaluation.
>
> LaPage's team has already identified two firms that might be good acquisition candidates for TTS. One is Aragon Metals, and the other is Brittany Engineered Products. A member of the staff asks Clamon about types of takeover defenses that might by employed by either Aragon or Brittany. Clamon replies that these fall broadly into two categories: pre-offer and post-offer defenses. As examples of pre-offer defenses, he describes staggered boards and supermajority voting provisions. As an example of post-offer defenses, he describes the sale of significant assets. He notes that, obviously, TTS must take care to account for the ramifications of the presence of any takeover defenses.

1. The three categories of cash flows that are typically associated with a capital project are:
   A. financing, operating, and terminal year.
   B. initial investment outlay, operating, and financing.
   C. initial investment outlay, operating, and terminal year.

2. Suppose that there are two scenarios for projects Andover and Baltimore. Under Scenario 1, the projects cannot be replicated, while under Scenario 2, the projects can be replicated. Which project should be accepted?

	Scenario 1	Scenario 2
A.	Andover	Baltimore
B.	Andover	Andover
C.	Baltimore	Andover

3. When the value of a given project is contingent upon future decisions of management, the project can be *best* described as containing:
   A. real options.
   B. flexibility options.
   C. timing options.

4. Suppose that the firm has a project code named Richmond. The dollar amount of the investment in Richmond is $40 million. Last year, Richmond's EBIT was $6 million. If the relevant tax rate is 35%, what was Richmond's economic profit during the past year?
   A. $900,000.
   B. $3,900,000.
   C. $2,100,000.

5. With regard to the list of sensible motives for undertaking a merger cited by Clamon in Johnson's case study, he is:
   A. correct with regard to operating inefficiencies, and correct with regard to diversification.
   B. correct with regard to operating inefficiencies, but incorrect with regard to diversification.
   C. incorrect with regard to operating inefficiencies, but correct with regard to diversification.

6. With respect to the takeover defenses described by Clamon, he is:
   A. incorrect with regard to the pre-offer defenses listed, and incorrect with regard to the post-offer defense listed.
   B. incorrect with regard to the pre-offer defenses listed, but correct with regard to the post-offer defense listed.
   C. correct with regard to the pre-offer defenses listed, and correct with regard to the post-offer defense listed.

TOPIC ASSESSMENT ANSWERS: CORPORATE FINANCE

1. **C** The three typical categories regarding capital project cash flows are initial investment outlay, operating, and terminal year. (Study Session 7, Module 20.1, LOS 20.a)

2. **A** If the projects cannot be replicated, then the project with the greatest NPV should be selected, and this is Andover. If the projects can be replicated, we can evaluate the projects using either a least common lives approach or an equivalent annual annuity approach. The least common multiple of the projects' lives is 40 years, and the replacement chain NPVs are \$75.25 million for Andover and \$77.83 million for Baltimore (e.g., total NPV of Andover repeated five times over 40 years = $35 + 35/1.075^{8} + 35/1.075^{16} + 35/1.075^{24} + 35/1.075^{32} = \$75.26$). The equivalent annual annuity values are \$5.975 million for Andover and \$6.179 million for Baltimore. Both methods indicate that Baltimore should be chosen if the projects can be replicated. (Study Session 7, Module 20.2, LOS 20.c)

3. **A** When a project's value is a function of managerial decisions that must be made in periods following the investment, the project is said to contain real options. The other answers are simply types of real options that may be present in a project. (Study Session 7, Module 20.3, LOS 20.f)

4. **A** The economic profit is calculated as:

   EP = NOPAT – \$WACC = \$6(1 – 0.35) – \$40(0.075) = \$0.9 million

   (Study Session 7, Module 20.3, LOS 20.i)

5. **B** Pursuing a merger where the underlying rationale is to eliminate operating inefficiencies is generally considered sensible. A merger in pursuit of diversification is generally not seen as sensible, because it is ordinarily much more cost-effective for shareholders to diversify on their own. (Study Session 8, Module 25.1, LOS 25.b)

6. **C** In both cases, Clamon has correctly provided examples of pre-offer and post-offer takeover defenses. (Study Session 8, Module 25.2, LOS 25.f)

FORMULAS

Study Sessions 5 and 6: Financial Reporting and Analysis

funded status of the plan: funded status = fair value of plan assets – PBO

total periodic pension cost
= contributions – (ending funded status – beginning funded status)

PROFESSOR'S NOTE

Not all of the following ratios are used in this book. However, this list includes most of the common ratios that you are likely to encounter on exam day.

current ratio $= \dfrac{\text{current assets}}{\text{current liabilities}}$

quick ratio $= \dfrac{\text{cash + marketable securities + receivables}}{\text{current liabilities}}$

cash ratio $= \dfrac{\text{cash + short-term marketable securities}}{\text{current liabilities}}$

defensive interval ratio = (cash + short-term marketable investments + receivables) ÷ daily cash expenditures

receivables turnover $= \dfrac{\text{net annual sales}}{\text{average receivables}}$

inventory turnover $= \dfrac{\text{cost of goods sold}}{\text{average inventory}}$

days of sales outstanding (DSO) =

average receivable collection period $= \dfrac{365}{\text{receivables turnover ratio}}$

days of inventory on hand $(\text{DOH}) = \dfrac{365}{\text{inventory turnover}}$

payables turnover $= \dfrac{\text{purchases}}{\text{average payables}}$

number of days of payables $= \dfrac{365}{\text{payables turnover}}$

total asset turnover $= \dfrac{\text{net sales}}{\text{average total assets}}$

fixed asset turnover $= \dfrac{\text{net sales}}{\text{average fixed assets}}$

cash generated from operations (CGO)
= operating cash flow + cash interest + cash taxes
= EBIT + non-cash charges – increase in working capital

accruals^{CF} = NI – CFO – CFI

$$\text{accruals ratio}^{CF} = \frac{(\text{NI} - \text{CFO} - \text{CFI})}{(\text{NOA}_{\text{END}} + \text{NOA}_{\text{BEG}})/2}$$

Study Sessions 7 and 8: Corporate Finance

outlay = FCInv + NWCInv

after-tax operating cash flow (CF) = (S – C – D)(1 – T) + D
= (S – C)(1 – T) + (TD)

TNOCF = Sal_T + NWCInv – T (Sal_T – B_T)

economic income = cash flow + (ending market value – beginning market value)

or

economic income = cash flow – economic depreciation

economic profit: EP = NOPAT – $WACC

market value added: $NPV = MVA = \sum_{t=1}^{\infty} \frac{EP_t}{(1+WACC)^t}$

residual income = net income – equity charge

project cost of equity $= R_F + \beta_{project}\left[E(R_{MKT}) - R_F\right]$

weighted average cost of capital: $WACC = \left[r_d \times (1-t)\left(\frac{debt}{assets}\right)\right] + \left[r_e \times \left(\frac{equity}{assets}\right)\right]$

MM Proposition I (no taxes): $V_L = V_U$

MM Proposition II (no taxes): $r_e = r_0 + \frac{D}{E}(r_0 - r_d)$

MM Proposition I (with taxes): $V_L = V_U + (t \times d)$

MM Proposition II (with taxes): $r_e = r_0 + \frac{D}{E}(r_0 - r_d)(1 - T_c)$

static trade-off theory: $V_L = V_U + (t \times d)$ – PV(costs of financial distress)

change in price when stock goes ex-dividend: $\Delta P = \frac{D(1-T_D)}{(1-T_{CG})}$

effective tax rate = corporate tax rate + (1 – corporate tax rate)(individual tax rate)

expected increase in dividends = [(expected earnings × target payout ratio) – previous dividend] × adjustment factor

FCFE coverage ratio = FCFE / (dividends + share repurchases)

Herfindahl-Hirschman Index: $HHI = \sum_{i=1}^{n} (MS_i \times 100)^2$

free cash flow: Net income
+ Net interest after tax
= Unlevered net income
± Change in deferred taxes
= Net operating profit less adjusted taxes (NOPLAT)
+ Net noncash charges
± Change in net working capital
− Capital expenditures (capex)
= Free cash flow (FCF)

terminal value: $TV_T = \frac{FCF_T(1+g)}{(WACC_{adjusted} - g)}$

or

$TV_T = FCF_T \times (P / FCF)$

takeover premium: $TP = \frac{DP - SP}{SP}$

post-merger value of an acquirer: $V_{AT} = V_A + V_T + S - C$

gain to target: $Gain_T = TP = P_T - V_T$

gain to acquirer: $Gain_A = S - TP = S - (P_T - V_T)$

price of target in stock deal: $P_T = (N \times P_{AT})$

gross profit margin $= \frac{\text{gross profit}}{\text{net sales}}$

operating profit margin $= \frac{\text{operating profit}}{\text{net sales}} = \frac{\text{EBIT}}{\text{net sales}}$

net profit margin $= \frac{\text{net income}}{\text{net sales}}$

return on assets $= \frac{\text{net income}}{\text{average total assets}}$

return on capital $= \frac{\text{EBIT}}{(\text{interest bearing debt} + \text{shareholders' equity})}$

return on total equity $= \frac{\text{net income}}{\text{average total equity}}$

$$\textbf{financial leverage ratio} = \frac{\text{total assets}}{\text{total equity}}$$

$$\textbf{long-term debt-to-equity ratio} = \frac{\text{total long-term debt}}{\text{total equity}}$$

$$\textbf{debt-to-equity ratio} = \frac{\text{total debt}}{\text{total equity}}$$

$$\textbf{debt-to-capital ratio} = \frac{\text{short-term debt} + \text{long-term debt}}{\text{short-term debt} + \text{long-term debt} + \text{total equity}}$$

$$\textbf{interest coverage} = \frac{\text{EBIT}}{\text{interest expense}}$$

$$\textbf{payout ratio} = \frac{\text{dividends paid}}{\text{net income}}$$

retention ratio = 1 – payout ratio

$$\textbf{earnings per share} = \frac{\text{net income} - \text{preferred dividends}}{\text{average common shares outstanding}}$$

$$\textbf{book value per share} = \frac{\text{common stockholders' equity}}{\text{total number of common shares outstanding}}$$

INDEX

Q

R

S

T

U

V

W

Z

Notes

Notes

Notes

Notes

Notes

Notes